D1426730

ROBERT SOUTHWELL AND THE MISSION OF LITERATURE 1561–1595

Robert Southwell and the Mission of Literature, 1561–1595

Writing Reconciliation

P. ROBERTVS SOVTHVELL. Soc. Iesu
Londini pro Cath. fide suspensus et sect
tus. 3. mar. 1595.

Scott R. Pilarz, S.J.

ASHGATE

Published by
Ashgate Publishing Limited
Gower House
Croft Road
Aldershot
Hants GU11 3HR
England

Ashgate Publishing Company
Suite 420
101 Cherry Street
Burlington
Vermont, 05401–4405
USA

Ashgate website: http://www.ashgate.com

British Library Cataloguing in Publication Data
Pilarz, Scott R.
    Robert Southwell, and the Mission of Literature, 1561–1595: Writing
    Reconciliation
    1. Southwell, Robert, Saint, 1561–1595 – Criticism and interpretation
    2. Christianity in literature
    828.3'09

US Library of Congress Cataloging in Publication Data
Pilarz, Scott R. 1959–
    Robert Southwell, and the Mission of Literature, 1561–1595: Writing
    Reconciliation / Scott R. Pilarz, S.J.
        p.   cm.
    Includes bibliographical references and index.
    1. Southwell, Robert, Saint 1561?–1595 – Criticism and interpretation.
    2. Reconciliation – Religious aspects – Christianity – History of doctrines –
    16th century. 3. Christianity and literature – England – History – 16th
    century. 4. Christian poetry, English – History and criticism. I. Title

    PR2349.S5Z85 2003
    821'.3–dc22   2003057862

ISBN 0 7546 3380 2
This book is printed on acid-free paper.
Printed and bound in Great Britain by TJ International Ltd, Padstow, Cornwall

Contents

Acknowledgments

Several communities made Robert Southwell's work possible, and that is true of this book as well. The Georgetown University Jesuit Community, along with Jesuit friends further flung, supported me throughout the process of researching and writing. I want to especially thank Dean Bechard, Joe Feeney, Chuck Frederico, Brian McDermott, Joe Ritzman, Matt Ruhl, Kevin Wildes, and the late George Reilly for their encouragement. Joseph Haller and Joseph Tylenda deserve the credit for the illustrations featured here, and other of my Jesuit brothers did me the tremendous favor of reading this work at various stages: Ryan Maher, Bill McFadden, Ron Murphy, Alvaro Ribeiro, Chris Steck, Jim Walsh, and my great friend and mentor of twenty-five years, Otto Hentz. Others at Georgetown, especially members of the English Department, also helped this project along: my two generous chairs, Leona Fisher and Joe Sitterson; my mentor, Jason Rosenblatt; colleagues, including Paul Betz, John Glavin, Wayne Knoll, Patricia O'Connor, John Pfordresher, and Bruce Smith, and my former teacher and cherished friend, Joan Holmer. My new colleagues in the University Chaplain's office saw this project to completion, including Meghan Simons, Tabby Noorbakhsh, and the fabulous Susan Buckingham. Also fabulous are the Georgetown students and alumni in whose lives I have been privileged to share. This book began under the tutelage of some inspiring professors and good friends at the Graduate Center of the City University of New York: Marlene Clark, Pam Scheingorn, the late Martin Stevens, Scott Westrem, Joe Wittreich, and Rich McCoy. Rich also led an NEH seminar at the Folger Shakespeare Institute, which inspired much of my thinking about Southwell and sixteenth-century literature. When I was able to spend time in our own century, I enjoyed the company of many wonderful Washington friends: John P. "Jack" Carroll, Mabel and the late Wesley Horstman, Jim Hemelt, Tom and Joan Kiely, Patty Prince, Ed Quinn, and Caroline Scullin. Patty and Caroline were even kind enough to slog through endnotes and bibliographies. One friend in particular, Chris Stamboulis, listened to my laments and latest ideas during long runs along the Potomac. That was far more painful than shin splints, and I thank him for his patience. One other Washington friend, Carey Smith, translated two Latin accounts of Southwell's martyrdom. My family watched and worried and wondered and waited while I wrote this book. Southwell's work was inspired by his immediate and extended family. So was mine: the late Bob and Mary Simons and my courageous Simons cousins; Carolrae, Lou, Stephen, Michael, and Chris Surovick; Susan, Joe, Carly, and Joey Lappin; and most of all, my mother and father. Most of this book was written at their summer home in North Wildwood, New Jersey, which I made my own for more than a year. They can have it back now, along with a whole lot more of my time, attention, and love. This book is for them, but it pales in comparison to all they keep giving to me.

Scott Pilarz, S.J.
Georgetown University,
Washington, D.C.

List of Illustrations

Prologue

> Sixteenth-century religious leaders were not marginalized intellectuals writing for a narrow scholarly audience, preaching to the converted, with little, if any, impact on their society's wider culture or politics ... As active pastors and moralists, their deep influence on the broader society and culture resounded for centuries, and by the disagreements they engendered, they helped to shape fundamentally the course of Western, and indeed world, history. (Gregory 345)

Elizabethan authorities dramatically and definitively silenced Robert Southwell on 21 February 1595. Or such was their intention. The state required that his allegedly destabilizing voice be stifled, so John Popham, Chief Justice of the Queen's Bench, sentenced the thirty-three year old Jesuit priest and author "to be drawn to Tyburn upon a hurdle, and there to be hanged and cut down alive; his bowels to be burned before his face; his head to be stricken off; the body to be quartered and disposed at her Majesty's pleasure" (Foley *Jesuits in Conflict*, 372).[1] The government also went to great but futile lengths to deprive Southwell of an audience in death. An account of his execution notes that "care was taken not to let the people know beforehand the day he was to die, to hinder their concourse on that occasion." For good measure, "a famous highwayman was ordered to be executed at the same time in another place, to divert the crowd from the sight of this last conflict of the servant of Christ. But these precautions availed nothing; great numbers, and amongst them many persons of distinction, flocked to Tyburn to be witnesses to his glorious martyrdom" (Challoner 214–17). Before his death, as Southwell prayed and professed loyalty to the Queen, a sheriff shouted, "Make an end!" (Devlin 321). His command epitomizes the efforts of many since to quiet an early modern voice that has long made audiences uncomfortable enough to suppress its articulations, often disregarding their content. When C.S. Lewis delivered the Clark Lectures at Trinity College, Cambridge in 1944, he said of the poet-priest, "we never read him without wondering why we do not read him more" (546). The end of Lewis' wonderment is found, in good measure, in an account of endeavors to muzzle or minimize the importance of the young Englishman's voice.

...

The original silencing of the martyr was a protracted effort. Government agents hunted him for six years after he returned from Rome having completed his

Jesuit studies. Southwell left England in 1576 for a Catholic education at Continental schools established for English exiles. While matriculating, he entered the Jesuits in 1578 and was ordained a priest six years later. By an Act of Parliament in 1585, barring from the realm subjects ordained abroad since Elizabeth's accession, Robert could not legally return to England. At his own request, and with his religious superiors' permission, he did so nonetheless in July 1586. The Queen's most determined priest hunter, Richard Topcliffe, monomaniacally dedicated himself to capturing a man deemed a traitor on account of his priestly ministry, which included writing poetry and prose. After Southwell's arrest in 1592, Topcliffe, with royal approval, tortured him for thirty-six months. Finally, at the request of his family who wanted to end his suffering, and following a show-trial staged by the government, the prisoner played the role of martyr for which he had long been rehearsing. On the scaffold he managed to be heard over his executioners' opposition: "I am come hither to play out the last act of this poor life" (Devlin 321).

The rest, however, is not silence. Southwell, who frequently described himself in theatrical terms, provided for encores and revivals. As a result, he has managed to be heard, albeit faintly, despite resistance. As assiduously as authorities tried to obliterate all vestiges of him, the poet left traces that cry out for recognition. He left physical traces: relics, which, according to William Allen, were inestimably prized:

> ... the Catholics of Italy, Spain, France, and namely (which is less to be marveled at), England, more than the weight in gold would be given for any piece of their relics, either of their bodies, hair, bones or garments, yea or anything that hath any spot or stain of their innocent and sacred blood. Wherein surely great diligence and honorable zeal hath been shown by diverse noble gentlemen and virtuous people, that have to their great danger obtained some good pieces of them, to satisfy the goodly greedy appetite or holy persons of diverse nations making extreme suit for them. (*Briefe Historie*, sig. [c7v])

When Henry Garnet, S.J., reported on Southwell's death, he had on his desk a handkerchief with which the young man had wiped his face before dying. The similarity of this handkerchief to Veronica's legendary veil, like the coincidence that both Southwell and Christ died at thirty-three, heightened the typology recognizable both in the actual event of Southwell's martyrdom and in accounts of it. The condemned priest made an article for veneration, cognizant that Catholics desired such objects and that the government wanted to eradicate them.[2] He balled up the cloth and threw it into the crowd. The handkerchief became a prized possession of Southwell's confreres. For example, it served as Garnet's inspiration and as a physical connection with his dead companion. Ultimately, the Jesuit Superior General ordered that the cloth be sent to Rome where it heartened future missionaries. Less willfully on Southwell's part, but as significantly, bystanders dipped their own handkerchiefs in the blood that sprayed as his body was hacked apart. Others bribed executioners for pieces of bone or locks of hair. These relics had powerful resonance among English Catholics for generations to come.[3]

Southwell deliberately left other traces of himself as well, texts, which resonated among future generations despite efforts by political, religious and aesthetic authorities to render them inaccessible or inconsequential.[4] Along with fifty-two lyric poems and a long poem entitled *Saint Peter's Complaint*, he kept a journal published as *Spiritual Exercises and Devotions*; four major prose works, *Mary Magdalene's Funeral Tears*, *An Epistle of Comfort*, *The Triumphs Over Death*, and *Short Rules of a Good Life*; and letters to fellow Jesuits, relatives and prominent Elizabethans. The government penalized those who printed or possessed copies of the poet's writings, as well as those of other Catholic authors.[5] In 1602, for example, James Duckett was hanged for publishing Southwell's *Humble Supplication to Her Majesty the Queen*. The Jesuits also strove for a time to limit the circulation of this conciliatory work. Superiors were embarrassed into such action when their opponents in the Archpriest controversy, an argument among Catholics over the church governance in England, used Southwell's appeal for clemency to undermine the efforts of other Jesuits.[6] Subsequent generations of critics have also discouraged for various reasons the reading of Robert Southwell, sometimes ignoring him, sometimes dismissing him on account of anti-Catholic prejudice, sometimes judging unfairly his literary accomplishments, and most recently treating him with skepticism for his alleged psychological extravagance. Martyrdom makes little sense to postmodernists.[7] Recent detractors regard the author's life as an incomprehensible instance of alterity.[8] His works, they argue, especially his poetry, represent a shallow eddy removed from the Elizabethan mainstream. His prose escapes censure only because it is so seldom read.[9] F.W. Brownlow, the author of the only book-length treatment of Southwell produced in the last decade, adopts a characteristically dismissive tone, stressing the Jesuit's "eccentricity" and "isolation." "Southwell made the decision," Brownlow writes, "in some ways an extremely arrogant one, to be one of the absolutely excluded" (xii). Brownlow confirms Southwell's long-standing consignment to obscurity on account of his allegedly unintelligible convictions.

Unfortunately, the poet's relegation to insignificance has precluded research that can offer fresh perceptions of early modern culture. As a survey of scholarship entitled "Recent Studies in Southwell" concludes, "a comprehensive critical biography of Southwell has yet to be written, [and] further examination of [his] prose writings would be helpful, as would the study of Southwell's mastery of various literary genres and styles and an analysis of his political views" (King *ELR* 13.2 [1983], 221–27). This book aims to advance some of these overdue investigations, arguing that Southwell's life and works mark the point of convergence of aesthetic, theological, political and personal influences that shaped him and his age. The Elizabethan establishment and later literary judgment may push the martyr toward the cultural sidelines, but his life and works can be understood as efforts to claim or construct a center by promoting reconciliation. Far from marginalizing himself by entering the Jesuits and returning to England as a missionary, Southwell deliberately incorporated, for the sake of establishing common ground, the principal energies that inform his era. He absorbed these energies and, as a result, he embodies some of the period's central oppositions. This embodiment made him aware of the need for reconciliation on a variety of levels, and he tried to reconcile in himself many things at once: a nascent English nationalism and an allegiance to the Roman church; the exercise of priestly ministry and the production of literary texts; loyalty as a son and obedience as a member of a religious order; and the constraints imposed by vowed celibacy and the complicated emotional attachments accruing to ardent friendship. He also negotiated and combined a variety of literary styles and theories. Caught among these contradictions, Southwell attempted through reconciliation to make meaning for himself, his family, his nation, his religious order and his church. This meaning, he hoped, would promote coherence when it seemed to be waning.[10]

Southwell's physical body and the body of his work serve as sites for making meaning. These bodies occupy privileged positions from which the poet-priest adapts, negotiates and integrates resistant and competing ways of thinking, writing, believing and being. Attempts to understand Southwell's bodies can afford readers similar opportunities. When executioners broke open his corporeal body at Tyburn, they unintentionally reanimated the Jesuit mission, the English Catholic community, and support for the English cause among Continental Catholics. Likewise, breaking open Southwell's texts advances early modern studies. Examinations of his poetry and prose enhance our understanding of his world in all its complexity. Southwell's voice, often difficult to hear in the centuries since his death, contributes significantly to conversations among scholars committed to appreciating the intricacies of early modern culture. His voice, calling for reconciliation, deserves to be recovered, reevaluated and heard in its historical context.

...

Southwell's contemporaries, persecutors and promoters alike, appreciated his place among them. This acknowledgment made Topcliffe and others adamant about his capture. Thomas Wilson, keeper of government records and sometime foreign intelligencer, in a letter of 22 May 1591 to Robert Cecil, names Southwell, along with Garnet, as "the [two] principal priests in England" (*Dom. Eliz.* ccxxxviii, no. 179). Richard Young, Justice of the Peace, singles him out among prisoners in the Tower as a "notorious traitor" (*Dom. Eliz.* ccxlviii, no. 68). On the night of Southwell's arrest, Topcliffe writes to the Queen bragging about his invention of a special means for torturing his prized prisoner: "It may please your Majesty to consider that I never did take so weighty a man: if he be rightly used" (Lansdowne ms. 72, [fn] 113 "Burghley Papers 1592," printed by Christobel Hood, *The Book of Robert Southwell*, 48). Given this estimation, Topcliffe grew anxious to kill Southwell after years of attempting to extort information from him. The latter refused to reveal names or whereabouts of other Catholics, and his resistance both antagonized and inspired his jailors. When his opponents tried to silence him, he turned silence as a weapon back on them. Cecil, the most powerful figure in Elizabeth's government, who had been present at Southwell's interrogation, admitted, "they boast about the heroes of antiquity ... but we have a new torture which it is not possible for a man to bear. And yet I have seen Robert Southwell hanged by it, still as a tree-stump, and it had not been possible to make him utter one word" (Janelle 66–67). Early on in the trials to which the Crown subjected Southwell, Topcliffe boasted how "he would, if he were able, gather together in one bundle, all the Jesuits in the world, and consume the entire wicked race in flames, and scatter their ashes to the winds" (Foley *Records*, VI, 361). At the poet's last appearance before Chief Justice Popham, an exasperated Topcliffe asserted to his captive, "I would blow you all to dust if I could" (Southwell *Unpublished Documents*, 333–37). Ashes and dust are apt images for that which Topcliffe and other state agents ardently wished: the annihilation of Robert Southwell. Such vehemence attests that the priest's enemies recognized his importance. If Southwell's first biographer, Diego de Yepez, can be believed, even the Queen acknowledged his significance. "Having heard [of Southwell's trial and death]," Yepez writes, "the Queen answered that she had been deceived with false reports, when she had been told that the said father had come to raise sedition in the realm; she showed that she lamented his death, and much more so after she had seen a book that the same father had composed of various pious and devout subjects in the English tongue" (646–47, cited in Janelle 86).

Southwell's proponents were equally aware of his significance and were energetic in advancing his cause. Surveying the first half of the seventeenth century, Thomas Fuller writes in *The Worthies of England* (1662) that Southwell was "cried up by men of his own profession for his many Books in Verse and Prose" (344). Fuller refers to the fifteen editions of *Saint Peter's Complaint, With other Poemes* published in a span of forty years. There were at least two London editions in 1595, another in 1597, and a third in 1602. That same year an edition appeared, with theological emendations, in Edinburgh under the sponsorship of the Puritan R. Waldegrave, and London publishers presented other editions, expurgated or otherwise, throughout the 1630s and 1640s.[11] Even before his death, Southwell authorized an edition of *Mary Magdalene's Funeral Tears* because it was circulating in corrupt versions. In an "Address to the Reader" affixed in 1591, he writes:

> And if necessity (the lawless patron of enforced actions) had not more prevailed than choice, this work, of so different a subject than the usual veil, should have been no eye-sore to those that are pleased with worse matters. Yet sith the copies flew so fast and so false abroad, that it was in danger to come corrupted to the print, it seemed a less evil to let it fly to the common view in the native plume and with its own wings, than disguised in a coat of bastard feather, or cast off from the fist of such a corrector as might haply have perished the sound, and imped in some sick and sorry feathers of his own fancies. (Thurston *The Month* LXXX [1895], 383)

Imping is a term borrowed from falconry. The process requires adding feathers to a bird that has lost its plumage. Southwell appropriates the term in describing his efforts to protect his work's integrity. Since copies of the text were inaccurate, he had intermediaries work with Gabriel Cawood, a printer, to supply an official version which was entered at the Stationers' Register on 8 November 1591. The registration's irony merits its citation: "Master Cawood. Entered for his copie under the hand of the Lord Archbishop of Canterbury. A booke entitled *Mary Magdalen's Funerall Teares*." The Archbishop hardly intended to make available a Jesuit fugitive's work, but the book proved so popular that subsequent editions were published in 1594, 1596, 1602, 1607 and 1609. Southwell's poems were later included in editions published in 1616 and 1620 at Douai, and in 1620, 1630 and 1634 at London.

Along with impressive literary production, Southwell's personal merits and intercessory powers were advertised broadly, mostly by other Jesuits, for the edification of Catholics in England and throughout Europe. John Gerard describes him as "excelling in the art of helping and gaining souls, being at once prudent, pious, meek and exceedingly winning" (*The Condition of Catholics Under James I*). Recounting his 1597 escape from the Tower, Gerard remembers invoking Southwell's name.[12] "So commending myself to God," he writes, "to our Lord Jesus, to the Blessed Virgin, to my Guardian Angel, to all my patrons, particularly Fr. Southwell, who had been imprisoned near this place for nearly three years before his martyrdom ... I took the rope ... and so descended towards the outer world and freedom" (*Autobiography*, 287). The prayer is effective; so much so that Gerard expresses envy that Southwell met with martyrdom while he, "unworthy of so great a good, was left to run out [his] days, and so supply for [his] defects by washing [his] soul with [his] tears, since [he] deserve[s] not to wash it with [his] blood" (*Autobiography*, 287).[13] Garnet, Southwell's closest companion, echoes Gerard's praise. On the day of his comrade's death, Garnet sent a letter to the Jesuit General, Claudio Aquaviva, knowing that the Society's custom was to circulate such missives among the order's houses:

> Behold, now at length I present to his Paternity [i.e., Aquaviva] a lovely flower gathered from his gardens, the sweetest fruit from his tree, a priceless treasure from his bank, silver weighed, tried, and sevenfold purged from earthly dross in the fire; an invincible soldier, a most faithful disciple, and courageous martyr of Christ, Robert Southwell, my former most beloved companion and brother, now my patron, a king reigning together with Christ. (Foley *Jesuits in Conflict*, 376)

This attention provoked attacks from unsympathetic quarters, and the marginalization of Southwell took on literary and theological dimensions. As a young man at Cambridge, Joseph Hall, a future Anglican bishop, challenged Southwell's use of poetry to express religious thought and feeling. Hall's first satires, *Virgidemiae*, published in 1597, argue that verse trivializes spiritual matters. Raised under Puritan influence and educated at the Calvinist-dominated Emmanuel College, Hall became suspicious of things Catholic and Jesuit. Though he later adopted moderate positions and collaborated with Laud and Donne, Hall writes his satires while sympathizing with rigorous reformers. He criticizes the practices of Rome:

> Who says these Romish Pageants bene too hy
> To be the scorne of sportfull Poesy?
> Certes not all the world such matter wist
> As are the seven hills, for a *Satiryst*? (Hall ll. 69–72)

Hall describes the Catholic church as "Pestred with mungrell Saints, and reliques dere" (74), and accuses Southwell of "recklesse poesy" (7), profaning the muses' "sacred hest" by his "presuming tongue" (10). Satire VIII of Book One advances objections to Southwell. In an apostrophe to his opponent he begins, "Hence ye profane." Then Hall proceeds to a posthumous instruction of his martyred rival:

> mell not with holy thing
> That *Sion* muse from *Palestina* brings.
> *Parnassus* is transform'd to *Sion* hill,
> And *Iu'ry-palmes* her steep ascents done fill. (19)

Given Hall's objection to "melling" or mixing the sacred and secular, he oddly begins his satire on religious poetry by echoing the *Aeneid* VI, 258. He willingly uses pre-Christian literature to attack religious expression but not to promote it. His point is that Southwell debases his subject matter by treating it in verse of a classical cast: "Now good Saint *Peter* weeps pure *Helicon,/* And both the *Maries* make a Musick mone:" (19). He judges the "musick" of *Saint Peter's Complaint* and *Mary Magdalene's Funeral Tears* irreverent because it is innovative and, therefore, poorly suited for hallowed subjects. The tendency to "transform" sacred experiences into secular patterns of expression, a trend which Hall claims Southwell introduced to England, transgresses boundaries that Hall would reenforce. The second "Marie," whose "mones" Hall likewise finds objectionable, is probably the creation of Thomas Lodge. Lodge, who likely knew Southwell personally, published *Prosopopeia, containing the Teares of the holy, blessed and sanctified Marie, the mother of God* in 1596.[14] In his Preface, Lodge references Robert when he writes, "[o]thers have wept at Peter his apostasy, Mary her loss and miss of Christ, their tears wrought from them either for reent or love" (Lodge *Complete Works* III, 10). As Herbert Thurston notes, "this close collocation of the subjects of the two best known writings [of Southwell] cannot possibly be accidental" (*The Month* LXXX [1895], 392). Moreover, Lodge regrets having earlier penned profane poems, a conversion that "may have been a result of Southwell's exhortations to the men of letters of this time" (Thurston *The Month* LXXXIII [1895], 242).

Hall assumes that Southwell, Lodge and others who "mell" the things of Sion with those of Parnassus incline toward "the mightiest Ink-hornismes [they] can thither wrest" (12). Such poets, in striving to impress readers, resort to pedantic terms, occluding their subject matter's religious significance.[15] Doing so makes no sense to Hall, who concludes with a pun on the insane asylum, Bethlehem Hospital, or "Bedlam," both to mock and to marginalize Southwell and his imitators. His pun derides a Catholic tradition according to which angels transported the Virgin Mary's home from the Holy Land to the Italian city of Loreto. Hall contends that religious subjects are as likely to be well-served by verse settings as houses are apt to fly:

> Ye *Sion* muses shall be my deare will,
> For this your zeale, and far-admired skill,
> Be straight transported from *Ierusalem*,
> Unto the holy house of *Betleem*. (ll. 13–16)[16]

Hall's censure of Southwell secured his place as a controversial figure among the contentious Elizabethan literary set. Southwell became a weapon for critics who were less interested in him than they were in settling scores among themselves. The playwright John Marston, whose "immoral" satires were burned by the Archbishop of Canterbury, responded to Hall (Morse A. Allen 6). As one nineteenth-century historian observes, Marston "begins to call names in the first line, and with the tenacity of [his] country's bulldogs, continues to worry his game down to the very end" (Marston ed. Davenport, 202). Marston asserts that "No Jew, No Turk, would use a Christian [i.e., Southwell]/ So inhumanely as this Puritan." Then he adapts Hall's pun on Bedlam, undermining the latter's point. Marston worries that if Hall has his way, he will "ding" religious poets "down from Ierusalem,/ And mew them up in [his] deserved Bedlam" (*Virgidemiae*, ll. 45–46). He compares Hall to "*Grillus*," a character in the *Odyssey* who prefers to remain among Circe's swine. Hall, like Grillus, with his "subtile-smelling swinish snout" (l. 31) undervalues Southwell's efforts. Marston, although unsympathetic to Catholicism, defends Robert's pious poetry in the fourth of his earliest satires, *Reactio*, by espousing a principle similar to Southwell's own:

> Shall Painims honor, their vile falsed gods
> With sprightly wits? And shall not we by gods
> Farre, farre more strive with wits best quintessence
> To adore that sacred ever-living Essence? (ll. 47–50)

Southwell, too, admits that "among the Heathens, ... Gods were chiefly canonized by their Poets, and their Painim Divinitie Oracled in verse" ("The Author to his loving Cosen," ll. 8–10). But both he and Marston see in poetry the potential for promoting piety. Poetry is not inimical to Christianity because pagans employed it to worship their gods.[17] On the contrary, Marston defends religious poetry by extending the "Painim" paradigm to Catholicism:

> So have I heard an Heretick maintaine
> The Church unholy, where *Iehovas* Name
> Is now ador'd: because he surely knowes
> Some-times it was defil'd with Popish showes.
> The Bells profane, and not to be endur'd,
> Because to Popish rites they were inur'd. (ll. 63–68)

Marston's point is that poems, like bells, can serve Protestant purposes. Arguing otherwise, as Hall does, is "Pure madness": "Fie inconsiderate, it greeveth me/ An Academick should so senceles be" (ll. 69–72). The Oxford-educated Marston tweaks his Cambridge-trained opponent. Secondarily, and surprisingly, he vindicates the literary intentions, if not the religious beliefs, of an alumnus of the Collegio Romano:

> Come daunce yee stumbling Satyres by [Hall's] side
> If he list once the Syon Muse deride,
> Ye *Granta's* white Nymphs, come and with you bring
> Some sillabub, whilst he doth sweetly sing
> Gainst *Peters* teares, and *Maries* moving moane,
> And like a fierce enraged Boare doth foame
> At Sacred sonnets. O daring hardiment! (ll. 33–39)

This description of Hall's ferocity is more amusing as it follows an early reference to a dish popular among dairy maids. The association of "sillabub," a concoction made of cream, curdled by the addition of wine, with Hall's "enraged" criticism of Southwell renders Hall ridiculous.[18]

Both to make the case against Hall and to defend Southwell, Marston accords significance to the Jesuit's two long poems because they are "moving." Almost accidentally, he is the first to recognize Southwell's emotional effectiveness, and he is echoed by Gabriel Harvey who recommends Robert on the same account; but Harvey, like Marston, cites Southwell to ridicule his rival, Thomas Nashe.[19] Harvey describes *Mary Magdalene's Funeral Tears* as "elegantly and pathetically written," taking umbrage that Nashe bases *Christ's Tears Over Jerusalem* (1593) on Southwell's model. Nashe claims his poem constitutes a public penance for personal misdeeds, and in an "Epistle to His Readers," he apologizes to Harvey for attacking him in earlier works. Without even reading the poem, Harvey accuses Nashe of crying "the tears of a crocodile" (*Works* I, 287). In his *New Letter of Notable Contents* Harvey writes:

> Now he hath a little mused upon the *Funeral Tears of Mary Magdalene* and is egged on to try the suppleness of his pathetical vein, in weeping the compassionatest and divinest tears, that ever heavenly Eye rained upon the Earth; Jesu, what a new work of Supererogation have they achieved? ... What say you, to a Spring of rankest Villany in February: and a Harvest of ripest Divinity in May? (*Works* I, 272–73)

Harvey uses Southwell's work, without naming him, to accuse Nashe of insincerity. Keeping alive among critics the Jesuit's reputation for emotional effectiveness is an unintended effect of Harvey's attack. Nashe responds by withdrawing his apology and freshly assaulting Harvey in the second edition of *Christ's Tears*, without acknowledging his indebtedness to Southwell.

While Marston and Harvey glancingly allude to their fellow poet's ability to move readers, other early critics begrudgingly praise his diction and syntax. Francis Bacon writes to his brother Anthony after the publication of Southwell's *Humble Supplication*, urging him to copy it as a stylistic lesson:

> Good Brother — I send you the *Supplication* which Mr. Topcliffe lent me. It is curiously written, and worth the writing out for the art; though the argument be bad. But it is lent me but for two or three days. So God keep you.
> From Gray's Inn, this 5th of May.
>   Your entire loving Brother,
>   Fr[ancis] Bacon
>   (Bacon II, 308)

Twenty years later, in Part IV of Edmund Bolton's 1618 *Hypercritica*, entitled "Prime Gardens for Gathering English, according to the true gauge or standard of our tongue, about fifteen or sixteen years ago," the author urges that "never must be forgotten *Saint Peter's Complaint* and those other serious poems said to be Father *Southwell's*; the *English* whereof, as it is most proper, so the sharpness and Light of Wit is very rare in them" (Spingarn vol. 1, 110). Likewise, Ben Jonson confessed to William Drummond that "Southwell was hanged, yet so he had written that piece of his, the Burning Babe, he [Jonson] would have been content to destroy many of his" (Spingarn vol. 1, 213).[20]

Robert's Jacobean admirers failed to influence succeeding generations of commentators. Despite Bolton's warnings, Southwell goes largely unmentioned and unpublished in the eighteenth century. Except for an edition of *Mary Magdalene's Funeral Tears* printed in 1772, his works are never reissued between the middle of the seventeenth century and the second decade of the next. When his name appears again in literary histories written after 1820, it mostly receives short and scornful shrift.

Most literary histories written before 1900, including George L. Craik's *A Compendious History of English Literature and of the English Language from the Norman Conquest, with Numerous Specimens* (1863); James Baldwin's *An Introduction to the Study of English Literature and Literary Criticism* (1882); Maude Phillips' *A Popular Manual of English Literature* (1885); Donald T. Mitchell's *England's Lands Letters and Kings* (1890); J.J. Jusserand's *A Literary History of the English People* (1894); and J. Scott Clark's *A Study of English Prose Writers* (1898), omit any reference to Southwell. Charles Cleveland is typical of the few nineteenth-century critics who do refer to him. Cleveland alludes to three unspecified poems by the Jesuit, noting that "they have not many of the endowments of fancy" (89). Robert receives slightly more attention from Alfred Welsh in his 1882 *The*

Development of English Literature and Language. Welsh lists Southwell among "the lesser poets who swarmed in the second half of the sixteenth century." "No useful purpose," writes Welsh, "could be served here by more than passing comment on [him]" (128). Welsh claims him to be a "didactic poet." Echoing Hall, Southwell's earliest detractor, he asserts that the martyr's "poetry was excessively poetical for its sacred and solemn theme," because "the movement and music outweigh the spirit and at times [i.e., in *Saint Peter's Complaint*] becomes almost voluptuous in its verbal languor" (131). The sensuality of Southwell's religious verse unnerves Welsh, as it will others.

Several nineteenth-century writers repeat objections made against various aspects of Southwell's poems. Henry Hallam observes how they "wear a deep tinge of gloom, which seems to presage a catastrophe too usual to have been unexpected" (*Introduction to the Literature of Europe* II, 565). John Alfred Langford describes *Saint Peter's Complaint* as a "strongly religious poem," though, he qualifies, "often its strength is at the expense of its verse":

> It is generally harsh in its construction, and lacks the sweet flow and noble ring which frequently marks the efforts of contemporary poets. It is direct; full of a fierce energy which is out of keeping with the character of the Apostle whose complaint it confesses to be. It is finely exaggerated, and deals in hyperbole to an extraordinary extent. (142)

Perhaps Southwell, unlike Langford, remembered the passage in scripture describing how Peter, after denying Christ, "went out and wept bitterly" (Matthew 26:75).

Writing in 1880, John W. Hales detects in the same poem "genius run riot." Hales, no stranger to hyperbole himself, criticizes the poet for "heap[ing] up metaphor on metaphor" such that "Southwell's defects spring not from poverty but from imperfectly managed wealth; or, to use a different image, the flowers are overcrowded in his garden, and the blaze of colors is excessive" (vol. 1, 480–81). The prevailing taste makes readers suspicious of what appears to be licentious, carnal and seductive in the Jesuit's poetry. Their preference for modesty is offended by what they judge to be his literary promiscuity. Given the anti-Catholicism of the era, which produced numerous literary representations of lascivious priests, a certain amount of slippage may be occurring here.[21] Nineteenth-century Protestant critics attribute to Southwell's verse that which they suspect of Catholic clergymen: an alarming lack of control. Even when his Catholicism does not arouse these suspicions, other critics argue that religion explains his personal and literary idiosyncracies. J.J. Jusserand's *A Literary History of the English People* contends that "Southwell's Catholicism isolated him among the Englishmen of his period"

(329). This separation accounts for poetry full of "pious effusions" and "marred by preciousity." Jusserand claims that "forced similes, paradoxes and antitheses" abound in Southwell's works, while his Protestant contemporaries showed that "a great and truly Christian poetry was possible" (329).

Nineteenth-century denigrations are not exclusively European. Southwell's reputation suffers among the few Americans who read him. This is evident in James Russell Lowell's essay attacking the principles of selection employed by John Russell Smith in volumes entitled *The Library of Old Authors*. Lowell asserts that Smith was guided by "the old-maidenly genius of antiquarianism" in reprinting Southwell's verse along with the poems of Drummond of Hawthornden, *Piers Ploughman*, the dramatic works of Marston, Webster and Lily, and the *Hymns and Sonnets* of George Wither. Lowell alleges that readers of the *Library* might "forget, in their fanaticism for antiquity, that the dust of never so many centuries is impotent to transform a curiosity into a gem, that only good books absorb mellowness or tone from age, and that a baptismal register which proves a patriarchal longevity cannot make mediocrity anything but a bore, or garrulous commonplace entertainment" (249). After suggesting that Wither be assigned as "penal reading," Lowell trains his sights on the Jesuit, opining that "Southwell is, if possible, worse" than Wither. William B. Turnbull, who edited the Southwell volume for Smith, anticipated such attacks. He introduces his volume by expressing "surprise and regret that no modern and complete edition of the poetical works of Father Southwell should have been submitted to the public," but he admits that his "appreciation of the intrinsic worth of the poems" is shared only by "the few living individuals who are conversant with them" (ix). He then cites the poet himself to forestall critics such as Lowell: "Many carps are expected, when curious eyes come a-fishing" (*Mary Magdalene's Funeral Tears*, ix).

Lowell first carps about *Saint Peter's Complaint*, in which he claims Southwell makes "that rashest and shortest-spoken of the Apostles drawl through thirty pages of maudlin repentance, in which the distinctions between the north and northeast sides of sentimentality are worthy of Duns Scotus." Lowell's characterization of St. Peter as taciturn is as debatable as Southwell's depiction. Each constructs the saint to advance his own agenda, though the earlier writer might have scripture on his side considering numerous passages wherein the apostle appears outspoken. Southwell's rendering promotes reconciliation with God through contrition and firm purpose of amendment. There is an emotional aspect to these requirements for a good sacramental confession, and Robert accentuates them so that Peter becomes a model penitent. Lowell renders Peter solemn and detached, attacking the Jesuit's figuration. In reaction to the whole of Southwell's poetry, Lowell utters "an earnest protest ... against the wrong done to the religious sentiment by the greater part of what is called religious poetry, but which is commonly a painful something misnamed by the noun and misqualified by the adjective" (253). He ends his screed by comparing Southwell to George Herbert. He will not be the last critic to do so, but while others find affinity between the two priestly poets, Lowell distinguishes sharply between them:

> to regard these metrical mechanics as sacred because nobody wishes to touch them, as meriticious because no one can be merry in their company, ... nay, to set them up beside such poems as those of Herbert, composed in the upper chambers of the soul that open toward the sun's rising, is to confound piety with dullness, and the manna of heaven with its sickening namesake from the apothecary's drawer. (254)

Finally, though, Lowell finds one redeeming quality in Southwell, admitting that he may be admired for his courage; but Lowell finally equates reading him with a kind of martyrdom: "We would almost match the fortitude that quails not at the good Jesuit's poems with his own which carried him serenely to the fatal tree." "The stuff of which poets are made," Lowell concludes, "is of a very different fibre from that which is used in the tough fabric of martyrs" (253).

Despite this reaction, Southwell garners sympathetic attention from a few late nineteenth-century publishers and pundits. The most important and accurate edition of his poems published since the years immediately after his death appears in 1872 under the supervision of Alexander Grossart. Unlike Turnbull, who, according to Grossart, availed himself of manuscripts that "swarm with mistakes of every conceivable sort," Grossart bases his version on an edition then held at Stonyhurst College, a Jesuit boarding school in Lancashire (Southwell *The Complete Poems of Robert Southwell*, xxvi). Grossart, a Protestant minister, sounds an ecumenical note uncharacteristic of his age when he writes, "there is no monopoly on martyrdoms." He confesses that he "must rejoice that the Reformation in England was not undone" by Southwell's efforts, but he decries the use of violence for religious purposes: "I have that faith in Truth that makes me confident that it was no righteous way to preserve the Reformation to 'persecute' and slay cruelly and meanly those who held to the 'old Religion' in its old forms" (xliv). He publishes the poet to make amends for the treatment the latter received from Grossart's Protestant forebears, which, in Grossart's estimation, amounted to "judicial murder" (lxv). "I should blush for my Protestantism," he admits, "if I did not hold in honor, yea reverence, [Southwell's] stainless and beautiful memory, all the more that he was on the 'losing side,' none the less that beliefs and forms and observances that were dear to him are errors, and more, to me" (lxv–lxvi). Grossart brought forth a limited edition of one-hundred copies of Southwell's poems prefaced by an account of his life. The biography is meant to solicit sympathy for the martyr leading to admiration for his verse. Grossart considers himself a failure if his rendering of Southwell's character has "not won an extrinsic interest and transfiguration for his books" (lxvii).

Grossart's efforts succeeded, at least among Catholic readers. His edition resulted in a series of articles in *The Month*, a periodical published by the English Jesuits. Herbert Thurston, author of several essays on Southwell which appeared at the turn of the century, anticipates the critic Louis Martz when arguing that the priest's literary influence has been underestimated. Tracking Southwell's popularity among his peers, Thurston concludes that "apart from the direct work of the ministry pursued with untiring zeal, the talent so generously surrendered with all its brilliant promise left a mark upon the age" (*The Month* LXXX [1895], 397). Thurston perceives the poet's victory in terms of promoting piety:

> It is something to have induced Nash [*sic*], even for a time, to turn aside from his ribaldry, and to have enlisted such pens as those of Lodge, Breton, Rowlands, and Markham in the cause of morality and religion ... the new interest thus created can hardly have failed to lend its aid in stemming the tide of licentiousness and atheism which threatened to sweep everything before it, amid the convulsions of the change of religion. (397)

But Thurston also intuits that Southwell effected the sound, structure and sense of better-known poets:

> Neither do we know what the indirect effects of this new taste for devotional poetry may have been, nor how much we are indebted to it for the work of Milton and of Crashaw, of George Herbert, and the seventeenth-century divines. This much at least the evidence seems to me clearly to establish, that there *was* such a fashion, which manifested itself in the last ten years of Elizabeth's reign, that the initiative may be traced without hesitation to the writings of Father Southwell, and that the influence which the new fashion exerted cannot have been otherwise than good. (397)

The tone with which Thurston writes about Southwell's sanctity sets the precedent for subsequent pious biographies. These include: Christobel Hood's *The Book of Robert Southwell* (1926), containing a useful compilation of historical sources; Sr. Rose Anita Morton's *An Appreciation of Robert Southwell* (1929); an essay in Sigrid Unset's *Stages in the Road* (1934), a book written "with the object of making Norwegian readers acquainted with pages of history with which, for good reasons, the public in a Protestant country has been kept in ignorance" (viii); and D.H. Moseley's *Blessed Robert Southwell*

(1957), written to inspire Catholic boys. The most recent and sophisticated of such works is Philip Caraman's *Saint Robert Southwell and Henry Garnet: A Study in Friendship* (1995). Caraman describes what he considers to be "the best documented friendship in Elizabethan annals" (3), though he sets the tone for his small volume by noting in the introduction that Henry VIII "is now acknowledged to have put to death a proportionately larger number of his subjects than did Stalin in our own time" (viii).

More serious and less sectarian scholarship on Southwell dates from the 1935 publication of Pierre Janelle's *Robert Southwell, the Writer: A Study in Religious Inspiration*. Janelle measures his subject's works against the ideals of the Counter-Reformation, and argues that Southwell shares more with his Anglican contemporaries than previously thought. Janelle, bucking the dominant historiography, presents a prescient hunch later proved by historians such as Christopher Haigh and Eamon Duffy. According to Janelle, Southwell is undervalued because "it is not generally realized how hard Catholicism died in England, and what a considerable influence the Counter-Reformation exerted in the field of devotional literature and practice" (283). He believes that Southwell's texts, especially his prose, helped sustain Catholicism. Janelle praises Robert's later prose for its "unique blend of classical and native elements," but he is unenthusiastic about his poems, the quality of which is not so "uniformly sustained" (286). According to Janelle, because Southwell "complies too obediently with the directions of some of the Jesuit literary theorists," his poems "treat emotion and passion with distrust." Turning the tables on critics who complained about the poet-priest's emotionalism, Janelle thinks that the poems' structures obscure feelings. "The pleasure they provide," he concludes, "is merely of an intellectual kind." Nevertheless, Janelle admits that "such a type of poetry need not be invariably or absolutely despised [because] ... the mind can take some pleasure in observing close-packed thought neatly and aptly expressed" (286). In those rare instances when Southwell "delights in humanizing" religious figures, "bringing them into actual existence upon earth, in surrounding them with real objects, in making them into daily friends and companions," he reveals his "definitively English," as opposed to Jesuit, quality (287). This assertion displays Janelle's ignorance of Jesuit spirituality.

If Janelle disregards Southwell's spiritual formation, he is even less cognizant of his literary legacy; but Louis Martz makes advances on both these fronts in *The Poetry of Meditation* (1954). Like Janelle, who admits that Thurston's articles are the "starting point" for his work, Martz cites the contributions of the nineteenth-century Jesuit as inspiring him "to modify the view of literary history which sees a 'Donne tradition' in English religious poetry." After studying seventeenth-century religious lyrics written by

Catholics and Protestants, Martz concludes that there is, instead, "a meditative tradition, which found its first notable example not in Donne but in Robert Southwell" (3). Martz's argument is familiar to students of this period: Southwell's poems may not be in the style of the seventeenth century, "but in [their] meditative methods, in [their] theme of tears, in [their] use of conventions from profane poetry, we may see in [them] the seeds of the poetry of meditation soon to follow" (210). He points to a basic Ignatian meditative pattern informing contemporary poetry, a pattern that Southwell learned while making the *Spiritual Exercises* during his Jesuit formation. Whereas Southwell's first critic, Bishop Hall, condemned him for being an innovator, Martz praises him for writing methodologically inventive verse through which "the Counter-Reformation penetrated to English Literature" (13).

Likewise familiar are Barbara Lewalski's objections to Martz. These two scholars are unintentionally responsible for a binary still obtaining to much criticism of early modern religious literature. Lewalski rarely refers to Southwell in *Protestant Poetics and the Seventeenth-Century Religious Lyric* (1979). Given her argument that "the poetics of much seventeenth-century religious lyric derives primarily from Protestant assumptions about the poetry of the Bible and the nature of the spiritual life," this scarcity is expected (5). Advancing her case, contra Martz, that "the primary poetic influences" upon Donne, Herbert Vaughan, Traherne and Taylor are "contemporary, English, and Protestant," and that "the energy we respond to in much of this poetry has its basis in the resources of biblical genre, language and symbolism, the analysis of spiritual states, and the tensions over the relation of art and truth which were brought into new prominence by the reformation," Lewalski sidelines Southwell (5). She cannot number his works among "the superb religious lyrics" which "reflect in various ways the heightened Protestant regard for biblical figurative language as a principal vehicle for uniting divine truth and the truths of human experience" (104). While admitting that "basic Christian tropes" such as the marriage and pilgrimage metaphors and the light–darkness antithesis "had considerable currency" in Southwell and other Catholic poets, Lewalski contends that Protestant poets "exploited biblical metaphor even more intensely" (104). Southwell, by implication at least, employs basic tropes in conventional ways while ineffectively expressing truths, divine and human.

...

A new reading of Southwell's life and works can move beyond the Reformation/Counter-Reformation binary inadvertently installed by Martz and Lewalski. This reading will necessarily consider the sea-change in the historiography of the period, which complicates previous understandings of denominational affiliations during Elizabeth's reign. Religious identity in Southwell's England was more fluid than once imagined, and this fluidity affected the poet's family. For example, his grandfather, father, brothers, uncles and cousins moved in and out of the established church. It is difficult to determine where they stand at any given moment, and this difficulty applies to his wider audience as well. As a result of this fluidity, Lewalski's argument with Martz needs reevaluation. Given that many Englishmen known to Southwell, though fewer English women, were Catholic and Protestant by turns, it may be fruitless to worry over which religious tradition had greatest influence. In fact, recent scholarship insists that there were several religious traditions competing for adherents in the late sixteenth century. It makes more sense to discuss Catholic traditions, Anglican traditions and Puritan traditions than it does to speak as though three univocal monoliths were pitted against each other. Southwell encountered a religious landscape more variegated than previously imagined, and in traversing it he had more tools than Martz knew. While Martz rightly stressed Robert's "Jesuitness," he did some injustice both to the poet and to his religious order. For example, Loyola's *Spiritual Exercises* is not the last word in understanding Southwell. His motivation has, as Martz suggests, much to do with the mission of the Society of Jesus, and while the formative value of the Ignatian *Exercises* should never be underestimated, it is not necessarily the exclusive influence on the labors of a given member of the order, especially a man such as Southwell, who faced ministerial contexts that are highly unusual even by Jesuit standards. While Martz masterfully discovers in Southwell's poems the Ignatian meditative pattern, it is often the case that issues to which Loyola's *Exercises* attend hardly or not at all engage the poet's energies. To read him then, as Martz has done, as a poet of the *Exercises*, is to ignore much that animates his work, including a poetics of pious utilitarianism grounded in the Jesuits' *Constitutions* and other foundational documents.[22] Moreover, Southwell negotiates terrain for which his Jesuit formation could never have prepared him. Perhaps these negotiations are most interesting and informative in showing how a study of this neglected author illuminates early modern realities. When Southwell attempts through reconciliation to make meaning against the background of confusing aesthetic, political, personal and religious developments, we are privileged to watch a keen early modern mind at work. Rather than avoiding developments which would stretch him, figuratively and literally, beyond the breaking point, Southwell deliberately engaged them. This is not to say that he was fearless. He admitted his anxieties and terrors, and in this, too, we hear a revelatory voice. Southwell was hardly close in to Elizabethan circles of power; nonetheless, he never imagined himself far from the center of important cultural movements, which he wanted to influence. His contemporaries' testimonies, those provided by friends and, even more clearly, those of his enemies, indicate that his conciliatory voice was far more articulate and effectual than critics of subsequent centuries have allowed it to be.

Notes

[1] On trial, Southwell testified "that he was neare about the age of our Savioure, who lyved uppon the earth 33 years, and he him selfe was as he thought neare about 34 yeares." Topcliffe "hereat ... seemed to make a great exclamation, fearinge he compared him selfe to Christe." Southwell's assertion and Topcliffe's reaction underscore their awareness that they were playing out a familiar script.

[2] Southwell also gave his cap to his jailer before being dragged to Tyburn. When Robert's friends asked for the relic, the jailer would not part with it (Moseley 179). Another "second class relic" was Southwell's Breviary, through which Garnet discovered that the tortured priest was deprived of writing implements in prison since he "found not one single sign made with ink ... one can just see the word 'Jesus' scratched with a pin" (Janelle 69).

[3] C.A. Newdigate reprints in *The Month* a chapter from *Lives of Philip Howard, Earl of Arundel, and of Anne Dacres his Wife*, which tells how the Countess of Arundel gained one such relic: "After his death she obtained by mediation of some friends one of the smaller bones belonging to his feet, the which she caused to be set in gold, kept it as a relique of great esteem, and wore it continually about her neck even until her dying day, leaving it then as a legacy unto F. Richard Blount, Provincial at that time of the Society [of Jesus] here in England, and she esteemed it the more because she found much help thereby for the easing of sundry pains and infirmities to which she was subject" (251). See "A New Chapter in the Life of Blessed Robert Southwell, S.J.," in *The Month* CLVII (Mar. 1931), 246–54.

[4] See Gregory 300, on the relationship between texts and relics: "Relics reenforced writings by and about martyrs—both were *monumenta martyrum*."

[5] Garnet complained to the Jesuit General that "the greater part of the editions [of Southwell's *Humble Supplication*] must have fallen into the hands of the Queen's officers" after its publication in 1600. As a result, he could not find one to send to Rome. The few extant copies of the text were probably seized by the Archbishop of Canterbury in his role as *censor librorum* (Thurston *The Month* LXX [Mar. 1895], 388). State Papers record the seizure of books by Southwell, including the record of the examination of John Bolt, a musician, who confessed to borrowing Catholic books: "And (this examinate). saith that the one book bound in parchment ... and also one little book written called *Saint Peter's Complaint* is his, but of whose writing he knoweth not, but borrowed it of Mr. Wiseman" (*Dom. Eliz.* vol. 248, [fn] 37). Owing to influential friends at court, where he had been among the Queen's favorite performers, Bolt escaped conviction and later became a priest (Hood 72).

[6] See the Introduction to R.C. Bald's edition of the *Humble Supplication* on the use of the text by Jesuits' opponents.

7   See, for example, Ronald J. Corthell's "'The Secrecy of Man': Recusant Discourse and the Elizabethan Subject" in *ELR* 19.3 (1989), 272–90. Invoking Steven Greenblatt's *Renaissance Self-Fashioning*, Corthell argues for "the highly paradoxical character of martyrdom, a social action at once self-consuming and self-dramatizing" (279). Comparing Southwell to Hamlet, he suggests that the Jesuit represents a "radically divided subject, one socially constituted and therefore powerfully related to the experience of subjection" (290). See also Seymour Byman, "Ritualistic Acts and Compulsive Behaviors: The Pattern of Tudor Martyrdom," *American Historical Review*, 83 (1978), and Richard Marius, *Thomas More: A Biography* (New York: Alfred A. Knopf, 1984), 517–18.

8   Brad Gregory masterfully exposes the inability of contemporary theory to "get" martyrdom (101), on account of "self-indulgent presentism" (351): "Christian martyrs in early modern Europe will remain opaque to the extent that their religiosity—with all that that entails—remains alien, obscured by modern and/or postmodern assumptions" (8). Moreover, "[i]f our objective is to understand these people rather than to judge them ... then we ought to declare a postmortem for poststructuralism and avoid its dead end ... In fact, all reductionist theories evince an impoverished historical imagination, one insufficient to understand the lived realities of the past" (10).

9   Even Christobel Hood's hagiographical *Book of Robert Southwell* dismisses his prose as "perhaps too much in the nature of 'tracts for the times' to appeal to us at the present day." "The heavily ornamented style," she concludes, "which so pleased his contemporaries, is tedious to readers in the twentieth century" (70).

10   John Donne, who knew of Southwell through his mother and her two Jesuit brothers, concludes in "An Anatomy of the World" in the "First Anniversary" that "all coherence [is] gone." Critics who study this perception include William J. Bouwsma ("Anxiety and the Formation of Early Modern Culture," in *After the Reformation: Essays in Honor of J.H. Hexter*. ed. Barbara C. Malalent [Manchester, UK: Manchester UP, 1980], 215–46), and Malcolm MacKenzie Ross (*Poetry and Dogma: The Transformation of Eucharistic Symbols in Seventeenth-Century English Poetry* [New York: Octagon, 1969]). In describing the late sixteenth and early seventeenth centuries, Ross relates how "the [English] firmament becomes a whirling jumble of every conceivable dogmatic stress" (55).

11   For example, Waldegrave limits Mary's role in the poem. Whereas Southwell's St. Peter bemoans that he has been "a traitor to the Son, in Mother's eyes," Waldegrave's Peter considers the reaction of God the Father (Thurston 398).

12   His invocation shows that Southwell's contemporaries "widely perceived their recent martyrs as new saints who were in God's presence, regardless of the status of their canonization proceedings" (Gregory 297). Remarkably, "[n]ot a single person killed for his or her religious commitments in the early modern period was canonized before 1700" (252).

13   See Lake and Questier (206) for an explanation of Gerard's envy: "the point was also reached when a priest's escape from jail might be viewed by some catholics [*sic*], as a sign of serious moral and spiritual weakness."

14   Janelle reports "we have proof that [Lodge] knew Southwell's works and admired them." Moreover, "he may also have moved about in the Arundel circle, since about 1596, he married one Mrs. Aldred, 'a Catholic lady, who having been used by the government to slander the imprisoned Earl of Arundel to his wife, was wholly gained over, it seems, by the sweet gentleness of the Countess, and remained ever afterwards her devoted adherent'" (55).

15   See Hall 171.

16   Hall willingly "wrest[s]" the details of the legend, moving Mary's house from Nazareth to Bethlehem.

17 As Joan Holmer points out in *The Merchant of Venice: Choice, Hazard and Consequence*, early modern authors such as Southwell and Hall understood the notion of "Egyptian gold," i.e., "gold is gold regardless of the camp in which it is mined" (xiii). See also D.W. Robertson's *A Preface to Chaucer: Studies in Medieval Perspectives* (Princeton: Princeton UP, 1962), 340–42.

18 Arnold Davenport dates the earliest use of "sillabub" to describe writing to 1706, though he does note that Harvey speaks of Nashe and "the sillibub of his stale invention" (Marston 244).

19 For a full account of the Harvey–Nashe quarrel, see pp. 67–110, vol. 5, *The Works of Thomas Nashe*. ed. Ronald McKerrow (London: Sidgwick and Jackson, 1910).

20 This is high praise from Jonson who criticized Shakespeare in *Timber; or, Discoveries Made upon Men and Matter*: "The players have often mentioned it as an honor to Shakespeare that in his writing (whatsoever he penned). he never blotted out a line. My answer hath been, 'Would he had blotted a thousand.'"

21 Examples abound of this nineteenth-century association between priests and sexual license. Among the most famous is *The Awful Disclosures of Maria Monk*, originally published in 1836. According to John Wolffe in *The Protestant Crusade in Great Britain 1829–1860*, "this notorious book purported to be the memoirs of a renegade nun from the Hotel Dieu in Montreal, and alleged that nuns regularly performed sexual services for priests." Wolffe shows that "the book had a great impact in stirring anti-Catholicism in the United States" (125). Another example, and one specifically critical of Jesuits, is W.W. Collins' *The Black Robe*. Published in 1881, this novel is one of many that parodies Catholic confession practice with regard to sexual sins. Considering Collins' work and those similar to it, Wolffe observes, "in its crudest form, the Protestant didactic novel was more propaganda than art, but in skillfull hands the scheming Jesuit or tortured Catholic conscience could provide the basis for some not unsubtle characterization ... In this context, the Victorian Jesuit should be seen as in some respects the precursor of the twentieth-century German or Russian spy" (312).

22 See my essay "'To Help Souls': Recovering the Purpose of Southwell's Poetry and Prose," in *Discovering and (Re)covering the Seventeenth Century Religious Lyric*. ed. Eugene R. Cunnar and Jeffrey Johnson (Pittsburgh: Duquesne UP, 2001), for a definition of Southwell's pious utilitarianism.

Chapter 1
Reconciling Family:
The Epistle to His Father

Southwell's desire to claim or construct a center by promoting reconciliation initially resulted from affection for a family that presented symptoms of falling apart.[1] His relatives occupied provisional and precarious positions all over the English religious landscape during "an era of unprecedented disorder and dislocation" (Walsham 2). Often, the same relative could be found serially, or simultaneously, in a variety of credal corners; and while their inconsistency provoked criticism from contemporaries, including fellow Jesuits, Southwell found his family's plight sympathetic.[2] This sympathy inspired his vocation as a Jesuit writer. Among his priorities as a priestly author was the mediation of his responsibilities as a son of the church with those attendant upon the youngest member of a religiously complicated family. In this task, Southwell had company. Many English Jesuits in the late 1500s, including the poet's cousin, John Copley, could admit that "their parents, siblings and close relatives were conformists, and confess … to having complacently spent their own childhood and youth in 'schism'" (Walsham 77). Moreover, Southwell, like other contemporary poets, including John Donne, George Herbert and Richard Crashaw, was cognizant of his enmeshment in challenging family faith dynamics. He responded to that challenge by promoting religious, personal and political reconciliation.

. . .

Southwell's relatives merit attention not only because he, like all of us, is shaped by family history, but also because their lives reveal the conflicting cultural forces operative at the time. The following narratives display a world in which compromises and vacillation were regular features. In addition, Robert was committed to his family and so had to negotiate their religious fluidity in light of the sharp contrasts made during his education. For example, his engagement with his father's religious identity illustrates how the poet himself maneuvered. Southwell's works show that his approach reflected both an orthodox Roman view, on the one hand, and a pastoral engagement with the complexities of the situation which allowed a latitude not always present in ecclesiastical texts. In this case, his Jesuit formation and, in particular, Loyola's *Spiritual Exercises* equipped him for reconciling theological rigor and pastoral sensitivity. The result is a response at once aligned with Catholic tradition and modern in its commitment to religious truth while underscoring the need for decisions made in freedom and integrity.

. . .

Among Southwell's Roman papers is a copy of a 1582 letter he wrote to Robert Persons concerning his relatives. Persons, from England, had reported the effects of Edmund Campion's martyrdom (Southwell *Unpublished Documents*, 301–303). The poet responds in code in order to confuse state agents should they intercept his letter; however, the sense is clear.[3] He hopes that, through Persons' ministrations, Campion's death will edify rather than unnerve his family. Following his superior's instructions, he addresses Persons using his alias, Eusebius.[4] The letter's controlling metaphor, a favorite of Southwell's, is the buying and selling of "jewels," with which Persons can "enrich" the Southwells. "One request I particularly make," he writes, "is that you would contrive by all means possible to dispose of some [jewels] to the relatives of your friend Robert S., for I remember that at one time they were very keen about that quality of goods, and kept a factor who was occupied solely in searching for such gems." This "factor" is a Marian priest whom the family supported. The "gems" stand for sacraments and other ministries. Southwell worries that Campion's execution will frighten his family into apostasy. "Possibly now," he speculates, "after seeing the great losses others have sustained, they may have changed their minds, a circumstance which, if true, would grieve me sorely." This moves Southwell to ask a favor:

> I earnestly beg you to persuade them, if possible, either yourself or through another, not to lose heart because of any small loss that may happen; for such is the lot of merchants, at one time to rejoice over the amassing of wealth, at another to bear patiently the loss of some small barque. A strong suspicion for fearing that they may have withdrawn from this line of business is occasioned by my never hearing of their having the same success as some others have had, who have persevered and still persevere, even with an occasional loss, knowing full well that in the end it is more lucrative than any other sort of enterprise. (*Documents*, 302)

ROBERT PARSONS,
Jesuit

1.1 Engraving of Robert Persons (by courtesy of
the Woodstock Theological Center Library,
Georgetown University, Washington, D.C.)

Southwell's suspicion settles upon his immediate family, especially his
brother, Thomas; and he tells Persons he would be "much obliged if
[Persons] could possibly prevail on some one to visit" them and "see if
there be any of them who is disposed to accept your advice in this matter."
Thomas "once had dealings" with Persons "in this particular [line of]
business, though what he decided to do I have not been able to ascertain."
　　Lack of certainty makes Southwell anxious for news:

> If not convenient to you, Sir, I should feel obliged if you would let me
> know in what frame of mind he and my other relatives are, in order that, if
> there be no other resource, I may recommend them more earnestly to our
> Lord, begging that He would open their eyes to the evil that will result, if

> they thus retire from the business which for so many years they have
> carried on so profitably. (303)

Robert's familial concerns ultimately motivate his desire to return to
England. He awaits "some future day, if health and means permit, and
Signor Claudio [Aquaviva, the Jesuit Superior General] will give leave,"
when he "should like to join" Persons and "share both in [his] toils and
profits" (303).

. . .

Southwell's incentive for entering the Jesuits shows how religious
motivations are reshaped around family issues. On the one hand, he
exhibits normal sixteenth-century reasons for entering religious life: he
wants to save his own soul, stating as much in *Spiritual Exercises and
Devotions*:

> The first foundation which I lay down by the aid of God's grace and, by
> the help of the same grace, will maintain until my last breath, is this: By
> the special love and mercy of God, I have been singled out from all my
> family and kindred and called to enter the Society of Jesus, in which I
> am determined, as I wish to be saved, to persevere during life and until
> death. (33)

As his works show, Southwell remains always acutely aware that his soul
hangs in the balance. But so, by the same account, hang the souls of his
family members, and their spiritual welfare is never far from his thoughts.
His reason for choosing the Jesuits, over other orders, has to do with
them. "My aim in entering religion," he writes, "[is] that by constant
mortification of self and by submitting myself to all men for Christ's
sake, I might become as like to my crucified savior as I could." The poet
understood such constancy in apostolic terms: "my aim in choosing the
Society in preference to other religious orders ... was that I might not
only have the opportunity of carrying out these objects, but in addition
labor with all my strength for the salvation of my fellow-men" (*Spiritual
Exercises and Devotions*, 34).[5]

Southwell's sense of the range of his "fellow-men" narrows down
in the course of his life. Early in his Jesuit formation, before his return to
England was assured, he writes about commitment to family. After
entering the novitiate on 17 October 1578, Robert heard from Persons
how unlikely his homecoming might prove, given anxieties generated
among Jesuit leaders about an English mission. "Why," the young exile

writes in reaction, "why, then, should God have drawn me to the Society—and not to the Carthusians or some other solitary order—and drawn me with this one and only argument, namely that only in the Society and not in these other Orders, could I be of any use to my country, to my kinsfolk, to my friends, etc., who do so seem to need my help?" (*Spiritual Exercises and Devotions*, 93).

Two of Southwell's prose works disclose his perceptions of his family's need for help. The lengthier of the two, *An Epistle of Robert Southwell unto his Father, Exhorting Him to the Perfect Forsaking of the World*, is dated 22 October 1589. The second, perhaps addressed to his brother, Thomas, bears no date, and lacks internal evidence to place it chronologically.[6] Both texts, however, underscore Southwell's affection for relations and his awareness of their recent history. He writes to his father to produce "effectual significations" and "yield proof" of his "thankful mind" (3). Gratitude moves him to write this *Epistle*, even if his father and other relatives are reluctant to benefit from his ministries. He describes them as "more willing to hear of me than from me, and readier to praise than use my endeavors" (4). He notes how friends, on the other hand, understand "the right persuasion of [his] present calling," his Jesuit vocation, on account of "descent and pedigree." His priesthood is "in manner hereditary" (3). Moreover, in the letter to his brother, he implies that family loyalty provides motivation for martyrdom. To convince the letter's recipient to return to his "former liberty in God's Church," Southwell expresses a self-abnegating wish: "I would I might send you the sacrifice of my dearest veins to try whether Nature could awake remorse and prepare a way for Grace's entrance" (*The Triumphs Over Death*, 65–67). In large measure, the writer ministers as a Jesuit priest and contemplates death as a martyr for his family's sake.

. . .

Southwell's fidelity is surprising given the inability of men in his family to stay any course in religious matters.[7] But it reveals his dedication to people challenged with sustaining religious identity in the sixteenth century.[8] Robert knows this challenge personally and from his earliest years. More than property and prestige, anxieties about religious allegiance are part of his patrimony. Southwell's family, with its muddled religious affinities, first figures in English history after the Tudor accession. His great-great-grandfather, Richard, acquired property in Norfolk through marriage. Henry VII befriended Richard's sons, Robert and Francis, appointing them to high offices. Francis, auditor of the exchequer, left two sons, Richard and Robert, and it is this Richard, the Jesuit's grandfather, who provides the best example of how the Southwells negotiated England's "piecemeal," "discontinuous," "parallel" and "blundering" reformations, "which most did not understand, which few wanted, and which no one knew had come to stay" (Haigh 13–14). Richard Southwell, in his dodges and manipulations, exemplifies "men [who] may seem hypocrites, *politiques*, and cowards."[9] But, we should remember, "they lived in confused and dangerous times, when ideas and power structures were unstable." As a result, "they did not know, and could not yet know what it was to be Catholic or Protestant. So they did not elect for or against 'the Reformation' in one great do-or-die decision; rather, they made a number of lesser choices in particular contexts" (Haigh 14).

Among Richard Southwell's choice-making contexts was his relationship with Thomas Howard, Duke of Norfolk. Upon his father's death, Richard Southwell went to be raised in Norfolk's household, along with his cousin, Norfolk's son, Henry Howard, Earl of Surrey. The two became close friends; so close that Southwell was poised to bring Surrey down when, in 1546, Henry VIII suggested he do so. Raised under Norfolk's tutelage, Southwell learned survival skills inherited by his heirs, with the exception of his martyred grandson. These skills were similarly lost on Norfolk's own son, who had a talent for trouble. Southwell, however, acquired the Duke's dexterity. For example, he ably aided Norfolk during the trials of his nieces, Anne Boleyn and Katherine Howard, both of whose royal marriages Howard had arranged.[10]

Proximity to power well suited Richard Southwell, and he readily enjoyed the attendant benefits, rarely allowing conscience or religious conviction to impede his rise. For example, his connections helped him prosper at the expense of England's monastic establishments. Despite the Catholic inclinations of Norfolk and his supporters, they took advantage, sometimes with feigned reluctance, of the proceedings against the monasteries.[11] In one instance, Southwell, in 1536, interceded with Cromwell on behalf of an abbey at Pentney:

> We beseech your favours for the prior of Pentney, assuring you that he relieves those quarters wondrously where he dwells, and it would be a pity not to spare a house that feeds so many indigent poor, which is in a good state, maintains good service, and does so many charitable deeds … If you will prevent it, your labor will not be without remembrance. (Gasquet 191–92)

His politicking is typical of the times, during which "the King gave [monastic spoils] as presents, as stakes in a game of dice" (Constant 190). Usually, Southwell was a willing player. When his labors on Pentney's behalf failed, he acquired the property.

Richard, along with his younger brother, Robert, both commissioners for the suppression, investigated monasteries, mostly precipitating their closure. Robert, for example, writes in 1538 to Cromwell condemning the priors of St. Andrew, Northampton: "There have growne no decay by this priour that we can lerne, but surely his predecessours plesured moche in odoryferous savours, as it shulde seme by their converting the rentes of their monastery, that were wonte to be paide in coyne and grayne, into gelofer flowers and roses" (Wright 172). In a subsequent report on the priory of Twynham in Hampshire, Robert relates how "in thys churche we founde a chaple and monument curiously made of Cane Stone, preparyd by the late mother of Raynolde [Cardinal] Pole for herre buriall, whiche we have caused to be defacyd and all the armys and badgis clerly to be delete" (Wright 231–32).[12]

Currying Cromwell's favor, Robert Southwell ruined a tomb. Richard, with greater subtlety, but for identical reasons, ruined the reputation of Walsingham monks by reporting their allegedly occult experiments. "Emoung other thinges" found in the priory, Southwell describes:

> ... a secrete prevye place within the howse, where no channon nor onnye other of the howse dyd ever enter, as they saye, in wiche there were instrewmentes, pottes, belowes, flyes of suche strange colers as the lick non of us had seene, with poysies, and other thinges to sorte, and denyd gould and sylver, nothing ther wantinge that should belonge to the arte of multyplyeng ... Of this moultiplyeng it maye please you to cawse hem to be examined. (Wright 138)

Such reports pleased Cromwell and, more importantly, the King, who, after introducing the bill for the suppression of the monasteries in Commons in 1536, referenced the "salacious tidbits" provided by the Southwell brothers (Haigh 131).

Their evidence secured the bill's passage, though the King was of several minds on monasticism. He needed funds which the suppression supplied, and ambitious courtiers, including the Southwells, desired properties. On the other hand, Henry resisted moving against traditional religion beyond the prescriptions of the Ten Articles of Religion, which were themselves a "compromised compromise" (Haigh 128).[13] The King's religious confusion in the 1530s explains Richard Southwell's adjustments. Cromwell and Cranmer intended to undermine the sacramental system presupposed and promoted by monastic life. Henry, however, and men like Southwell, believed in masses for the dead, the necessity of confession, and Christ's "substantial" presence in the eucharist (Haigh 131). They willingly dislodged contemplatives, especially from smaller monasteries, and sold their treasures. But they never endorsed the eradication of monasticism, much less Catholic sacramental teaching.

The Southwells also grasped the political consequences of such destruction, intuiting the resistance that culminated in the conflicts of 1536. But when northern rebels finally rebelled against the suppression, the Southwells rallied around the King. "On 23 December 1536," M.H. Dodds reports, "Richard Southwell announced that he had arrested two priests who were circulating copies of the rebels' oath, [and] his brother, Robert, reported about Easter 1537, the execution of two priests who were taken in Sussex and were perhaps the same men." In April 1538, the people of Walsingham planned to defend the town's abbey. Hearing of this "most serious plot," Cromwell dispatched Richard Southwell to Norfolk (Elton 144). Southwell interrogated conspirators, including two Carmelites and three secular priests, and the investigation ended in fifteen executions (Elton 150–51).

These efforts assured Richard Southwell's appointment as receiver to the Court of Augmentations and his Parliamentary election in 1539. Richard was joined at Westminster by Robert, who, at Cromwell's instigation, was seated for King's Lynn. Cromwell's promotion of the Southwells was not reciprocated, however. They shifted allegiances to "a distinctly conservative block in Commons that was of crucial importance to Norfolk, Gardiner and the conservative party that steered the Act of Six Articles through this session despite Cromwell's opposition" (Head 266–67). Gardiner, leading this faction, used "court connections, parliamentary elections and ecclesiastical patronage to bolster his defense of orthodox Catholicism." The Southwell brothers supported them, so long as Gardiner and Norfolk remained in the King's graces, which they did long enough to see Robert knighted in 1537 (Strype *Annals* II, 1, 6). Richard was knighted five years later.

. . .

Richard Southwell's affinity for authorities sympathetic to Catholicism predates his election to Parliament and provides another chapter in his history of religious obfuscation. On 12 May 1535, Richard Rich, accompanied by Southwell, visited Thomas More in the Tower. Their ostensible purpose was to confiscate More's books on account of his obstinate refusal regarding the Oath of Supremacy. According to Roper's *Life of More*, Rich, at More's trial, claimed it was upon this occasion that More denied Henry's authority as Head of the Church (Roper 245). But Roper recounts how, at the climax of More's trial, Southwell failed to corroborate Rich's testimony:

> Master Rich ... caused Richard Southwell and Master Palmer, that at the time of their communication were in the chamber, to be sworn what words had passed between them. Whereupon Master Palmer, upon his deposition, said that he was so busy with the trussing up of Sir Thomas More's books in a sack that he took no heed to their talk. Sir Richard Southwell likewise, upon his deposition, said that because he was appointed only to look upon the conveyance of his books, he gave no ear unto them. (248)

Roper's account is suspect. He wrote twenty years after the fact and was not an eyewitness. Oddly, other trial records omit Southwell's inability to produce evidence. As G.R. Elton observes, "Admittedly, if the Crown had really invented some damning statement and then produced two witnesses who denied hearing it, the prosecution's incompetence passes the limits of the probable." "Can we," Elton asks, "trust the story of those defaulting witnesses?":

> Their collapse seems to have impressed nobody, not even the original reporters, who quite failed to mention it, and certainly not the jury. More oddly still, those broken reeds came to no harm at all. Nothing much is known of Palmer, except that he was a servant of Cromwell's, but Richard Southwell, a careerist client of his, continued serenely on his successful way to wealth and a little power. (414)

. . .

If the More episode is clouded, Richard Southwell's tendency to identify and serve the powerful is incontrovertible when he betrays Henry Howard. Toward the end of Henry VIII's reign, debates raged about a regent for Prince Edward. Henry Howard promoted his father, despite Norfolk's diminishing influence at court. The ascendant Seymore faction undermined what chance Norfolk had by bringing charges against his ambitious son. After years of living with Surrey, Southwell sided with the Earl's enemies, positioning himself for prominence in the coming reign. The case brought by Southwell alleged Surrey's misuse of heraldic devices. Informed against Surrey, Southwell claimed that the Earl added the arms of Edward the Confessor to his escutcheon painted on the walls of the family's manor, Kenninghall. This decoration belonged exclusively to the Prince of Wales.[14] Those seeking Norfolk's demise convinced the King that this meant treason. Surrey was arrested, along with his father, who was arraigned as an accomplice. Southwell searched Kenninghall for evidence against the family who had raised him on the estate he was now working to confiscate from them. At trial, he admitted finding no trace of the escutcheon; but even without physical evidence, his word caused his friend's death.

Religion also figured in the Howards' downfall, and again Southwell's behavior contradicts his Catholic inclinations. The Howards represented the old religious regime, and their incarceration occasioned Protestant celebrations. One reformer, John Burcher, writes to a colleague, "[t]he Duke of Norfolk ... —a most bitter enemy of the word of God—has been imprisoned, with his son, with whom he made a secret attempt to restore the Pope and the monks; but their design was discovered" (Padelford 39). The more factual discovery was Southwell's sacrifice of religious and personal commitments for political advantage.

Surrey reacts to Southwell's treachery in a translation of Psalm 55, describing the "unbrydled tungs" of "that coniured league" (13) which "bray so lowde" in "their malice bent" (3–4). Southwell led the "league," assisted by others whom Surrey accuses of practicing "wickidnes with craft," and explains how they caused his fall because they had been so close: "It was a friendly foo, by shadow of good will, Myne old fere and dere frende, my guyde that trapped me" (22–23). Surrey hopes that God will "stryke with hevy hand" those who should suffer from "conscyence unquyet" (36).

His hope was misplaced. Southwell gained higher office, and when Surrey's father was reinstated by Mary Tudor, Richard befriended him again. Perhaps the Duke found a kindred spirit in Southwell since Norfolk, too, cooperated in his son's demise. To save his life and property, he confessed concealing his son's use of heraldic symbols. This sealed Surrey's doom, but Norfolk's appeals for clemency postponed his execution long enough for the King to die (Head 228). Norfolk spent seven years in prison, but this was to his good: "[f]or the Catholic and conservative Thomas Howard, the Tower may have been the safest place to spend Edward's reign" (Head 228).

While Richard Southwell joined Norfolk in prison by Edward's death, early in the reign he prospered because of his role in Surrey's fall. He was named an assistant executor in Henry VIII's will, which made him a member of the Privy Council (Pollard *England Under Somerset*, 38). The King likely signed this last in a series of wills on 30 December 1546, naming as executors representatives of several religious factions to establish balance in the coming reign. But after Henry's death even conservatives, such as Southwell, cooperated with Somerset's reformist circle. Most Council members earned gifts and titles in exchange for accepting religious changes, which they understood as a limited program "to consolidate royal supremacy and extend lay control of the Church rather than as an effort to move the Church in a thoroughly Protestant direction" (Loach 47).

Later in the reign, Southwell and others resented the reformist agenda. After popular uprisings in 1549, he joined the opposition organized by John Dudley, Earl of Warwick. Warwick convinced Southwell that if they united, Cranmer's innovations could be undone. Looking back on Warwick's coup, the Protestant bishop, John Ponet, describes the conspirators:

> When Wriothesley, Arundell and Southwell conspired with the ambitious and subtle Alcibiades of England, the earl of Warwick ... to pull the good Duke of Somerset, the King's uncle and protector out of his authority, and by forging a great many false letters and lies to make the Protector hated, brought to pass Warwick's purpose: who then for awhile but they three? And Wriothesley that was before banished the Court, is lodged with his wife and son next to the King ... Arundell, is promised to be next to the King, groom of his stool, or comptroller of his house at least. Southwell (for his whisking and double diligence) must be a great councilor in any wise. (Hudson 134)

Though Ponet accurately credits Southwell for duplicity, he was ultimately duped by Warwick, who switched sides, replacing Somerset as Protector. In the wake of his treachery, most who had sided with him were executed. Southwell, though, fortunate as ever, was merely imprisoned (Jordan 28). Ponet bemoans how "Southwell is committed to the Fleet, where being examined, he confessed enough to be hanged for, and had gone very near it, had not his examiners upon hope of his amendment breaking out of his eye, but not out of his heart, obtained their favour" (Hudson 135). Given Southwell's guile, his examiners can be exonerated.

Surviving another crisis, Southwell spent Edward's reign waiting for the tide to turn. At Edward's death in 1553, he was among the first who rallied around Mary Tudor at Kenninghall, the former Howard estate. He arrived two days after her accession, even though, hedging his bets, he also signed Letters Patented for Jane Grey to be Queen (Markham 204). While Northumberland had Jane Grey proclaimed Queen in London, Southwell and others amassed strength in East Anglia, Oxfordshire, Buckinghamshire and the Thames Valley. These men "were not magnates, but immediately they formed the nucleus of a well-disciplined military camp" (Loades 176). When Mary triumphed, she constituted a Council from among those at hand, including Southwell.

Southwell generously served his Catholic Queen. A "work horse," he sat on twelve royal commissions, most dealing with "the tricky disciplinary problems created by the change in religious policy" (Loades 82). During Wyatt's rebellion he commanded troops in defense of St. James' Palace and asked the Queen's permission to pursue the traitors in London's streets. Mary also sent Southwell to bring Elizabeth to London under suspicion that she instigated the attempted coup (Strype *Annals* III, 1, 129). John Foxe, who often alludes to Southwell in *Acts and Monuments*, describes Southwell's leadership during "the unreverent and doleful dealings" of the Lords with Elizabeth, who claimed to be too ill to travel. Southwell found a physician loyal to Mary who ruled that the Princess was well enough to go to London despite her protestations.

If Southwell punished Protestants as enthusiastically as Foxe claims, this is a rare moment when he acts on his religious convictions. According to Foxe, Southwell participated in the trials of at least four men burned for heresy, including one who was already dead.[15] In a section of *Acts and Monuments* entitled "The Ridiculous Handling and Proceedings of Bishop Bonner and His Mates against John Tooley," Southwell recommends the trial of a man already executed for theft (Foxe VII, 90). On the scaffold, the thief, John Tooley, recited lines from Cranmer's Litany, asking God to save him from "the Bishop of Rome and all his detestable enormities." Southwell participated in a subsequent Council meeting which decided that "the Pope's holiness should be avenged with fire and faggots" (VII, 91), and he signed a letter to Bishop Bonner urging that "such a matter should not be overpassed without some example to the world" (VII, 92). Bonner summoned Tooley for examination. When he failed to appear, he was tried in absentia, and turned over to the sheriffs of London who exhumed and burned his corpse on 4 June 1555.

After Wyatt's rebellion, Southwell collaborated with Gardiner in opposing Mary's marriage to Philip. As a result, he almost forfeited his seat on the Council at Philip's request (Prescott 288). The Queen, however, rewarded Southwell's loyalty during the rebellion by making him Master of the Ordinance (Strype *Ecclesiastical Memoirs* III, 1, 351). He returned the Queen's favor by urging Parliament to acknowledge one of Mary's imagined pregnancies.[16] Southwell, according to Foxe, represents the worst of the Marian regime, but the fortunes of the Southwell family did not turn immediately upon Elizabeth's accession. Richard remained Master of the Ordinance for three years, and he prospered despite growing royal disfavor, dying a wealthy man.

. . .

Richard established the paradigm for generations of Southwells who moved frequently and in different directions across England's intricate religious terrain. Robert Southwell grew up knowing that religious identity could prove complex, fluid and potentially life threatening. Even personal geography served as a reminder. He was raised at St. Faith's, a former Benedictine priory, which his grandfather obtained during the suppression. The poet's father, the elder of Richard's illegitimate sons, inherited the property, enabling him to marry Bridget Copley.[17] As a Jesuit novice, Robert remained mindful of, and perhaps defensive about, his family's involvement in the suppression, making monastic corruption a spur to his own vocation. "See," he records, "what has happened in England, in Germany or anywhere else, where nowadays for most people the names of 'monk' and 'scoundrel' have the same meaning." As a result, "[i]t is our duty therefore—we who last of all have enrolled ourselves as Religious under the most Holy Name of Jesus ... so to shine upon the world to lift up the *Res Christiana* that now droops so sadly, and to build up again from the ruins what others by their vices have brought low" (Devlin 10). Robert's vocation can never be disentangled from Southwell family history.

. . .

Religious complexities also disoriented Southwell's maternal relatives, the Copleys. His uncle, Thomas Copley, was raised Catholic, but owing to relations between the Copleys and the Boleyns, Thomas supported Elizabeth's claim to the throne. As his granddaughters, Mary and Helen, both of whom became nuns, describe him, "in his youth he fell into heresy, although he had been brought up a Catholic ... and [he] continued a hot heretic in the time of Queen Mary, when all were Catholics" (Morris *Troubles* I, 51–52). At the commencement of Elizabeth's reign, Copley was a rising star, a position secured when the Queen stood as godmother to his first son, named Henry after her father, on 8 June 1561. Then, abruptly, he returned to Catholicism.

Biographers attribute his conversion to reading Jewell's *Apology for the Church of England.*[18] Persons describes Copley "examin[ing] certain leaves [of Jewell's book] and finding many falsehoods therein which were inexcusable," raising the matter with Jewell over dinner:

> And receiving certain trifling answers from Mr. Jewell, he waxed more hot, and urged the matter more earnestly; which Jewell perceiving told him in effect that papists were papists and so they were to be dealt withal: and other answer he could not get. Which thing made the good gentleman to make a new resolution with himself, and to take that happy course which he did to leave his country, and many great commodities which he enjoyed therein, to enjoy the liberty of conscience and so both lived and died in voluntary banishment. ("A Relation of a tryal made before the king of France an. 1600 between the Bishop of Evreux and the Lord Plessis Mournay," 1604, *Letters and Memorials*, 53–54).

Persons' contention that Copley "happily" gave up his commodities meets with contradiction in the latter's letters to Elizabethan officials. After Thomas left England in 1570, Parliament passed an Act stipulating that if any subject left the realm without the Queen's license, and did not return within six months after warning or proclamation, he shall forfeit to the Queen the profits, lands and properties. As a result, Copley's property was in jeopardy. He argued that his exile was lawful "by reason of his freedom in the staple; which gave him liberty to pass and repass the seas at his pleasure" (Strype *Annals* II, 1, 379). In the meantime, to support his family, he entered military service under Continental monarchs and was rewarded with titles referring to his English estates (Copley *Letters*, xxix). In 1577, Henri III of France made him a Baron, allowing Copley to refer to himself as "Lord." Intuiting the Queen's objection, Copley explained his acceptance of foreign honors on account of "[his] poore wyfe, seing w[i]th what lovingnes and patience she hathe made herselfe a voluntary partaker of all [his] travayles" (Copley *Letters*, 107). Moreover, he argues in a letter to Burleigh, "my doings tende to myne owne particular, and to the helping of my selfe, and not to any practice against my Prynce or Contrey" (110).

1.2 Portrait of Richard Southwell, grandfather of the poet (by courtesy of the National Portrait Gallery, London)

Protestations of loyalty fill Copley's correspondence, but he remained suspect for the remainder of his life, as did his wife, Katherine, who survived him. After Thomas' death, she returned to England, but before departing, she wrote "to my very loving Nephew, Mr Robert Southwell, of the holly Societie of Jhesus, at the Inglish Colledge at

Rome," which is the only family correspondence among Southwell's papers (Devlin 87). Her name appears on a list compiled two years later of those who housed missionaries, and she was arrested in September 1586, after Nicholas Smith, her nephew and a classmate of Southwell's at the English College, Rome, testified that she harbored him at Roughey and at Gatton. Her financial situation was dire. Southwell reported to superiors that the "poor dear lady ... has so much to bear and was reduced to such straits that I had to lend her ten pounds" (Southwell *Unpublished Documents*, 318). Katherine Copley fled England after her release from prison. An unsigned 1589 letter notes that she has "obtained the favor of entry into the kingdom" from the Duke of Alva and that she is using her resources to "instruct the said Jesuits, one of whom is always with her." The letter also recommends her interrogation because "she is such a great bigot she will know their [the Jesuits'] rendezvous" (*S.P. Dom.* 1580–1625 Cal. 311).

Ties between the Copleys and the Jesuits grew intense, and in some cases knotty, in future generations. Thomas Copley's eldest son, Henry, was taught by Jesuits at Douai. William, his brother, studied under Jesuits at Rheims. His oldest son, Thomas, entered the Jesuits and volunteered for the order's Maryland mission in 1634; and, as noted, two of his daughters joined the convent of St. Monica, Louvain, which was under the influence of Jesuit spiritual directors. Several of William Copley's siblings are entangled in Jesuit history. His sister Margaret and her husband, John Gage, were arrested at a Mass said by George Beesley, a priest who was hanged in June 1590. The Gages were condemned as well, but two years later they were pardoned on the scaffold.

Topcliffe mentions this pardon in a note written after Southwell's arrest to the Queen regarding the most complicated of the Copleys, Thomas's third son, Anthony:

> Young Anthony Copley, the most desperate youth that liveth, hath most familiarity with Southwell. Copley did shoot at a gentleman last summer and did kill an ox with a musket, and in Horsham church threw his dagger at the parish clerk ... there liveth not the like I think in England for sudden attempts; nor is there one upon whom I have good grounds to have more watchful eyes for his sister Gage's and his brother-in-law Gage's sake, of whose pardon he boasteth he is assured. (Landsowne ms. 2, [fn] 13)

A biography of the Jesuit Thomas Copley speculates that "the black sheep Anthony ... exchanged the life of his sister for that of his cousin and benefactor, i.e., Robert" (Dorsey 71). However dubious this claim, Robert Southwell was very solicitous of Anthony, referring to him

in one letter as "my Anthony" (Southwell *Unpublished Documents*, 319).
Anthony, too, acknowledges their relationship, confessing in the Tower in
1590 Robert's "love towards [him]" (Strype *Annals* IV, 1, 12).

. . .

Anthony Copley, born in 1567, joined his parents in exile after several
years under the charge of Thomas Southwell, Robert's brother (Strype
Annals IV, 1, 12). In 1584 he entered the English College in Rome, where
Robert Southwell was Prefect of Studies. Anthony's College career was
checkered. To secure his admission, Southwell obtained a papal pension
for his cousin; even after Southwell left Rome, he watched after Anthony.
In December 1586, he wrote to the College rector on behalf of Copley's
mother:

> His mother begged me earnestly to write to him that he must not think
> about leaving the College, solemnly adding only that she did not know
> what would become of him if he returned hither ... Relying on your
> kindness, I told the mother that Anthony would be kept at the College
> without any charge to her, or the seeking any pension from his other
> relatives and that he should stay there till he had finished his course of
> studies. I praised him in the old words of praise, which he so well
> deserved at his first arrival, though, as I afterwards learnt from his mother,
> he has dimmed that praiseworthiness by his letters, asking to be allowed
> to leave. It pained me to hear this, but I made the best excuses for him I
> could, so as to spare sorrow to one in affliction. I hope for the best
> regarding him: may God convert hope into reality. (*Unpublished
> Documents*, 318)

Despite these pleas, Copley, whom Persons calls "that wanton
boy," was expelled from the College after standing in the pulpit with a
rose between his teeth (Devlin 257).[19]

Returning illegally to England, Anthony ingratiated himself with
officials. Under arrest, he flirted with conforming to the established
church (Strype *Annals* IV, 1, 14). Moreover, he intimated that he might
spy on other Catholics: "And good sirs, I beseech you, let my honourable
good lords of her majesty's council, ... be satisfied in my faith and truth
to my prince and country; and to make proof thereof in whatsoever they
shall please to employ me" (Strype *Annals* IV, 1, 14). Copley also
distanced himself from relatives thought to be enmeshed in foreign plots.
"Perchance," he acknowledges, "my father's and my brother's demerits
may make against me, but I refer myself to the favour of my good lords."

. . .

Exactly what his good lords' favor assigned Copley is unclear. Perhaps "owing to Southwell's influence, he spent the next six years in seclusion, writing poetry and trying to cultivate a philosophic calm" (Devlin 257).[20] Evidence of both activities exists in *A Fig For Fortune*, Copley's 1596 parody of *The Faerie Queen*.[21] This lengthy allegory makes an argument, similar to that advanced five years earlier in Southwell's *Humble Supplication*, for the possibility of loyalty to the Queen and the Catholic church. In an opening prose argument, Copley explains how he will expose "the insults of Fortune, whom I have named Doblessa in respect of the double danger both of her luring and lowering inconstancy" (5–6). What he actually exposes, by means of a narrator identified as an exiled "Elizian," is the error of the English church, even while praising its head.

As in Spenser's original, Copley's language is archaic, at times annoyingly so. As one critic remarks, "he seems to have been as bad a poet as he was a man" (Dorsey 71). C.S. Lewis avoids moralizing, but singles out for opprobrium one of Copley's neologisms, "to cravin-cockadoodle it" (84) (Lewis 464). The poem's worst passages include lines such as "What manhood is it still to feed on Chickins/ Like infant nurse-boys in nice Fortune's kitchins?" wherein Revenge personified distinguishes between masculine and feminine glory (18); and:

> Contrarie-wise whatsoever Sionite
> Doblessa could with flight or fight enthrall
> She led away into eternall night
> Blind-folding their eyes to make them fall
> Into a thousand helles and offendickles
> Thrice fatall lapse from Grace into such pickles. (79)

This awful stanza establishes the poem's opposition between Doblessa, Copley's figure for the English church, and Sion, the Catholic church. Prior to this contest, however, Copley's speaker, "exild from joy" (7), entertains two options, suicide or revenge, to end his misery. Cato's ghost presents the first possibility, praising suicide's merits.

Suicide appeals to the Elizian when Cato encourages him to "flip out [his] life at glories window" (10). Should he do so, Cato argues, "[Jove] will imbosome thee in his embrace,/ And Joy-embalme thee in his Heaven-delights" (14). Cato advertises his remedy in a manner congruent with contemporary discourse on death, describing suicides as "Fame's choicest Martyrs" (14). Should the poem's protagonist join them, then "will we [Cato and other suicides together with Jove] magnifie thy happie woundes/ and high applaud thee with Crownets and crowns" (14). Copley, in decorating suicide with the accoutrement of martyrdom, recognizes that in early modern England one man's martyrdom is another man's self-murder; and his exile rejects this course when, after drawing out his "emboldened blade,/ Resolved to massacre my loathed life," the ghost departs, leaving behind "such a sulphur stench ... / That I in dread thereof shook every limb" (14).[22]

"Reflecting on [Cato's] stink," the speaker rides until he meets Revenge's "shape of shame" (16). This "Medusa like ... Bug" (16) advertises herself as "the Phoenix of Adversitie" (17), predicting the exile will see his foes "in downe disgrace" (21). Revenge prescribes "politicke dissimulation/ Of contrarie language, and contrarie face" (22), and requires "chameleon-like" qualities (23). Behaving otherwise reveals "foole-sincerity and want of wit" (23). Finally, Revenge reveals herself a creature of darkness who loathes the light. She "suddenly ... vanisht out of sight/ Because now in the East it dawned daylight" (25). This disappearance disenchants Copley's Elizian, who notes that "such is not the instinct of Paradize" (25).

Copley maintains loyalty to the Roman church and his earthly ruler, but obviously not all Catholics did. He diplomatically distances himself from those who heed Revenge's advice. Some Catholics saw the end of Elizabeth's reign as an opportunity for retaliation. Revenge's lines, such as "what greater glory can betide the Vale/ Then force the mountaintop adowne to fall" (21), would resonate in these quarters. At this point in Copley's career, however, he clings to the possibility of conciliation, a position he shares with his cousin Robert. His poem, like Southwell's *Humble Supplication*, attempts to avoid the extremes of martyrdom and regicide.

At the poem's midpoint, the Elizian seeks this middling approach, exchanging his sable steed for a snow-white jennet named Good Desire, who knows the way to "a penal place ... brighter than the Noony Zodiak." Here the exile meets Catechrysius, a hermit, who leads him on a pilgrimage toward orthodoxy. Zion appears as "a Rock in shining glorie" (27), an allusion to the primacy of Peter, and the catechist assembles elements of Catholic piety:

> There kneeled a Sophie all in teares
> With needle-pointed discipline correcting
> His flesh's frailty. Oh how he besmears
> The place with penal blood, and blubbering:
> His heart was wholly fixed on Christ his Passion,
> So shewed his Crucifixe-contemplation. (28)

This crucifix becomes an object of tear-soaked veneration in following stanzas when it is knelt before and kissed, controversial gestures in the Elizabethan context. But Catechrysius' homage to England's Queen allays the poem's contentious aspects. Even when exposing her church's fraudulence, he upholds Elizabeth's political legitimacy.

Catechrysius delivers a distinctly Catholic sermon in which he praises suffering in *imitatio Christi*. Jesus established "a prescedent/ Of passive Fortitude, and Lamblihead" (52), which the exile should follow. Copley's advice on suffering is like Southwell's own. Catechrysius, for example, advises the exile to stand on "Reasons haughty Promontorie," above the vicissitudes of Fortune (42). Reasoned contentment is the goal of Christian living, for "without content all glorie is but gall,/ And with content disgrace is festivall" (44). In articulating this theory, Copley echoes the two poems by his cousin which mention fortune in their titles, "Fortunes Falsehood" and "From Fortunes Reach." Moreover, his desire for contentment recalls Southwell's "Content and Rich," a parody of Edward Dyer's "My Mind to Me a Kingdom Is." In "Fortunes Falsehood," Southwell describes fortune's vagaries:

> No wing so chaungable, no sea so wavering,
> As giddy fortune in reeling varieties:
> Now mad, now mercifull, now fearce, now favoring:
> In all things mutable, but mutabilities. (ll. 37–40)

Given this, Southwell makes recommendations much like Copley's. In "From Fortunes Reach" he urges readers to "[l]et fickle fortune run her blindest race": "I have settled an unremoved mind:/ I scorne to be the game of phancies chase,/ Or vain to shew the chaunge of every winde" (ll. 2–6). And finally, in "Content and Rich," Southwell ends where Copley does:

> My conscience, is my crowne:
> Contented thoughts, my rest:
> My hart is happie in it selfe:
> My blisse is in my brest. (ll. 9–12)

If, as Devlin suggests, Southwell had sway, both personally and poetically, over Copley during the years following his release from prison, the similar sentiments they express reveal the depth of Southwell's influence.

Catechrysius also invokes the emblematic image of the Pelican, underscoring the vulneral accent typical of current Catholic prayer.[23] This devotion to Christ's wounds is characteristic of Ignatius Loyola, who places the *Anima Christi* prayer at the start of his *Spiritual Exercises*. In the prayer, Loyola has an exercitant say, "O good Jesus hear me; Within thy wounds hide me." Similarly, Catechrysius explains the Pelican emblem:

> So shew'd his Pellican content to die
> To give thee life, the gore adowne his breast
> To wash away thy sin impuritie:
> His dolor was thy everlasting rest,
> His bitter wounds the ever open gates
> Of grace, and glorie to thy rankest fates. (53)

The exile is told to "behold [Christ's] image on the Crosse,/ See how he droops and dies and damnes Revenge" (54). After seeing the crucified Christ, he ought to "die in [his] Saviors wounds, and there an end,/ There prick the Period of thy moody wander" (55). This emphasis establishes further similarity between Copley and his cousin. Schooled in the same spiritual tradition, Southwell writes of Christ's wounds in "Man to the wounds in Christs side," in which the speaker apostrophizes the gash made by a Roman soldier's spear:

> O Pleasant port! O place of rest,
> O royall rifte, O worthy wound,
> Come harbour me a weary guest,
> That in the world no ease have found. (ll. 1–4)

Southwell's speaker contemplates the wounds before entering them: "Here would I view that bloudy sore,/ Which dint of spitefull speare did breed" (ll. 17–18). But he is not content until gaining access:

> O happy soule that flies so hie,
> As to attain this sacred cave:
> Lord send me wings that I may flye,
> And in this harbour quiet have. (ll. 25–28)

Sealing the exile's redemption, an angel appears, performing a ritual of investiture, complete with "heaven-inchanted tackle." The Elizian is grateful for graces received, especially the sacraments, "the streams that tril from *Iesus* wounds/ Into the seven-fold cisterns" (62). This numerical reference challenges Spenser's image of the Catholic church as the seven-headed beast of Revelation. Next the Elizian enters a temple, and nearing the sanctuary, Catechrysius exclaims, "O *Elizian*/ See what it is to be a Christian" (64), comparing unfavorably the English church to Sion, while carefully praising Elizabeth as "the lords dear daintie," "the phoenix of true Principalitie/ The feast of peace and sweet saturitie/ Unto the people of her Emperie" (65). "But," he insists, "such her glories are but eare-delightes." The citizens of Sion "are no *Elizium*-bred wightes." They hunger for sounder truths and more substantial spiritual fare: "We have oure joyes in another kind/ Ghostly innated in our soule and mind" (65).

After describing the Temple's architecture, epitomizing the full fury of the baroque, the poem reaches its climax during a Mass presided over by "the high Sacrificator at the Altar/ Victiming with holie rites his maker" (72). This terminology is conspicuously Catholic, and Copley inserts other vocabulary, as well, to challenge Protestant readers. "There saw I," he tells his audience, "sacred imposition/ Of hands, and grace abundantly imparted,/ Chrisme, and authentic sanctification/ and Exorcism of such as were possessed" (67). He implicitly undermines the legitimacy of Anglican orders and defends the practice of exorcism for which Jesuit missionaries were famous.[24] Finally, Copley stresses the unity among Catholics, setting them apart from "*Babell*-Biblers ... scambling for the Ghospels bread" (73).

Before the battle between the churches, Copley digresses about Doblessa's resistance to missionaries. "How manie Sionites of choise esteem," he asks, "Brave men of wonders have been sent from thence/ To teach *Doblessa* (Errors Dreary Queen)/ Their sanctimonie and innocence?" (74). Not even martyrs impress Doblessa: "How manie worthies have dispent their blood/ To doe th'unkind *Doblessa* so much good" (74). Copley concludes that Doblessa is "a Witch, and Queen of all the Desert/ From *Babell*-mount unto the pit of Hell" (74):

> She had no Altar, nor no Sacrament
> No Ceremonie, nor Oblation,
> Her school was Cavill and truthlesse babblement
> Riot her Raigne, her end damnation;
> This was the haggard whore of *Babylon*
> Whose cup invenym'd all that drunk upon. (77)

In this stanza, Copley turns back upon Protestant polemicists their favorite image for the Catholic church. But this whore needs to be narrowly understood; it is not Elizabeth, as Copley points out when the battle ends.

Signaling the poem's conclusion, the narrator explains how "thus began the holie warres of *Sion*/ Against the rampant Haag and whoore of *Babylon*" (79). Sion's troops are orderly. "It was a heaven to see the good array/ And unity of *Sion* in this conflict," the exile reports (81). The opposition, on the other hand, "fightes/ Without all discipline or good array" (79). Protestant discord reveals a fatal flaw, recalling Jesus' admonition that "a house divided against itself cannot stand." Given such divisions, Doblessa can merely entrap a few Sionites "by hooke or crooke" (82), and in a desperate effort to make traitors, "[s]he can with Magick-spels and sorcerie/ Faire Virgin-like to falsifie her figure" (83).

This is the first of several confusing references in the poem's last stanzas to appearances made by virgins, and the perplexity allows for Copley's profession of dual allegiances. After the false virgin's retreat, the Sionites stage a procession during which the exile sees "a Virgin in bright majesie" descending upon a silver cloud (88). This virgin showers down red and white "Roses most odiferous" (89), and the Sionites are left "a scambling/ For such her sweets" (90). The exile assumes the Virgin is Elizabeth, but Catechrysius explains that this "was an Easterne Dame," namely the Virgin Mary. The red and white roses exacerbate the exile's uncertainty about the virgin's identity. As Roy Strong shows, "roses ... are *par excellence* the flower of the Queen." "She is," according to Strong, "both the white rose of York and the red rose of Lancaster; she is the double Tudor rose epitomizing in her person the Tudor *pax* brought about by the union of the two houses" (68). Previously, as Strong also notes, the rose featured in medieval art celebrating the Virgin Mary, and those responsible for promoting "the cult of Elizabeth" appropriated the symbol, whether consciously or not. Copley may be undermining this appropriation by restoring the symbol to its original object of association. At the same time, however, the poem shows him zealous for the well-being of England and Elizabeth.

Copley's Catholicism, compounded by his concern for England, lands him in controversy throughout his life. While there is scant evidence of the poem's original reception, there exist many references to its author's unstable political and religious affiliations. In *A Fig For Fortune*, for example, Copley praises Jesuit missionary activity. After Southwell's death, however, he distanced himself from the controversial religious order, siding with England's secular clergy in their struggles against the Society. In 1601 he wrote a pamphlet entitled "An Answere to a Letter of a Jesuited Gentleman, by his Cosin, Maister A.C., concerning the Appeale, State, Jesuits," and later he elaborated his case in "Another Letter of Mr. A.C. to his disjesuited Kinsman concerning the Appeale,

State, Jesuits. Also a Third letter of His Apologeticall for himself against the Calumnies contaned against him in a certain Jesuiticall libel intitled A Manifestation of folly and bad spirit." The controversy between the priests, Jesuits and seculars, which drove a wedge between rival factions of English Catholics, concerned the authority of the Archpriest, George Blackwell, and the alleged "hispanolization" of the Jesuits. The latter issue arose after Persons' *A Conference about the Next Succession Concerning the Crown of England* was printed in English in 1595.[25] The work argues that religion, rather than heredity, should determine Elizabeth's successor, and evaluates the competing claims of potential rulers. Many readers, including Copley, thought Persons advocated a Spanish successor instead of James VI of Scotland.[26]

Copley's penchant for controversy drew him into the 1603 "Bye Plot," a scheme to kidnap James before his coronation. Under the kidnappers' influence, they hoped James might convert to Catholicism. The plot's details are mostly gained from reading Copley's confession made after the plan was foiled. He traces the plot's origins to failed negotiations between James and Catholic visitors to his court. Once James secured the support of Cecil and the majority of England's Protestant peers, he refused to meet with Catholic emissaries. Copley reports, imitating the King's burr, how James informed his advisors, "Na, na, gud fayth, wee's not neede the papists now!" (*Dodd's Church History* IV, I). Disappointed Catholics thought the King ungrateful and disrespectful of his mother, Mary Queen of Scots, whom Southwell canonized in his poem "Decease, release." "Upon these grounds," Copley contends, a group of conspirators, "associates of the best sort," took an oath and vowed secrecy for fear that either the government or the Jesuits would discover their intentions. The Jesuits, known as "the Spanish faction," were "distasted with the King," and sure to be designing their own plot. According to Copley, the conspirators merely wanted "to present unto his majesty ... by the hands and the *viva vox* of some eighty or hundred of the chiefest [Catholics], a supplication."

After the plot failed, Copley, in exchange for incriminating evidence about his co-conspirators, had his death sentence commuted to banishment, probably agreeing to furnish information about Catholics on the Continent. Later reports concerning him are ambiguous. After some time in France and Brussels, Copley returned to Rome in 1606, interrupting his residence there for a visit to Naples where he reconciled with Persons. In a letter to the latter he praises the Jesuit's "singular endeavors in God's cause and our country's," and credits him with changing his life. Copley received a written testimonial verifying his change of heart, and he spoke in Roman churches, repudiating his anti-Jesuit pamphlets as "false and scandalous" (Edwards *Robert Persons*, 307). All the while, though, he wrote letters asking for permission to return to England.

. . .

While Southwell's family may seem eccentric for its shifting religious affinities, recent scholarship reveals that they had company among Englishmen of their stature. As Walsham reports, "[t]hese redirections in research suggest that the sharp polarities in Church and society indicated by labels like 'Catholic' and 'Protestant' are, in many respects invalid in the early modern environment" (8). Haigh, studying the aftermath of "the theological revolution of 1559," instigated by the Act of Uniformity and a new Prayer Book, concurs that denominational lines are difficult to draw. The Southwells, then, and Robert's responses to them, need to be considered in the context of an England in which "clear-cut divisions between 'Catholicism' and 'Protestantism' did not pass into being ... as smoothly or as rapidly as the legislation of that year" (Walsham 14). Members of the poet's family and others like it "instinctively" and understandably "temporized": "After the abrupt religious reversals under Henry VIII, Edward VI and Mary, Elizabeth's new reformation was widely anticipated to be an equally impermanent affair" (Walsham 14).

Southwell and his Jesuit companions placed their apostolic hopes on such impermanence, in light of which they formulated missionary strategies. When Mercurian, the Superior General, sent Jesuits to England, he circumscribed their work. Jesuits were to "confirm Catholics in their faith, to absolve the lapsed, [and] not to fight with heretics" (Basset 40). This approach could exploit the weakness of the Elizabethan Settlement without antagonizing non-Catholics. Jesuits were to privilege pastoral work over polemic; and while not all Jesuits obeyed the last of these instructions, Southwell avoided controversy, attending instead to the General's first two tasks. This attention came naturally to him, since his relatives needed to be confirmed in their faith or reconciled to it. Reading the signs of the times, a requirement for effective ministry, meant, for Southwell, reviewing the behaviors of those closest to him. If he proved more patient with temporizers than other Jesuits or Continental Catholic writers, it is a result of his allegiance to and compassion for relatives. Circumstances situated Southwell at the center of his family's religious struggles. From that vantage point, he produced comparatively mild and generous texts. Family loyalties smooth the rough edges of religious polemic, even while Southwell remains an articulate spokesman for Catholicism. On account of natural affections and religious commitments, he reconciles contradictions that created tensions for many of his contemporaries.

. . .

Southwell composed two letters for relatives in states of religious flux. Both encourage reconciliation with his larger, mostly observant family, and the Catholic faith; and his approach, in comparison to his contemporaries, is tempered and moderate. Southwell labors in these letters to mediate his loyalty to and love for compromising relatives and his increasingly exacting religion. As noted, the longer of these works, the *Epistle unto His Father*, is dated October 1589 and appeared in print in 1596 with *A Short Rule of Good Life*. The 1589 date is debated, however, since Nancy Pollard Brown argues that a copyist mistakenly rewrote the original date of 1586 (*Two Letters*, *xxiii*).[27] She bases her speculation on the fact that the name "Richard Southwell of St. Faith's, whose son is a Jesuit" appears on a list of recusants composed in 1588 (*CRS* XXII, 120). If the poet's father reconciled with the church in that year, the earlier date of 1586 seems likely. In either case, Henry Garnet, writing in 1600, confirms that reconciliation occurred: "Mr. Southwell, Robert's father, died a Catholic" (Devlin 203).

If Southwell's letter reconciled his father with the Catholic church, its effect on other readers varies greatly. Early critics applaud its style and content. Grossart's praise is effusive. "I know of nothing comparable," he writes, "with the mingled affection and prophet-like fidelity, the wise 'instruction, correction, reproof,' the full rich scripturalness and quaint applications, the devoutness, the insistence, the pathos of the letter" (Southwell *Complete Poems*, lxxvii). Janelle notes its "quiet conciseness," describing it as "sincere and moving" (229). Southwell writes out of "natural affection being strengthened by religion": "The Jesuit's spiritual attitude here is definitely optimistic" and akin to that of "devout humanists" such as Francis de Sales.[28] The *Epistle* is "a masterpiece of English religious prose; and it would no doubt have won early recognition as such, had not its Catholic character prevented its dissemination" (232). Devlin concurs. "There is no note of scolding in the letter," he writes. Moreover, "it is a masterly mingling of the stern warnings of a priest … with the loving loyalty of a younger son" (202). Brown, editor of the Folger manuscript copy of the letter, introduces it by claiming "[Southwell] writes to his father as to a man of education and sensitivity." The text contains "earnest pleading" combined with "striking imagery to bring his work to a series of emotional climaxes" (*v*).

Southwell's most recent critic, F.W. Brownlow, on the other hand, describes the young Jesuit's voice as "officious." "Officiousness was inseparable from his position," Brownlow argues, "because [Southwell] was a priest by office, endowed in his own eyes with supernatural power" (47). As a result, "the higher authority" [i.e., priestly as opposed to patriarchal] "empower[s] filial emotions of anger, disappointment and even shame" (48). What Southwell produces, according to Brownlow, is "an exercise of power in literary form," such that "most twentieth-century readers will shrink from the contemplation of a son preaching hell-fire to his father, trying to frighten him into Catholicism by dwelling upon his failures and his approaching death, and never throughout a long letter ever expressing any but the most formal respect for him, let alone love, sympathy, or admiration." Brownlow compares Robert to Hamlet, "bullying his mother with a mouthful of metaphors and a head too full of cliches to admit any real idea of what her life might actually be like." As a consequence of this "often outrageous exercise of power," "Richard Southwell emerges as a more sympathetic figure than his son" (49).

Reading the *Epistle* against the background of related documents, however, uncovers the work's conciliatory tone. So many authors wrote to reconcile schismatics that such texts comprise a genre to which Southwell contributes significantly and uniquely. Earlier examples of these works, most by clerics on the Continent, "clarified for the anxious and doubtful 'the quality of this sin' of conformity" (Walsham 27). These authors take a rigorous stance toward conforming to the established church. Their arguments and imagery are stark and chilling. A 1578 *Treatise of Schisme* by Gregory Martin states that "the sin of schism has been more grievously punished in scripture than infidelity or idolatry" (Bruno 7). Martin is the first author who threatens that the earth will swallow up schismatics. He counsels "cold Catholics" that schism is "a cancer that infecteth those it touches," and morbidly highlights the dangers of attending Protestant services. Those divided from the Catholic church by conformity are "dead members withered to be cast into the everlasting fire of hellish pain and woeful misery" (14). He bolsters his argument with references to scripture and church history, and refers to the Council of Trent and Jesuit scholars in Rome, concluding that conformity amounts to collaboration with Satan:

> The enemy, Satan, being overthrown by the coming of Christ, seeing idols forsaken, and that his Sees and Temples were left desert, by reason of the

great multitude of faithful people, he devised a new subtlety, under the
very title and name of Christianity, to deceive the unwary. He found out, I
say, heresies and schisms, whereby he might overthrow faith, corrupt the
truth [and] divide the unity of the Catholic church. (121)

Heretics, therefore, can be unfavorably compared to non-
Christians: "The Jews stumbled at the beginning when the Church began:
but heretics stumble now at it, when it filleth the whole world. If then
they be worse than the Jews, ergo much more than the Pagans which are
infidels only ... because they have not heard of Christ and his Church"
(125–26). Even their humanity is jeopardized: "Whatsoever [heretics]
speak and think they say to the praise of God is the howling of wolves and
the bellowing of mad kine" (159). If Martin and others conflate heresy and
schism, it is because "[s]chism is the highway unto heresy" (7).[29]

Thomas Hide expounds similar points in his 1560 *Consolatorie
Epistle to the Afflicted Catholikes*, adding reasons against conforming for
practicalities such as preserving property. "Seeing then," he urges, how
"religion is the sovereign honor and the only supreme service that you
owe to God ... respect of no creature, love of no felicity, fear of no
adversary, should withdraw you from this cause." Moreover, "love of
parents and country, love of wife and children, love of goods and honors,
love of livelihood and life, must give place to this" (17). Typical of such
tracts, Hide summons dramatic language when addressing this issue:
"Though thy mourning mother with rent hairs and blubbered cheeks show
thee her paps wherewith she gave you suck, though thy feeble father cry
at thy threshold, pass by thy father, pass by thy mother with dry eyes, and
hasten to the Cross of Christ ... Cruelty in this case is the only kind of
piety, and piety for God is no cruelty" (19). He, too, imagines schismatics
being swallowed by the earth, but he adds how they, in fact, "die alive"
because "they live without faith, without charity, without Church, without
Altar, without Priest, without sacrifice, without God" (45). He urges
patience in the face of persecution in whatever degree, including "the
secret martyrdom of the mind." Patience is necessary because "he cannot
be a saved Christian that is not a pure Papist" (50).

Persons addresses his contribution to this genre, *A Brief Discors
Contayning Certayne Reasons Why Catholiques Refuse to go to Church*,
to the Queen herself, arguing here, as elsewhere, for Catholic loyalty.
After referring to Elizabeth as "the substitute and Angel of God" and
trying to convince the Queen that among her subjects Catholics are "most
in number," Persons contends that the Roman church "teaches her
children true obedience to their Princes, for conscience sake, even unto
God himself, whose room they do possess, and to whom they are bound,

under the pain of mortal sin, and eternal damnation, patiently to obey, how hardly soever they deal with them in their government otherwise" (13). This implicit and possibly disingenuous plea for toleration precedes Persons' no tolerance policy on conformity. Catholics will not go to church "for the avoiding of manifest peril of eternal damnation." Those who conform "for fear or favor or some other worldly cause" are "wicked and out of all doubt damnable" (3). For Persons, too, schismatics are the living dead: "albeit he be yet quick upon the earth, yet he is, in the Providence of God, dead and damned in hell" (4). The schismatic merits "that heavy sentence of everlasting fire" on two counts: first, "a Catholic going to the churches, services or prayers of them of the contrary religion cannot but commit the great sin of scandal in the highest degree" (14); and second, they break the unity of the Catholic church though they know "how perilous and dreadful a thing it is" (18). "Of all the enemies that God hath in the world," Persons concludes, "there is none in so high displeasure with him as he who once knowing the truth and being received into his house (the Catholic Church) runneth out again" (29). Those who leave the church lose their humanity: "[t]heir minds are so overgrown with the rank weeds of Carnality, that there is no difference betwixt them and a brute bullock: for as much as the one followeth his passions as the other" (43).

. . .

In comparison to these texts, Southwell's *Epistle* stands out. The circumstances surrounding the letter may contribute to its measured tone. The Southwells' finances in the 1580s continually worsened. Richard Southwell, once wealthy enough to raise £9,000 by mortgaging properties, was imprisoned for debt (Brown *Two Letters*, *xxiii*). Legal expenses aggravated his condition. Probating the will of the poet's grandfather proved intractable and expensive. It is understandable then, that Richard Southwell conformed to avoid recusancy fines. Robert acknowledges these problems in the *Epistle*, reminding his father that the world has treated him harshly: "To serve the world you are now unable, and though you were able, you have little cause to be willing, seeing that it never gave you but an unhappy welcome, a hurtful entertainment, and now doth abandon you with an unfortunate farewell" (178–82).[30] This acknowledgment serves as the first practical argument as to why his father should shun the world and follow "God's merciful inspirations, proceeding from an infinite love and tending to your assured good" (536–37).

Southwell's pragmatism also explains the letter's timing. He previously held back, he writes, for his family's protection. "The care and jealousy of their safety" justified his careful distance (31). Now his father's advancing years sway his "sincere and dutiful mind" (37). Spiritual urgency outweighs physical peril. He writes so as to "open a vent for [his] zealous affection" (38–39). The start and close of the letter, in particular, attest to his depth of feeling; and he hopes his excesses will be excused on account of his emotions. He knows he risks alienating his father by writing with conviction, but he "humbly desires that [his] sincere affection might find excuse of [his] boldness" (578). Robert informs his father that some of his other children also worry about his soul. He speaks for them, "whose humble wishes are here written with my pen" (539). They concur on "the thing we have chiefly in request, that we may be as near linked in spiritual as we are in carnal consanguinity, and living with you in the compass of one Church we may to our unspeakable comfort enjoy in heaven your desired company" (558–61).

Robert writes for the family because he alone enjoys a dual relationship with his father. Not only is he bound by nature "to remember the root out of which [he] branched" (11), but he also exhorts his father as a priest, "the viceregent of God" (534). Southwell several times in the *Epistle* clarifies his understanding of the complementary relationship between nature and grace, an understanding that informs much of his writing. "Nature by grace is not abolished," he insists, "but perfected; ... neither are her impressions quite razed or annulled, but suited to the colors of faith and virtue" (48–50). His filial duties, therefore, are augmented by his priesthood. Whereas authors of other tracts against conformity stress the insignificance of family compared to religious faith, Southwell sees his religious obligations as strengthening the ties that bind him to his father. Priesthood has not separated Robert from his family. It places him at its center as primary spokesman and promoter of reconciliation. Religion, for Southwell, does not alienate but incorporates, making familial relationships spiritually substantial.

As a priest he can also administer sacraments to his father. "I have traveled far," he explains, "and brought home a freight of spiritual substance to enrich you" (76–77). Employing mercantile language here as in his 1582 letter to Persons, Southwell explains how he can personally attend to the same business. He has already done so for "strangers" (72), and now, he wants to help the man who provided for him from his earliest years. "How," he asks, "can the child owe so very great service to any as to him whom he is indebted to for his very life and being?" (74–76). Throughout the *Epistle* Southwell invokes biblical typologies to explain his relationship with his father, and in this case he claims to be a type of Old Testament Joseph who can provide for the latter, who stands in the place of Jacob in Genesis 47:12: "I have, in this general famine of all true and Christian food, with Joseph prepared abundance of the bread of angels for the repast of your soul" (81–83). "My desire," he tells him "is that ... my provision feed you, by whom I have been ... delighted and fed myself, that your courtesies may in part be countervailed and my duty in some sort performed" (83–86). The food here is the eucharist, which Robert has the power to confect, though he never specifically refers to this or any other priestly faculty.

In fact, Southwell shows acute awareness that his priesthood might intimidate rather than console his father, and he works to eliminate the possibility. Rather than insisting on priestly prerogatives, he mentions ordination in the context of a family joke. After citing St. Climacus on priestly service to relatives, the *Epistle*'s first Patristic reference, he lightens his tone by reminding his father "that even from my infancy you were wont in merriment to call me 'Father Robert' which is the customary style now allotted to my present estate" (149–51). Despite his clerical status, Southwell regards Richard as his spiritual equal: "Yet if you consider our alliance in the chief portion, I mean our soul, which discerneth man from inferior creatures, we are of equal proximity to our heavenly father, both descended of the same parent and no other distance in our degrees but that you are the elder brother" (110–14). As a son, he will not insist on his priestly due if his father cedes the privileges of age. After establishing their essential likeness, "our equality upon the soul, which is man's main substance," Southwell almost apologetically raises this issue of his religious expertise:

> [T]hink it I pray you no dishonor to your age or disparagement to your person if with all humility I offer my advice unto you. One man cannot be perfect in all faculties, neither is it a disgrace to the goldsmith if he be ignorant of the milliner's trade. Many are deep lawyers and yet shallow divines; many very deliver in feats of the body and curious in external complements, yet little experimented in matters of their soul and far to seek in religious actions. I have studied and practiced these many years spiritual physic, acquainting myself with the beating and temper of every pulse and travailing in the scrutiny of the maladies and medicines incident unto souls. If therefore I proffer you the fruits of my long studies and make you a present of my profession, I hope you will construe it rather as a dutiful part than any point of presumption. (118–30)

Comparing priesthood to the practice of law or medicine, and even more so to the proficiency of tradesmen, is remarkable in the context of current views on ordained ministry. Since reformers insisted on the priesthood of all believers, Catholics responded by exalting sacerdotal status. The Twenty-third session of the Council of Trent declares:

> Sacrifice and priesthood are so joined together by God's foundation that each exists in every law. And so since the new covenant of the Catholic church has received the visible sacrifice of the eucharist from the Lord's institution, it is also bound to profess that there is in it a new, visible and external priesthood into which the old has been changed. The sacred scriptures show, and the tradition of the catholic church has always taught, that this was instituted by the same Lord our savior, and that power was given to the apostles and their successors in the priesthood to consecrate, offer and administer his body and blood, as also to remit or retain sins. (Tanner II, 742)

Advancing this view, authors cited above note that Protestant churches lack priests, rendering their worship null and void. They liken it to "the howling of wolves and the bellowing of mad kine" (Bruno *Treatise of Schisme*, 159). Southwell, instead, moves toward the center of the debate, accommodating what he imagines as his father's anxieties, while at the same time upholding church teaching. Far from sounding "officious," he strikes a conciliatory tone on a contentious issue. For his father's comfort, Southwell avoids polemical language. He reverts to the exercise of wit, employing a paradox to resolve any residual tension between generations and states in life: "He may be a father to the soul that is a son to the body" (130–31). This paradox is not insulting, since he uses a similar device to describe the relationship between Jesus and his mother: "BEHOLDE the father, is his daughters sonne:/ The bird that built the nest, is hatched therein:" ("The Nativitie of Christ," ll. 1–2).

Southwell likewise apologizes for any insult caused by his youth, hoping to "avoid all touch of presumption in advising my elders" (104–105). The letter discusses this at length gently. To avoid strain, its author again employs typologies, likening himself to youthful Old Testament figures such as David and Daniel. The case of David has special resonance because he, like Robert, is the youngest of his brothers, yet he plays a significant role in a critical situation, namely that Southwell's father is "in the waning, and the date of [his] pilgrimage is well nigh expired" (162–63).

The poet's references to his father's mortality echo the *memento mori* tradition of late medieval and early modern piety.[31] Southwell, in fact, borrows from classical and contemporary sources, pointing out how "the young may die quickly, but the old cannot live long" (168–69).

These words occur in Thomas More's *Dialogue of Comfort against Tribulation*, and More might have found them attributed to St. Augustine in Girolamo Cardano's *Cardanus Comfort* or in Cicero's *De Senectute* (Brown *Two Letters*, 107, n. 22). There is also an aphoristic quality in this portion of the letter. He instructs his father, "if green years must sometimes think of the grave, the thoughts of sere age should continually dwell in the same" (171–72). Later he reminds him, "[f]or life is to be measured by merits than by number of days, seeing that most men by many days do but procure many deaths and others in short space attain the life of infinite ages" (201–203).

These are conventional sentiments, and through them Southwell introduces an exercise he encountered as a Jesuit novice. He wants his father to consider death as the context for making a choice or election. The choice should be made well, in freedom and with clarity of mind. There is something modern about what Southwell recommends, which stands in stark contrast to how others were trying to force decisions through theological, economic, political or legal threats. He does refer to the threat of damnation, but his overriding emphasis is on a well-made, autonomous, decision. To do so, he employs familiar scriptural references in framing his father's situation:

> You have long sowed in a field of flint which could bring you nothing forth but a crop of cares and affliction of spirit, rewarding your labors with remorse, and affording for your gain eternal damages. It is now more than a seasonable time to alter the course of so unthriving a husbandry and to enter into the field of God's Church, in which, sowing the seeds of repentant sorrow and watering them with tears of humble contrition, you may reap a more beneficial harvest and gather the fruits of everlasting comfort. (182–89)

References to confession occur in all that Southwell writes, owing to the sacrament's preeminence in Jesuit practice. In this case, the poet wants his father, in the context of an imagined deathbed scene, to confess freely his sins. He lets the character of the sins remain general, referring to schism only four times (293; 507; 551; and 565). Texts described above are more specific, with the words "heresy" and "schism" occurring on every page, if not in every line. For Southwell, sin in general should generate enough concern for his father to make an Ignatian exercise leading to a life-defining choice.

In the Second Week of the *Exercises*, Loyola provides guidelines for making important decisions, noting how "in every good election, as far as depends on us, the eye of our intention ought to be simple, only

looking at what we are created for, namely, the praise of God our Lord
and the salvation of our souls" (Loyola *Spiritual Exercises*, 169).
Southwell intimates the same manner of thinking when encouraging his
father to "seriously consider the terms [he] stand[s] in and weigh
[him]self in the Christian balance" (*Epistle*, 155–56). According to
Loyola, he can learn in one of three ways the direction his life should
take: first, "when God our Lord so moves and attracts the will, that
without doubting or being able to doubt, such devout soul follows what is
shown;" second, "when enough light or knowledge is received by
experience of consolations and desolations, and by the experience of the
discernment of various spirits;" or third, "when one considers for what
man is born ... and desiring this chooses as means a life or state within
the limits of the Church, in order that he may be helped in the service of
our Lord and the salvation of his soul" (*Spiritual Exercises*, 175–77).
Southwell recommends this last method to his father. Specifically, for
Loyola and for Southwell, this requires the imaginative contemplation of
one's own death and judgment before God. The person facing a choice
should envisage that "[he] were on the point of death, the form and
measure which [he] would then want to have kept in the way of the
present election, and regulating [him]self by that election, let [him] make
[his] decision in everything" (*Exercises*, 186).[32] Then Loyola prescribes a
more dramatic context for deciding, which Southwell also urges upon his
father: "looking and considering how I shall find myself on the Day of
Judgment, to think how I would want to have deliberated about the present
matter, and to take now the rule which I would then wish to have kept, in
order that I may then find myself in entire pleasure and joy" (187).

Consideration of Doomsday comprises "the principal drift" of
Southwell's discourse, wherein, echoing Loyola, he instructs his father
that "[d]eath in itself is very fearful, but more terrible in regard of the
judgment that it summoneth us unto" (*Epistle*, 248–49). Standing squarely
in the Jesuit spiritual tradition, Robert questions his father:

> If you were laid on your departing bed, burthened with the heavy load of
> your former trespasses and gored with the sting and prick of a festered
> conscience, if you felt the cramp of death wresting your heartstrings and
> ready to make the rueful divorce between body and soul, if you lay panting
> for breath and swimming in a cold and fatal sweat, weary with struggling
> against your deadly pangs—O how much would you give for an hour of
> repentance, at what rate would you value a days contrition? (249–60)

This interrogation means to conjure in his father's imagination
what Loyola names a "composition of place," the aim of which is to

engage fully the imagination, describing scenes in detail, so as to move the heart and mind to proper relationship with God. Southwell stirs strong feelings in his father for the sake of bringing him to a firm purpose of amendment. Early in the *Exercises*, Loyola urges a particular method of prayer. "Here it is to be noted," he begins:

> ... that, in a visible contemplation or meditation—as, for instance, when one contemplates Christ our Lord, Who is visible—the composition will be to see with the sight of the imagination the corporeal place where the thing is found which I want to contemplate ... In an invisible contemplation or meditation—[such as] on the Sins—the composition will be to see with the sight of the imagination and consider that my soul is imprisoned in this corruptible body, and all the compound in this valley, as exiled among brute beasts. (*Exercises*, 47)

This method of prayer accounts for Southwell's description of hell. Having made the *Exercises* as a novice and revisiting them during annual retreats, he knew how Loyola saw this particular "corporeal place," and this familiarity influences his rendering of what might await his father after he is "stripped of [his] mortal weed and turned out of the service and houseroom of this world" (*Epistle*, 269–70). In the meditation on hell Loyola spares no sensory detail in elaborating the tortures of the damned. "The first Prelude," he begins, "is here to see with the sight of the imagination the length, breadth and depth of hell." "The second," he continues, is "to ask for what I want: it will be here to ask for interior sense of pain which the damned suffer, in order that, if, through my faults, I should forget the love of the Eternal Lord, at least the fear of the pains may help me not to come into sin" (*Exercises*, 65). For Loyola, and Southwell after him, love trumps fear as the preferred motivation in the spiritual life, but both men employ the latter as a last resort. To that end, Loyola prescribes five "points" for prayer, which inform Southwell's discourse on damnation:

> The First point will be to see with the sight of the imagination the great fires, and the souls as in bodies of fire. The second, to hear with the ears wailings, howlings, cries, blasphemies against Christ our Lord and against all his Saints. The third, to smell with the smell smoke, sulphur, dregs and putrid things. The fourth, to taste with the taste bitter things like tears, sadness and the worm of conscience. The fifth, to touch with the touch; that is to say, how the fires touch and burn the souls. (66–70)

Typically, Southwell takes a moderate tone in working through this exercise in the *Epistle*. Encouraging his father to stand before God, he again invokes mercantile language to describe the process of judgment. He compares his father's conscience to "a perfect register of all [his] misdeeds," as a result of which his father will be his own sharpest "appeacher." "What would you do in these dreadful exigents," he asks, and then presents a milder version of the hell he discovered in Ignatius' *Exercises*: "What would you do ... when you saw that ghastly dungeon and huge gulf of hell breaking out with most fearful flames, when you saw the weeping and gnashing of teeth, the rage of those hellish monsters, the horror of the place, the rigor of the pain, the terror of the company, and the eternity of all these punishments?" (*Epistle*, 279–84). The poet takes his father on a relatively brief tour of hell. The point is not to remain there but to render him well disposed toward arguments for reconciliation.

Southwell's rhetorical strategy in the rest of the *Epistle* appeals to his father's acknowledged sagacity. Asking why he delays reconciliation, Robert credits the older man's acumen: "It cannot be fear that leadeth you amiss seeing it were too unfitting a thing that the cravant cowardice of flesh and blood should daunt the prowess of an intelligent person, who by his wisdom cannot but discern how much more cause there is to fear God than man, and to stand in more awe of perpetual than of temporal penalties" (310–15). Later he describes his father as "a sound and sensed man," who would never make "an ungrounded presumption of the mercy of God" (316–19). Citing Patristic authorities, with whom he intimates his father is familiar, he argues for the value of the human person, which he describes as "a creature of so incomparable a price" (469). This, perhaps, is where Janelle finds similarities between Southwell and other "devout humanists." The Jesuit relies upon a shared appreciation for the dignity of the soul in convincing his father to be reconciled. Given this appreciation for the worth of persons, it is rational and just, according to the poet, that God would be angry with anyone who puts his soul at risk. Nevertheless, the God of Southwell's *Epistle*, who is neither "impotent" nor "weak-witted," remains predisposed toward salvation, even in the face of human transgression.

In these arguments, Southwell respects his "dearest" father's "merits," which have "fastened" his children's affections. Conversely, he never compromises his own understanding of the truth. Along with writers of similar tracts, Robert echoes St. Cyprian's assertion that "[h]e cannot have God for his father that refuseth to profess the Catholic Church for his mother [and] neither can he achieve to the Church Triumphant that is not a member of the Church Militant here in earth" (503–506). But he stands apart from other authors in several respects. Unlike them, he eschews theological speculation, giving his father credit for appreciating the state of religious controversy. He also avoids criticizing the English church and its worship. Others specialize in such attacks. Southwell, in obedience to his religious superiors, here and in most of his writing, forgoes denominational strife.

In the *Epistle*, as elsewhere, Southwell fashions a metaphor for his literary efforts. He imagines himself "baiting hooks" in order "to draw a soul out of the puddle of schism" (654–55). A puddle is an unattractive image, but other authors use far more vitriol in describing faiths other than their own. Moreover, he likens his attempt to fishing, an activity traditionally associated with apostolic efforts, and angling for souls does not involve force or compulsion. Southwell tries to lure his father into reconciliation with the Catholic church, and the close of the letter, signed "your most dutiful and loving son," ends with characteristic equilibrium, literary quality and personal tenderness:

> Howsoever, therefore, the soft gales of your morning pleasures lulled you in slumbering fits, howsoever the violent heats of noon might awake affections, yet now in the cool and calm of the evening retire to a Christian rest and close up the day of your life with a clear sunset, that leaving all darkness behind you and carrying in your conscience the light of grace, you may escape the horror of an eternal night and pass from mortal day to an everlasting morrow. (570–76)

Southwell never pretends that his father can be saved outside the church, so there is no avoiding the reference to the judgment. No sixteenth-century Jesuit, nor ardent believer of whatever persuasion, could stretch beyond that point.[33] However, his tactics in the *Epistle* illustrate characteristics that inform his other works. Southwell appreciates his audience because he stands at the point of convergence of many potent cultural and personal forces. Writing to his father on behalf of his family, he weaves together out of affection, spiritual expertise and intellectual rigor, a letter of significant literary quality that speaks not only to his addressee but also to several of the principal anxieties of his age.

Notes

[1] Southwell's genealogy appears in Southwell (*Complete Poems*, xxxv–xl); Foley (*Records* I, 3000); Hood (i); and Devlin (5–7).

[2] See Persons' *Brief Discourse containing Certain Reasons why Catholics Refuse to go to Church* (1580). Persons and other Jesuits "vigorously campaigned against church-papism, sensing the damage that English Catholics did to their cause by attending apparently innocuous Protestant worship" (Houlistan 297).

[3] See Haynes (21–24) on the widespread use of codes and ciphers in Elizabethan England.

[4] In 1587, Aquaviva warned Southwell to exercise caution in writing letters: "Do not say so much in plain and open terms lest [if what you write fall into others' hands] danger should thence arise either to others or to yourself; men there being as wicked as they are, and the suspicions of creditors and debtors [i.e., persecutors and persecuted] being so great" (*CRS* I, 320).

[5] Southwell echoes the Jesuit *Constitutions*: "The end of this Society is to devote itself with God's grace to the salvation and perfection of the members' own souls, but also with that same grace to labor strenuously in giving aid toward the salvation and perfection of the souls of their fellow men" (Loyola *Constitutions*, 3).

[6] Confusion about this letter's recipient endures. Nancy Pollard Brown publishes it in Appendix D of her edition of *Two Letters and Short Rules of a Good Life*, arguing that it was a second letter to his father.

[7] Southwell's female relatives prove more faithful in part because male temporizing made possible female recusancy: "A husband's concentration on protecting the family's resources and reputation could both enable and necessitate his wife's assumption of a more energetic role in safeguarding its spiritual integrity. Ironically, a woman's inferior public and legal identity afforded her superior devotional status, fuller membership of the Roman Catholic Church" (Walsham 80–81).

[8] Walsham's *Church Papists* is a valuable scholarly work on this challenge, and her research proved enormously helpful for understanding Southwell's family.

[9] The Southwells were representative figures: "Probably the majority instinctively temporised" (14). This majority included clergymen who were "biconfessional incumbents ... prepared to say clandestine masses, prior to publicly administering communion according to the new rite" (Walsham 14–15).

[10] At the trial's close, "Norfolk pronounced sentence, weeping as he did so." Underscoring Norfolk's characteristic duplicity, Ives adds, "and is it cynical to wonder whether they were more tears of relief than sympathy?" (387).

[11] The sincerity of those involved in the suppression is questionable. Since they sometimes gained from their work, self-interest could trump their religious instincts. But, "[e]xemption from suppression was not a straightforward financial transaction ... The houses allowed to stand were often those for which the royal commissioners made a special case." As Haigh notes, "Sometimes these intercessions worked, sometimes they did not" (144–45).

[12] See Gregory (268) on the martyrdom of Margaret Pole, one of forty Catholics executed for refusing to subscribe to the Oath of Supremacy between 1537 and 1544. She is featured, with More and Fisher, in the martyrological frescoes in the chapel of the English College, Rome.

[13] The Articles "have been variously described ... as a victory for Lutheran opinion, and as a Catholic resistance to theological innovation," and, [Haigh] concludes, "they were both" (128).

[14] See Padelford (36–37).

[15] The three other men are John Rogers, who was burned on 4 February 1555 (Foxe VI, 591); John Bradford, described by Southwell as "an arrogant and stubborn boy," burned later the same year (Foxe VII, 151); and Thomas Rose, who at his examination in 1558 is quoted as saying, "[h]owbeit one Sir Robert Southwell, still accused me for my prayer, and said I did put a difference between lady Mary and lady Elizabeth, for that I prayed in King Edward's faith, and prayed that he would confirm lady Elizabeth in that which was well begun in her" (Foxe VIII, 585).

[16] See Foxe VI, 580.

[17] Richard Southwell fathered two sons by Mary Darcy while married to her cousin, Thomasine Darcy. After his first wife's death, he married the mother of his sons.

[18] Much material concerning Copley reads as hagiography. For example, his granddaughters describe him as "another Job," who "exercised the virtue of patience in suffering for so good a cause" (Morris *Troubles* I, 53). Copley's letters, however, reveal an un-Job-like anxiety about his lost fortune.

[19] That Anthony was preaching does not indicate ordination. Students at the College were preparing for ministry, and this included delivering pious talks in the chapel.

[20] Of the relationship between Southwell and Anthony Copley, Janelle observes, "The two men were strikingly different in temper ... Nevertheless [Copley's] work bears unmistakable traces of Jesuit influence, and is sprinkled with reminiscences of Southwell's poetry" (55).

[21] Copley had earlier penned *Wits fittes and fancies*, based on a collection of Spanish stories, and *Love's Owle: An idle conceited dialogue between Love and an Old Man*, also a translation. Regarding Copley's parody of Spenser, it is notable that Anthony's sometime nemesis, Persons, also uses Spenserian imagery in defending Catholicism (Houliston 296).

[22] This discourse reaches its apex in John Donne's *Pseudo-Martyr* (1611). Donne, a descendant of Thomas More and the nephew of two Jesuit missionaries, was raised in a context like Copley's. "I have," he writes, "beene ever kept awake in meditation of martyrdom, by being derived from such a stock and race, as, I believe, no family (which is not of farre larger extent, and greater branches,) hath endured and suffered more in their persons and fortunes, for obeying teachers of Roman Doctrine, than it hath done" (310). He concludes, as Copley does, that we ought "not to urge and provoke, and importune affliction so much, as to make those punishments just, which otherwise have been wrongfully inflicted on us. We are not sent into this world to suffer, but to do and to perform the Offices of society, required by our several callings" (316–17).

[23] See Gregory (62) for the rationale of such an accent: "The only excess and obsession here lay not in late medieval devotion ... but in God's love: all the visual and verbal depictions of the sweat of Gethsemane, the blood of Golgatha, the wounds of Christ's lacerated body and its scourges of pain put together could never adequately express the infinite reality they proclaimed."

[24] According to a 1586 letter of Southwell's, exorcisms were an integral part of the Jesuits' strategy: "Some extraordinary occurrences, as I gather from ocular witnesses, have taken place here in the case of possessed persons, which have had the effect of converting many to the faith, and greatly rallying the wavering." He also acknowledges Protestant opposition: "The priests, whose piety and extraordinary power in these exorcisms has been most conspicuous have been styled magicians and sorcerers by the heretics, with the object forsooth of slanderously imputing to diabolical artifice and not to priestly power, facts which they cannot deny" (Southwell *Unpublished Documents*, 309).

[25] The book was published under the pseudonym R. Doleman, but Persons gained notoriety for its authorship even though the work was probably written by several prominent exiles. See L. Hicks, "Father Parsons and the Book of Succession," *Recusant History* 4 (1975), 104–37.

[26] See Edwards *Robert Persons* (172) on debates about the work's authorship.

[27] The title of the *Epistle* varies according to manuscript and printed traditions. Brown lists the six extant manuscripts in her Textual Introduction (xlvi) and explains how all but one of the first seven printed editions bear the heading "An Epistle of a Religious Priest unto His Father, exhorting him to the perfect forsaking of the world." A

superscription follows in each case: "To the worshipful his very good father, R.S., his dutiful son R.S. wisheth all happiness" (*xlviii*).

[28] See Richard Strier's "Sanctifying the Aristocracy: 'Devout Humanism' in Francois de Sales, John Donne and George Herbert" in *Journal of Religion* (1989), 36–58. According to Strier, "the Jesuits concentrated their efforts on the social elite, and it was out of this emphasis and the anti-ascetic strands within Loyola's teachings that the movement known ... as 'devout humanism' took its orientation." Strier defines devout humanism as a "movement that set out to show Christianity to be fully possible within the bounds of ordinary and recognizable aristocratic life" (37).

[29] Heresy (literally "a choice") is the denial of dogma, i.e., a doctrine promulgated according to the highest level of magisterial authority. Schism is any rupture of unity within the church by a group or community. Usually this involves breaking communion with the Pope.

[30] These numbers refer to lines in the Brown edition.

[31] See Gregory (55) on the relationship between this tradition and martyrdom: "The values and practices of the *Ars Moriendi* were directly relevant to martyrdom ... When crowds gathered to witness the execution of religious criminals, town squares replaced the domestic intimacy of the deathbed. Spectators scrutinized the condemned, looking for behavior to which the *Ars Moriendi* had sensitized them for more than a century."

[32] Loyola possibly drew inspiration from Thomas A Kempis. See Gregory (53): "This advice was self-conscious, pragmatic and starkly unromantic. Death was a sure thing. Its undeniable certainty plus life's manifest uncertainty unmasked the unprepared as foolish, negligent or both."

[33] See Gregory (346–47) on the impossibility of religious tolerance in the sixteenth century: "To imply that religious toleration was a sort of missed opportunity in the Reformation era implies that early modern Christian leaders should have made peaceful coexistence a priority over God's truth ... To suggest that the course and character of early modern Christianity might have been completely different—with the divergences and intensity, but without the disagreements, conflict and violence—is to imagine early modern Christians who never existed in a world that never was."

Chapter 2
Reconciling Martyrdom:
The Epistle of Comfort

Robert Southwell lived in three formative environments outside his family and prior to his missionary career. The first of these was the English Catholic community of his boyhood; the second was schools established for English exiles at Douai and Paris; and the third consisted of his spiritual and intellectual formation as a Jesuit in Rome. All three situated him at critical points of convergence where he encountered and incorporated in himself energies that need to be appreciated for understanding the period in which he worked. Because Southwell was so positioned, he provides access to sometimes-obscured aspects of sixteenth-century culture as it was emerging in England and on the Continent. Some of these energies were at odds with one another, requiring the poet to reconcile differences or live with contradictions. Furthermore, in each environment he developed loyalties to individuals and, through them, to institutions and intellectual positions. These occasionally conflicting loyalties defined the context in which he made meaning while standing at the center of a rapidly changing world. If H.C. White is correct that Southwell was "educated and trained, not to hold on to a vanishing order, but to meet the challenges of a new age with the resources of a new age," then it was in these environments that he acquired those resources (202).

...

Before traveling to Douai in 1576, Southwell developed loyalties to a community of Catholic men, including relatives but also extending beyond them, who shaped his imagination and provided him with aesthetic, intellectual and spiritual resources. Unlike his grandfather, father and brothers, these men modeled constancy. Such models, epitomized in Philip Howard, Earl of Arundel, were also the audience for his first major prose work, *An Epistle of Comfort*, written in 1587. His early acquaintance with this community accounts for the text's style and substance.

The men constituted a circle with ties to the Copleys and Southwell's other cousins, the Cottons, among whom Robert likely lived after the Copleys went into exile in 1572. While it is difficult to ascertain where Robert lived between the ages of eleven and fifteen, Christopher Devlin provides strong evidence, if admittedly circumstantial, that he spent these impressionable years among "a wide semi-circle of his mother's kinfolk that stretched along the South Downs to the fringes of the New Forest: Shelly of Michaelgrove and Shelly of Petersfield, Gage of West Firle and Gage of Bentley, Cotton of Warblington and many other allied families, who were soon to prove a most formidable rampart of recusant Catholicism" (11). Several facts support his connection to the Cottons. His sister, Mary, married Edward Bannister, resident of a town near the Cottons' home. Secondly, Southwell arrived at Douai with John Cotton, where they joined John's older brother, Richard.[1] Finally, after returning to England, Robert used "Cotton as his alias. When Topcliffe arrived at the Bellamy home to arrest Southwell, he demanded, 'Now will you hand over this Cotton, or shall I pull this foul nest of yours about your ears, beam by beam?'" (Devlin 280).

Warblington Castle on Chichester Harbour belonged to George Cotton, cousin to Southwell's mother and the father of John and Richard. According to Michael Hodgetts, this was "almost certainly the point from which Southwell and John Cotton crossed the channel in 1576" (113). George Cotton belonged to a group of Catholics organized by Henry Wriothesley, second Earl of Southampton, and Cotton's castle features in recusant history. As Hodgetts records in *Secret Hiding Places*, a study of "priest-holes" to which missionaries, including Southwell, repaired for safety, "Thomas Lister from Hindslip was here in 1603, and so ... were two other Jesuits, William Baldwin and Thomas Singleton ... and during a search in 1613 part of the body of the martyr Mark Barkworth was found in a reliquary ... in John Cotton's study" (113). Wriothesley's leadership gave this group financial and social advantages. Thomas Stephens, another member of the circle who became a Jesuit missionary in India, describes the father of Shakespeare's patron as "the most illustrious and leading Catholic in England, and a great supporter of the faithful" (Letter of Thomas Stephens, Stonyhurst ms., *Collectio Cardwelli*, [fn] 16). Wriothesley and Cotton, along with Wriothesley's nephew, Thomas Pounde, established secret Mass centers and promoted Catholicism, especially among young men. Pounde, in particular, was enthusiastic early on about the Jesuits whom he knew through reading the order's *Relations*, or reports on missionary efforts. He counts among the first Englishmen to promote the Jesuits' cause, and he eventually took vows, although secretly, as a lay brother in the Society in 1578.[2]

Pounde is representative of the men who earned Southwell's admiration during his adolescence, and his biography, as reported in Foley's *Records*, "seem[s] rather the product of a clever imagination than the sober and truthful record of simple facts" (III, 568).[3] His dramatic career inspired a romantic enthusiasm for the recusant cause in Southwell and others of his generation. According to Foley, Pounde was "always a Catholic at heart," but like many he conformed to the established church "to gain a better footing at Court" (III, 571). In 1559, Pounde entered Lincoln's Inn, on behalf of which he wrote two masques; and in 1560, he was appointed esquire to the body of the Queen (Chambers III, 468).[4] As a courtier he played Mercury in Gascoigne's masque performed for Elizabeth at Kenilworth in 1565. On this occasion he also penned verses for the Queen, of which he later reminded her when suing for clemency while imprisoned for recusancy (Simpson, *The Rambler*, 95).[5] His artistic efforts earned him a charismatic reputation. Edmund Simpson describes how Pounde "made himself conspicuous as a fascinating lady-killer ... and a sharpshooter in battles of wits" (*The Rambler* VIII [July 1857], 24). But his fame ended when he embarrassed himself while performing an encore of an intricate dance step in a 1569 Christmas revels, which was played before the Queen. After he fell during the dance, Elizabeth, who had earlier applauded his agility, called him "Sir Ox" (Foley *Records* III, 572).

This embarrassment apparently caused a conversion. Pounde avoided court, and spent two "penitential years," after which he was reconciled with the Catholic church. Later, as a proselytizer and protector of missionaries, he regained the Queen's attention, and her government frequently imprisoned him. Between incarcerations, he collaborated with Wriothesley and Cotton in recruiting young noblemen to the Catholic cause.[6] According to Foley, "it afforded him wonderful joy and consolation of soul when at times he beheld twelve or sixteen young men of rank, whom he had collected together, hearing the Mass which he had secretly procured to be said in his private oratory, and going to Communion along with him" (III, 582). If Devlin is correct, Southwell numbered among these participants. Pounde also "got men to entertain conferences of the priests [and] inveigled youths to fly over sea to the seminaries" (Foley III, 627).

Pounde hosted an especially notable conference in 1573 when a Portuguese Jesuit, Henry Alvarez, arrived in England on his way from Rome to the missions in the West Indies. He was carrying copies of the *Relations*, which he read to Pounde and those he had assembled. These letters that inspired Pounde and Southwell were a hallmark of the early Jesuits' way of proceeding, and later, while in Rome, Southwell wrote and published news of the English mission and, in particular, of its martyrs. Discussing the quantity of letters produced by early Jesuits, John O'Malley records that "by 1565 the Society numbered approximately 3,500 members, who were exhorted or obliged to maintain regular correspondence with each other and especially with the Jesuit leadership in Rome" (2). The Jesuit *Constitutions* insisted on correspondence as a means to achieve the *esprit de corps* necessary for effective work. According to the *Constitutions* and other foundational documents, rectors of local communities were to write weekly to regional superiors. Regional superiors were to do likewise for Roman officials. As O'Malley shows, "besides conveying information and seeking or giving advice, some letters or parts of letters were meant by deliberate design to do something more":

> They had a professedly edifying purpose either for Jesuits themselves or for others ... Jesuits especially looked forward to letters from their brethren in the "Indies" and read them at table in Jesuit houses. In September 1553, for instance, Nadal enthusiastically informed Ignatius that four ships had arrived from Lisbon carrying letters from those parts and that they were being copied for distribution—"They are very edifying! The Jesuits circulated letters of this kind to silence enemies, win friends, attract recruits and for their own enthusiasm for their vocation. (63)[*]

Prior to Alvarez' visit, most Englishmen were unfamiliar with the Society.[7] If they knew anything of the order, they were probably suspicious of it. As Thomas McCoog observes, "even though there were no Jesuits in England, they were ... feared." As early as 1561, McCoog reports, "Everard Mercurian relayed to Diego Lainez that the Society had been the subject of sermons in England [and that] Protestant preachers warned their congregations that the Jesuits were eager to enter their country and that, at once, they would be in terrible harm" (101). Letters of the sort which Alvarez provided improved this reputation. Readers, including Southwell, absorbed the energies contained in the *Relations*. As a result, their sense of themselves, their world and their church became more expansive and imbued with potential for the exciting, even exotic work that needed doing. When Pounde and his recruits read about missionaries in India or the Americas, they developed enthusiasm for the Society and the church it served. According to Devlin, "now came the exciting realization that the Old Religion had renewed its youth like the eagle and was no longer on the defensive" (17).

Thomas Clancy, in his study of "The First Generation of English Jesuits," supports Devlin's claim with facts gleaned from Jesuit catalogues. Based on his findings, Clancy concludes that "the [English] Jesuits who entered from 1570 on tended to be much more enthusiastic than their predecessors":

---

[*] Reprinted by permission of the publisher from *The First Jesuits* by John W. O'Malley, Cambridge, Mass.: Harvard University Press. Copyright © 1993 by the President and Fellows of Harvard College.

EVERARDVS MERCVRIANVS IIII.
In NOMINE tuo faluum me fac.

P. EVERARDVS MERCVRIANVS, *Leodius,*
Societatis IESV *Præpositus Generalis quartus, Obijt Romæ,*
Kal. Augusti, anno Christi CIƆ. IƆ. LXXX. *Ætatis* LXV.

Et pius, & prudens, Eburonum natus in oris,
Quartus eras Socijs, MERCVRIANE, parens.

2.1 Engraving of Everard Mercurian, General of the Society
of Jesus 1573–1580 (by courtesy of the Woodstock
Theological Center Library, Georgetown University,
Washington, D.C.)

Some had caught the fire of missionary zeal from reading the letters of
Xavier and the other accounts of the Jesuit missionaries in the New World and
the Far East. That was the inspiration of Stephens and Pound [*sic*]. Others who
longed to go on the missions were Southwell, Cottam and Yates. Even Persons
volunteered for the Indies. (144)[8]

CLAVDIVS AQVAVIVA NEAPOLIT V GENERALIS

2.2 Engraving of Clavio Aquaviva, General of the Society of Jesus 1581–1615 (by courtesy of the Woodstock Theological Center Library, Georgetown University, Washington, D.C.)

A life of Southwell written by his close Jesuit friend, John Deckers, entitled *Narratio Martyri*, reveals the poet's early desire to serve in India (Devlin 341). When he first entered the Society, Southwell was under the spell of the missions, and the *Relations* informed his prayer. For example, in his journal he reproves himself by writing:

> Consider thy companions at present in the service of the Lord and see how
> fervent they are, how regular in their observance, how eager for perfection.
> Think of the virtues of those members of the Society who … in India …
> devote themselves to the salvation of souls with the greatest zeal amidst
> extraordinary difficulties. Some lie in their dungeons in chains, amidst
> squalor and filth indescribable, but bear all with astonishing cheerfulness and
> desire to suffer still more. Set on the one side their gratitude, their love, their
> constancy, their truly religious fortitude, and on the other thy tepidity, thy
> ingratitude, thy inconstancy, thy cowardice. (*Spiritual Exercises and
> Devotions*, 88)

Colored with the hyperbole typical of an enthusiastic novice, Robert's notion
of missionary heroism spurred remorse. To the end of his life he feared
showing cowardice when confronting pain, and the example of missionaries
fortified him. He drew apostolic energy from the *Relations*.

Letters written by John Yates provide examples of such "edifying"
reports. Born in 1550 and entering the Society four years before Southwell,
Yates was the first Jesuit missionary to Brazil, where he arrived in 1577 and
remained until his death. Three of Yates' letters are reprinted in Foley's
Records, one each to Fr. William Good, Fr. Richard Gibbons and Sir Francis
Englefield. The letter to Good, dated 2 February 1589, describes Yates' work,
and it is evident why it inspired men such as Southwell.

Yates intends to provide "some news of me and my accustomed
ministries in the Company [of Jesus]." First, though, he apologizes that his
reports infrequently arrive in Europe, blaming pirates, who because they
capture his readers' imaginations are often the objects of his epistolary
attention. The only compatriots with whom he has personal contact are these
"certain heretical pirates [who] come into these parts of the world, to exercise
their piracy and irreverence to churches and images" (*Records* II, 279), and the
only information he has of England comes from Jesuit letters. He notes, for
example, that "of the not so lamentable but glorious death of the most Catholic
Queen of Scots we have present news," and he thanks Good for sending him
the very sort of publications that Southwell was producing in Rome. Good has
sent him "the description of the English persecution, eight leaves of images of
the saints, … the history of the twelve English martyrs in the English tongue,
and *Trophae Ecclesiae Anglicanae*, with the book *de Decem Rationibus Patris
Campiani*" (II, 289). Remarkably, Yates receives the publications circulating
in Europe to promote vocations, sympathy for and benefactions to the English
mission. The "history" to which he refers is likely William Allen's *A Briefe
Historie of the Glorious Martyrdom of Twelve Reverend Priests, Father
Edmund Campion and His Companions*, published in 1582. The *Trophae* is a
collection of prints based on paintings in the chapel of the English College,

Rome; and the *Decem Rationes* was written and published by Campion in 1581. This tract gained notoriety when Oxford scholars found it on their benches during a convocation that same year. Thanks to Good, Yates is cognizant of "the miserable state of Europe and specially England," and he returns the favor of news in his letters (II, 293).

His letters' purpose, as per the Jesuit *Constitutions*, is to spur a copious consolation. Related to this benefit, Yates seeks advice on how to better "write to our countrymen as touching the persuading of them to enter religion and change of life" (II, 287). Though he claims to lack expertise, he packs his letters with the kind of news that inspired Pounde, Stephens, Southwell and others to join the Society. Yates relates how, until recently, he lived "in the village of Christian Brazils (which beareth the name of St. Anthony), exercising the common functions of our Company with them for their salvation ... wherein the knowledge and speaking of their language (which I have much more perfected than when I did last write), is to me a great aid." His letter to Englefield also mentions his linguistic skills, a common accomplishment among early Jesuits. "I do enjoy exercising among these silly souls in their language," he writes, "which I understand and speak almost as well as my native speech, as also the Portuguese tongue, the ordinary ministries of our Society" (II, 293).[9] To edify readers he summarizes these "ordinary ministries," noting that since his last letter he performed 300 baptisms, heard 6,500 confessions, distributed first communion to 2,600 people, and witnessed 90 marriages.

Yates also exercised two extraordinary ministries. The first was a mission to the "Eugines," where he worked among people "who have no other remedy for to save themselves than that which Almighty God doth give unto them by our means, by which they be brought to the knowledge and love of their Creator from their foolish and blind superstitions, and to live according to His Holy High commandments." Yates describes the second mission in detail. He traveled "500 miles ... unto a country of those Brazils of the same language called Rari ... in which the mission first going thitherward not passing by villages, ... but by lands of diverse sorts of infidels of different speeches and customs, many of them living in the fields and woods, like unto wild beasts." "We passed many dangers of death," he adds, such as "hunger and thirst for lack of victuals and water, making peace with the ignorant and beastly people for to pass more safely (nevertheless they killed four of our disciples, Christians); and lying every night in the fields and woods, passing also *pericula fluminorum* [dangers of rivers] upon rotten trees and not in boats" (II, 289). The purpose of this daring and arduous trip was to convert indigenous people who lived inland and bring them to the coast where they were safer from enslavement by Portuguese colonizers. In this, however,

Yates admits defeat: "And I likewise was constrained for the safety of the lives of our disciples ... to turn home ... bringing with me no more than two hundred infidels, of more than a thousand that would have come with me if the said Portuguese had not hindered them in the way" (II, 290).[10]

Yates' letters, filled with exotic details, brave accomplishments and quixotic reverses, aimed to stir his readers' affections. The same was true of the *Relations* that Pounde and his circle read. In Foley's biography of Pounde, he describes the result of such reading:

> He had also read letters from our Fathers in the Indies, giving an account of their labors and sufferings, and the numerous conversions of those barbarous infidels to the faith, whom God in his mercy had drawn to himself. The reading of these letters greatly increased his desire of entering the Society, and of devoting himself wholly to it as a servant and son. (*Records* III, 573)

...

Pounde never left England, though he was permitted to take secret vows as a Jesuit through the efforts of Stephens.[11] Pounde and Stephens had planned to leave England for Rome, though Pounde was arrested *en route*. However, from prison, he promoted the Catholic cause through writing, and, according to Foley, "his literary productions were by no means contemptible" (*Records* III, 589). Chief among these was his *Six Reasons*, arguing against Protestant reliance on scripture alone in determining doctrine. Thomas wrote this tract in the wake of Campion's famous *Brag*, which Campion produced at the latter's insistence.[12] Pounde, worried about the effect of anti-Jesuit polemic, urged Campion and Persons to write descriptions of their ministries, which would be published only in the event of their arrest. These descriptions would exonerate the Jesuits, Thomas thought, against charges of political intrigue. Prior to Campion's arrest, however, his *Brag* circulated, possibly at Pounde's instigation. According to his biographers, Pounde, like Campion, enjoyed altercations, which the circulation of the *Brag* provoked.[13] As Simpson puts it, "Poor Pounde! Hot combustible fellow that he was, he had better have put a stick of phosphorous into his pocket than that 'Brag and Challenge' of Campion's" (*The Rambler*, 32). Pounde's *Six Reasons* contributed to the controversy surrounding the *Brag*. "Muse not at this challenge as on a counter-buff," Pounde warns his opponents:

> For it is made in the further behalf of a perpetual corporation and succession of most learned fathers without comparison in the world [i.e., the Jesuits] with the aid of another good race besides [i.e., seminary priests] which cannot die, who have all vowed as chastity hath inflamed them either to win

this realm again to the Catholic faith, and that without any bloodshed except their own at God's permission, or else to die upon the pikes of your sharpest laws, and win heaven for themselves. (Cited in Simpson *The Rambler*, 36)

This resembles, in tone and diction, the *Brag*, which concludes:

> Many innocent hands are lifted up to heaven for [the Queen and her Council] daily and hourly, by those English students whose posterity shall not die, which, beyond the seas, gathering virtue sufficient knowledge for the purpose, are determined never to give you over, but either to win you over to heaven or to die upon your pikes, And touching our Society, be it known unto you, that we have made a league—all the Jesuits in the world, whose succession and multitude must overreach all the practices of England— cheerfully to carry the cross that you shall lay upon us, and never to despair your recovery while we have a man left to enjoy your Tyburn, or to be racked with your torments, or to be consumed by your prisons. The expense is reckoned, the enterprise is begun; it is of God, it cannot be withstood. So the faith was planted; so it must be restored.

Pounde, unlike the more articulate Campion, never achieved martyrdom. He did, though, remain an organizer among recusants, even from prison, where he continued to produce works aimed at confirming and consoling Catholics.[14] In this he provided a model for Southwell and others. Though none of Pounde's works ever got beyond the manuscript stage, they circulated widely, and, in imitation of the Jesuits who inspired him, he was a prolific letter writer (Guiney 185). His best known poem had the same purpose as many of Southwell's verses, and is aptly entitled "The Cheerer: A Consolation for Afflicted Catholycs." The practical-minded Pounde laid no claim to literary merit, and his deserved self-criticism exceeds the humility tropes found in poetry of the period. He apologizes for his "homely meters rude" and his "lamed lines," and, he explains, "For zeal, not skill, did make me take my pen/ To stir myself by stirring other men." In his zeal he addresses the audience for whom Southwell also writes, "You blessed men who suffer for belief," urging them to "pluck up their hearts." He has "happy news" for them, he claims: "Your state is bliss, yea treble blessed it is/ To see our Church yield such an imp as this." In lines more similar to those of Anthony Copley's *Fig For Fortune* than any of Southwell's, Pounde reminds recusant readers how "elephants will be provoked to fight/ ... When blood of grapes is set before their sight" (cf. 1 Maccabees 6:34). Therefore, they have cause for courage "When [they] behold the blessed martyr's blood,/ And call to mind our case and quarrel good." But after awkwardly comparing papists to elephants and the blood of martyrs to grape juice, he produces, as Southwell can, an elegant biblical typology, seeing in "the tribe of Ruben," which preceded the other tribes of Israel into the promised land, a figure for the English martyrs, who already "seized have the skies," where they "Present your prayers, your tears, your groans and cries,/ To him of helps the only help which is." Also anticipating Southwell, Pounde invents images to clarify and ornament his arguments. At the start of one of the poem's fifty-one stanzas, he asserts that "ith Christ in heaven, if that you hope to be./ With Christ on earth you must endure annoy;/ As none at once both heaven and earth can see,/ So none in both can pleasures sweet enjoy." Then, in the final couplet, he explicates the experience of grace by employing the language of the sun: "Shade shrouds the back when sun beshines the face;/ When wordly comforts lack, men have light of grace."

While Southwell surpasses Pounde's literary accomplishments, he finds in the latter a precedent for his work. Thomas, prior to his conversion, produced literature to entertain the Queen and her court and, ultimately, advance his career. After reconciling with the church, his poetry serves the Catholic community. He employs his skills as a writer to edify rather than simply entertain, aiming to advance the Catholic agenda at significant personal risk, which he takes because he sees poetry's apostolic potential. Southwell, when he returns to England, never harbors doubts about poetry's apostolic merits. He is confident that literature is an effective part of his ministry, and he owes some degree of this confidence, as well as the content of his arguments, to Pounde. Animated by Pounde's example, Southwell embraces literature as an integral part of his work as a Jesuit priest.

...

Pounde's legacy to Southwell extends beyond the ministerial efficacy of literature. Through Thomas and his associates Robert learned the aesthetic and spiritual expectations of his future audience. His familiarity with these men enabled him to sustain relationships he would later as a missionary form with others of similar style, substance and fate. Philip Howard, for example, whom Southwell never met but for whom he wrote *An Epistle of Comfort*, strikingly resembles Pounde.

Like Pounde, Howard was an attractive figure at court, and given his family's rank, the Earl was even more conspicuous. At Philip's birth in 1557, his father was England's only Duke; and at his baptism, Philip of Spain, for whom he was named, stood as his godfather. After his father's death, Philip became the ward of William Cecil, who saw to it that his charge acquired a courtier's range of expertise. Philip naturally fulfilled the requirements of the position. His earliest biographer describes him at the age of eighteen as "tall of stature, yet ever very straight, long visaged but of a very comely countenance

… his memory was excellent, his wit more than ordinary [and] he was naturally eloquent and of a ready speech." Like Pounde he employed these talents writing poetry and acting. As Margaret Waugh notes, "[h]is name appears on every page of the Court chronicles in entries describing little gifts to the Queen, entreaties describing entertainments, plays in which Philip took a leading part" (Southwell *An Epistle of Comfort*, 8). Howard counted among Elizabeth's favorites at the time of the proposed French marriage, but when the Queen foreclosed that option, he fell from grace as precipitously as Pounde had. The young earl also came under Campion's influence while witnessing the Jesuit's disputations with officials in the Tower. In Pounde's case, familiarity with Campion shaped his literary agenda. In Howard's, Campion caused his conversion, or, at least, started him down the path of reconciliation with the Catholic church and his estranged wife, Anne Dacres.[15] As a result, Howard, like Pounde, developed affection for Jesuits, and, years after he was received into the church by William Weston, he would write, "I call God to witness I have, and do principally in my heart most affect, reverence and honor for your [Jesuit] vocation above others, for that I have seen, heard and read, as also in respect that from one of that calling I received the greatest good which I ever tasted" (Pollen *CRS* 21, 96).

After his conversion, Howard attempted to travel to the Continent, possibly at the urging of William Allen, who hoped to make use of this celebrated convert.[16] Howard, too, was betrayed and imprisoned; but whereas Pounde was occasionally released, the Earl spent the rest of his life incarcerated. From prison he, too, produced edifying works in prose and verse. He also sent letters to his wife and to Southwell, who enjoyed Anne Dacres' patronage, perhaps even sharing her home. The poet's care for the Howards is no coincidence. The Southwells and the Howards were long associated, even if the grandfathers of Robert and Philip had a falling out, resulting in the death of Henry Howard. Though not of the Howards' stature, the Southwells claimed a degree of nobility, which made for similarities between Robert and Philip.[17]

Southwell appreciated the importance of Howard's conversion, and he reports on the Earl in one of his first missives to Rome. In a letter to Aquaviva dated 25 July 1586, the poet writes that he has safely arrived in England and ascertained the condition of his co-religionists, among whom Arundel stands out. Given his prominence, the government enticed Howard to conform. According to Southwell:

> It was proposed to the Earl of Arundel by the ministers of the state, and I believe by the Queen herself, that if he would only consent for honor's sake to bear the sword as usual before the Queen to church and there wait till the end of the service and of evensong, he should be set free. (*Unpublished Documents*, 307–308)

How Southwell obtained this information is unclear, nor is it known how he met Anne Dacres. Devlin repeats an anecdote recorded in a seventeenth-century biography penned by an anonymous Jesuit, who was Anne's spiritual director for the last years of her life. According to this source, Anne inquired of her relatives, the Vauxes, about priests available in London. This inquiry came after the capture of Martin Array, who had ministered to her household. The Vauxes, who first welcomed the newly arrived missionary, recommended Southwell to the Countess. Their initial meeting, as recorded years later, was marked by a fortuitous misunderstanding.[18] Arundel's wife never intended to invite Robert to live with her "by reason of the inconveniency of her house, and the small number of Catholics about her" (Devlin 134). She knew that he would be in danger at her house in the Strand. The poet, however, was too new on the scene to recognize the peril and inquired about moving in. "He began upon occasion," the biography reports, "to speak of procuring some secret convenience to be made in some part of the house [i.e., a priest hole], wherein himself and his few books together with the Church stuff might be hidden in case any sudden search should happen to be made, as it was usual in most Catholic houses where any priest had residence" (Devlin 134). According to her biographer, Anne was too polite to refuse his request.

Whether or not this anecdote is accurate, Southwell began to correspond with Howard, who secreted letters out of prison by hiding them among legal documents. These letters show remarkable honesty on Howard's part. He uses them as an informal, but no less intimate form of confession. For example, he writes to Southwell about his treatment of Anne:

> I call our Lord to witness that as no sin grieves me any thing so much as my offenses to that party [Anne], so no worldly thing makes me loather to depart hence than that I cannot live to make that party satisfaction according to my most ardent and affectionate desire. *Afflictio dat intellectum*, affliction gives understanding. God I hope of his infinite mercy who knows my heart and has seen my true sorrow in that behalf has remitted all, I do not doubt, and so has the party of my singular charity to my unspeakable comfort. (Pollen *CRS* 21, 315)

A letter from Howard to his wife attests to his candor with Southwell regarding infidelities:

> I must now in this world make my last farewell of you, and as I know no person living whom I have so much offended as yourself, so do I account this opportunity of asking you forgiveness as a singular benefit of Almighty God, and I most humbly and hartily beseech you even for His sake, and of your charity to forgive me all whereinsoever I have offended you, ... and I call God to witness it is no small grief unto me that I cannot make you

recompense in this world for the wrongs I have done you; for if it had pleased God to have granted me longer life, I do not doubt but you should have found me as good a husband to my poor ability by His grace, as you have found me bad heretofore. (Pollen *CRS* 21, 315)

Howard also writes to Southwell about making recompense for his behavior. After explaining that he has had no "carnal relations with any woman but [his] wife since his conversion, he makes plans to distribute to the poor all the money gained by selling the gifts he had received from former lovers (Southwell *Epistle of Comfort* ed. Waugh, 9).

The pace and intensity of their epistolary exchange increased after Howard was sentenced to death. The months surrounding the Armada saw increased hostility against Catholics, thirty-one of whom were executed in 1588–1589. Given Philip's station, the government could not ignore its most famous Catholic prisoner. An aged priest named Bennet, imprisoned with the Earl, when threatened with torture confessed that the latter had requested him to offer a votive Mass of the Holy Ghost for the success of the Spanish cause. Though Bennet retracted the accusation, based upon his testimony Philip was sentenced to death. In his own defense, Howard insisted that as a recent convert to Catholicism, he did not even know what a votive Mass was, much less how to request one.

A letter from Henry Garnet to the Jesuit General, likely based on details supplied by Southwell, records reaction to Howard's sentencing:

> On my arrival [in London] I found all, of all classes, in a terrible state of affliction and disquiet, on account of the condemnation of a certain noble Earl, who being taken when endeavoring to leave the kingdom, has spent four years entire in prison, apart from his family with no comfort but that of a good conscience, inasmuch as he aimed at nothing else but to be a good Catholic, and to betake himself to a land where he might live as one. (Translated and reprinted by J. Gerard, *The Month* no. 404 [Feb. 1898], 124–25)

...

Howard's lack of comfort was soon supplied by Southwell. In their correspondence the need for "comfort" becomes a theme in response to the young nobleman's anxieties. He feared that he might conform, which the state offered him ample opportunities to do. In one instance, his keeper in the Tower, a Mr. MacWilliams, assured him that if he would only read Protestant books, he would be released. In a letter to his wife, Philip considers the possibility, but worries about causing scandal:

I know it is not unlawful if a man have leave, and I am sure by the grace of God that none of their false Books shall make me as much as once stagger in my faith. Wherefor I pray let some zealous, learned, and discreet man be talked withall, and sue for leave for me at his hands if he shall think it lawful, and that I may do it without any scandal in the world to the Church; otherwise I would rather choose to lie here all the days of my life than by any act for my liberty offend or scandalize the smallest member of the Catholic Church. (*Life*, 147–49)

He also consults Southwell about scandal, and his worry elicits a quick response. "It is my daily Prayer," writes Howard, "that I may continue constant in the profession of [God's] Catholic Faith ... And He knows, who knows the secrets of all hearts, that I am fully resolved to endure any death, rather than willingly yield to anything offensive to His Divine Majesty in the least respect, or to give just cause of scandal to the meanest Catholic." This letter and others like it show Howard's awareness of his responsibility to the church as well as of his weaknesses and fears. The frequency with which the young man mentions scandal, and his understandable desire to see his family, cause Southwell concern, out of which he writes a letter containing the seeds of *An Epistle of Comfort*.

Southwell opens with theological propositions. He notes, as he often will in *An Epistle of Comfort*, that "amongst the most certain proofs for the immortality of the soul, of a future life, and of a general judgment, this specially is ranked, that we see the good here oppressed and the wicked exalted, virtue loaded with afflictions, vice with honours." This is counter intuitive, the poet admits, if God governs the world providentially; but, he argues, "there is, therefore, another time for the due adjustment of this inversion of things, another life, another place, in which vices which here are lauded will be there punished, and virtue here oppressed will be there adorned with merited praise and reward." Southwell then proposes the proper perspective on the time and place that Howard currently occupies: "But they who are taught in the school of Christ know certainly that this life is a warfare, a pilgrimage and an exile; they truly understand that neither upon this journey is rest to be found, nor in exile their country, nor is the crown to be expected before the combat is finished." Robert's argument here, as well as his lengthier discussion of similar topics in the *Epistle*, echoes Christian teaching dating back to scripture and Patristic writers, who counsel similar attitudes on this passing world and the sufferings which are part of it. Echoes of the Letter to the Hebrews, for example, are discernible in the poet's text, especially passages where the letter's author urges fortitude. Southwell employs traditional wisdom contained in passages such as Hebrews 12:5–13:

> Brothers and sisters, you have forgotten my exhortation addressed to you as
> children: "my son, do not disdain the discipline of the Lord or lose heart
> when reproved by him; for whom the Lord loves he disciplines; he scourges
> every son he acknowledges." Endure your trials as "discipline"; God treats
> you as sons. For what "son" is there whom his father does not discipline? At
> the time, all discipline seems a cause not for joy but for pain, yet later it
> brings the peaceful fruit of righteousness to those who are trained by it. So
> strengthen your drooping hands and weak knees.

Southwell also employs typological relationships to Old Testament events,
implicitly comparing those who conform for the sake of "present ease" to
"those to whom it is sweeter to eat the garlic of Egypt in idleness than to be
satiated with milk and honey in the land of promise though to be gained only
by present labor." Finally, he sketches a theory that he develops in the *Epistle*.
Present suffering is good for the soul: "Truly the base goods of this life are far
removed from and an unequal reward to virtue; eternal punishments likewise
are heavier than the expiated sins of the pious deserve, if you consider how
much they have here mourned and repented them. Therefore their faults are
corrected in this present life by affliction; merits are preserved to be
recompensed by eternal rewards."

Halfway through the letter, Southwell specifically addresses Philip.
First, he points out that Howard has less reason to fear death than most, since
he knows when, where and how it will occur. Moreover, "the recompense to
follow, by the assent of the universal Church, [is] indubitable." "The present
condition of Howard's soul," as one suffering for the faith, means that death
"will not be so unpleasant on account of the loss it will bring, as delightful on
account of the miseries it will cut off." This argument recurs in Southwell's
Epistle and in his many poems on the advantages of martyrdom. So, too, does
the poet's contention that, as a martyr, Philip offers the church the greatest
possible service: "Men everywhere predict that your constancy in death, your
humility in suffering will profit the Church of God far more than the labors of
a long life, so indignant are all men with this iniquitous sentence."

As in his *Epistle to His Father*, Southwell acknowledges the
temptations to which a man of Howard's rank is prone. "Let therefor neither
fury nor fiction nor the sword, nor glory of splendid attire, nor bribes, nor
entreaties, nor any other violence seduce thee from the charity of Christ," he
warns. As an encouragement to resist these attractions, he notes that
martyrdom offers special benefits for Howard, who, as his letters reveal,
remained anxious about his sinful past. "If thou hast sinned," Robert reminds
him, there is "no sacrament more powerful than such a death, no satisfaction
more valid." Southwell offers consolation tailored to his audience. Martyrdom
assures that God will forgive all: "Your desire of confessing [sacramentally],

the means being now precluded, and the contrition of a humble heart, expressed by shedding your blood in this cause, will be a full remission of sins and of all punishment due for them, as in baptism, so great is the prerogative of martyrdom."

...

This letter serves as a precis of the claims asserted in *An Epistle of Comfort*. Since some assertions in both texts might strike readers centuries later as stark and insensitive, it is not surprising that this *Epistle* generates debate similar to that attendant upon the *Epistle to His Father*. Also not unexpectedly, Southwell's most recent critic finds more fault with *An Epistle of Comfort* than do earlier ones. Robert's contemporaries, who were familiar with the genre and theses of the *Epistle*, valued it so much that it was reprinted immediately after the poet's death, then in 1605, again in 1616 and possibly in 1608.[19] F.W. Brownlow, however, writing four centuries later, criticizes the *Epistle* because in it Southwell "steps completely into the martyr's looking glass world in which things are their opposite: prison is freedom, violence is love, and death is life" (30). His sympathies lie with Philip Arundel, whom he imagines "reading his director's instructions in the Tower of London." The text is tedious, according to Brownlow, "and there is no word in it of sorrow, regret or sympathy, no mention of the wife and children he would never see again" (31). By Brownlow's lights, Howard, "in solitary confinement, under sentence of death, isolated from the ordinary flow of human life and contact," is "the perfect embodiment of the Southwellian man, his comfort a sheet of paper assigning him to the absolute as rigorously in its own way as his judges' sentence" (34). Finally, according to Brownlow, the *Epistle* is "a triumphalistic work taking no account of the changed realities of his country."

H.C. White, however, offers a more sympathetic and sophisticated reading of the work based precisely on Brownlow's last point. In illustrating the differences between the literary styles of Southwell and Campion, White notes that recent changes in England, namely the Babington Plot of 1586, which Robert condemns in *A Humble Supplication*, and the anticipation of the Armada, shaped the poet's text. Southwell describes the effects of the changes in a letter to Aquaviva dated 12 January 1587. He writes, "There is weeping almost unto death among wives who have no husbands, and families with no support, where religion has no champions, and chapels no loving hands to tend them" (*Arch. Rom. S.J. Gesuitico* 651). "It is significant of the changed time," White points out, "that the first literary fruit of the new mission was ... no challenge or manifesto [e.g., Campion's *Brag* or Pounde's *Six Reasons*], but an epistle of comfort to the sufferers of persecution" (242). In the *Epistle*

Southwell responds to the growing sense of hopelessness among Catholics, and in doing so, White asserts, he employs one of the classical types of martyrological literature. White also illustrates that in appropriating this traditional genre, the poet has company among his contemporaries across denominational boundaries. White does not mention it, but Southwell engages some of these works in the *Epistle*. In a chapter on the unhappiness of schismatics, for example, he cites John Foxe, who, along with Southwell, argues that people should not be forced to attend church services (*Epistle*, 200). White underscores Southwell's desire to show "reverent affection" towards "God's prisoners," which he, like writers of similar works, does by "systematically enumerating the grounds of consolation for those who suffer." White outlines the *Epistle*, highlighting the poet's methodology. In every chapter he presents a thesis, which he then supports with references to scripture and Patristic writers. Comparing Southwell's work to those of his contemporaries, she concludes that the *Epistle* "may fairly be counted the most impressive Recusant contribution to the classic martyrological type of encouragement to martyrdom" (249).

Other sympathetic readers agree with White's assessment of the *Epistle*'s method, and they appreciate Southwell's originality despite the expectations characterizing the ancient genre. Janelle praises Southwell's use of natural imagery, which he thinks reveals a growing acceptance by the poet of English versus Continental literary styles.[20] Southwell is maturing, he observes: "Manliness, plain, straightforward and square dealing is now uppermost. The harder spiritual realities have to be faced, and the Jesuit makes no attempt to gloze them over, in his advice to the Catholics, or in his warnings to their adversaries" (199). Despite the *Epistle*'s rigor, and contrary to Brownlow's criticism, Janelle asserts that an "intense lovingness is displayed in the *Epistle*," in which the poet "tranquilly and composedly" addresses even his persecutors. "From end to end," he writes, "the tone is of supreme serenity," caused in part by "natural, forcible and poetic imagery" (201). He applauds Southwell for incorporating "realistic observation" and "the merest touch of sly humor" into a centuries-old genre.

Geoffrey Hill also recognizes Southwell's originality, which he ascribes to his "mystical pragmatism" (19). Hill calls Robert a "mystic" because, while "hedged 'round' with violence," he experiences "foresuffering [of] his own agony even as he rises serenely above the fear and violence" (28). The poet's pragmatism consists in his "achievement of a style ardent yet equable, eloquent and assured, yet without 'panache.'" Compared to others who describe persecution, Southwell attains "eloquent moderation" largely on account of what he leaves out. According to Hill, "style is not simply the manner in which a poet 'says what he has to say'"; it is also the manner of his choosing not to say (27). Southwell, he thinks, is "absolutely reasonable" in comparison with other writers of the period because he chooses not to say much that is violent, coarse or disgusting. While not ignoring the Jesuit's pointed passages written about or for heretics and schismatics, Hill concludes that "one of the achievements of [Southwell's] polemical style is its ability to turn both injustice and 'revenge' in the direction of equity; towards the reparation of wrongs rather than the punishment of offenses" (32).

Christopher Devlin is primarily interested in the *Epistle*'s publication history, and he anticipates the authoritative work done by Nancy Pollard Brown on secret presses in England, upon which the *Epistle* was printed. In terms of the work's merits, Devlin believes it to be "of rare value and scholarship"; moreover, "it revived in the language of his own day the grand tradition of English medieval devotion, like the restoring of a great Cathedral window before the art of those glowing colors had been forgotten" (145). Devlin's praise is typically effusive, but in locating the *Epistle* in the medieval tradition, he denies its proper connection to older Christian sources. Among the earliest works produced by Catholic authors was the address of consolation and encouragement to church members facing persecution, and as H.C. White observes, "particularly is this type moving when [as in Southwell's case] it emanates from one who is to be a martyr, ... for then the voice of the teacher comes with the deepening authority of the witness" (8). This "deepening authority" likely accounts for the republication of the *Epistle* after Robert's death.

Southwell seems aware of his work's potential to gain posthumous authority, noting the likelihood of his execution at the start. He admits that he, as a candidate for martyrdom, can benefit from the work as much as his readers. As a likely martyr, he writes the *Epistle* "for his good and [his reader's] comfort," and he includes himself when describing the conditions of death. "So let them draw us upon hurdles," he writes, "hang us, disembowel us, mangle us, boil us and set our quarters upon their gates to be meat for the birds of the air as they used to handle rebels" (*Epistle of Comfort*, 156). That he was eventually so treated enhanced the *Epistle*'s influence. As White points out, "if later the writer himself joined the ranks of the martyrs, then the message of encouragement would take on an especially persuasive and even sacred character" (8).

Writing as a candidate for martyrdom, Southwell consciously stands in the tradition of Ignatius of Antioch, the first author in this hagiographic genre, who in approximately 110 A.D. wrote letters to the Church of Rome while on his way to die in the Coliseum. Robert frequently quotes Ignatius, and toward the end of his *Epistle* he does so conspicuously by citing the latter's famous passage likening martyrs to "God's wheat." Imploring Roman

Christians not to interfere with his martyrdom by exerting influence on government officials, a possibility which Southwell also faced by virtue of his relationship with powerful Elizabethans, Ignatius writes, "I beg you, do not show me unseasonable kindness. Suffer me to be the food of wild beasts, which are the means of my making my way to God. God's wheat I am, and by the teeth of wild beasts I am to be ground that I may prove Christ's pure bread" (*The Epistles of St. Clement of Rome and St. Ignatius of Antioch* ed. James A. Kleist, 54). Southwell fits the passage to his situation, erasing the distance between the church's earliest martyrs and the audience whom he hopes to console and reconcile to their fate. "We are the wheat of Christ, as St. Ignatius said," he writes, "and are ready, if you will, to be ground with the teeth of wild beasts, or if you will not suffer that, with the mill-stones of your heavy persecution, that we may become pure and clean bread in the fight of Christ" (*Epistle of Comfort*, 229).

Southwell borrows more than imagery from his sources. He also adopts their arguments. Principally, he echoes Ignatius and Origen, the author of an *Exhortation to Martyrdom* written in 235, underscoring that fear, affection for family and concern for property should not sway one from the martyr's course. The ultimate benefits of "the baptism of blood," such as the total remission of sins, outweigh these concerns. And like Cyprian, another Patristic author whom he cites, Robert addresses his persecutors with whom he hopes to be reconciled. Cyprian wrote an entire work, entitled *The Lapsed*, considering the fate of those who weaken during persecution or who perpetrate it. Southwell abbreviates his similar consideration in the *Epistle*'s two briefest chapters, and while he follows Cyprian in providing examples of how God exacts retribution on the church's enemies, he avoids the earlier writer's rigorist approach to persecutors.[21] As in the *Epistle to His Father*, Southwell's outlook is comparatively gentle. Near the end of *An Epistle of Comfort*, he expresses care for his opponents. "To your hatred we render goodwill," he writes, "for your punishments, prayers; and we would willingly purchase your salvation with our dearest blood" (240). He underscores the possibility of reconciliation elsewhere as well. "God is ready again to receive you," he insists in a chapter entitled "The Unhappiness of Schismatics and the Lapsed": "Wherefore whoever hath fallen, let him now rise" (206–207). This concern for his persecutors marks the first of the *Epistle*'s many attempts to achieve reconciliation on several levels.

Southwell also hoped to reconcile his readers to their unexpected fate, and his knowledge, gained from early experiences among them, proved advantageous in doing so. His audience, as epitomized by Philip Howard, had much in common with the persecuted churches for whom Ignatius, Origen and Cyprian wrote. As Margaret Waugh observes in her introduction to the

Epistle, "the Christians in North Africa in the time of Cyprian offered the nearest analogy to the position of Catholics in England in the last decades of the sixteenth century" (xii). As a result, they found the same literary genre helpful in accepting their predicament centuries later. Helen White describes these similarities, pointing out how "the great persecutions ... came as a shock to many Christians, many of whom were solid citizens in every sense of the solid citizenship of the Roman Empire." "Many of these Christians," she continues, "upon whom the terror of the great persecutions fell were men and women who had been gently and even luxuriously nurtured with a great deal in the way of human satisfaction to sacrifice." Consequently, "they doubtless thought of [martyrdom] as something remote, appertaining to beings of less delicate nerve or lively imagination than theirs, and here it was upon them" (6). In composing his *Epistle*, Southwell deliberately takes these circumstances into account. Throughout it is obvious, for example, that he is addressing sophisticated readers used to power, privilege and prestige. He warns them about being tempted by "syrens' sweet notes," luring them to recover through conformity all that they had lost. "The devil kisseth where he meaneth to kill," writes the poet, "he giveth us a draught of poison in a golden cup, and in a sumptuous and stately ship wafteth his passengers upon the rocks of eternal ruin" (*Epistle*, 24). He lists the temptations facing men such as Howard, pointing out "how unhappy are they, who, in order to save their goods, credit, temporal authority or other such worldly respects, forsake the glorious and divine honours and purchase a most lamentable and ignominious style" (195). "With whatsoever jewels or ornaments you are set forth," he reminds his formerly prosperous readers, "without Christ's beauty, you are deformed" (205).

Southwell's knowledge of his audience also determines the *Epistle*'s allusions and figurative language. Through the community that recruited his loyalty as a boy, he acquired the resources necessary for meeting his readers on their own ground in order to reconcile them to his paradoxical theses. He understands the nuances of their experience as well as their aesthetic and spiritual expectations. For example, after explaining in the first chapter how persecution reveals that Catholics are out of the devil's power, he refers to falconry. Presuming upon their expertise in the sport, he likens God to a falconer. Southwell, who spent so many years abroad, was initially uneasy about using English sporting imagery. As John Gerard reports, "frequently as [he and Southwell] traveled together, [Southwell] would ask me to tell him the correct terms, and worried because he could not remember and use them when need arose" (*John Gerard*, 218). The second chapter of the *Epistle* reveals that Robert was an able student. "The falconer that hath a hawk of great price on his fist," he insists, "be he never so fond of it, yet he will not let it loose. Yea, the more he loveth it, the more care he hath to keep it hooded, to have good jesses at the legs and to hold it fast" (*Epistle*, 15). God likewise binds his favorites with the jesses of persecution to keep them close to him. Because of his fondness for England's Catholics, God deprives them of "vain and superfluous pleasures," as the skilled huntsman deprives his birds of liberty. According to Southwell, "so God, like a careful keeper of our soul, lest our whole mind should be employed in vain and superfluous pleasures, cutteth them from us so that our wits which would have been diffused in them without profit, being kept in compass by troubles, may be fitter to work and bring forth fruits of eternal salvation" (25). Later, in the *Epistle*'s ninth chapter, on the comforting nature of death to good people, the poet again employs hunting imagery. England's Catholics are like a "chased hart," who, to avoid their persecutors, figured as "greedy hounds," run to the hunter, namely God, trusting in his mercy. Death, according to Southwell, which leads to God, is a comfort in comparison to being chased by pursuivants. The point, though stark, is simple, but Robert employs an elaborate and class-conscious rhetorical strategy appropriate for his audience. He renders the paradox more palatable by couching it in familiar terms.

John Gerard also tutored Southwell in horsemanship, another aspect of his readers' lives. Describing Jesuit work in England, Gerard notes that when they had to sit at table with gentlemen, especially Protestants "who had practically no other conversation except obscene subjects or rant against the saints or the Catholic faith ... there is often the chance of bringing the talk round to some other topic simply by throwing out a remark about horses or hounds or the like" (*John Gerard*, 15). Southwell, bringing his readers round to constancy in their faith, throws out an allusion to buying horses. "It were a great folly," writes Southwell, "in one that seeing a horse fair to the eye, of a good color, of a proper make, and set forth with a gorgeous furniture, would straight buy it at an unreasonable price, neither considering its pace, courage, force or soundness." So, too, his readers would understand, "were it extreme madness to buy the advancements of this world with loss of eternal joy, only for the fair show and flattering delights, not weighing the slipperiness, the vanity and the danger of them" (210).

In reconciling his readers to their fate, Southwell appeals to their sensitivities. In chapter three of the *Epistle*, Southwell alludes to courtly literature. "An enamoured knight," by analogy, "hath no greater felicity than to do that which may be acceptable to his paramour":

> And the fading beauty of a fair lady's countenance is able to work so forcibly in men's minds that neither loss of riches, danger of endurance, menacings of torments, no not present death is able to withhold where she inviteth, or make the bark ride at anchor that is wafted in her streams. Every peril undertaken for

her seemeth pleasant, every reproach honorable, all drudgery delightsome, yea the very wounds that come from her or are suffered for her are void of smart: and the wounded wretch rejoices more with the hope that his hurt will purchase favour than feels aggrieved that his body hath received such a maim. (40)

Men such as Philip Howard were accustomed to this language of love and to the description of the paramour's beauty accompanying it. For such a lady's sake the proper knight would lay down his life. If this is the case, Southwell contends, then believers should do the same for Christ. In fact, Southwell's Christ is physically beautiful, though Southwell mentions this only in passing. "I will not stay upon Christ's corporal seemliness," he demures, "though indeed he were *white and ruddy, a choice piece out of thousands* (Canticles 5:10), and *comely in feature above all the sons of men* (Psalm 44:3), and in that respect more amiable than any other" (41).

More important than his beauty is Christ's "excessive love," which Southwell's readers can experience by engaging in an Ignatian contemplation on "the last tragical pageant of his Passion" (43). Southwell's audience can view Christ on the cross "with the eyes of [their] heart[s]" (44). "We shall discover a most lamentable sight," he continues. Invoking the favorite tropes of affective piety, Southwell describes the vision's content: "We shall see his head full of thorns, his ears full of blasphemies, his eyes full of tears, his mouth full of gall, his body full of wounds, his heart full of sorrow." The sight will cause them to be "deeply ravished by the love of God," such that they will "so settle [their] minds therein that [they] think it [their] chiefest happiness in life to embrace all hazards, disgraces and misfortunes in his quarrel and find most comfort, when for his glory, [they] are in the most bitter pangs" (42).

Other references to Christ's death also show Southwell appealing to the sharp minds, as well as to the soft hearts, of his readers. He cites the example of St. Paul, "who being enflamed with the force of so unusual an example [i.e., Christ's Passion] labored himself to be a perfect scholar in this doctrine, esteeming it the highest and most needful point of Christian knowledge to understand the value, necessity and manner of patient sufferance." Southwell encourages his audience to have "no other university but Jerusalem, no other school but Mount Calvary, ... no other reader but the crucifix, no other letters but his wounds, no other commas but his lashes, no other book but his open side, and finally no other lesson but *to know Christ and to know him crucified*" (1 Corinthians 2:2). In preparation for this knowledge, they should consider their prisons as classrooms. "So we see," he contends, "how prison is a school of divine and hidden mysteries to God's friends" (126), and "considering these things, let us take our prison as a preparation and as a private school of exercise to train and instruct us for public, serious and most sharp affrays" (130).

...

References to familiar aspects of his readers' lives set the stage for Southwell's ultimate appeal, which he presents as a call to arms on behalf of an incomparably noble cause. Employing dramatic, martial terms, he summons men such as Howard to fight on Christ's side in a daunting battle, but one in which victory is certain. Addressing them as "you who professed to be Christ's champions," he writes, "your life is a warfare; your weapons, patience; your Captain, Christ; your standard, the Cross. Now the alarm is sounded and the war proclaimed" (158). Here Southwell draws on the "Meditation on Two Standards," a centerpiece of Loyola's *Spiritual Exercises.* Loyola, too, describes Christian life as a battle and Christ as "the supreme and true Captain" (*Spiritual Exercises*, 139). On the one hand, Satan, who has "seated himself in that great field of Babylon," bids "innumerable demons," who "cast out nets and chains; that they have first to tempt with a longing for riches ... that men may more easily come to vain honor of the world, and then to vast pride." On the opposing side, we should "consider the discourse which Christ our Lord makes to all his servants and friends, whom he sends on this expedition, recommending them to want to help all." Loyola imagines Christ recommending three kinds of humility which will render his followers more helpful:

> First ... the highest spiritual poverty, and—if His Divine Majesty would be served and would want to choose them—no less to actual poverty; the second is to be of contumely and contempt; because from these two things humility follows. So that there are to be three steps; the first, poverty against riches; the second, contumely and contempt against worldly honor; the third humility against pride. And from these three steps let them induce to all other virtues. (*Exercises*, 146)

Southwell uses this Ignatian resource in his *Epistle* believing that it will resonate with his readers' aspirations for glory, if not in this world, then in the next. If they are humbled here, they will be exalted in heaven; though he also holds out the promise that in fighting and dying for Christ, martyrs will gain the prizes accorded great military men. They, too, will win monuments in the shape of churches, gain the attention of famous writers, and they will exert great power through intercession and miracles (*Epistle*, 187–94). In his usual fashion, Southwell uses the things of this world such as falcons, horses and the promise of lasting fame to lure readers to otherworldly pursuits.

To reconcile men such as Philip Howard to the prospect of martyrdom, Southwell appeals to their deepest desires, even when those desires are tainted by worldliness. Given his early experiences among such people, he knows how to make them enthusiastic about accepting the worst of circumstances. Several times he invokes famous Jesuit missionaries, including Francis Xavier. In chapter six of the *Epistle* he refers to Xavier's sanctity and success as evidence that "the cause we suffer for is the true Catholic faith." "In our days since Luther rose up," the truth of Catholicism is made evident by "the Reverend Father Francis Xavier of the Society of Jesus, in the Indies." Xavier's miraculous efforts should inspire English Catholics to fidelity. "What greater certificate can we have," Southwell asks, "of the goodness of our quarrel, since we are sure that God, the only author of these supernatural effects, cannot witness to any kind of untruth?" (104). Elsewhere he refers to the contents of "epistles and stories of India," to show how heretics cannot be martyrs. Even though infidels willingly die for their false gods, as missionaries report in their letters, they are not saints. Christian missionaries, surrounded by so much horror and suffering for the sake of Christ, provide the best examples for Englishmen facing persecution (215).

...

In reconciling his readers to their plight, Southwell never minimizes the risks they face. He is brutally honest, perhaps even hyperbolically so; and the hyperbole may be what his readers want. At the *Epistle*'s start, he admits that "when we come to the service of Christ, we come to a rough profession, which is bound to have continual defiance and enmity with the pleasures, vanities and praises of this world" (10). Moreover, the opposition is formidable. Again invoking imagery from the Jesuit *Relations* and other forms of travel literature, Robert likens Protestants to pirates. "The pirates," he writes, "used in the dark night to set lights in the shallow places so that the ships thinking to find some sure haven, should direct their course by these lights, and thus be guilefully drawn to their own ruin." In the same way, his audience's persecutors, "setting the light of scripture and counterfeit piety upon the rocks of heresy, allure under the color of truth the simple passengers of this life to their own perdition" (97). Southwell wants, though, to describe his readers' task as more onerous, and more glorious, than that of explorers. To this end, he compares them to ancient martyrs. "But if comparison to saints be not presumption," he continues, "this, for our great comfort we may say: that though the cause of religion were always honorable, yet it is in us more worthily defended than of any martyrs of former ages." The reason being, "they defended either against epicures and heathens, or against the Jews and rabbis, or against some one heretic and his offspring." But his readers "are now in a battle not only against men of our times, who are epicures in conditions, Jews in malice, and heretics in proud and obstinate spirit, but against the whole rabble and generation of all heretics that since Christ's time have been in league with Satan." He concludes that "in combating them we challenge all the old heretics onto the field ... sustain[ing] a multitude of enemies, jointly assaulting us, every one of whom hath, in times past, made work enough for diverse doctors in several ages, according as they did rise one after another" (98). Southwell uses this argument to prove that England currently faces the direst of threats, namely atheism. "The variety of religion hath abolished almost all religion," he warns, "it is indeed true that this uncertainty among so many beliefs hath made the greatest part of our country believe none at all" (100).

"Combat" against atheism requires extraordinary "soldiers" (29), and the poet recruits his readers by reminding them that they are England's last, best hope:

> You are the choice captains whom God hath allotted to be chief actors in the conquest. Your veins are conduits out of which he meaneth to derive the streams that shall water his Church. He hath placed you as the fairest and surest stones in the forefront of his building to delight his friends and confound his enemies with the beauty and grace of your virtuous life and patient constancy. (112)

After flattering them, he puts his plan for spiritual combat in traditional parlance. "For if in a serious and earnest battle upon which the state of the commonwealth depended, the King himself were in complete harness [i.e., armor], and in person ready with his weapons to fight for his kingdom, if then," Southwell asserts with the wry humor Janelle observed, "any of his nobles came into the field with a fan of feathers instead of a buckler, and a posy of flowers instead of a sword, ... the king could not but take it in very evil part" (117). Christ, he insinuates, is in just such straits, and he requires "true soldiers ... ready as our King and Captain to venture our lives in the same quarrel" (117). Moreover, he appeals to their instincts and experience. They know, for example, that many men have willingly suffered even death for "a puff of vainglory" (148). How much more, then, should they willingly suffer for "eternal felicity"? Reminding them of their courtly past, he asks, "how often, for a point of honor, have we been ready to challenge our counterpeers' into the field?" "Now," he instructs them, "we ought to renew that wonted courage, and be as careless of our lives when they are to be well spent, as we were when we would have spilled them for vanity" (153).

Addressing his readers in terms and a tone that they would have found accessible and attractive, Southwell can take his argument in an unexpected direction. The "combat" to which he summons them turns out to be an interior one. While never denying the reality of outside opposition, faithful to his Jesuit superiors' instructions he does not himself nor does he encourage his readers to "do battle with heretics." Instead, he wants them to engage in a process of transformation or, in his word, "transfiguration" (157). The battle is within: he and his readers must "war against our vain desires and appetites, when they draw us away from the cross towards delight and pleasure" (31). It is a process in which they choose to participate, but one which God controls, even making heretics his unwitting agents. For their part, English Catholics must accept whatever tribulation God sends. It is, he contends, for their good. God is "more desirous to have [them] affectionate than fortunate children," so he "delighteth to see our torturings, rackings, chains and imprisonments for his sake (which are assurances of our love), than to see us swim in his temporal gifts" (39). In the third and fourth chapters of the *Epistle*, he argues that their sufferings are less than what he and his readers deserve on account of "the estate and condition of [their] life" and their manifold iniquities. Consciousness of sin should make them patient in adversity, he claims, and "since God of his mercy has not permitted such punishments [as they deserve] but laid a soft and easy hand upon [them], [they] have more cause of thanksgiving than of any just complaint" (70).

...

Beyond counting the benefits awaiting those who will be personally transformed by suffering, Southwell argues that England will be transfigured through persecutions. The *Epistle* is a work in which the poet's nationalism surfaces, and in the text he works at reconciling his patriotic attachments and his loyalty to the church. Though he is at odds with Elizabeth's government, he expresses his affection and hopes for her people. In chapter two, for example, he claims that England is among God's favorite nations. In fact, he finds in Israel a typological forerunner for his own country. Citing the second book of Maccabees, he writes, "I beseech them that shall read this book not to be terrified by these adversities but deem those things which have happened to be rather to the amendment than destruction of our nation" (2 Mac. 6:12). He further reads the signs of the times as pointing toward God's special care for England. According to Southwell, providence operates in England as nowhere else. "For God dealeth not with us as with other nations," he contends, "whose sins he leaveth to the last day to be punished together; for though he chastiseth us, he never removeth his mercy from us and never forsaketh us in our trouble" (19). England is a sinful nation, so God causes some to suffer in order that many might ultimately be saved; and in the context of their suffering, God causes miracles to occur. He mentions "the wonderful stay and standing of the Thames on the day Fr. Campion and his company were martyred." To those who would dispute this occurrence, he responds, "although some will impute these accidents to other causes, yet as they happened at such special times when so open and unnatural injustice was done, they cannot but be interpreted as tokens of God's indignation" (235). The age of miracles has not passed in England. Even out of anger God deals separately with his favorite nation. Moreover, Southwell wants to prove that the present, on account of persecution, is the best possible time to be an Englishman and, most especially, to be a priest in England:

> This is the time that many of your forefathers have desired to live in, so that they might not only profit the Church by example of their life and by virtue of their preaching, but also (which they counted most to be desired) by the effusion of their blood. When England was Catholic it had many glorious confessors. It is now for the honor and benefit of our country that it be also well stored with numbers of martyrs; and we have (God be thanked) such martyr-quellers now in authority, as mean (if they have their will) to make saints enough to furnish all our Churches with treasure, when it shall please God to restore them to their true honors. (247)

To bolster confidence among his readers and in his own mind that a restoration is possible, the poet predicts a future in which persecutors "or their posterity shall see the very prisons and places of execution, places of reverence and great devotion, and the scattered bones of those that suffered in this cause, which are now thought unworthy of Christian burial, shrined in gold" (247). His patriotism equips him for making meaning out of the suffering of Catholics. Those loyal to England's ancient faith are actually agents for the nation's best interests. Robert reconciles his love of nation and church by means of a paradox. From his perspective, Elizabeth's persecuted subjects are also her most patriotic supporters; and later, in his *Humble Supplication*, he encourages her to recognize this truth.

···

Along with reconciling religious opponents, candidates for martyrdom to their fate, and his own nationalism to his Catholic identity, Southwell wants to maintain convictions about scriptural and Augustinian indifference toward the world while incorporating in his thought a humanistic approach to present life. He knows the strain in Catholic piety that urges believers to consider themselves exiles on a perilous journey through an evil world. The tradition is grounded in scriptural texts, such as Hebrews 11:13–16, in which Old Testament figures, including Abel, Noah, Abraham and Moses, know that they "were not yet in possession of those things promised, but had seen them far ahead, and confessed themselves no more than pilgrims or passing travelers on earth." "Those who use such language," the letter's author argues, "show that they are looking for a country of their own": "If their hearts had been in the country they had left, they could have found opportunity to return. Instead we find them looking forward to a better country—I mean a heavenly one. That is why God is not ashamed to be called their God, for he has a city ready for them." Southwell espouses this attitude, telling his readers:

> As for you, the world hateth you, and therefore how can you love it, being hated of it? We are here pilgrims and strangers, and how can we but willingly embrace the death that assigneth us to our last home, delivering us out of these worldly snares, and restoreth us to Paradise and the Kingdom of Heaven? Our country is heaven; our parents, the patriarchs. Why do we not hasten to come speedily to our country and salute these parents? (160)

Implicit in his argument is St. Augustine's division between the City of God and the City of Man.[22] Often in the *Epistle* Southwell endorses Augustine's assertions about the relationship between Christians and the world. Christians by grace are "aliens" on earth who "wander as on a pilgrimage through time looking for the kingdom of eternity" (*City of God* bk. XV, ch. 1). Southwell employs this terminology in chapter four, for example, reminding readers that they are "wandering stranger[s] in this far and foreign country, ... drudge[s] in the miry farm of this world" (*Epistle*, 50). "We are here in a place of exile," he continues, "in a hospital of Lazars, in a channel of ordure, in a dungeon of misery, in a sepulchre of dead carcasses, finally, in a vale of tears" (51). As a result of such thinking, believers should adopt certain attitudes such as disdain for the body. "If we consider our body," he writes, "what is it, how brittle, how frail, how subject to corruption, how full of horrible diseases, stuffed with loathsome excrements, miserable in life and abominable after death, how can we take pleasure in a fountain of so much pain or not find it tedious to serve and to feed so noisome a thing?" (53). The body is "a most filthy prison" in which the soul is "exiled ... from her native country and in a most lamentable sort debarred from her kingdom, like a captive fettered, ... like a forlorn and left widow deprived of her spouse's fellowship" (53–54). Therefore, he concludes, the "easiest and only remedy" lies in "the severing of body and soul asunder." Because the martyrs have experienced this severing they are, according to Southwell, "thrice happy" (54).

Despite this Augustinian otherworldliness, the poet throughout the *Epistle* enjoys referring to the things of this world and, especially, to English things. As Margaret Waugh observes, "as he proceeds it can be seen how every aspect of English life in Elizabethan England provided material for his meditations: there are similes drawn from the marble quarries and foundaries, from the lives of husbandmen, embroiderers, portrait-painters and sea-faring captains" (*Epistle*, xvii). Waugh intuits that Southwell is practicing the Ignatian exercise of seeking God in all things. This possibility, and Southwell's use of material reality to point out God's presence in the world, grows out of a passage at the start of Loyola's *Spiritual Exercises* entitled the "Principle and Foundation." In it Loyola explains that all "things on the face of the earth are created for man and that they may help him in prosecuting the end for which he was created," namely, "to praise, reverence and serve God our Lord, and by this means to save his soul" (*Exercises*, 23). "From this it follows," according to Loyola, "that man is to use them as much as they help him on to his end, and ought to rid himself of them so far as they hinder him as to it." This "Principle and Foundation" qualifies the Augustinian perspective, giving the world a clear though relative affirmation, exemplified in Robert's positive use of worldly imagery, in his commendation of hospitality, and in his reverence for personal relationships. In achieving his *Epistle*'s end, the poet uses things at his disposal so that his readers can be reconciled to their fate, their persecutors and God. Though all three will remove them from the world they know, Southwell invokes that world to the point of celebrating it. Although "all nations and islands advanced to great power and sway have decayed in time," he is adamant that God loves England uniquely and best. Though we should consider ourselves as exiles during earthly life, the poet encourages hospitality. In fact, he makes "for proof of the sincerity of our religion" the claim that Catholics surpass Protestants in "friendly conversation" and "their large hospitality in housekeeping" (*Epistle*, 106). He regularly celebrates friendship both in the *Epistle* and in other works. In chapter three of the *Epistle* he describes it as propaedeutic to friendship with God. He reached this conclusion as a Jesuit novice. In the journal he kept during the noviceship he writes:

> If thou dost love thy friend so tenderly, if N. and N. are so pleasing to thee that thou acceptest willingly whatsoever they may bid thee to do and findest the greatest delight in conversing with them and in speaking to them of thyself and all thy sorrow; with what greater confidence oughtest thou not to commend thyself to Almighty God, to speak with him and to expose before him all thy needs and miseries, since He has greater care of thee than thou hast of thyself, and is more intimately present to thee even than thou art to thy self. (*Spiritual Exercises and Devotions*, 66)

There is a world-affirming quality to this appreciation of human relationships, and the same attribute extends to his treatment of the stuff of experience. He is attuned to how human work and its products mirror God's ways. He compares God, for example, to a "cunning artificer" (*Epistle*, 173) and a "cunning embroiderer" (236). In a warning to persecutors, he describes in human terms how God operates through martyrdom:

A cunning embroiderer, having a piece of torn or fretted velvet for his ground, so contriveth and draweth his work that, as fretted places are wrought over with curious knots or flowers, they far excel in show the other whole parts of the velvet. So God working upon the ground of our bodies, by you so rent and dismembered, will cover with unspeakable glory the ruptures, breaches and wounds which you have made. (236)

Elsewhere in the *Epistle* Southwell expands this celebration of the body's potential for beauty and enjoyment in the afterlife, and his tone approaches rapture. He describes heaven in very worldly terms:

For first all the comforts, joys and delights that are here scattered in diverse creatures and countries, any beauty and comeliness that any worldly thing here hath, shall be there united and joined together in every saint and they shall be without any of these imperfections wherewithal they are here copied. (219)

Moreover, "in heaven all the senses are evermore and without fear of loss fully satisfied with their several pleasures and drowned in the depth of unspeakable delight." He also insists that his readers will enjoy their heavenly companions. "Now for your company," he reassures his sophisticated audience, "you must not think that because the lame, blind, poor and despised objects of this world are those that go to heaven [and] therefore all the best company is banished from heaven and only the rejects of mankind left to fill up the seats of the fallen angels" (220–21). They will be joined by "all those of all estates and degrees whose company shall be grateful," and will be comfortable in heaven because it will be a perfected version of the courtly life they once enjoyed. For example, "it shall be lawful to love whatsoever we like, and whatsoever we love shall be perfectly enjoyed; and not only love, but be also loved so much as we ourselves will desire." Love will come easily because people will be attractive. "And for our bodies," writes Southwell, "they shall be of most comely and gracious feature: beauteous and lovely, healthy without all weakness, always in youth, flower and prime of their force, personable of shape, as nimble as our thought, subject to no penal oppression, incapable of grief, as clear as crystal, as bright as the sun, and as able to find passage through heaven, earth or any other material stop as is the liquid and yielding air" (222–23).

Southwell's description of heaven and its citizens results from Patristic influences and Renaissance humanism. As such, it nuances the determinative teachings of Augustine and Thomas Aquinas that argue for a theocentric heaven in which human relationships, desires and bodies are subordinated. In Southwell's heaven both God and people, especially people who have suffered, get what they desire and deserve. In describing heaven he reverts to a model expounded by Irenaeus, a second-century bishop of Lyon, who wrote for a community facing martyrdom. As Colleen McDannell and Bernhard Lang suggest, "the church of the martyrs, which Irenaeus represented, did not reject the world." Instead, "it resented the fact that Roman persecution had made it impossible for Christians to enjoy God's gift to humanity fully." Therefore, "the will to survive in a hostile civilization despite persecution and martyrdom led to an understanding of heaven as the compensation for lost earthly privileges" (McDannell and Lang 47). Irenaeus, like Southwell, offers suffering readers a heaven that is, in fact, "a glorified material world" that "would offset" earthly limitations" (48). Irenaeus' readers resemble Southwell's. Many were prosperous, professional people. "They did not," McDannell and Lang assert, "march bravely to death because they hated the world." "Contrary to our assumptions that those who die for Christ despise the world," they claim, "Christian martyrs accepted the goodness of their material lives, [and] they expected that after martyrdom they would experience an improved earthly existence."

Only after the age of martyrdom did Christians, especially Augustine, find inspiration in world-renouncing Greek philosophies such as Neoplatonism. As a result, "they rejected the compensational heaven of Irenaeus and predicted that life after death would entail the culmination of their ascetic, spiritual lifestyle" (McDannell and Lang 48). Southwell shows the influence of Augustine often in his *Epistle*, but he is not constrained by it. Instead, he wants to achieve equilibrium between Augustinianism and more world-affirming strains in Christian thought. For example, whereas Augustine "insisted on the irrelevance of social joys for real happiness" in heaven (McDannell and Lang 58), Southwell notes how "besides men, we shall have the company of many choirs of angels, of our Blessed Lady, Christ and the most Blessed Trinity; and these so beautiful to see and so amiable and loving to converse with that we shall have no less joy of our company than of our own glory" (*Epistle*, 221). Whereas in Augustine's heaven only God's glory and our contemplation of it exist, in Southwell's heaven, "everyone's wish shall be fulfilled in himself, in all other creatures, yea and in almighty God." "And so shall all be absolute kings," the poet concludes, "because everyone's pleasure and will shall be fully accomplished" (222). The promise of attaining royal status must have pleased readers like Philip Howard who were deprived of their legitimate nobility. In heaven their rights and prerogatives will be restored.

Humanism adds to Southwell's notion of heaven. Because of that pervasive cultural movement, McDannell and Lang argue, "Renaissance theology insisted that as noble beings we are invited to enjoy rather than renounce the world" (112). This exceeds Irenaeus' compensational approach to the afterlife. During the Renaissance, "since God and humans were seen as being in harmony rather than competing as rivals, the human side of heaven gained prominence" (112). This counters the authoritative scholasticism of Aquinas, who, like Augustine, insisted that God must be the primary, if not exclusive, source of happiness in heaven. The only activity necessary in Aquinas' heaven is contemplation. Renaissance thinking, however, allows other pursuits. According to McDannell and Lang, "in its boldest form, the new theology envisioned heaven as a place of erotic human love in the bucolic setting of a comfortable natural landscape," so that "without losing its divine center, heaven became more worldly, more human" (112). Southwell moves in this direction when he writes:

> Our sight shall feed on the most glorious and eyesome majesty of the place and on the glory and beauty of the company. The ears shall always be more solaced with most sweet and angelic harmony. The smelling shall be delighted with heavenly scents and odors. The taste shall be pleased with incomparable sweetness. The feeling shall be satisfied with a perpetual and unknown pleasure. Finally, every parcel, joint, sinew, vein and member of our body shall have his several and peculiar delights. (*Epistle*, 223)

This passage, along with other points in Southwell's *Epistle*, resonates with McDannell and Lang's conclusion that "courage, discipline, perseverance and a kind of Renaissance optimism about the human condition and the value of human endeavor became the hallmarks of the Catholic reform mentality" (160). Robert understands that his sophisticated audience needs to be encouraged to those first three qualities, and he effectively addresses them because he possesses the fourth.

Because of his familiarity with men like Philip Howard, Southwell, when writing for them in *An Epistle of Comfort*, produces effective discourse. He engages them by invoking the particularities of their lives and the milieu in which they were raised. In doing so he brings together pre-existing literary, spiritual and theological traditions, some at odds with others, to make something new for his readers. The product, therefore, is not without contradictions. While his aim is reconciliation, he never resolves all of these tensions. He and his text live with them, and this can be perceived as a limitation. But as he later admits in the preface to his poems, "The Author to his loving Cosen," whatever degree of originality he claims resides in his ability to take cultural and religious materials available to him and "weave a new web." Once in England, he never enjoys the leisure required to create something out of nothing. The needs of his audience are too pressing. The conditions in which he lives and works are too dire and dangerous. Nevertheless, these needs and conditions inspire on Southwell's part prodigious creativity if not entirely unmarred products.

...

Southwell's literary efforts were not limited to authorship. In the case of *An Epistle of Comfort*, the poet, with the help of associates, built and ran the secret press which reproduced the text. Printing had been taken up by Campion and Persons, who arrived in 1580 with canonical faculties to set up presses. They were granted an exemption from the Tridentine canons which forbad the anonymous publication of works by Catholic authors. The Council's fourth session, in declaring the Latin Vulgate edition of the Bible authoritative, wanted to police all Catholic books to ensure orthodox interpretations of scripture. The session's second decree read, "no one may print or have printed any books on sacred subjects without the name of the author, nor in the future sell them or even keep them in his possession, unless they have first been examined and approved by the local ordinary, under pain of anathema and fine" (Tanner II, 665). Since England lacked bishops, the directive was unenforceable. Furthermore, Jesuit superiors recognized the uniqueness of the missionaries' situation, and made provisions for publication.

Those responsible for the mission understood the ministerial potential of printed works. Given the difficulty of supplying the needs of English Catholics by personal priestly attention, printed material provided spiritual sustenance in lieu of sacraments, sermons and other services ordinarily provided by local clergy. Moreover, Jesuits already recognized publishing as an apostolate. Early in Jesuit history, Loyola charged Jeronimo Nadal with explicating the phrase "any other ministrations whatsoever of the word of God," which defines the scope of Jesuit works in the "Formula of the Institute," an epitome of the *Constitutions*. "Without a word of elaboration," according to John O'Malley, "[Nadal] mentioned ... the writing of books, either to refute heretics or to 'help souls'" (114). In a short while, "it was inevitable ... that Jesuits would turn to the printing press, and Ignatius himself gave an impetus":

> He came to support especially two categories of publication—writings to refute the heretics and writings to aid Jesuits in their ministry. In a letter to Canisius, 13 August 1554, he encouraged Jesuits in Germany to counter Protestant pamphlets with their own, and he did the same in a letter to Nadal the next year. He encouraged Polanco to compile a manual for Jesuit confessors, Canisius to write his catechism, and Lainez to write a compendium of theology adapted to pastoral needs. The categories began to broaden even in Ignatius' lifetime and surely with his approval. (114–15)

Jesuit schools stimulated this broadening of categories. Schools required affordable textbooks, and Ignatius purchased a press for the Collegio Romano at its opening. On this press and others like it at colleges around the world, Jesuits produced books on grammar, rhetoric, and the Latin and Greek classics, as well as philosophy and theology.[23] Southwell and others educated at the Roman College were trained to consider publishing as part of their Jesuit and priestly work.

The establishment of presses and the distribution of Catholic printed materials in England, though, were difficult projects.[24] During Elizabeth's reign, the government issued proclamations against the importation or ownership of unapproved religious texts on 1 March 1569, 1 July 1570, 14 November 1570, and 28 September 1573 (Hughes and Larkin II, nos. 561, 577, 580 and 598). In addition, publishing books required supplies not usually available to priests hiding for their lives. Nevertheless, the need for a press became acute in the face of anti-Jesuit polemic responding to Campion's "Brag." With the help of laymen such as Stephen Brinkley, Persons clandestinely bought and assembled a press in Essex, since one in London would have been easily discovered. As it was, Persons' press needed to be moved twice to elude pursuivants. Producing Catholic books was costly as well as dangerous because they could not be sold. Persons needed to raise funds to cover expenses, and supporters of the mission such as George Gilbert, another layman associated with Pounde's circle, responded generously. Even with benefactions, the work remained difficult. As Nancy Pollard Brown reports in an article on Southwell's "mission of the written word":

> As it was the equipment was hardly adequate to the tasks that were planned. The press was so small that only half-sheets could be printed; there was no Greek fount, and some types were in such short supply that substitutes from mis-matched founts had to be used; completed forms had to be printed off before the next pages could be set. In view of this limited operation, it is not difficult to understand why as many as seven printers seem to have been needed at a time. ("Robert Southwell: The Mission of the Written Word," in *The Reckoned Expense* 195)

Printers gathering in an out-of-the-way spot would arouse suspicion, so Persons made his associates wear disguises. He also needed to exercise caution in collecting paper. Supplies arrived in small amounts, slowing the process.

After Campion's arrest, Persons stopped the press, and no Jesuits would write or print books in England until the homecoming six years later of Southwell and Garnet; but they, too, made publishing a priority, and they so successfully hid equipment that their base of operations remains a mystery. In arguing against the seventeenth-century account of Anne Dacres' interactions with Robert, Brown engages in detective work which illuminates the situation surrounding the Southwell and Garnet presses. She concludes that Southwell never lived in Arundel House, but that the Countess provided him with another refuge where he produced *An Epistle of Comfort*, identifying this location as the Countess' house in Spitalfields. According to Brown, "the enclosure [at Spitalfields] offered its inhabitants the sort of privacy to be justly valued in houses so close to the busy city, to be carefully guarded if they chose to follow an unorthodox way of life" ("Paper Chase: The Dissemination of Catholic Texts in Elizabethan England," 125). The location, Brown suggests, also supplied Southwell with accomplices. Recusants inhabited the area, including members of the poet's own family and neighbors from East Anglia.[25]

Christopher Devlin shares Brown's views, except that he places the press at another home of the Countess' in Acton, Middlesex. He also cites evidence provided in John Gerard's autobiography. Describing his return to England in 1588, Gerard writes:

> We then had few friends in a position to help us. Fr. Southwell alone had a great benefactress, and ... he was able with her help to maintain himself and some other priests, as well as keep a private house where he usually received the Superior on his visits to London. It was there that I first met them both; there too that Father Southwell had his printing press, where his own admirable books were produced.

In claiming or constructing a center from which he could reconcile cultural forces, Southwell embraces available technology despite personal risk. Acknowledging this embrace corrects views of the poet which see him cut off from the Elizabethan mainstream. He never waited in the wings while events played out before him. Instead, he contributed to the often vitriolic national and international exchanges occurring around him, and typically his contributions are more measured and conciliatory than those of his "counterpeers," to use a neologism introduced in the *Epistle*. Moreover, he hazards his life ensuring that his contributions can be heard. Despite images of him hiding in priest holes, keeping himself at a safe distance from the days and works of Elizabethans of his class and education, Southwell claims a congregation of men and women like himself. To engage them, he draws on personal, aesthetic and religious resources supplied by his early acquaintance with the English Catholic community. In addition, he enhances those resources with an overlay of Jesuit spirituality and the kind of learning to which he was exposed at Douai, Paris and Rome. To reach his audience, he employs the most sophisticated technical means available, and in doing so he shows himself to be a man moving toward, if not in, the center of early modern culture.

Notes

[1]   The College Diary reports that on 10 June 1576, "Mr Cottonus et Mr Southwellus, nobiles utrique adolescentes, per communem quendam Angliae nunciam ad nos adducti sunt" (Mr. Cotton and Mr. Southwell, also noble young men, are brought to us through a certain common agent of England.) (Knox, *Diary of the English College, Douai* I:105). According to Foley, the Cotton brothers remained active in the recusant cause. John was "a great sufferer for his faith [and] he had been so involved in the various storms of persecution, that scarcely any portion of his life, even to extreme old age, had been exempt from troubles" (*Records* I, 284). Moreover, "he was always sincerely attached to the Society, and his house was for many years a constant hospice, opened not only for its members, but for his Catholic neighbors of every grade. It went by the name 'Common Refuge'" (284). State Papers attest to Southwell's use of Cotton's homes as a refuge (*Dom. Eliz.* V. ccxli, no. 35, Jan. 1592).

[2]   The General explains the need for secrecy in a letter dated December 1578. Accepting Pounde into the Society, he cautions him to "neither run into danger" nor "destroy your health and strength." Therefore, writes the General, "this one thing ... I greatly desire of you, that you publish to no one this your determination regarding our Society, neither by habit or dress, nor by discourse, but that you keep your secret to yourself until better times beam forth, when this your desire, by the grace of God, may be openly followed out." (See Foley *Jesuits in Conflict*, 50–52.)

[3]   Guiney in *Recusant Poets* describes Pounde as "the most typical figure in this book as a Recusant, though not, it is to be hoped, as a poet" (182).

[4] .   According to Chambers, Pounde's first masque was written for the wedding of his cousin Henry, Earl of Southampton in 1566. The second, also written for a wedding, can be found with the first in *Bodlien Rawlins* ms. 108.

[5]   Chambers notes this development: in 1580 Pounde wrote from his prison in Bishop's Stortford to Sir Christopher Hatton (*S.P.D. Eliz.* cxlii. 20) commending a petition to the Queen, "'for her poeticall presents sake, which her Majesty disdayned not to take at poore Mercuries hands, if you remember it, at Killegeworth Castle'" (III, 468).

[6]   This group was eventually blessed by Gregory XIII in 1580 as a pious association. As Simpson reports, "These men soon became known as 'subseminaries; conductors, companions and comforters of priests;'" ... out of whom the Jesuits were accused of getting "either all or most part of their riches" (223).

[7]   The only exception to this, Clancy points out, was the number of English clerics in exile beginning in 1559. "A good portion of these," Clancy observes, "were university men, mostly from Oxford, and there was a steady stream of them entering the Society" (140) (*AHSI* 57, 140).

[8]   O'Malley underscores Xavier's preeminence. Xavier went to India in 1540, the only original companion of Loyola to leave Europe. According to O'Malley, he "sent letters back to Europe that electrified his brethren and any one else who read them." "Although few Jesuits from this first generation labored outside Europe," O'Malley asserts that "those who did fulfilled the evangelizing aspirations of the first companions, and they set a powerful example for the generations to come" (76).

[9]   Thomas Stephens was the first Westerner to study Canares. He also learned Hindustani, Marathi, Konkani and Sanskrit. As a result, he produced religious works for indigenous people, some of which are considered classics. Stephens also wrote inspirational letters, including one to his father in 1579, which is reprinted in Hakluyt's *Voyages* (Foley *Records* IV, 703).

[10]   Commenting on this brand of missionary activity, John O'Malley asserts, "although these efforts smack of paternalism and a misguided sense of European superiority, with all their

attendant evils, they were not engaged in by the Jesuits without some feeling of mutuality, and they contrast with the attitudes and practices of many other Europeans who had settled in these places. In Brazil Jesuits took courageous stands against the abuses of slave raids and evoked great wonderment from the natives as word spread through the jungles that among the Portuguese there were some who defended them" (78).

[11] Stephens' letter on Pounde's behalf is found in Foley *Jesuits in Conflict*. After describing Pounde's life, Stephens concludes, "the only relief for this his two-fold grief, and affliction of soul, is that your Paternity will be pleased to give him your fatherly consent to his petition, to regard his sighs, his prayers and desires, now these four years daily poured out before God, and would persuade yourself (which is most true), that Thomas Pounde has been so disposed towards the Society for the past seven years, that he would esteem all labours light to him were he but admitted to it" (49).

[12] Campion's work is sometimes called his "Challenge." As Geoffrey Hill observes, "'Brag' was itself a term of abuse foisted by the opposition on Campion's apologia" ("The Absolute Reasonableness of Robert Southwell," in *Lords of Limit* 21).

[13] For more on the controversial nature of Campion's "Brag," see Thomas McCoog, "'Playing the Champion': the Role of Disputation in the Jesuit Mission," in *The Reckoned Expense: Edmund Campion and the Early English Jesuits*, ed. Thomas McCoog (Woodbridge, UK: Boydell, 1996), 119–40.

[14] Pounde never lost his taste for sparring with religious adversaries, or as Simpson puts it, "touching the shield of every opponent [he] met with the sharp end of his argumentative lance" (32). Among his polemical works, for example, is a poem entitled "Jesus, a Challenge unto Foxe, the Martyrmonger."

[15] For much of his career at court, Howard lived apart from his wife, who was also his stepsister. The third wife of Howard's father, the third Duke of Norfolk, who was executed in 1572 for his alleged connection with the Ridolphi Plot, was the widowed mother of Anne Dacres. Philip and Anne were betrothed at twelve and married two years later. Only after his conversion did Philip live with his wife, who bore him a daughter in 1583 and later a son, whom Philip would never see (Devlin 132).

[16] It is possible that government agents, at Elizabeth's instigation, forged the letter from Allen to Howard to gather evidence against the latter.

[17] For example, they were both raised on former monastic properties; in Philip's case, the Charterhouse in London, a Carthusian establishment, which his father purchased after the monks were martyred.

[18] See C.A. Newdigate's "A New Chapter in the Life of Blessed Robert Southwell, S.J." in *The Month*, no. 801 (Mar. 1931), 246–54.

[19] These editions are noted in Janelle, who admits that the 1608 publication, though mentioned by Joseph Gillow in *A Literary and Biographical History or Biographical Dictionary of the English Catholics* (1885), has never been found.

[20] Margaret Waugh also describes as "a fascinating curiosity" the number of metaphors Southwell draws from natural history, arguing that "at the time Southwell wrote his *Epistle* there was a widespread interest in animals, stimulated partly by the zoo, then housed in the Tower of London, but still more by a popular work compiled by John Maplet, *A Greene Forest or Naturall Historie* which appeared in 1576" (*Epistle*, xiv). One instance of borrowing on Southwell's part has to do with Maplet's observation on beavers, which "when they are hunted, they, espying the huntsman earnestly pursuing them … the male is reported to bite off his own stones and to geld himself, and by that means becometh very swift" (74). Waugh points out Southwell's use of the story in the *Epistle*: "When beavers are hunted and see themselves straitened, they bite off their own stones, for which by kind they know themselves to be chiefly pursued, so that the hunter having his desire may cease to follow them any further. Now if nature hath taught these

brute things so painful a means to save themselves from bodily danger, how much more ought reason and faith teach us to forgo willingly not only liberty and living, and purchase thereby the life of our souls, and deliver ourselves from eternal perdition?" (158).

21   For example, he reminds his readers of the "sudden and horrible death of one Younge, an apostate and pursuivant, who pursuing a Catholic at Lambeth fell down on the sudden, ere he could lay hands on him that he persecuted, and foaming at the mouth, presently died" (233).

22   This notion can be found in earlier Christian texts such as The Epistle to Diognetus, which describes Christians as living "in countries of their own, but as sojourners." The anonymous author then anticipates the division, which Augustine made famous: "They share all things as citizens; they suffer all things as foreigners. Every foreign land is their native place, every native place is foreign ... They pass their life on earth, but they are citizens in heaven." See *The Early Christian Fathers: A Selection from the Writings of the Fathers from St. Clement of Rome to St. Athanasius*, ed. and trans. by Henry Bettenson (Oxford: Oxford UP, [1959] 1984, ed. 7), 54.

23   O'Malley notes that "in 1556 the Jesuits introduced printing to India by installing a press at their college at Goa. Thus the first book printed in India was Xavier's *Doutrina Christam*" (115). This press also produced Thomas Stephens' works.

24   Documenting the work of laymen involved in Catholic publications, A.C.F. Beales observes, "Throughout the reign [of Elizabeth] as press after press was captured or dispersed, there were printers forthcoming to fill the breach. Some were executed: William Cater, taken to the Tower in July 1582; James Duckett, at Tyburn in April 1602; John Collins, at Tyburn in 1601. Some fled and resumed work abroad: John Fowler of Winchester and New College (to Louvain to Laurence Kelham); Rowland Jenks (in Oxford as late as 1578); Stephen Brinkley, to Rouen when the press in Stonor Park ceased, when he went to replace George Flinton; Christopher Plantin at Rheims; Richard Verstegan at Antwerp; and Persons' own press at St. Omer" (54–55).

25   Brown discovered that Southwell's father and second wife, Mary Stiles, lived nearby in Clerkenwell. His sister, Elizabeth, was married in 1600 to Dr. Edward Gray in the neighboring parish of St. James ("Paper Chase," 132).

Chapter 3
Reconciling Vocation: Secular Form and Religious Matter

When Robert Southwell arrived at Douai in 1576, the English College he entered had been established for eight years and had already experienced a reorientation in its mission in response to the needs of English Catholics. Established as a house of writers, it grew under William Allen's leadership into a seminary for missionary priests. As such it graduated 33 archbishops and bishops, 169 authors, mostly of controversial works, and 160 martyrs (Beales 42). This reorientation, and the changes in curriculum and spiritual practice it required, shaped Southwell in several ways. At Douai, and briefly in Paris, he was again inculcated with missionary zeal, now colored by a stress on the possibility, even the desirability, of martyrdom in England. The College produced its first martyr in 1577, when one of its alumni, Cuthbert Mayne, was executed. Faculty and students greeted the news with sadness as well as gratitude and enthusiasm.[1] Southwell also enrolled in a practical-minded Jesuit curriculum grounded in the humanists' conviction that literature, especially classical secular literature, was congenial with and conducive to Catholic faith. Finally, and perhaps most importantly, he discovered an affinity for Jesuit spirituality, with its emphasis on reconciliation. While his sense of the Society's spirituality grew and deepened during his Jesuit formation at Rome, this first experience of the Spiritual Exercises helped him discover his vocation. Southwell also experienced personal crises at Douai. He developed an attachment to another student, John Deckers, causing him to question the role of affections and passions in religious life. Then he was rebuffed several times in seeking admission to the Jesuits. In both situations he relied on resources provided by his academic and spiritual training to reconcile tensions, resolve doubts and make meaning through the process of writing.

...

William Allen founded what became the English College when he rented a house in Douai in 1568. He intended to provide a residence for scholarly English exiles close to a university. He envisioned that these men would read and produce controversial literature, which would circulate among their peers, other professional theologians, in England and on the Continent. Douai, home to a newly established university and close to the French coast, provided a suitable location. Officially opened in 1562 by Philip II of Spain, in whose dominions it was situated, the Pontifical University of Douai was already home to prominent English academics with ties to their nation's universities, especially Oxford.[2] The University's first rector was Dr. Richard Smith, professor of divinity and formerly a fellow of Merton College. While Allen initially lived in Louvain after leaving England, he was drawn to Douai by familiar and distinguished English company engaged in controversial theology.[3]

After acclimating to his new setting and assessing the situation of English Catholics, Allen realized the need to establish a College for future priests. His hope was "to draw into this College the best wits out of England, that were either Catholikly bent or desirous of more exact education than is these days [practiced] in either of the [English] universities" (*An Apologie*, 22). The original purpose of the College, however, was not to train missionaries who would return immediately to England. The first missionaries from Douai were not sent to England until 1574. Instead, Allen wanted to maintain an English clergy abroad that would be ready to return home upon Elizabeth's death or other circumstances favoring a Catholic revival. He articulates this purpose in a letter to Dr. Jean de Vendeville, a professor of canon law and later bishop of Tournay:

> Our first purpose was to establish a college in which our countrymen who were scattered abroad in different places might live and study together more profitably than apart. Our next intention was to secure for the college an unbroken and enduring existence by means of a constant succession of students coming and leaving; for we feared that, if the schism should last much longer, owing to the death of the few who at its beginning had been cast out of the English universities for the faith, no seed would be left hereafter for the restoration of religion, and that heresy would thus obtain a perpetual and peaceful possession of the realm, there being no one to make reclamation, even though an opportunity should offer at the death of the Queen or otherwise. For we thought it would be an excellent thing to have men of learning always ready outside the realm to restore religion when the proper moment should arrive, although it seemed hopeless to attempt anything while the heretics were masters there. (Knox *Letters of Allen*, xxvi)

By the time of Southwell's arrival, however, Allen had altered the College's purpose. Owing to increasingly severe penal laws and the diminishing number of Marian priests functioning in England, he adopted the position that newly ordained English priests should return home immediately. In addition, the College grew from the top down. Originally intended to prepare mature men for priesthood through the study of philosophy and theology, the College began accepting younger students, such as Southwell, who received basic training in the humanities, enabling some of them to prepare for ordination. The difficulty for English Catholic families to provide Catholic education for their sons at home influenced this decision. The government harassed English schoolmasters suspected of Catholic sympathies, and the availability of private tutors, many of whom were Marian priests, was limited.[4] Government anxiety about Catholic education culminated in 1583 with Cecil's plan to remove Catholic children from their parents (Beales 58). As A.C.F. Beales notes, "the curve of admissions of little boys, *pueri*, in the Douai Diary, rises steeply after each new penal act in England" (116).[5]

Southwell joined an English College student body of more than 100, attached to a University numbering approximately 1,000. He lived among Englishmen but took classes taught in Latin by members of the Society of Jesus. This placed him in two worlds. On the one hand, the English College maintained the traditions in which men such as Allen had been trained at Oxford. Allen had only recently left a post at Oxford, and, according to Janelle, he "consistently endeavored to preserve the English character of the College" (8). For example, sermons were regularly preached in English, so that alumni would be proficient at the task upon their return. "[Allen] had a clear perception," according to Janelle, "of the hold which Protestant preachers and controversialists had gained upon the common people at home, owing to their mastery of the vernacular" (9). After admitting that "perhaps indeed it would have been more desirable that the scriptures had never been translated into barbarous tongues," Allen writes:

> On every Sunday and festival English sermons are preached by the more advanced students on the gospel, epistle or subject proper to the day. These discourses are calculated to inflame the hearts of all with piety towards God and zeal for the bringing back of England from schism to the path of salvation. We preach in English, in order to acquire greater power and grace in the use of the vulgar tongue, a thing on which the heretics plume themselves exceedingly, and by which they do great injury to simple folk. (Knox *Letters of Allen*, xl)

While Southwell was reminded of his Englishness in the residential College, his classroom experience and his spiritual formation, which Allen entrusted to Jesuits, transported him into a new and foreign environment. In his plan for the College, Allen urged students to "enter into a holy union with these fathers," referring to the Jesuits on the faculty. This union was academic as well as spiritual, and during his tenure at Douai, and later at Paris, Southwell took advantage of the relationship between Jesuits and their students. The academic milieu was highly personal. Each grade or "form," as opposed to each academic subject, had its own master, so there was close contact throughout the school day between a teacher and his students. In this respect, "the Jesuit teacher was something new, a definitive innovation among sixteenth century pedagogues … His attitude towards his students was invested with reverence [and] the Jesuit could and did devote himself to the education of the will [as well as of the intellect]" (McCabe 8). "Better educated and motivated on the whole than most … schoolmasters almost anywhere in Europe," Jesuits "tried to influence their students more by their example than by their words." Moreover, "they repeatedly inculcated in one another the importance of loving their students, of knowing them as individuals, of enjoying a respectful *familiaritis* with them" (O'Malley 225). The atmosphere was intellectually progressive as well, exposing students to curricular innovations sweeping the Continent. As Janelle describes it, "Douai College was inspired by a new spirit, that of the Council of Trent, [and] it embodied a scheme of education which in its main features had been first outlined in the *Constitutions of the Society of Jesus*" (7). According to Janelle, this "was a departure from the medieval and early humanistic traditions which had persisted and were to persist in England undisturbed by the new influences at work on the Continent" (7).

Southwell arrived at the English College as an adolescent, so he did not study philosophy and theology. Those disciplines occupied him later in Rome. At Douai, and briefly in Paris, he was enrolled in a curriculum common to Jesuit schools all over Europe (Beales 118). Students in these schools, divided into "forms," progressed from the study of rudimentary Latin, through grammar, major and minor syntax, poetry and rhetoric. These "forms" did not consist of a prescribed length of time. Students were promoted when they mastered material, and Robert moved quickly through the courses. According to Beales, "these five grades, through which the boy completed his humanities, were universal throughout all the colleges, [and] they were indeed the course established by the Jesuit system" (133). After acquiring basic Latin, students were promoted to a grammar class in which they studied Alvarus, Terence and the *Epistles* of Cicero. Describing a typical class, "the professor would first declaim a passage, ... then he would analyze the artistic structure with stress on style rather than erudition, descending from the ethical power of the piece as a whole down to the rhythm and nuances of particular words and phrases" (Devlin 25). Southwell reflects this emphasis on style for the sake of "ethical power" in his later work. In the third form, a student would finish the *Epistles* of Cicero and move on to *De Senectute* and *De Amicitia*. In the fourth, Virgil's *Aeneid*, the *Odes* of Horace and Caesar's *Gallic Wars* were the objects of study, with emphasis on the rules of poetry and metaphor. Finally, in rhetoric class, students learned Virgil's *Bucolics* and *Georgics*, along with the satires, epistles and *Ars Poetica* of Horace (Beales 132–33). The pedagogical emphasis throughout was on the spirituality formative potential of secular literature learned through imitation and exercises of literary mimicry, skills which Southwell employs when writing verse. His imitative poems, in particular, provide evidence of how influential the Douai curriculum proved to be.

...

There are several examples of Southwell applying what and how he learned about literature at Douai, including his imitations of English love poems, such as "Love's servile lot," "Lewd love is loss," and "Love's gardyne grief." In each of these, Robert imitates the figures and tropes common in contemporary poetry, many of them borrowed from the tradition established by Petrarch; but as he invokes them, he inverts their intentions. Southwell reworks lyrics on amorous or erotic love, making them argue for moral and spiritual reform. In doing so, he reverses the Petrarchan tendency to apply religious language when illuminating secular experience. Not only does he wish to reform his readers, he also wants to reform poetry, which, he believes, is being wasted on subject matter beneath its dignity. In "Love's servile lot," for example, he personifies love as a woman and uses Petrarchan language to describe her influence over men. At first, love seems irresistibly attractive. "A honnie shower raines from her lippes,/ Sweet lights shine in her face," writes the poet, with Petrarchan emphasis on the power of her gaze (13–14). Moreover, "Her loving lookes, are murdring dartes" (51). "Her watery eyes have burning force," and "Her clouds and flames conspire./ Tears kindle sparkes, sobbes fuel are:/ and sighs to blow her fire" (33–36). His readers would recognize this imagery through Petrarchan imitators such as Wyatt, Sidney and Surrey. Like their works, Southwell's is filled with language about love's elusiveness, and the "cruell woundes shee geves" (41). Love's victim typically experiences

"Moodes, passions, phancies [and] jelous fits." Simultaneously, in Petrarchan fashion, love makes "thy hart to frie,/ and yet to freeze within thee" (23–24). But whereas most poems in this vein celebrate love despite the contrary emotions it inspires, Southwell's criticize it, dissuading readers from pursuing objects unworthy of their attention. Observing Petrarchan lovers, he argues, "Yet few know whom they serve/ They recken least how little love/ Their service doth deserve" (2–4). Such love, according to the Jesuit, is "corrupted in the core" (8); "shee doth kill" (12); and she possesses "the mind of viper race" (16). To the poem's end he employs Petrarchan terms, but he convinces the reader to reorder his life's purpose and direction:

> Plow not the Seas, sow not the sands,
> Leave off your Idle paine,
> Seek other mistres for your minds,
> Loves service is in vain. (73–76)

Perhaps the best examples of Southwell using extant poems for purposes opposite of the originals are his line-by-line reworkings of Sir Edward Dyer's "My Mind to Me a Kingdom Is" and "A Fancy." His choice of poems by Dyer typifies Southwell's embrace of early modern culture even while modifying it. While mostly unknown now, Dyer enjoyed prominence in the sixteenth century. His biographer, Ralph M. Sargent, describes him as "the complete gentleman of the English Renaissance" (vii). Born in 1543, Dyer, like Southwell, grew up on the grounds of a former abbey, and his father named him after Henry VIII's son in gratitude for the property. Educated at Oxford, Dyer moved in courtly circles under the Earl of Leicester's patronage. His poems, which he never published during his lifetime, circulated among friends, including Philip Sidney and Edmund Spenser. Dyer served as Sidney's mentor on matters courtly and poetic. At the latter's funeral, he served as a pall bearer, and after the burial he composed an epitaph describing Sidney as "the wonder of our age" (Sargent 198–200).

In life, Dyer and Sidney revolutionized English poetry. They took up verse at an inauspicious time in the genre's history. Despite the publication of *Tottel's Miscellany*, English poetry was in decline. According to Sargent, "the promising Italianate verse of Wyatt and Surrey had been succeeded by the earthy maxims of Thomas Tusser and the pedestrian exercises of Nicholas Grimald and Barnabe Googe" (10). Dyer represented something new:

In Dyer his contemporaries quickly discovered the true lyric gift. Striking upon ears accustomed to rude or monotonous verses, his songs with their easy grace must have been genuinely moving. As the earliest of the Elizabethan "courtly makers," Dyer brought forth possibly the first fine lyrics of the great Renaissance in England. (11)

Dyer and Sidney set out to reform poetry, making it suitably entertaining for courtiers. To accomplish this they composed something akin to rules for poetry, anticipating Sidney's *Defense of Poesie*, published in 1599. Spenser calls them "Areopogites," because they had "a mission to teach poetry once more to speak courtly" (Sargent 61). Later Thomas Nashe writes of Dyer, "[he is] the first (in our language). I have encountered, that repurified poetry from Arts pendantisme, and that instructed it to speak courtly." According to Nashe, Dyer is "our Patron, our first Orpheus or quintessence of invention … ; wherefor, either let us jointly invent some worthy subject to eternize him, or let Warre call back Barbarisme" (*Works*, ed. McKerrow, III, 76–77). John Davies confirms this opinion in his *Microcosmos*, published in 1603:

> Thou virgin Knight that dost thyselfe obscure,
> From Worlds unequall eies, and faine wouldst *dy*
> *Er'* thy *name* would be knowne to Worlds impure,
> From our new Worlds desert out-searching Eie.
> Great Sidneies love (true proofe of thy great worth).
> Live now, for now thou maist not living die;
> Vertue must use thee, then (*Dyer* Knight). come forth
> To haile thy vertues Loadstarre from the North. (17)

Davies' line, "Vertue must use thee," captures Southwell's purpose in appropriating Dyer's poems. Robert wants to show "how well verse and vertue sute together," as he explains in "The Author to his loving Cosen," so he infuses the latter's poems with religious themes. He deliberately chooses to imitate Dyer: Dyer set out to reform English poetry for the sake of his audience; Southwell reforms a reformer for the spiritual welfare of his readers and for the sake of the medium itself. For Southwell, entertaining courtiers is not enough. He wants to move beyond entertainment to edification. He adopts the style and structure of Dyer's originals, and in them reconciles secular form and religious matter.

Southwell judges the contents of Dyer's verse to be inappropriate. This is especially true regarding the latter poet's speakers. As Sargent observes, "[Dyer] helped to set the Elizabethan fashion of self-conscious melancholy" (9), and while Southwell is not opposed to the sentiment, he criticizes the motive for melancholy among Dyer's speakers, namely the illusion of love. Both of the Dyer poems which Robert imitates feature lovelorn speakers who have been inexplicably spurned. Elizabethan readers favored this figure, and as Anthony À. Wood notices, "[Dyer's] excellency in bewailing and bemoaning the perplexities of love were observed by his contemporaries" (*Athenae Oxoniensis* I, 740). Southwell, too, features dejected speakers in his imitative works, but his are moved to mourning because of their sinfulness, as opposed to having been sinned against.

Dyer's speakers are autobiographical, which he signals when he names himself toward the end of "A Fancy" (Sargent 187).[6] His relationship with Queen Elizabeth was subject to frequent and sudden changes. For example, he was often banished from court, most notably around the time of the proposed marriage to the Duke of Anjou, which Dyer and his patron, Leicester, opposed. The Queen resented their opposition, so Dyer retreated to his country estate, waiting for opportunities to reassure the Queen of his loyalty and affection. He had company in this predicament, and his works expressed feelings common among Elizabeth's rejected courtiers.

"A Fancy" presents a courtier who has been jilted by his lover and banished from court. The speaker, maintaining his innocence, bemoans his undeserved reversal of fortune. He cannot understand why he is no longer the darling of the "Powers" that control his fate (31), and he is unable to appease them, even though he offers his suffering as a sacrifice. The poem's purpose is to help him accept his fate while proving that he is worse off than any other man, which is a typical self-dramatizing Petrarchan strategy. To prove the latter, he invites other sufferers to compare their woes to his: "He that his mirth hath lost,/ Whose comfort is dismaid,/ Whose hope is vain, whose faith is scorned,/ Whose trust is all betraid;/ ... Come let him take his place by mee: He shall not rue alone" (1–8). The speaker in Southwell's version of the poem, entitled in manuscripts "Dyers (Master dires A) phancy turned to a Sinners Complainte," is similarly bad off, but the causes of his misery are markedly different. Dyer's speaker is sinned against; Southwell's confesses himself to be the worst of sinners. Robert signals this change by altering the verbs from Dyer's passive forms to active voice in his first stanza: Dyer's distressed lover "is scornd," and "all betraid." Southwell's sinner has lost his mirth through his own fault.

Many of the poems' parallel stanzas appear exactly the same. Southwell adopts the style and substance of Dyer's work, imitating him word for word. This is especially the case when the two speakers describe their emotions. Both wish for the death of the body, for example, which they equally consider kinder than the "death of the mind," as they experience it (17–24). Both speakers "live in shewe,/ and inwardly do die" (25–26), but the couplet with which Southwell completes this thought illustrates how his subtle changes alter the purpose of Dyer's poem. After admitting to inward death, Dyer's speaker describes himself as one "Whose knowledge is a bloody field,/ Where all help slaine doth lie" (26–27). For Southwell's sinner, knowledge is also a "bloody field," but one in which "virtue slaine doth lie." Jilted by the "Powers" who decide the fate of courtiers, Dyer's speaker considers himself beyond help through no fault of his own. His lack of responsibility only increases the depth of feeling. He is a victim. Southwell's speaker, on the other hand, brought on his own demise.

The next stanza clarifies that Robert's speaker worries about divine rather than human judgment. He is not banished from court. He is estranged from God, and can find no way back into God's graces. Closely following Dyer's original, Southwell employs religious imagery to magnify feelings of estrangement and frustration, likening his heart to an "altar." But where Dyer's spurned lover vainly offers his sorrows upon the altar of his heart as sacrifices to appease his former beloved, Southwell's frustrated sinner fears God's "revenge" (31).

Both speakers take refuge in nostalgia. Dyer's lover remembers when he was one "whom love and fortune once advaunced" (43). Southwell's sinner recalls how he was "advaunced" as well, but by "grace and vertue" that "nowe sinne hath cast away" (43–44). They are alike in that both are currently all the unhappier because they once enjoyed great happiness: by the loss of "the peace, the rest, the life,/ That I enjoyed of yore," now "my smart doth sting the more" (57–60). However, once they move beyond expressing emotion to identifying the causes of their present conditions, the two speakers, and the poems with them, move in different directions. Dyer's speaker meditates on human and especially female inconstancy, enrolling his poems among numerous similar efforts by other contemporary poets:

> O fraile unconstant kynde,
> And sake in trust to noe man!
> Noe woomen angels be,
> And loe, my mistress is a woeman. (92–95)

Southwell's speaker, on the other hand, meditates on his sinfulness:

> O fraile inconstant flesh,
> Soone trapt in every ginne;
> Soone wrought thus to betray thy soule,
> And plunge thyself in sin. (93–96)

In doing so, he turns Dyer's poem from an exercise of wit in the wake of being jilted into a spiritual exercise modeling remorse. In fact, Dyer uses the word "exercise" to describe the activities in which his speaker henceforth occupies himself, and Southwell seizes the opportunity to give the word its Ignatian value. Both poems end with speakers resolving to spend their lives in places of retreat, namely "the solitary wood" (125). Dyer's lover will pine away for the woman to whom he pledged himself: "I cannot set at nought/ That I have held soe deare:/ ... Nor shall it ever faile/ That my word have in hand: I gave my word, my word gave me; Both word and guift shall stand" (109–20). He realizes that in order to be true to himself, he must remain true to the beloved, even though she rejects him. He plans to spend his days reveling in sorrow: "Mine Exercise naught ells/ But raginge agonies,/ My bookes of spightfull fortunes foiles/ And drerye tragedies:" (137–40). Southwell's speaker pines away as well, "To moane a sinners case/ Then which, was never worse" (101–102). A realization likewise inspires his moaning, but in his case, he grasps that God remains true to him despite the distance he puts between himself and God: "Yet Gods must I remain,/ By death, by wrong, by shame;/ I cannot blot out of my hart,/ That grace wrought in his name" (109–12). Acknowledging God's fidelity moves the speaker to resolution: "But since that I have sinn'd,/ And scourge none is too ill;/ I yeeld me captive to my curse,/ My hard fate to fulfill" (121–24). This "fate" consists of making spiritual exercises: "My exercise remorse/ And doleful sinners layes,/ My booke remembrance of my crimes,/ And faults of former days." He takes up penitential practices, including preparation for the general confession prescribed in the First Week of the *Spiritual Exercises*. In the end, Southwell redirects Dyer's poem, while leaving its style and structure intact. Instead of rehearsing a Petrarchan lover's complaint, he substitutes a model penitent in his place. Whereas Dyer's speaker bemoans the rigors of love and the inconstancy of women, Robert's shows readers how to seek reconciliation with a faithful God.

When Southwell reworks Dyer's "My Mind to Me a Kingdom Is," he is possibly reclaiming a classical source that had been originally translated by another Jesuit. According to Sargent, Dyer's poem "may well have been suggested by a reading of Seneca's *Thyestes*," which, in 1560, was Englished by Jasper Heywood, former superior of the English mission. Heywood, reports Sargent, uses in his translation a ballad measure similar to that of "My Mind to Me a Kingdom Is." The translation includes such lines as "Great kyngdome is to be content,/ without the same to lyve,/ Yet should it not refused be, if god the kyngdome gyve," and "They never might the truthe hereof denye,/ it is the mynde that onely makes the kyng."

These appeal to Dyer during another period of banishment from court. The poem's speaker tries to convince himself that he prefers rustication. From his new perspective, he claims to have acquired wisdom: "I see how plenty suffers ofte,/ and hasty clymers sone do fall:/ I see that those which are alofte/ Myshapp dothe threaten moste of all" (13–16). Dyer is describing his own predicament. Throughout his career he backed losing sides in political intrigues, and paid the price. The highest office he attained came late in life, and even that was less influential than he hoped. He served as Chancellor of the Order of the Garter, which enabled him to be called "Sir Edward," but he was not a member of the Order, merely its servant. More often, he was far from the center of power, but in the poem he claims to find happiness in contemplation:

> No princely pompe, no wealthy store,
> No force to wine the victorye,
> No wilye witt to salve a sore,
> No shape to feade a lovinge eye;
> To none of these I yealde as thrall:
> For why? My mind dothe serve for all. (7–12)

Much of the poem argues for relinquishing the assets Dyer labored to attain throughout his life. Conspicuous accomplishment, he contends, creates anxiety: "They get with toylle, they keepe with feare;/ Such cares my mynde coulde never beare" (17–18). He even claims to pity those misdirected souls who seek status. "Some waye their pleasure by theyre luste," he observes, "Their wisdom by theyre rage of will:/ Their treasure is theire only truste,/ A cloked crafte theure store of skyll" (37–40). He, on the other hand, has attained the moral high ground, which he recommends to his readers: "But all the pleasure that I fynde/ Is to mayntayne a quiet mynde ... Thus do I lyve, thus will I dye;/ Would all did so as well as I" (41–42; 47–48).

Dyer's poem proved popular based on the number of references to it by other authors. Sargent notes that Ben Jonson, Thomas Deloney, Nicholas Breton, John Davies, John Taylor and George Withers all cite it (218). Along with Southwell's imitation, Dyer's original is reworked by Robert Greene in *Greenes farewell to folly*. The poem was also set to music by William Byrd, who, in 1588, is responsible for the first printed version of the work. Perhaps it is through Byrd that Southwell knew the poem. Byrd, who composed music for both Anglican and Catholic services, was familiar with English Jesuits.[7] Southwell, in adapting "My Mind to Me a Kingdom Is," claims a cultural commonplace. He retitles the work "Content and Rich," and in the first stanza he acknowledges the original's courtly setting while introducing his religious agenda: "I dwell in graces courte,/ Enrichde with vertues rights:/ Faithe, guides my wit: love, leads my will:/ Hope all my mind delights" (1–4). Given the final couplet's reference to the three theological virtues of faith, hope and love, Southwell means "grace" in its religious sense. His poem, like Dyer's, concerns wisdom, but Robert moves beyond philosophical arguments about finding a mean and maintaining equilibrium in defeat. In the second through the fourth stanzas, he echoes Dyer's advice on wealth and power. "My seely shroud true honor brings,/ My poore estate is rich," he claims, and then concludes, "I make the Limites of my power,/ The bondes of my will." But in stanza six, he returns to the religious concerns with which the poem began: "I have no hopes but one,/ Which is of heavenly reign" (21–22). Both Dyer's poem and Southwell's are about power. Dyer reconciles himself to the loss of whatever political advantage he once enjoyed. Southwell writes on God's power which is manifest in spiritual paradoxes: poverty is wealth, weakness is strength, loss is gain, death means life.

In Dyer's poem, the speaker implicates an enemy in his fall, but he never reveals his attitude toward those responsible for his demise. Southwell uses his poem to address this issue in unambiguous terms. In doing so, he advises his readers on how they ought to deal with persecutors. The speaker makes himself an example: "I wrastle not with rage/ While furies flame doth burne:/ It is in vaine to stop the streeme,/ Until the tide doth turn" (37–40). Writing for recusants he counsels patience amid persecution. He also advises them to avoid attracting attention. "Sith sayles of largest size/ The storme doth soonest teare:/ I beare so low and small a sayle,/ As freeth me from feare" (33–36). When Southwell compares recommended behaviors to natural forces such as streams and storms, he ornaments Dyer's work, which lacks figures of speech. He pursues the same literary strategy when urging reconciliation: "But when the flame is out/ And ebbing wrath doth end:/ I turn a late enraged foe/ Into a quiet friend" (41–44). This eleventh stanza of "Content and Rich" summarizes Southwell's approach to opposition, an approach that he articulates throughout his career and most conspicuously in *An Humble Supplication to Her Majesty*. He avoids controversy, preferring reconciliation instead, and he uses Dyer's entirely self-referential poem to encourage his readers to reach out to their opponents. This adds another religious theme to the original poem. Serenity is not enough for Southwell. His speaker moves beyond self-concern and befriends enemies.

In Southwell's versions of Dyer's poems enemies are reconciled to one another; sinners are reconciled to God; and poetry is restored to its proper function, as the poet himself understands it. Southwell learned at

Douai that literary imitation is not so much a form of flattery as a means to make literature serve religion. He mines Dyer's poems for style and structure, substituting his own arguments. He uses "the faining Poets stile," as he calls it in "The Author to his loving Cosen," to articulate spiritual truths. He learned at Douai to appreciate literature's potential to encourage moral behavior, and he applies this lesson in his ministry. He learned to read secular, classical literature with an eye toward its unintended spiritual substance. When he takes up writing, he reworks extant poems, creating in them spaces for consciously expressing that same substance. In works such as "A Phansie turned to a sinners complaint" and "Content and Rich," Southwell sacrifices originality; and while he is more creative in other poems which are entirely his own, there is a subtlety about his imitative efforts. In most cases, he substitutes a few words or phrases, leaving the poems stylistically and structurally inviolate while radically altering their sense. This is paradigmatic of Southwell's work. He does not set himself apart from the dominant culture. He embraces the elements of his culture when he can. In his imitative poems, as in *An Epistle of Comfort*, Southwell employs worldly means to spiritual ends. To do so, he immerses himself in those means, laboring to understand how they work on their own terms before making use of them on his. His studies at Douai, with their emphasis on the spiritual potential of literature learned through imitation and mimicry, prepared him for this immersion. He reconciles important aspects of this culture to his religious beliefs, creating a common ground from which he can approach his readers.

...

Douai's influence on Southwell extends beyond imitative verse. The atmosphere and curriculum at Allen's College contributed to the poet's appreciation of zeal for mission and martyrdom, and the need to proceed practically when devising pastoral responses to the recusant predicament. Both issues inform Southwell's work. He writes poems, for example, that inspire zeal in his readers, responding to the difficulties they experience in sustaining enthusiasm, courage and determination. He also produces a practical guide for Christian living entitled *A Short Rule of Good Life*, rendering Loyola's *Spiritual Exercises* more readily accessible for English lay men and women.

Zeal and practicality were especially important to William Allen whose letters reveal how his concern for the restoration of Catholicism animated the College at Douai. He regularly writes on themes that Southwell takes up. One typical passage underscores the need for these two qualities, and Southwell's works reveal that the lessons were not lost on him:

> Our students, being intended for the English harvest, are not required to excel or be great proficients in theological science, though their teachers ought to be as learned and prudent as possible; but they must abound in zeal for God's house, charity and thirst for souls. True it is that the more knowledge they possess concerning the scriptures and controversial divinity, and the greater the prudence and discretion they couple with this knowledge, so much the more abundant will be their success. Still, when they have burning zeal, even though deep science be wanting, provided they always know the necessary heads of religious doctrine and the power and nature of the sacraments, such men ... also do good work in hearing confessions and offering sacrifice, which are the points to which we especially direct our instructions according to the gifts and abilities of each one. (Knox *Letters of Allen*, xxxviii)

...

Many of Southwell's works aim to stir up such ardor among readers as well as in himself. Obviously, *An Epistle of Comfort* ranks among these efforts, and poems such as "New heaven, new warre," "New Prince, new pompe," and "Christs sleeping friends" share this purpose. They respond to Allen's desire to "breed [in English Catholics] zeal ... even in these days, when they can look for no worldly honor, lucre, preferment or promotion thereby, but manifold dangers, disgraces, persecutions and vexations" (*An Apologie*, 25). "New heaven, new warre" addresses this situation by stressing the hardships surrounding Christ's birth. The poem belongs to a group of four that concern the nativity. The others are "A childe my Choice," "The Burning Babe," and "New Prince, new pompe." All of these poems underscore Christ's poverty, suffering and seeming helplessness in the face of inhospitable, dangerous conditions. Southwell wants readers to identify with these circumstances so that they can enter into the meditative dynamic which the poems introduce, a dynamic that promotes resolve, enthusiasm and courage despite opposition.

There is some scholarly disagreement about the unity of "New heaven, new warre," but the preponderance of evidence is on the side of McDonald, Brown, and Joseph D. Scallon, who think it is two separate but similar, even parallel poems.[8] Martz, however, believes that it is a unified whole comprising an Ignatian meditation. It consists, he contends, of a prelude running through the first four stanzas, followed by an application or analysis in stanzas five through seven, and a colloquy in stanza eight.

Certainly the Ignatian paradigm is at work in the piece, especially in the final colloquy; but if most critics correctly separate the poems, then the first works as a call to arms. The speaker summons angels to earth at the Incarnation. Heaven is here now in that the angels' only desire is to dwell with God who has become man. Men, unfortunately, "their homage doe denie," therefore, the speaker beckons angels to do that which humans can or will not: "Come Angels all their fault supplie" (6). The poem portrays a needy Christ child: "His chilling cold doth heate require" (7). "This little Ark no cover hath" (9); "this Babe must eat" (11). The speaker then calls out to individual angels and types of angels, identifying each according to the work that he or they can do. Seraphs, for example, provide heat "in liew of fire" (8). The cherubs' wings can be used for covers (10). Raphael brings food as he once did for Tobias (11–12).

In the second stanza Southwell introduces angels who perform gentlemanly tasks. These duties would have appealed to the kinds of readers whom the poet knew in the England of his youth. He figures Gabriel as Christ's "groom." Michael is given his usual martial role when Robert orders him to "stand in [Christ's] defense" (15). The fourth and final stanza urges them to "agnize" or recognize their transformed reality. The mighty God whom they served in his "heavenly seate" is reduced to a nursing infant. Christ depends on them, and they must rise to the occasion with zeal tempered by appropriate tenderness. Their service, even when strenuous, begins with an act of love. They are invited to "Come kisse the maunger where he lies" (23). Southwell's readers could put themselves in the place of the angels described in these lines. Their reality has been similarly transformed, since they no longer enjoy prominence. Their church, as well, has been reduced and needs various kinds of help. The poem's figurative and typological language works to include its readers. The services the angels render to Jesus prefigure works they themselves can do for the church.

If the tasks seem daunting, the second poem, or second half of a unified poem, bolsters confidence. Southwell, through a series of paradoxes, shows how Christ and the angels are deceptively strong. Though the Christ Child "himselfe for cold do shake," the less obvious truth is that "all hell doth at his presence quake" (27–28). While the opposing odds seem overwhelming now, Christ and his cause will triumph: "For in this weak unarmed wise,/ The gates of hell he will surprise" (29–30). In these stanzas the angels are replaced by Southwell and his readers. The lines reassure and remind them how Christ prevails through weakness rather than shows of strength. They are encouraged to develop zeal not for a war of arms but for spiritual battle, which will be won by tears shed amid poverty:

> With teares he fights and winnes the field,
> His naked breast stands for a shield,
> His battring shot are babish cryes,
> His Arrowes lookes of weeping eyes,
> His Martiall ensignes cold and neede,
> And feeble flesh his warriers steede. (31–36)

The final stanza, a colloquy between the speaker and his soul, brings to a crescendo the call to zeal:

> My soule with Christ joyne thou in fight,
> Sticke to the tents that he hath plight;
> Within his crib is surest ward,
> This little babe will be thy guard:
> If thou wilt foil thy foes with joy,
> Then flit not from this heavenly boy. (43–48)

The emphasis on "joining," "sticking" and "flitting not" shows Southwell encouraging readers to stay their course even when indicators point to defeat. They need the kind of passion and commitment recommended by Allen to Robert and his fellow students at Douai.

This same call to zeal occurs in a companion piece entitled "New Prince, new pompe." Again, Southwell calls attention to the conditions of Christ's birth "in freesing winter night" (2). But readers are invited to see through the hardships surrounding the event and appreciate its deeper, paradoxical significance. The birth of Christ inverts established orders, upending political and social hierarchies: "This stable is a Princes Court,/ The Crib his chaire of state" (17–18). There is reason for hope even amid squalid conditions, and the poet couches this argument in language that would appeal to his aristocratic readers. "This Prince himselfe is come from heaven," he assures them, bringing "royal liveries" and a new order of "pompe." As a result, his readers have reason for encouragement, even joy. The poem's final stanza calls them to rally around their monarch, much as readers were summoned to spiritual battle in *An Epistle of Comfort*. Southwell requires courage of his readers, which they can prove by performing an act of fealty: "With joy approach o Christiain wight,/ Doe homage to thy King" (25–26). Moreover, they need to align their values with Christ's. Filled with zeal for the Saviour and his kingdom they will "highly prize this humble pompe" (27). In this poem, as in "New heaven, new warre," Southwell, like Allen, understands his readers' apprehensions, and he wants them to identify with Christ at his birth. Rather than shrinking back in cowardice and conforming, they can be confident of ultimately prevailing as Jesus did.

Southwell also draws on Christ's passion to encourage zeal. In "Christs sleeping friends," one of several Southwell poems set in the Garden of Gethsemane, he describes the disciples in a moment of weakness. They sleep through a miracle, even though Christ three times told them to watch and pray with him. Southwell describes the miracle itself in a companion poem, "Christs bloody sweat," employing a series of unnatural occurrences to illuminate how Jesus "unforced prevents in shedding blood/ The whips, the thornes, the nailes, the speare, and rood" (5–6). Here, "prevents" means anticipates, and the miracle is that without being physically wounded on the Mount of Olives, Christ bleeds as he sweats. As the speaker in "Christs bloody sweat" meditates on this miracle, he is inspired to reciprocate the Son's sacrifice with the Holy Spirit's help. He prays, "O sacred Fire come shewe thy force on me/ That sacrifice to Christe I may retorne" (19–20). The disciples in "Christs sleeping friends," on the other hand, miss the inspiring moment on account of their "heavy eies" and "heavy mindes" (6). They sleep even though "the sunne [i.e., Christ] the brightest shew doth make" (9). Jesus' enemies are far more attentive: "they did watch to worke their cruell spight" (11). Southwell employs two biblical types in differentiating between Christ's friends and foes. Like Jonah who slept through a storm, the disciples need to be aroused from their torpor, so they can witness and respond to the events unfolding around them. And like Judas, the enemies of Christ work diligently. Judas is compared to a "blustering gust" that "doe[s] stirre the furious sea." As a storm, Judas threatens Christ, "the barke of all our bliss" (20–23).

Southwell stretches the Jonah conceit in the fifth and sixth stanzas, recalling the story of Jonah asleep under a fig tree that withers overnight, devoured by a worm. The disciples, like the inattentive prophet, take for granted the source of their protection. The poet compares Christ to the fig, which in England becomes "ivy" (26). His enemies are "a cankered worme that gnawen the root away,/ and brought the glorious branches to decay" (30). The penultimate stanza makes an apostrophe to Christ, the "gratious plant," who shades his disciples from harm. When trouble comes, "they with Jonas fall asleep" (35). The last stanza issues the clearest call to zealous action in any of Southwell's works. It begins, "Awake ye wights lift up your eies, ... Arise and guard the comforte of your lives" (37–40). This stanza startles readers, coming as it does after a string of conceits which can cloud the poem's purpose. Elaborate figures of speech might make readers share the disciples' "heavy eies" and "heavy minds." But the poem's last six lines sound a clarion call. Southwell's readers, like Christ's disciples, will lose all if they lack zeal for the church: "No Jonas ivy …/ Were to the world so great a loss as he" (41–42). They must understand the stakes in the battle they fight and be on "guard." Like Allen who recommended zeal to his students at Douai, Southwell advocates the same virtue in these poems. The needs of English Catholics, to which Allen introduced Southwell, consistently surface in poems the latter produces a decade later. In fact, those needs become more pressing by the time Southwell returns to England, as does the requirement to proceed practically in response to virulent opposition.

…

As Janelle points out, at Douai, "the training of future priests was essentially practical," and this emphasis impressed Southwell (11). When he returns to England, his efforts are grounded in a keen sense of what is possible for him and the community he serves. He works within the limits prescribed by his circumstances. Even his use of pre-existing poems shows his practicality. Given the conditions under which he wrote he lacked the leisure to produce entirely original works. As a result, he settles for "weav[ing] a new web" on the already established poetic "loom" (Southwell *Poems*, 1); and his training in imitation and literary mimicry stands him in good stead. Obtaining and operating a press, as described above, also reveals his pragmatic side.

Allen's pragmatic emphasis was enhanced by the Jesuit scheme of education, which itself resulted from practical decisions. The Jesuit educational system grew out of experience rather than theory. Contrary to popular impressions, Loyola and his companions did not set out to form a teaching order. But as university men who met while studying in Paris, they cared greatly about the education of the order's members. They wanted future Jesuits to enjoy the same educational benefits they had, so they set up residences for young Jesuits in proximity to universities. Their operative conviction was practical: well-educated men are more effective in exercising ministries of the word of God. They held this especially true for preaching. Eventually, however, owing to the curricular disarray characteristic of many universities, Jesuits began to educate their own.[9] Unfortunately, it was difficult to convince benefactors to fund exclusively Jesuit schools while the benefactors' own children remained in inferior institutions. Bowing to pressure from donors and a practical need for benefactions, Jesuits admitted lay students into their schools, and soon some schools were mostly or entirely composed of non-Jesuit pupils.

By the time Loyola wrote the *Constitutions*, education was so significant an apostolate that he included a chapter on the schools. In it, he did not so much articulate a philosophy of education as attend to practical details out of which a more general approach to education would develop later in the order's history. Ignatius stipulates items such as class size, methods of discipline, the need for repetitions and public disputations, and the times and proper amounts of relaxation. His first concern is for what kind of schools the Society should administer, and he has a special regard for those best suited for "the improvement in learning and living not only of our own members but even more especially of those from outside the Society" (Loyola *Constitutions*, 440). He desires that recipients of Jesuit education "be able to teach with authority elsewhere what they have learned well in these universities of the Society." Based on his experience at the University of Paris, Ignatius gives priority to theology, but he also underscores the need for training in humane vernacular letters as well as Latin, Greek and Hebrew. This is not only because such training enables the study of theology, but also because "by their own nature" these disciplines lead to knowledge and love of God (450). He also spells out a Jesuit teacher's personal responsibility for each of his students, and anticipating the 1599 *Ratio Studiorum*, he looks forward to a fuller expression of this aspect of Jesuit education in some future document. In all this, Ignatius relies on incoming reports about what is already working in the Society's best schools. He and other Jesuits do not come at education with preconceived notions or, for that matter, original ideas. As John O'Malley observes, "as was often true of them in other endeavors, the Jesuits created relatively few of the components of their educational program, but they put those parts together in a way and on a scale that had never been done before" (225). The same could be said of Southwell's poetry and prose, proving again the influence of his education at Douai. Like the Jesuits who taught him and devised the curriculum of his College, Southwell was more an imitator and improviser than an inventor, and his literary efforts, like their educational ones, were driven by pragmatic concerns and determined by best practice.

As for the intended outcomes of their curriculum, Jesuits were equally pragmatic. As one historian of Jesuit education puts it, "Jesuits never meant to train scholars" (Beales 9). Aquaviva, writing as General, tells Jesuit teachers to "carry the students on at least as far as mediocrity in learning, so that they may go forth to their respective vocations ... qualified in some degree with a sufficiency of literary culture" (Beales 9). The need for literary culture grows out of Jesuit confidence in the power of good literature to cultivate solid citizens. This was a shared assumption among

European humanists, who were, according to John O'Malley, "vociferous" in their criticism of the medieval university's "failure to relate learning to a life of virtue and public service" (207). Because of their faith in the formative power of letters and their concern for the common good, "Jesuits looked more to the formation of mind and character, to *Bildung*, than to the acquisition of ever more information or the advancement of the disciplines" (O'Malley 214).

This explains Southwell's classical studies at Douai, with their emphasis on rhetoric as the capstone college class. It also explains why Loyola, in the *Constitutions*, prescribes classes in letters every day, while classes in Christian doctrine were held weekly (483). The point of the curriculum was to persuade students to accept their responsibilities as church members and as citizens. Among those responsibilities was the persuasion, through *eloquentia perfecta*, of others whom they would encounter when their studies were completed. Southwell and his fellow students were encouraged to such eloquence. Good style, they were taught, promoted good morals, in themselves and in others whom they would influence through speaking and writing. Understandably, Robert begins his literary career by demonstrating "how well verse and vertue sute together" ("The Author to his loving Cosen," 1), and several of his works reveal how prose texts, as well, could have the practical effect of aiding English Catholics to lead virtuous lives.

...

The work most illustrative of Southwell's practicality is *Short Rules of Good Life*, which, according to Henry More, was written for the Countess of Arundel in 1591–1592. This last year before Southwell's capture proved especially productive. During it he wrote *An Humble Supplication* and *Triumphs Over Death*, the latter of which he also penned for the Howard family. Southwell wrote *Triumphs* as a consolatory epistle to Philip Howard who was mourning the death of his half-sister, Lady Margaret Sackville. All three texts written in this year reveal Robert's practical side: each responds directly to pressing needs. In *An Humble Supplication* he acknowledges the conditions of the Catholic community under increased persecution, and appeals to the Queen for clemency, making a case for Catholic loyalty. In *Triumphs*, as Brownlow observes, "Southwell's stoicism is meant to be severely practical advice on maintaining presence of mind and a sense of proportion before impending death" (57). The poet makes Lady Sackville's death an opportunity to help Philip Howard and other Catholics prepare step-by-step for their own. Finally, in *Short Rules*, he provides a handbook for committed lay people, such as Anne Howard, which is steeped in Ignatian mysticism and cognizant of the realities of English life. In this work he reconciles the mystical strain in the *Spiritual Exercises* with the quotidian stuff of life in Elizabethan England.

Scholars debate the work's title because it varies in manuscript and print editions. In some cases it is entitled *A Short Rule*, as opposed to *Short Rules*, but in the end it may be impossible to discover which version Southwell intended. As Nancy Pollard Brown asserts in her introduction to the Folger edition, Southwell rarely gave his works formal titles (lvii). The plural form makes sense, however, since the poet writes for lay people rather than members of a religious order who follow a canonical constitution, or rule, by virtue of their vows. Southwell references his readers' lack of vows in the fifth chapter of the *Rules*, urging them to adopt a daily order of activities "though not by vow" (l. 30). *Short Rules* does not prescribe an all-encompassing code of behavior; it suggests how to establish Christian priorities in the midst of an active life.

Southwell is not following in the tradition of St. Benedict or other founders of religious orders. He is, instead, reinvigorating a medieval lay literary tradition, namely, he produces something akin to a primer. Such books, containing prayers based on the liturgical hours, methods for examining one's conscience, and other formulae for devotions, gained popularity in Reformation-era England. Primers supplied spiritual help for an increasingly literate audience in the absence of priests. Luis de Grenada, a Spanish Dominican whose devotional works were translated into English and whom Southwell cites in the *Rules*, referred to primers as "dumb preachers, which are neither tedious for length (because we may leave them off when we list), neither do they leave us with a greedy appetite by reason of their briefness" (trans. Richard Hopkins [Rouen 1586], sig. [2d] A6v.).[10] Robert, hoping to make available the principles of Loyola's *Spiritual Exercises*, employs a medium familiar to his readers, but in it he introduces a fresh approach to leading a good life.

The primer tradition lacked an organic structure. Primers were compendia of prayers and practices not necessarily related one to another. They were the spiritual equivalent of poetic miscellanies or personal commonplace books. Southwell takes this tradition and infuses it with the kind of order that Loyola imposes on his *Spiritual Exercises*. Loyola, too, borrowed from pre-existing spiritual traditions, and his genius, like Southwell's, is in organizing material under a new paradigm. According to O'Malley, "what made the *Exercises* special was not particular themes or their mode of articulation," it was "the coordination of the parts into an integral and novel totality" (46). Much in the *Exercises* corresponds to medieval devotions, but Loyola arranges his handbook in response to the early modern emphasis on personal freedom and decision-making.[11]

Southwell, in *Short Rules*, borrows liberally from Loyola. Both write in the first person so readers can identify with the voice of instruction and readily enter into the prescribed methods of prayer or types of behavior. Loyola divides the *Exercises* into four "weeks," or stages. Likewise Robert's *Short Rules* contains four sections, starting, as Loyola does, with a statement of first principles. The second section builds on these principles, outlining a Christian's duties to God, those in authority, neighbors, and self. The third and perhaps most practical section helps readers order daily events and responsibilities. Southwell ends his *Short Rules* by providing suggestions for spiritual growth in the face of inevitable temptations. Not only do the *Exercises* and the *Rules* have a similar four-fold structure, but both books also propose a logical progression that can help people move from one level of the spiritual life to the next, and both insist on the necessity of repetition as part of this growth. As Southwell puts it, "I must every week read some part of this rule, so dividing it that at month's end I may have read all, seeking to print these spiritual directions in my mind and endeavoring to put them into daily practice" (ch. 6, ll. 191–94). Repetition and progressive structure are the twin engines driving the vehicles for spiritual development that the *Exercises* and the *Rules* are meant to be.

Perhaps the greatest difference between the books is the brevity of the *Rules* compared to the *Exercises*, but this is not because Southwell's readers were busy lay men, whereas Loyola's were religious contemplatives. Loyola formulated and gave the *Exercises* before he was a Jesuit or a priest, and he continued to direct lay people throughout his life.[12] What accounts for Southwell's brevity is that his readers needed spiritual direction under increasingly difficult circumstances, including the unavailability of priests. Robert wants to make this formative experience available in as efficient and accessible a manner as possible.

In many ways, the *Exercises* are aptly suited for adaptation to the needs of ordinary people, even those in extraordinary circumstances. Loyola based his guidelines on personal experience. They are not the product of theory or theological speculation, and while he enjoyed mystical experiences, such as the gift of tears, he never assumes that others will. As a result, in the *Exercises* he provides for adaptation in light of differences occasioned by the concrete realities of life.[13] He states this policy in a note for those who give and receive these aids to improvement:

> The Spiritual Exercises have to be adapted to the dispositions of the persons who wish to receive them, that is, to their age, education or

> ability, in order not to give to one who is uneducated or of little
> intelligence things he cannot easily bear and profit by. Again, that should be
> given to each one by which, according to his wish to dispose himself, he
> may be better able to help himself and to profit. (*Spiritual Exercises*, 18)

He also makes provisions for the kinds of people for whom Southwell
writes his *Short Rules*. Loyola knew that not all those who can profit by
making the *Exercises* have the leisure to spend weeks in prayer and silence.
He acknowledges the benefits of isolation, but he also admits that there are
other ways to grow in a spiritual life shaped by his method of prayer: "A
person of education or ability who is taken up with public affairs or suitable
business, may take an hour and a half daily to exercise himself" (19).[14]
Loyola's willingness to accommodate the needs of busy people gives
Southwell license to fit the Ignatian tradition to the size of his readers'
lives. As Brown puts it, "the purpose of the *Short Rules* is to guide the
Christian who has resolved to serve God as a layman so that he may best
plan a life of virtuous action." "It is," she concludes, "a handbook of
spiritual life in the world, intended for a thoughtful and well-educated
householder who is willing to accept its directives and to live according to
the religious standards it imposes" (xxvi).

The centerpiece of Loyola's *Exercises* is a set of instructions for
choosing a state or way of life. John O'Malley contends, for example, that
"the *Exercises* were designed to enable one to make that choice with
objectivity and freedom of spirit and under the most immediate inspiration
of God." "It is obvious from the text," he continues, "that the decision or
election, lies at the heart of the *Exercises* when they are made in their full
integrity, which is foreseen as taking approximately a month in a situation
in which one could devote oneself exclusively to the purpose at hand,
removed from usual occupations" (38). This choice is situated at the end of
the retreat's Second Week, a series of meditations on the life of Christ up to
his passion. The placement of the "election," as Loyola terms it, is
purposeful. He hoped that after days spent in prayerful imagining of
Christ's ministry, a person making the *Exercises* will follow him by
forsaking riches, honor and pride, and embracing the evangelical counsels.
When a Jesuit novice makes the *Exercises*, for example, this can be the
point when he confirms his decision to enter the order.

When Southwell conceived of his *Short Rules*, however, he
understood the need to reorient this critical moment in the *Exercises* for an
audience that had already made life-shaping choices. He is writing for
married men and women, many of whom are raising children and running
households. In this reorientation, too, he can follow Loyola's lead, since the
latter made similar provisions. According to Loyola, "there are some things

which fall under unchangeable election, such as are the priesthood, marriage, etc." In this case, in which Anne Howard and many of Southwell's readers found themselves, "there is no reason for making the election anew, but let [the retreatant] perfect himself as much as he can in that already chosen" (*Exercises*, 173). This provides Robert's rationale in the *Short Rules*. His readers are not free to change their states in life. They are responsible to spouses and children. Nevertheless, they can perfect themselves by following the practices prescribed by the *Rules*.

As in the *Exercises*, the *Rules* open with a statement of first principles, but rather than simply repeat the principles articulated by Loyola, Southwell explains and expands them mindful of a particular audience. His diction and tone mirror Loyola's throughout the *Rules*, but especially so here at the start, where he avoids ornamentation. Readers across the critical spectrum agree on this assessment, with an admirer such as Janelle observing that there is "no room here for flowers of style; the essential quality to be aimed at was a convincing clearness" (152), and a detractor such as Brownlow agreeing that "the tone is sober, practical and subdued" (50). Imitating the clipped style of the *Exercises*, Southwell explains humanity's essential relationship with God:

> He made me of nothing, and that not to have a being only, as a stone, nor withal a bare kind of life or growing, as a plant or tree, nor moreover a power of sense or feeling only, as a brute beast, but a creature to his own likeness, endued with reason, or understanding, and free will; also, why he now preserveth me in this health, state, and calling; finally, why he redeemed me with his own blood, bestowed so infinite benefits upon me, and still continueth his mercy towards me. (*Rules* ch. 1, ll. 3–11)

This three-fold debt to the God who creates, preserves and redeems calls forth, according to Southwell, a response, which he describes as "rules that follow of this foundation." The first of such rules requires acknowledging that "I [am] only God's, not mine own; neither can I so bind or give myself to any creature but that I ought more to serve, love and obey God than any creature in this world" (ll. 19–21). Even married people, therefore, have a primary relationship to God which provides the context for fulfilling their obligations as spouses and parents. From this principle, others follow, and each has attendant "rules." For example, "seeing I was made to serve God … the salvation of mine own soul is the most weighty and important business and the most necessary matter wherein I must employ my body, mind, time and labor" (ll. 31–33). On the basis of this principle, "what diligence, labor, or cost I would employ in any other temporal matter of credit, living, or life, all that I am bound to employ in the service of God and the salvation of my soul, and so much more as the weight or worth of my soul passeth all other things" (ll. 39–42). In acknowledging that his audience has "other temporal matters of credit, living or life," he is following Loyola's lead in reaching out to worldly readers. He further appeals to their sensibilities, as he did in *An Epistle of Comfort*, by employing secular terms to explain their spiritual responsibilities. The service of God is their "principal business" (ll. 44–45). He also recalls the language of the *Epistle* when reminding his readers that they will encounter opposition to their efforts at spiritual growth. "Wherefore," he writes, "I must resolve myself and set it down as a thing undoubted that my whole life must be a continual combat with these adversaries" (ll. 52–53). According to the rule that follows from this principle, "I must prepare my body and mind to all patience and think it no news to be tempted but a point annexed necessarily to my profession." Moreover, "I must never look to be free from some trouble or other, but knowing my life to be a perpetual warfare, I must rather comfort myself with hope of a glorious crown for my victories than of any long or assured peace with mine enemies" (ll. 70–73).

After describing opposition to spiritual perfection, Southwell offers his readers a practical example of making a discernment. When faced with temptation, he suggests, "let me examine myself whether I would buy myself the fulfilling of mine appetite with being a leper, or full of the plague, or with death presently to ensue after it." "If not," he continues, "then much less ought I to buy it with the leprosy, loss, and death of my soul, which is of far more worth than my body" (ll. 87–90). And he follows this language of buying and selling by helping his readers reconsider their relationships to God in terms familiar to landowners: "Being God's creature ... I am only as bailiff, tenant, or officer to demain or govern these things to his best service."

Here he reaches out again to a specific readership by translating the starker and more theologically abstract Ignatian vocabulary into their own vernacular. The point, finally, is reconciliation, in this case with God. At the end of the first chapter, he recommends frequently recalling these principles and the rules based on them for the sake of examining one's conscience in preparation for sacramental confession:

> Let me often consider what bodily, ghostly and external gifts from God I have received; what in baptism and at other times I have promised; how profitable and necessary good works I have omitted; how many grievous and heinous sins I have committed; how much honor and how many souls I have robbed from God. And these things being well perused, let me seek to make that recompense and satisfaction for them which I would wish to

have made when death shall summon me before my heavenly judge to give up a most strict account of them. (ll. 109–18)

Once a reader reconciles with God through a general confession, a practice which Ignatius encourages in the *Exercises'* First Week, he must, according to Southwell, cultivate seven "affections."[15] This attention to feeling is classically Ignatian. According to O'Malley, for example, the text of the *Exercises* "manifests that the engaging of powerful emotions like grief, fear, horror, compunction, compassion, contentment, admiration, gratitude, wonder, joy, and especially love is the final and foreseen outcome of its various meditations and contemplations, especially its climactic ones" (41). Southwell evokes feeling by instructing his readers "to do all things as if I did see God visibly working and cooperating with me in every action, as in truth he doth" (*Rules* ch. 2, ll.12–14). This sense of God's immediacy is the first affection a reader needs to acquire: "a very fit mean I can use to please [God] is to bear always in mind his presence" (l. 5). Robert then suggests a practical means to this end. Aware that he is not writing for monks or for other Jesuits, he recommends "get[ting] a great facility in turning my mind and heart to [God] and in talking often with him by short and sweet prayers, which are the fuel of devotion" (ll. 23–25). Frequent, brief and sincere prayers can supply for hours in the chapel or cloister.

As a reader begins to appreciate God's presence to him, Southwell urges him to "endeavor to kindle in [him]self" other affections, the order of which is telling: "a sincere and tender love of [God]"; "a reverent and dutiful fear"; "zeal of God's honor"; "to take occasion of everything that I hear, see or think of to praise God"; "even in my ordinary actions ... to have a badge of Christianity"; "a perfect resignation of myself into God's hands"; and, finally, "gratitude and thankfulness." This ladder of affections, leading to spiritual perfection, closely mirrors the progress Loyola outlines in the *Exercises*. The First Week, for example, inspires love for God who creates and sustains and, subsequently, remorse on account of our sinful rejection of that love. In the Second Week, meditations on Christ's life promote zeal and a sense of how God labors for the good in all things. In response, exercitants want to imitate Christ and his disciples. The Third Week of the *Exercises* invites contemplation on Christ's resignation of self in his suffering and death; and the Fourth Week, ending with the Contemplation to Gain Love, underscores the reasons we have to be grateful to God, considering "how all good things and gifts descend from above" (*Spiritual Exercises*, 237). Southwell summarizes this complex dynamic, making it possible for ordinary people to participate in it. He restates the fundamental tenets of Ignatian spirituality, such as "seeking God in all things," without making them seem the stuff of which mystics are made. For example, he insists that the "ordinary actions" of life can be occasions of grace: "the fifth affection is to consider that I being a Christian, not only my faith and all my actions proper thereunto ought to be different ... but even mine ordinary actions of eating, drinking, playing, working, and suchlike ought to have a mark and badge of Christianity" (*Rules* ch. 2, ll. 91–95).

Southwell continues to make more concrete the consequences of the *Exercises* in the next three chapters of the *Rules*, which describe relationships with superiors, neighbors and self. The nature of these relationships is implied in Loyola's text, but Robert takes the further practical step of making it explicit. He also casts the relationships in the context of his readers' milieu. Loyola designed *Exercises* for the universal church; Southwell is far more specific; and on account of his specificity he addresses English issues. He opens, for example, by considering the proper relationship between subjects and secular rulers, an obviously vexed matter for his recusant readership. He fully explores this issue in *An Humble Supplication*, a text devoted to the loyalty Catholics owe Elizabeth and the clemency she owes them; but in the *Rules* the direction of his thinking is already apparent and characteristically conciliatory. He places duty to "superiors in temporal things" before that belonging to "spiritual superiors." According to Southwell, secular rulers are God's "viceregents and substitutes," adding carefully "in the things wherein I am subject to them" (ch. 3, ll. 1–3). This qualification leaves room for resisting Elizabeth's religious policies, and he reinforces his point in the following lines: "And first, to speak of these which are my superiors in temporal things, in all points belonging to their charge I am to yield them temporal duty, contenting myself with their appointment so far as with justice and equity they can demand, and by God's laws I shall be bound to yield unto them" (ll. 3–7). Southwell proposes a two-pronged argument. The first he will use in *An Humble Supplication* to make the case that Catholics are, in fact, Elizabeth's most loyal subjects because their relationship to her is guaranteed by divine warrant. The second defends a notion of limited government. There are constraints on royal authority, beyond which Elizabeth cannot assert her prerogative. Southwell does not define his use of the limiting terms "justice" and "equity." He will do so in his *Supplication*. Here he simply sketches the contours of his compromise: secular government can be reconciled to religious difference so long as the governed recognize the proper, divinely-sanctioned authority of the sovereign, and the sovereign acknowledges the parameters of her power.

Regarding spiritual authority, Robert comes closest to blurring the boundaries between lay and religious church members, employing language applicable to those under religious vows when addressing married people. He presents an ecclesiastical superior, even a spiritual director, as acting *in persona Christi*: "I must reverence and honor him as the viceregent of God, and consider Christ in his person, and do my duty to him as if in him I did see Christ" (ll. 26–28). These terms echo the Jesuit *Constitutions* in which Loyola defines the relationship between a religious superior and his subjects. The latter writer is unambiguous about the nature and importance of obedience in Jesuit life, stating "we should be ready to receive [a] command just as if it were coming from Christ our Savior, since we are practicing the obedience to one in His place and because of love and reverence for Him." Ignatius also employs the expression "blind obedience" in relation to Jesuits performing "with great alacrity, spiritual joy and perseverance whatever is commanded of them." Finally, he uses two similes to emphasize his point: "We ought to be firmly convinced that everyone of those who live under obedience ought to allow himself to be carried and directed by Divine Providence through the agency of the superior as if he were a lifeless body which allows itself to be carried to any place and be treated in any manner desired, or as if he were an old man's staff which serves in any place and in any manner whatsoever in which the holder wishes to use it" (*Constitutions*, 547). Such provisions make sense as Loyola is governing a far-flung religious order whose members are, through the *Exercises*, trained in the process of discernment in freedom.

It is difficult, but not impossible, to understand why Southwell insists on strict obedience among his readers. Robert avoids Loyola's dramatic figures of speech, but he imitates him in concluding that obedience to a superior or director, "or rather towards Christ's person in him," ought to be done "with these conditions: speedily, without delay; voluntarily, without constraint; simply, without questions or excuses; contentedly, without murmuring or grudging; stoutly, without despair or impatience; constantly, with perseverance to the end; [and] humbly, without pride" (*Rules* ch. 3, ll. 49–55). The adverse circumstances facing the English Catholic community explain this stringency. There was no obvious religious authority in place. The Catholic diocesan system had been abrogated, and Southwell acknowledges as much when he advises readers in choosing the religious authority under whom they will place themselves. That there is choice involved, even if by default, somewhat mitigates his hardline stance on perfect obedience. Unlike members of religious orders, such as the Jesuits, whose superiors are assigned to them, Southwell's readers select religious superiors. He urges them in doing so to "procure that [your] choice be of virtuous, grave, and mortified men, who having their own passions well subdued may better teach [you] how to bridle [yours]." This choice is critical, he writes: "it is the chief help and most profitable if my choice be good, and very dangerous if it be evil." Therefore, "I must make my choice with great advice and deliberation, using the counsel of some other persons of good and grounded judgment in such things" (ll. 9–15). Since the unity and permanency of the church in England depends upon allegiance to a religious authority, Southwell emphasizes the importance of this choice and its consequences. Again, he omits Loyola's starkest language, but he applies his practical-minded insistence on obedience in an extraordinary set of circumstances. Loyola demanded obedience in order to keep his Society organized and indivisible. Southwell shares these aims in his ministry among England's Catholics. He intuits that without obedience of a high order, the future of the English Catholic community is jeopardized.

The poet's tone lightens remarkably when he attends to the duty Christians owe their neighbors, and rarely does he sound more like an English aristocrat. In describing the householder whom Southwell addresses in this chapter, Brownlow observes, "he sounds more like a figure from the eighteenth century than the sixteenth century," and the chapter's instructions can be summed up in the phrase, "Be a Gentleman" (62–63). Robert instructs his readers on matters of courtesy such as countenance, gait, gesture, voice and apparel, recommending moderation in all these categories: "First, I must procure to remember that my external behavior ... and my outward actions be done with gravity, modesty and all decency; that I be not light, vain or too lavish in mirth, not too austere, or too much inclined to sadness, but with temperate modesty, rather composed to mirth than melancholy" (ch. 4, ll. 3–8). Given his readers' circumstances, such mirth would be a remarkable achievement, and Southwell several times repeats the need for it, encouraging people to "be rather bent to smiling than heaviness and free from frowning and unseemly distemper" (ll. 20–22). Similarly, they should avoid "all show of inward disquietness or unordered passions, which though I cannot choose but sometimes feel" (ll. 27–28). The final phrase in this injunction is typical of the poet's attitude throughout the *Rules*, in that he appreciates his readers' interior lives. He never dismisses or despises their feelings, and the depth of his understanding stems from personal experience. He has endured bouts of disquiet and unordered passions, so he empathizes with their struggles. For example, he urges readers to keep "free from affectation or singularity," a freedom which he struggled to achieve as a Jesuit. In his novitiate journal, *Spiritual Exercises and Devotions*, the temptation to "singularity" appears with regularity. On one occasion he writes, "in all this

... thou art to abide by custom and avoid singularity, as in everything else, for nothing is more harmful to community life" (*Devotions*, 42).

Much of his advice in this chapter of the *Rules* consists of commonplaces. Southwell strikes out on his own, however, in articulating the rationale for conventional comportment. The motivation for this behavior, as in obedience to superiors, is maintaining "mutual love and charity" among members of an endangered community (l. 62). Southwell's *Rules* encourage solidarity among England's Catholics, a solidarity upon which his life depends. He needs Catholics to support him, other priests and one another through hospitality, benefactions, and, most of all, confidentiality. To this end, his *Rules*, especially in this chapter on the duty owed to neighbors, cultivate a strong sense of community in which people never think, much less speak, ill of one another. Beyond acting like gentlemen and gentlewomen, Robert's readers need to "show ... compassion to others' miseries and ... joy at their welfare" (l. 66).

When Southwell writes on duty to oneself, he is especially practical, and this same quality extends to subsequent chapters on "How to Spend Every Day," "Rules in Sickness," "The Care of Servants," and "The Care of My Children." Chapter six recommends eight hours of sleep per night, and how "after I am up, for a good pretty space it is good not to talk" (ll. 3–4). While such quiet is characteristic of religious communities, its feasibility in large households is doubtful. The poet occasionally forgets that most people do not live as Jesuits do. In the silence of the ideal morning, he suggests causal conversation with God. Writing on prayer he recommends brevity: "I must think a few well said [prayers] better than many hastily shuffled over" (ll. 20–21). When readers enjoy leisure to pray, such as on feast days, he counsels Ignatian exercises such as "meditations on some part of Christ's passion or of his life, or of mine own sins" (ll. 22–23). Most days, though, he admits, are filled with work, which he endorses as a remedy against idleness, "the mother of all vices" (l. 26): "I must, if time and place will permit me, be always doing some profitable thing to avoid sloth, directing mine intention in all my exercises to this end, that I may avoid idleness and temptations and bestow my time in good sort to God's glory" (ll. 55–58).

This conviction that all days and works can glorify God is grounded in the Ignatian confidence that God can be sought and found in all things and activities—even eating, rules for which Southwell describes at length. In doing so, he builds on the "Rules for Eating" which Loyola appends to the *Exercises*. In Loyola's text, there are eight specific precepts on the subject, all sharing the same purpose. In eating, as in every aspect of life, a Christian aims to "get greater system and order as to how he ought to behave and manage himself" (*Spiritual Exercises*, 214). Mindful of this goal, Ignatius proposes strategies both practical and imaginative. Practically, he suggests deciding before mealtimes how much one will eat. "Beyond this," warns Loyola, "let him not go because of any appetite or temptation, but rather, in order to conquer more all inordinate appetite and temptation of the enemy, if he is tempted to eat more, let him eat less" (217). More imaginatively, he believes that meals can be occasions for a person to "consider as if he saw Christ our Lord eating with His Apostles, and how He drinks and how He looks and how He speaks; and let him see to imitating him" (214). Likewise, "while he is eating, he can take another consideration, either on the life of Saints, or on some pious Contemplation, or on some spiritual affair which he has to do, because, being intent on such thing, he will take less delight and feeling in the corporal food" (215). Southwell incorporates this exercise in the *Rules* when he encourages readers to imagine in "every room of the house ... in some decent place thereof a throne or chair of estate and dedicate the same and the whole room to God himself, that whensoever I enter it, I enter as it were into a chapel ... and therefore in mind do that reverence that is due to him" (ch. 11, ll. 359–64). In relation to eating, Southwell adds to Loyola's considerations a note on indifference, a quality to which he will return later in the *Rules*. "At meals," he suggests, "I must neither be too curious or doubtful of what I eat, neither too precise in the quantity, fineness or coarseness of the meat, but of that which God hath sent take a competent meal, measurable to my need and not hurtful to my health" (ll. 38–41).

Following meals, and again importing a custom observed in religious houses, Robert tells readers to take up spiritual reading. He insists that once a book is begun, it must be completed, and he also has a method in mind that is consistent with practices suggested in the *Exercises*: do not read as though "lightly running over" the book, "but pausing upon such things as move my affection and printing them well in mind and memory" (ll. 119–20). Southwell, in classic Ignatian fashion, provides a practical way to focus on one's interior life where God's will is manifest.

Another practical dimension of the latter chapters of the *Rules* is the poet's emphasis on planning. In a subsection of chapter six entitled "Every Week," he writes:

> In the beginning of the week I must foresee what holy days there are in the same that I might better prepare myself for them. Also in the beginning of the week I must think whether I have any extraordinary business, temporal or spiritual, to do, that having a foresight of it I may remember it and provide better for it. (ll. 178–82)

Planning becomes especially relevant, according to Southwell, when dealing with temptations. Readers should study the course of their lives to discover patterns of temptation. Once these patterns are discerned, they can be anticipated and avoided. "First," Robert writes, "I must learn to know when I am tempted, for if I can find my temptation I may reckon it half overcome" (ch. 10, ll. 1–2). This foreknowledge is described in chapter five as well:

> I must procure to foresee in every action, at least in all the principal, to forearm myself against those occasions of sin which will be offered in them; and where it lieth not in my power to avoid the occasion of any great sin, the more danger there is, and the greater the sin is that I am in danger of, so much more the preparation must I use to resist it and the more earnestly ask for God's grace. (ll. 10–15)

Even lesser sins can be anticipated. For example, one can guard against uncharitable conversation by imagining a social engagement before it happens:

> Always when I am to go to any company, either of my dwelling place or strangers, I ought to forecast their disposition and what talk or action is likely to be tendered unto me by their presence. If I fear detracting speeches, let me arm myself not to seem to approve of them, yea, rather to mislike them, and to turn the talk to some other matter, and so in all other kind of unlawful talk. Finally, for conversation let this be my chief rule: always to foresee and provide myself against the occasions that by every company are likely to be offered me, and in the beginning to direct mine intention to talk either for dispatch of necessary business, if there be any, or for maintaining mutual love and charity, if it be merry or ordinary talk. This foresight of occasions and faults likely to be committed is the principal remedy against all sin, and therefore especially to be noted and used. (Ch. 4, ll. 51–63)

Southwell also insists that one complement with perseverance this habit of anticipating sin. In a section of chapter eleven entitled "The last consideration, of the necessity of perseverance in continuing watchful over ourselves," he concludes, "seeing the sum and complement of all virtue consisteth in the continuance and progress in it, perseverance, of all other things, is most necessary in this business" (ll. 213–16). Despite a person's efforts at planning, he acknowledges, "I can never go on in virtue without falling" (ch. 5, l. 73). Therefore, "in the time of my desolation and disquiet of mind, I must not enter into any deliberation or go about to alter anything concerning the state of my soul or proposed course of life, but persevere in my former resolutions made in time of my good and quiet estate, wherein I was free from passion and better able to judge of things convenient to my good" (ch. 10, ll. 55–59). Loyola also endorses this common sense approach to decision-making in the *Exercises*. In his "Rules for Discernment of Spirits," upon which Southwell bases his own chapter ten, Ignatius writes, "In the time of desolation never to make a change; but to be firm and constant in the resolutions and determination in which one was the day proceeding such desolation, or in the determination in which he was in the proceeding consolation" (*Spiritual Exercises*, 318).

Southwell, like Loyola, introduces strategies for perseverance. For example, "in temptations and troubles of mind," readers should recall better times. This is not merely nostalgia, but a tactic for sustaining hope. What God has done in the past, God can do in the future. Southwell is also psychologically savvy about temptations. "Neither the multitude, continuance nor badness of any thought must breed any scruple or disquiet in me," he writes, "for not to have them is not in my power, but only not to consent unto them" (*Rules* ch. 10, ll. 71–73). He also encourages honest conversations with God when one is tempted. He includes a prayer at the end of this chapter, which serves as a model for his readers, and in it, he is blunt and demanding. "Why," he asks God, "dost thou set me contrary unto thee and make me grievous and a burthen unto myself?": "Didst thou create me to cast me away? Didst thou redeem me to damn me forever? ... Show thyself a Saviour unto me, and either take away mine enemies or grant me grace that without wound or fault, by thee and with thee, I may overcome them, sweet Jesus."

When urging perseverance Southwell is not always solemn, however. Several times throughout the rules he returns to the notion that religious people ought to be generally content in life, and genial even in difficult times. He suggests regular celebrations, for example. In the chapter on duties to self he plans to "celebrate the day of my conversion every year ... and some other principal feasts in the year, to call to mind the first fervor, devotion and zeal that God did then give me; and this to do very often at other times also" (ch. 5, ll. 78–84). He also reveals a light touch when he discusses sickness and raising children. Sick people, for example, need not pray beyond "in the morning commending [themselves] to God ... with short prayers such as 'Lord Jesus, save me,' 'Lord, strengthen me,' 'Lord, grant me patience,' and such like" (ch. 7, ll. 2–5). He also favors diversions and exercise in times of health: "I must also assure myself that I do God good service when I do any necessary thing and take any convenient recreation that may further my health" (ll. 14–16). Regarding children, he gives humane advice on teaching religion and applying discipline. "I must use them to devotion little by little," he resolves, "not cloying them with too much at once but rather seeking to make them take delight in it" (ch. 9, ll. 9–11). Moreover, "I must on the one side break them from their wills and punish them as they deserve, yet also remembering that they are young and not keeping them in too much subjection, which may breed in them base and servile minds and make their love less towards me" (ll. 16–20). And, finally, "I ought never to beat any child in mine anger" (l. 21).

Southwell ends the *Rules* by acknowledging the primer tradition to which he is indebted. He provides readers with lists such as "what good a soul loseth by mortal sin" and "how a soul is prepared to justification by degrees." These, as Brown points out, are taken from de Grenada's *A Memorial of a Christian Life* (119). He also includes "certain short prayers," many of them borrowed from St. Bernard, which readers can use to recall God's presence throughout the day. There is, as well, a traditional consideration of guardian angels, with whom "after a special devotion towards God we must procure to have a kind of reverent familiarity." Such an angel, according to Southwell, is "a most undivided and peculiar friend … When we sleep, he watcheth over us; when we wake, he attendeth on us; wheresoever we be, he guardeth us; withersoever we go, he assisteth us; and whatsoever we do, he hath still an eye to succor us" (ch. 10, ll. 325–335). Robert's practical-minded angels seem as busy as the audience for whom he writes the *Rules*.

...

The *Rules'* publication history shows that readers, editors and publishers found Southwell's work conciliatory in appealing to both Catholics and Protestants. Catholic readers regularly referred to the text after Henry Garnet published it upon the writer's death. The Garnet edition bears the title *A Short Rule of Good Life. To direct the devout Christian in a regular and orderly course. Newly set forth according to the author's direction before his death.* Garnet introduces the *Rules* with a preface addressing the "gentle reader," explaining that Southwell "is very well known unto thee as also for his learning, piety, zeal, charity, fortitude, and other rare and singular qualities, but especially for his precious death he is renowned in the world abroad" (ll. 19–22).[16] In describing that death, Garnet seems to recall Southwell's "Burning Babe": "and finally in his many several and most cruel conflicts with the enemies of Christ, he showed how strong and unconquerable the love of God is, whose burning heat never so many waters or gusts of most main floods may either quench or smother and who power the most powerable thing of all, which is death, cannot overcome" (ll. 46–51). Garnet urges readers to "enjoy these rules," and to help them do so, he explains Southwell's use of the word "must." Perhaps thinking of his friend's emphasis on obedience, Garnet writes, "whereas in these *Rules* thou shalt sometimes read that thou must do this or that, thou must not understand that word *must* as though thou wert bound to the performance of anything there expressed, but only that those actions do belong to the exercise of perfection, without any farther bond than either the laws of God or of Holy Church do impose" (ll. 94–97).

Those not bound by the laws of Holy Church also appreciated Southwell's *Rules*. They were printed on a commercial press by William Barrett in 1620 (STC 22965). Most specifically, Catholic references were removed from Barrett's edition, and as Brown asserts, "the texts contained little to indicate that they were the work of a Jesuit priest" (*Two Letters*, liii). For example, there are no references to the sacrament of penance or Marian devotions. But the adaptation preserves the dynamic of the Ignatian *Exercises* as rendered by Southwell, a dynamic that Protestants found helpful.

This use by Protestants of Southwell's originally Catholic text is not a unique case. Two years after Robert Persons published in 1582 his *First Book of the Christian Exercises, Appertaining to Resolution*, also based on Loyola's *Exercises* and the works of de Grenada, Edmund Bunny adapted the popular volume for use by non-Catholic Englishmen.[17] According to Victor Houliston, Persons' book "must count as one of the most influential prose works of Elizabeth's reign, a work not only eloquent in itself but remarkably successful as an instrument of Catholic revival" (159).[18] Bunny, Calvinist subdean of York and rector of Bolton Percy, was even more careful to remove and refute Catholic aspects of the text than was Southwell's Protestant editor, though Bunny acknowledged and praised the author of the original. In both cases, however, the degree to which Anglicans found congenial the Jesuit method of prayer is undisputed. Persons objected to what he considered the misuse of his book. As Houliston notes, "[Persons] refused Bunny's appended offer of pacification with contempt; his virulent, outraged response to this act of apparently benign piracy has been taken by many observers to provide further evidence of his legendary belligerence and intolerance" (160). He learned of Bunny's edition immediately after its publication, and he complained about its "infinite corruptions, maymes, and manglings." In the preface to a 1585 publication of his own *Directory*, Persons "is in controversialist mode, lampooning his adversary, mocking his name, ridiculing his arguments [and] indignantly flinging back in his face all irenic overtures"

(Houliston 170). In subsequent editions Persons added lengthy chapters proving that he and Bunny were theologically and stylistically worlds apart.[19] Persons would share no common ground with a Protestant. Southwell, characteristically inclined to reconciliation, would have been pleased that Protestants profited by his *Rules*.

Notes

[1]   William Allen includes an account of Mayne's martyrdom in *A Briefe Historie of the Glorious Martyrdom of XII Reverend Priests* (n.p. [Rheims], 1582). ARCR II, no. 7; STC 369.5. See also Michael E. Williams' "Campion and the English Continental Seminaries" in *The Reckoned Expense*, 285–99.

[2]   See A.C. Southern, "'The Best Wits out of England': University Men in Exile under Elizabeth I," *The Month* CXCIII (1952), 12–21.

[3]   The Papal Bull establishing the University stipulates its obligation to refute heretics and schismatics (Knox 267).

[4]   Beales reports in *Education Under Penalty* that twenty-one Catholic schoolmasters were executed during Elizabeth's reign (54).

[5]   Owing to the sizable number of young men and boys from England seeking admission, five other schools were established during Elizabeth's reign: Rome (1579); Eu (1582); Valladolid (1589); Seville (1592); and St. Omer (1593).

[6]   Dyer's poem is reprinted in *The Poems of Robert Southwell, S.J.* (135–38). The editors acknowledge that their text is based on a version in ms. Ashmole 781, which is given by Ralph M. Sargent in *At the Court of Queen Elizabeth: the Life and Lyrics of Sir Edward Dyer* (Oxford: Oxford UP, 1935), 184–87.

[7]   Southwell, in a letter dated 25 July 1586, describes a meeting of Jesuits at which Byrd was present (*Unpublished Documents*, 308).

[8]   For the McDonald and Brown argument, see Southwell *The Poems of Robert Southwell*, 124. Scallon's explication of the poem appears in his *The Poetry of Robert Southwell, S.J.*, 114.

[9]   Jesuits were disappointed to discover that universities other than Paris did not follow the curriculum known as the *modus Parisiensis*. For more on the *modus Parisiensis* and how Jesuits employed it, see Gabriel Codina, "The 'Modus Parisuensis'" in *The Jesuit Ratio Studiorum: 400th Anniversary Perspectives*. ed. Vincent J. Duminuco (New York: Fordham UP, 2000) 28–49.

[10] For the importance of de Grenada's works among English readers, both Catholic and Protestant, see H.C. White, *English Devotional Literature (Prose) 1600–1640* (Madison, WI: Wisconsin UP, 1931). According to White, "of all the Spanish devotional writers whose works were translated into English, none enjoyed a popularity like Luis de Grenada" (105).

[11] O'Malley lists some of the sources available to Ignatius in his formulation of the *Exercises*, including Ludolph of Saxony's *Vita Jesu Christi*, the *Meditationes vitae Christi* composed by a fourteenth-century Italian Franciscan, Alonso de Madrid's *Arte para servir a Dios*, Jean Gerson's *Monotessaron*, and Abbot Cisneros' *Ejercitatorio de la vida espiritual*. Ultimately, however, "the very commonplace nature of the ideas in the *Exercises* has rendered frustrating the search for their sources" (46).

[12] The list of those who made the *Exercises* ranges from church leaders such as Gasparo Cardinal Contarini, to secular rulers including Queen Catherine of Portugal, sister of

the emperor. According to O'Malley, "by 1564 Nadal had begun to advocate that all—
or at least the better—students in Jesuit schools not leave them until they had made the
Exercises in some form," and throughout Europe, Jesuit houses were reconfigured so
that they could handle large numbers or retreatants who put their names on waiting lists
in order to meet with spiritual directors.

[13]   As O'Malley reports, "the first generation [of Jesuits], under the influence of Ignatius,
knew they had in that book a unique instrument to 'help souls.'" In fact, "Polanco saw
the *Exercises* as a 'compendium' (*epilogus*) of all the means the Jesuits had for the
helping of souls in spiritual growth," [and] from Ignatius's example and from the text
itself, the Jesuits knew that the *Exercises* were an extraordinarily pliable instrument that
could be accommodated to a great variety of circumstances and individuals—
"'Multiplex est modus tradendi Exercitia,' said a contemporary source" (127).

[14]   According to O'Malley, this is probably how Ignatius usually gave the *Exercises*,
especially in the early years of his ministry (129).

[15]   "The *Exercises* do not propose [general confession] as a ritual obligation in order to be
shriven from one's sins," according to O'Malley, "for they presuppose that at least in
most cases that has already been done, perhaps many times." He maintains that "this
confession is something different": "It is the climax of the program of the first Week,
which has consisted of essentially two parts: first, a review, or moral inventory, of
one's life up to that point and, second, a deepening awareness of the mercy and love of
God, operative at every moment along the way, despite one's sins and failings." "In this
case," O'Malley maintains, "the confession is a dramatized statement to one's self, to
God and to another human being who here represents God that an important change in
one's pattern of thinking, feeling, and behaving is now desired with all one's heart and
is in fact underway" (39). The similarities to the role of confession in Southwell's
program are obvious.

[16]   Brown includes Garnet's "The Preface to the Reader" as Appendix A in her edition of
the Folger manuscript of the *Rules* (89–91).

[17]   Persons' book went through many adaptations and republications, both by Catholics
and by Protestants. Early on it was referred to as *The Book of Resolution*. It was then
enlarged and republished as *A Christian directorie guiding men to their salvation*
(Rouen: 1585). STC 19354.1; ARCR II no. 618. In other cases it was known as *A
Christian Directory*.

[18]   Houliston's article, "Why Robert Persons would not be Pacified: Edmund Bunny's
Theft of *The Book of Resolution*," appears in *The Reckoned Expense*, ed. Thomas
McCoog, 159–77. In terms of the book's scope of influence, Houliston observes that "the
original print run of 2,500 was immediately snapped up and read to pieces by a public
starved of books of devotion" (168). Moreover, Thomas Clancy shows in "Spiritual
Publications of the English Jesuits, 1615–1640" that a significant number of men entered
the Jesuits on account of reading it. (*Recusant History* 19 [1989], 426–46).

[19]   Houliston sympathizes with Persons' objections to Bunny's stylistic changes. "Persons
had good reason to resent Bunny's interference," he writes, "if only because of the
latter's clumsy prose": "This can frequently be seen in the mutilation of sentences,
where he upsets the balance and rhythm for the sake of theological correctness" (171).

Chapter 4
Reconciling Passions, Patriotism and Poetry

While Southwell was acquiring skills and resources at Douai, he also endured two crises. Both were related to vocational discernment, and a personal relationship occasioned the first. While deciding to enter the Jesuits, he met a peer, John Deckers, who, according to Southwell, instantaneously became an intimate friend and, later, a brother Jesuit. Their bond provided consolation to the poet in the course of his life, but his immediate attraction to Deckers raised questions that Robert labored to answer for several years. The depth of feeling prompted by meeting the other man made Southwell anxious about the appropriateness of passion in religious life. Rejection caused the second crisis. Complicating the young Englishman's life was Deckers' acceptance into the Jesuits directly upon making application, while superiors several times deferred Southwell's own entrance for reasons that remain unclear. Four documents reflect these crises: a letter written to Deckers two years after they met; the *Querimonia*, or "The Complaint of Robert Southwell when, after Petitioning to Enter the Society of Jesus, He was for a Long Time Deferred"; the notes Southwell kept as a novice and scholastic, published as *Spiritual Exercises and Devotions*; and a biography believed by some scholars to have been written by Southwell. The biography's subject is Edward Throgmorton, who died days after professing vows as a Jesuit in 1582. In all of these works, the poet attempts to reconcile or manage various loves and loyalties, consolations and desolations, and successes and failures.

...

Meeting Deckers, a Belgian, marked a turning point in Southwell's life. For the first time, and on his own, he developed a significant relationship beyond relatives and their circle. This experience simultaneously caused exhilaration and apprehension, raising personal and religious problems that he would solve in piecemeal fashion. Southwell's biographers base their knowledge of his relationship with Deckers on a letter sent by Robert to his friend in October 1580 (Southwell *Unpublished Documents*, 298).[1] The poet is replying to a letter of Deckers' written at the conclusion of his noviceship in Naples. Southwell, ultimately accepted into the Society, was about to pronounce his first vows in Rome, taking the occasion to reassess their friendship from his perspective as a soon-to-be vowed religious. He interprets Deckers' letter as "an interposition of God's providence" because it arrived just when he was thinking about "how great a boon through God's favor [friendship] had been to us" (298). He resolves to write so as to see their relationship "fostered, revived and strengthened by mutual interchange of letters."[2] Southwell "recall[s] to [Deckers] some things, the remembrance of which may serve to inflame our hearts with a more ardent desire of serving [God]," beginning with "the opportunity God made use of as a means of drawing us together." Moreover, he wants to "briefly state what first induced me to disclose my inmost thoughts and intentions to you."

While articulating conventional spiritual themes, the letter contains traces of anxiety generated by the attraction between the two men; and both the Society of Jesus, in particular, and early modern society, in general, form the context for and contribute to this distress. In the letter and in his *Spiritual Exercises and Devotions*, Southwell seeks to reconcile his natural attraction to Deckers to the affective constraints imposed upon all men by society-at-large and by the Society of Jesus upon its members. Vexing his project is that both cultures, early modern and Jesuit, sent mixed signals about the appropriateness of love between men; and similarly confusing to readers centuries later is the difficulty of decoding these signals from our vantage point. Understanding Southwell's struggles in the context of the sixteenth century, and especially religious life in the sixteenth century, requires caution and an appreciation for alterity.

...

In his letter, Southwell reminds Deckers of their meeting. At Douai, Robert felt increasingly attracted to religious life, but could not decide between the Carthusians, which he names "the bark of Bruno," referring to the order's eleventh-century founder, and the Jesuits, to whom he felt called as a boy. He never explains his attraction to the Carthusians, and the fact that no two religious orders could be more different heightens the challenge of comprehending his inclination. Carthusian life is contemplative, with time divided between prayer and manual labor. The monks gather several times daily to chant the Office of the Church, but the rest of their day is spent alone. Monks live in separate cells, and each cell door has a *guichet*, or small window through which food is passed.[3] This is vastly different from the Jesuits' "daily order," if their social and flexible "way of proceeding" can be termed such. Jesuits, like most religious, lived together in communities, but they pointedly differed from the others in that their "'best house' was their 'pilgrimages' and their 'missions,' that is their journeying for ministry." "In these various ways," according to O'Malley, "Jesuits followed more closely the lifestyle of the early preachers of the Gospel— 'The Apostles did not wear a monastic habit ... They did not spend their time [in choir] chanting psalms and hymns'" (67). Finally, "the essence of the monk was to flee the company of other human beings," while "the essence of the Jesuit was to *seek* their company 'in order to help them'" (68).

Perhaps the monks appealed to Southwell on account of their history in England, as well as the heroism of English Carthusians during the Reformation. The first English charterhouse was founded in 1178, followed by nine more establishments prior to the suppression of the monasteries. Carthusians resisted the suppression, and three of them, John Houghton, Robert Lawrence and Augustine Webster, executed in 1535, count as protomartyrs of the English Reformation.[4] Their executions were reported throughout Europe, and their relics were prized possessions among English Catholics at home and abroad. Fifteen more monks died by hanging or starvation in Newgate prison before the order was revived under Queen Mary. On Mary's death, the monks were exiled, but the community kept together in various locations in the Low Lands.[5] On the Continent, the monks relocated several times, often, as did Southwell, ahead of advancing Protestant armies. After nine years in Bruges, they moved to Louvain in 1578, stopping briefly at Douai, where Robert possibly encountered them.

Southwell, raised in a former monastery, might have found their situation sympathetic, and considered entering this order as an act of atonement for his family's appropriation of monastic property. Several years later, however, he reviews this temporary affinity for the Carthusians and decides that God chose him for the Jesuits because of his "natural gifts." In fact, Southwell believes this is universally the case: "No other reason can be given [for one's vocation] but that God, to whom all things are open and clear, and to whom the frailty and courage of each one is manifest, has decided that one mode of life is suited to them, but another to us" (*Spiritual Exercises and Devotions*, 94). After noting how "God usually adapts himself to the present state of men," he describes how "God saw that the solitude, the austerity, the silence, the abstinence of the Carthusians and the rules of other religious communities were unsuitable to thy character and thy state of health; and therefore He wished to call thee to the Society so that whatever the duties or position assigned to thee in it, thou mightest have no difficulty to excuse thee from the diligent performance of thy task" (93).[6]

4.1 Engraving of Leonard Lessius, Professor and Spiritual Director at Douai (by courtesy of the Woodstock Theological Center Library, Georgetown University, Washington, D.C.)

God's call to Southwell was not immediately clear, however. Writing to Deckers, the poet recollects months of wavering between the two orders:

> While still uncertain about my vocation, I was tossed to and fro by various interior impulses, wavering between the bark of Bruno and that of Ignatius, yet was unable to reach either, being well-nigh drowned by the beating waves of temptation ... Thus beset by daily assaults and uncertain where to find a haven of safety, I began to be worn out by the incessant struggle. (*Unpublished Documents*, 298)

In this state, Southwell turned to his spiritual director, whom Devlin identifies as Fr. Columb, a Jesuit from Devonshire (30).

Most people in spiritual direction meet monthly with directors, but Southwell, given his predicament, saw Columb more often. He recounts in the letter how, "shaping a prudent course, I frequently sought the advice of my soul's physician." Columb, following Loyola's Rules for the Discernment of Spirits, urged constancy: "He, with repeated arguments, exhorted me to follow steadily my first vocation, which was to the Society." Columb responded in Ignatian fashion to what he perceived as desolation on Southwell's part, and Robert later applies this lesson when consoling recusants in the *Epistle of Comfort*. In the *Spiritual Exercises*, Loyola describes desolation as "darkness of soul, disturbance in it, ... the unquiet of different agitations and temptations, moving to want of confidence, without hope, without love, when one finds oneself all lazy, tepid, sad, and as if separated from his Creator and Lord" (317). When one is in desolation, Loyola suggests the advice Columb gave Southwell:

> In time of desolation [urge the exercitant] never to make a change; but to be firm and constant in the resolutions and determination in which he was in the proceeding consolation. Because as in consolation it is rather the good spirit who guides and counsels us, so in desolation it is the bad, with whose counsels we cannot take a course to decide rightly. (318)

Following his director's instruction, Southwell also asked for what he thought would be "the one and only remedy for his case." He wanted Columb to "introduce [him] to some one who had desires similar to [his], with whom [he] could converse freely and explain his ever-recurring difficulties" (*Unpublished Documents*, 299). Robert's request is classically Ignatian. He desires what Jesuits call "devout conversation." This practice provides another context, in conjunction with direction, for discerning the "movement of spirits" by attending to and articulating feelings. This is especially important when making an "election" or choosing a state in life, as was the case for Southwell. At such a time "the reasons of the heart have primacy":

> The clearest and most important instance in the text [of the *Exercises*] of this confidence in affective response, under the right conditions, occurs when the *Exercises* describe three ways in which one makes a good election. The first two are not by a reasoning process but by a special and peremptory inspiration or by attending to one's feelings of consolation or desolation when confronted with the alternatives of a choice. The third way, which consists to a large extent in weighing the pros and cons of one's alternatives, is to be used in conjunction with the second or when the second has not led to a clear choice. (O'Malley 42)

Southwell wants to discuss the reasons of his heart with a peer in the form of "devout conversation," a Jesuit custom dating from the order's foundation and one that becomes a feature of the poet's missionary work. The *Constitutions* count the practice among "the ministries of the word of God."[7] Moreover, Jeronimo Nadal "underscored its importance by interpreting it as the very origin of the Society":

> By such conversations Ignatius gathered his companions at Paris, and only afterward did he guide them through the *Spiritual Exercises*. In the general design of Jesuit pastoral practice, Nadal therefore saw them as often the first step. According to him they were a form of ministry of God's word but ... they differed from preaching and were more effective because through them one endeavored to enter gently and with love into the thoughts of a specific individual. (O'Malley 111)

At the originating point of his own vocation, Southwell desires to share his thoughts with a like-minded companion, and he asks his director for a conversation partner. In his letter to Deckers, he details what for him was a providential concurrence: "At the very time I was speaking to him, the Divine Goodness arranged that you should be walking about with Master Leonard [Lessius], you whom our Lord had destined to be a helper to me, His poor combatant." Columb, according to Southwell, plays spiritual matchmaker: "The Father (Confessor), pointing you out to me said: 'There is one who for a year or more has been burning with a zeal like yours to serve God, and who, unlike you, has never betrayed any sign of inconstancy.'"

...

Southwell's reaction to Deckers strikes twenty-first-century readers as extraordinary for its passionate enthusiasm: "Transported with sudden joy at these words, I felt relieved of all doubt, so that rarely, if ever afterwards, have I had any misgivings as to the certainty of my vocation to the Society." Nevertheless, Robert hesitated about approaching Deckers, and asked Columb to act as a go-between. In his own words, "Forthwith, impatient of delay, I strongly urged him to obtain straightaway your consent to be my spiritual friend." Columb, too, approaches Deckers indirectly, asking the permission of his spiritual director, the Jesuit Leonard Lessius.[8] During these negotiations, Southwell "spent the whole of that day in suspense between hope and fear; fear because of our different nationality and tongue, hope because of the conformity of our wills in the same holy purpose." Throughout the letter Robert couches his attraction to Deckers in religious terms, though the natural element in his response is always evident, sometimes threatening to overwhelm his spiritualization of the relationship. He has yet to learn that, according to Catholic thought, grace can build on nature, and in the letter he uncomfortably yokes the two realms together, on account of anxiety about the depth of his natural attraction.

When Deckers consents to a "rendezvous," Southwell claims to be a changed man. Even before they meet, he feels radically altered, and reaches for the imagery of light and darkness to convey his thoughts and feelings: "an entirely new aspect of things presented itself to me, such an unwonted light shone on my mind previously clouded in darkness, that the confident hope of winning your consent, seemed to heal all the wounds of my preceding conflict." The news "filled [him] with joy," and he grew impatient to "relish the taste of the honey presented to [him]" in the person of the Belgian. When the two met, they "disclosed to each other the desires and secrets of [their] hearts." After their initial conversation, presumably in Latin, "no friend was then so dear to John as Robert, none so dear to Robert as John."[9] Again, Southwell tries to frame this admission of attraction in spiritual terms: when they were together "no delight in this world seemed greater than to enter the Society." But in the very next lines he slips back into the language of infatuation, noting how "Not a day passed, not an opportunity was lost [and] whatever free time we could steal for conversation together seemed all too short."

The two young men encouraged each other in ascetical practices, "private chastisements of the flesh to afford delight, and discipline to please exceedingly." When Robert writes to his friend two years later, he hopes these recollections will help them "strive to perform more fervently now the exercises we then practiced." He fears that apart from each other they have lost their first enthusiasm for religious life, but such ascetical practices performed so vigorously by Deckers and Southwell on their bodies may also confirm anxiety about their relationship. Such force in applying physical penances as preparation for entering the Jesuits, in particular, is odd. Among contemporary religious orders, Jesuits were known and criticized for penitential moderation. For example, while the *Spiritual Exercises* recommend during the First Week penances such as fasting, sleep deprivation and even "sensible pain, which is given by wearing haircloth or cords or iron chains next to the flesh, by scourging or wounding oneself," the Jesuit attitude toward discipline was relatively temperate (Loyola *Spiritual Exercises* no. 86). After recommending penances as a way to "grieve for one's sins," Loyola adds this characteristic qualification: "What appears most suitable and most secure to penance is that the pain should be sensible in the flesh and not enter within the bones, so that it give pain and not illness." Practically speaking, this means "scourg[ing] oneself with thin cords, which give pain exteriorly, rather than in another way which would cause notable illness within."[10] Again, Loyola recommends these activities only during the First Week of the *Exercises*, which focuses on recognizing one's own sinfulness. In the Fourth Week of the *Exercises*, however, the matter for prayer, such as Christ's resurrection and the Contemplation to Gain Love, makes penance unsuitable. "In place of penance," Loyola writes, "let one regard temperance and all moderation" (no. 229).

In a letter to Portuguese Jesuits written in May 1547, Loyola is similarly prudent, instructing them to forgo excessive penances for the sake of their studies:

> Spiritual infirmities such as tepidity are caused, not only by chills but often by fevers, that is, by excessive zeal ... "Nothing in excess," said the philosopher ... If one fails to observe this moderation, he will find that good is turned into evil, and virtue is turned into vice. I know that these and other holy follies have been profitably used by the saints and that they are useful to obtain self-mastery and bring down richer graces upon us, ... But for one who has acquired some mastery over his self-love, I hold that what I have written about bringing oneself to the golden mean of discretion is the better thing, provided one does not withdraw from obedience. (*Counsels for Jesuits*, 21–22)[11]

In the *Constitutions* he writes specifically about penances for novices: "the measure which ought to be observed will be left to the discreet charity of the superior and of those whom he has delegated in his place, that they may adjust them in accordance with the disposition of the persons and with the edification of each and every one of them for divine glory" (no. 269). In other words, there were to be no communal penances, as practiced by other orders, and superiors should be diligent about their subjects' health. In this sensitivity, Loyola "recurred to the idea that the body was the gift of God and should be cared for as such" (O'Malley 342). This attitude incurred criticism. The Dominican theologian, Melchor Cano, for example, "believed that the Jesuits' ... neglect for bodily penance made them as dangerous in Spain as Luther was in Germany" (O'Malley 292).[12] In this context, the penitential practices of Southwell and Deckers stand out for their uncharacteristic severity. Southwell's letter omits whether their "private chastisements" were approved by their spiritual directors, but given Columb's tendency to observe other tenets of Ignatian spirituality, such approval would be idiosyncratic. The young men may be acting on their own in response to emotional discomfort to which Southwell elsewhere alludes.

Later in the letter, Robert expresses hope that he and Deckers will reunite in the afterlife, anticipating the humanistic heaven described in *An Epistle of Comfort*; but here the thought of eternity reminds him that he and Deckers are currently "prisoners in the darksome dungeon of the body." When released from their bodies they can safely be together again, and he tries to sound confident that this will be the case: "For if the desire to converse about God was the origin of our intimacy, if our single-hearted wish to serve him drew it forward, why should not the result of our common desires put the finishing touch to our friendship?" His desired confidence, though, is undermined by an ambiguity which he acknowledges near the letter's end:

> The charity, forsooth, which by the seal of the Holy Ghost was impressed upon us, as though in as second baptism at our entrance into the Society, so far from being at variance with true friendship, extinguishes any lurking affection rising from flesh and blood, while it fosters, increases and perfects that which comes from God. But lest my communication outgrow due bonds, I will draw to a close. (*Unpublished Documents*, 300)

This nebulous hope, that somehow religious vows will purify their relationship, signals some disquiet on the poet's part.

...

Looking back two years later, Southwell still seems uncomfortable about his attraction to Deckers, and several factors might have contributed to this feeling, factors that affect as well other early modern men, especially other sixteenth-century Jesuits. Scholarship on the history of sexuality and friendship shows that male relationships in the Renaissance, whether emotional, erotic or both, were vexing phenomena; and from the order's origins, Jesuits were of several minds on the issue of affection.[13] On the one hand, the first Jesuits cared deeply about one another and were not afraid to show it. John Carroll Futrell writes, for example, that after professing vows at Montmartre in 1534, this band of young men "felt bound together in a new intimacy of mutual love grounded in their identical self ideal":

> Laynez remembered that from this time forward, although they did not live together, they would eat in the rooms of one another, besides having frequent visits and conversations which "inflamed their hearts with ardor." In retrospect, he saw this mutual familiarity and communication and unflagging attention to one another's needs, both spiritual and temporal, as the human bond of union which maintained their companionship for the aid of souls. (24)

Conversely, Jesuits became early on exceedingly careful about giving scandal on account of their relationships. The *Constitutions* state bluntly, "what pertains to the vow of chastity does not require explanation, since it is evident how perfectly it should be preserved through the endeavor in this matter to imitate the angelic purity by the purity of the body and mind" (Loyola *Constitutions*, 547). During his noviceship Southwell studied the *Constitutions*, and O'Malley finds that "'certain sins intolerable in the Society,' a circumlocution probably indicating sexual misdeeds," was a frequent reason for dismissal from the Jesuits (57).[14] Given Robert's disappointment when the Jesuits deferred his application, he would be understandably anxious about the possibility of dismissal on any count.[15] O'Malley also notes that "Ignatius, Nadal and others offered standard counsel on how to deal with temptations to lust" (348). Among these counsels are Loyola's 1555 "Rules of Modesty," or "Rules of Deportment," concerning looking or gazing at others. The second rule, for example, states that "[f]or the most part they should keep their eyes down, neither immodestly lifting them up, nor casting them now one way nor another." This same attention to gazing is expressed in a letter from Loyola to a young Jesuit named Emerio De Bonis. From Padua, De Bonis wrote to Loyola about temptations against chastity. In his reply, Loyola recommends several remedies:

> Besides your prayer, make it a point not to look at anyone fixedly in the face, which might cause you an uneasiness of heart. In general, when you deal with the neighbor, let your eyes be averted, and try not to think of this one or that one as handsome or ugly, but rather as the image of the

most Holy trinity, as a member of Christ and bathed in His blood. Moreover, do not become familiar with anyone. It will be enough if, in school, you fulfill your task in pure charity and obedience ... Also be on guard against those times and occasions when you are usually attacked. Briefly raise your mind to God. And above all, make a real effort to abide in His presence, frequently recalling that His Infinite Wisdom is present both to the inner and exterior man. There is no need to multiply remedies if you make faithful use of these. And do not forget the first, which concerns the eyes. You will, then, never complain with him who says: *my eyes cause me my grief* (Lamentations 3:51). (*Counsels for Jesuits*, 116–17)

Moreover, Jesuits "were not to show fraternal affection for each other by embracing, except upon departure for a journey or returning from one" (O'Malley 348). On journeys, Jesuits were also urged to be cautious about improprieties or occasions for them. Contrary to the custom of the time, when traveling, Jesuits never shared beds, even though this incurred extra expenses. Southwell knew and tried to observe these cautions, and he understood, as well, the sensitivities that gave rise to them. Jesuits and other religious needed to be vigilant about expressing affections against the background of Reformation polemics, and certain strains in Catholic spirituality also increased their wariness.

...

The Jesuits inherited from earlier Christian writers some of their ambivalence about personal relationships, and the circumstances in which the Society was founded, riddled by denominational vituperations fueled by charges of clerical promiscuity, aggravated the issue. The history of attitudes toward close or "particular" friendships between religious is long and contradictory. As Donald Goergen notes, "there is [in Christianity] a pluralism of theologies of friendship" (169), and he traces this pluralism to scripture. In John's Gospel, for example, Jesus models intimacy with his disciples, calling them friends (*philos*), as opposed to servants (*doulos*) (15:15). In Goergen's assessment, the Johannine teaching is that "true friendship is simply a love greater than which there cannot be" (166). Early commentators on religious life, however, did not hold friendship in high regard. For example, Cassian, a fifth-century writer, wanted monks to be wholly concerned with spiritual realities. The monk, according to Cassian, is not to seek anything, including friendship, beyond the Kingdom of God. Because he understood human intimacy as unworthy of religious, Cassian forbade monks to seek one another's company, to go off together, or to hold hands.[16]

As religious life evolved, others expressed opposite opinions on the matter. Aelred of Rievaulx, a twelfth-century Cistercian, defended friendship between religious. He produced a treatise *De Spirituali Amicitia*, according to which friendship between monks is both a result of human effort and a gift from God. He first distinguishes between Christian charity, which ought to extend to all people, and friendship: "Both enemies and friends are included in the former, while to those only to whom we entrust our heart and inmost thought, do we give the name of friend" (*Of Spiritual Friendship*, 18). Then he argues that friendships are necessary to authentic and fulfilling religious life. "There can be no genuine happiness," he argues, "without a friend." According to Aelred, "the man who has no one to feel glad of his success or to sympathize with him in sorrow, no one to whom he might pour out the perturbations of his mind, or with whom he might share such luminous thoughts as may come to him, that man can be likened to a beast" (29). Finally, Aelred ascribes a mystical quality to friendships, using language associated with marriage: "When a friend enters your life, you so unite your life to his as to become, in effect, one from two. You entrust yourself to him as another self. You neither hide nor fear anything from him" (47).[17]

Fear about friendships, however, resurfaced among early modern spiritual writers. Responding to real or imagined clerical licentiousness, otherwise humane writers, such as Francis de Sales, forbade intimacy in religious life. In his *Introduction to the Devout Life* de Sales warns against particular friendships:

> Let him absolutely curtail all particular familiarity, all private conversation, amorous looks, smiles, and, in general, all sorts of communication and allurement, which may nourish this shameful, smouldering fire. At most, if he must speak to another party, let it be only to declare, with a bold, short and serious protestation, the eternal divorce that he has sworn. I call upon everyone who has fallen into these wretched snares: Cut them! Break them! Tear them! Do not divert yourself in unraveling these criminal friendships; you must tear and rend them asunder. Do not untie the knots, but break or cut them. (128)

De Sales and other Catholic leaders were acutely sensitive to charges of sexual misconduct leveled against religious by Protestant propagandists. His reaction is typically defensive.

Such writers grasped a point that Alan Stewart makes in *Close Readers: Humanism and Sodomy in Early Modern England*. Commenting on the line, "Within the bownes of Sodomye/ Doth dwell the spirytuall clergy," from John Bale's *A Comedy concernynge thre lawes, of Nature.*

Moses, and Christ, corrupted by the Sodomytes, Pharisees & papystes most wicked, Stewart observes that Bale "was merely reiterating what had become a commonplace ... association between sodomy and the 'spiritual clergy,' the clerics in holy orders" (xv). "For centuries," Stewart continues, "they had provided a convenient target for accusations of sodomitical practices: the closed monastic houses, the vows of chastity, the segregation of the sexes, and the communal sleeping arrangements were all easy prey for anyone wishing to mock or attack the church's institutions" (xv). Bale's play, and more than a dozen others very much like it, advocated the suppression of the monasteries under Henry VIII. For instance, in *Thre Lawes*, the character Sodomy dresses as a monk in order to recruit audiences' sympathies away from monastic orders and to the Crown's policy.

Alan Bray considers this same topic in his groundbreaking book *Homosexuality in Renaissance England*. Commenting on the popular myth of the Popish Sodomite, Bray cites authors who declare the papacy itself to be "a second Sodom," "a new Sodom,"[18] "Sodom Fair,"[19] and nothing but "a cistern full of sodomy."[20] Clerical celibacy well-suited those who made such charges. Bray references the Scottish travel writer, William Lithgow, reporting, "Lo there is the chastity of the Romish priests, who forsooth may not marry and yet may miscarry themselves in all abominations, especially in sodomy, which is their continual pleasure and practice" (306–307).[21] "But it was the Jesuits above all," Bray claims, "who came to embody in popular mythology the identification of popery with homosexuality." "Were they not its open advocates?" he asks, quoting lines from John Marston's *The Scourge of Vilanie*, a satire attacking "falsed, seeming, Patriotes" returning from "Doway seminary," the "source of Sodom vilanie" in England "tainting our townes, and hopeful academes."[22]

In light of such accusations, Jesuits operating in the English context had good reasons to be sensitive about how critics perceived their relationships. In his *Spiritual Exercises and Devotions* Southwell acknowledges his awareness of these perceptions, some justified, concerning corrupt clergymen. He considers "what great harm has come to the Christian Commonwealth through the unworthiness ... of religious." As a result, he feels a special sense of responsibility for maintaining a reputation that is above suspicion. "The position now," he writes, "is that unless other religious by the holiness and innocence of their lives make up for the faults of their predecessors, ... the fire of heresy will very soon burst out, fed by the fuel of their scandals and vices." Since "others by their wickedness have branded the Catholic faith with a mark of shame," Southwell believes that Jesuits "must strive with all [their] strength to cleanse it from its ignominy and to restore it to its pristine glory" (107). His attraction to Deckers, however, may have shaken his convictions and compounded his emotional confusion.

...

As noted above, readers should exercise caution in assessing attractions and attachments between early modern men. For example, critics such as Alan Bray, Alan Stewart and Bruce Smith distinguish between charges of sexual misconduct leveled at institutions and the labeling of any individual as homosexual or any relationship as homoerotic. According to Bray, "to talk of an individual in this period as being or not being a 'homosexual' is an anachronism and ruinously misleading" (16). Moreover, "the terms in which we now speak of homosexuality cannot readily be translated into those of the sixteenth and seventeenth centuries." Therefore, "we need to carry our preconceptions lightly if we are to see in Renaissance England more than the distorted image of ourselves" (17). Bruce Smith concurs in *Homosexual Desire in Shakespeare's England*: "On one point of knowledge we need to be absolutely clear: in the sixteenth and seventeenth centuries, sexuality was not, as it is for us, the starting point of anyone's self definition" (11). "The essential fact about homosexuality," Smith continues, "was that it had no place in the Elizabethan world picture" (11).[23]

Nevertheless, Smith discovers "a startling ambiguity," which renders intelligible Southwell's anxiety-ridden feelings for Deckers. "The one salient fact about homosexuality in early modern England," he argues, "is the disparity that separates the extreme punishments prescribed by law and the apparent tolerance, even positive valuation of homoerotic desire in visual arts, in literature, and ... in the political power structure" (13–14). Smith suggests that there were opposing "scripts" for acting out male–male relationships in the period and that "competition between these modes of discourse was sharp" (56). On the one hand, "juridico-political and moral discourse" expressed absolute terror and intolerance on the subject of homosexuality. "The Renaissance moralists," Smith contends, "saw only chaos beyond the perfectly ordered heterosexual world of Christian dogma" (20). On the other hand, "literary, poetic and imaginative discourse" offered "a range of myths and models for articulating homosexual desire" (20). This was especially true, he points out, of classical literature, which constituted the curriculum at Douai. Southwell, caught between these two behavioral scripts, turns to literary models in expressing and managing his feelings. These models grant him license to explore the affective energy generated by meeting Deckers. As Smith observes, "poetic discourse can reflect much more accurately than moral discourse or legal discourse the inconsistencies or conflicts that are a fact of human social life" (56).

Southwell's position as an aspiring Jesuit compounded his need to explore via literary language the conflicting and seemingly dangerous emotions that surfaced at Douai. If Smith is correct that "the all-male power structure of sixteenth and seventeenth century society fostered male bonds above all other emotional ties," then such bonds would be even more privileged—and potentially destabilizing—in the exclusively all-male environment of a Jesuit school or community. "In any male dominated society," according to Eve Kosovfsky Sedgwick, "there is a special relationship between male homosocial (*including* homosexual) desire and the structures for maintaining and transmitting patriarchal power: a relationship founded on an inherent and potentially active structural congruence." "For historical reasons," Sedgwick claims, "this special relationship may take the form of ideological homophobia, ideological homosexuality, or some highly conflicted but intensively structured combination of the two" (*Between Men*, 25).[24]

In working out his own highly conflicted emotions, Southwell, in his letter to Deckers, seems to have relied on classical texts such as Cicero's *De Amicitia*, which was assigned to third-form students in Jesuit schools (Beales 133). In mining Cicero's text for style and content, Southwell was in good company, as humanists characteristically prized this treatise for providing a useful discourse of male–male relationships.[25] As Jonathan Goldberg notes, "the relationships between men which humanism claimed to forge and maintain were expressed in ... a rhetoric of intense emotional affect, which by the standards of the late twentieth century can often appear to be romantic, even erotic" (xxxiv). *De Amicitia* served for many as the font of this rhetoric.[26]

In the treatise Cicero records the feelings of Laelius for his recently deceased friend, Scipio, and his conversation concerns the ethical responsibilities incumbent upon friends.[27] Initially, Cicero is interested in the development of relationships, and from his own description Southwell's first feelings for Deckers sound strikingly similar to those of Laelius for Scipio. Laelius depicts "the springing up of a like feeling of love when one finds someone of manners and character congenial with our own, who becomes dear to us because we seem to see in him an illustrious example of probity and virtue" (24).[28] Likewise, Southwell's astonishment over his reaction to Deckers mirrors that of Laelius for Scipio: "what wonder is it when the minds of men are moved to affection when they behold the virtue and goodness of those with whom they can become intimately united" (25). Southwell's use of light imagery in describing Deckers' effect on him is also found in Cicero's text. Describing how "virtue both forms and preserves friendships," Cicero characterizes the discovery of friendship as an illumination: "When it has put itself forth and shown its light, and it has seen and recognized that same light in another, it draws near to that light and receives in return what the other has to give; and it is from this intercourse that love, or friendship—call it what you will—is kindled" (69).

Laelius also anticipates Southwell's depiction of the evolution of his feelings for Deckers. "Virtue attracts friendship," he says, and "since virtue attracts friendship, if there shines forth any manifestation of virtue with which a mind similarly disposed can come into contact and union, from such intercourse love must of necessity spring" (39). The reason for such love, according to the treatise, is that "nothing gives more delight than the interchange of friendly cares and offices" (39). Cicero's text also provides both a religious and a philosophical defense of friendship, arguing that it is a divine gift and that the capacity for it separates men from other creatures. Cicero acknowledges that some philosophers, like some later Christian writers, contend that intimate friendships should be avoided. "Yet," he responds, "if emotion be eliminated, what difference is there … not between a man and a brute, but between a man and a rock, or the trunk of a tree, or any inanimate object?" (38). "It is like taking the sun out of the world," he argues, "to bereave human life of friendship, than which the immortal gods have given man nothing better, nothing more gladdening" (37). Even setting the gods aside, according to Cicero, we need friends on account of our nature: "Thus nature has no love for solitude, and always leans, as it were on some support, and the sweetest support is found in the most intimate friendship." As a result, the Roman concludes, "as to those between whom there is, or has been, or shall be such an alliance, the fellowship is to be regarded as the best and happiest possible, in as much as it leads to the highest good that nature can bestow" (58). Southwell would find this argument congenial, since he wants to prove that his relationship with Deckers is conducive to personal and spiritual growth. Moreover, Cicero's text allows for relationships generated by external appearances. "To the requisites [of goodness and wisdom] there may be added," according to Laelius, "suavity of speech and manners, which is of no little worth as giving a relish to the intercourse of friendship" (50).

But *De Amicitia*, like Southwell's letter, also worries about the limits of friendship. After noting how a friend can be "another self" (57), Cicero warns that "those are in fatal error who think that in friendship there is free licence for all lusts and evil practices." "Friendship is given by nature," he points out, "not as a companion of the vices, but as a helper of the virtues, that, as solitary virtue might not be able to attain the summit of excellence, united and associated with another it might reach that eminence" (58). As noted, wariness about transgressing the boundaries of friendship colors Southwell's letter, and the same caution surfaces in his *Spiritual Exercises and Devotions*. After entering the Society, Southwell appears increasingly anxious about improper affections, and his novitiate notes hint that he is mostly unsuccessful in resolving the tension. In fact, as a novice and a newly professed Jesuit he moves away from the script made available by Cicero, taking refuge instead in the moralistic language of traditional piety; and this move is understandable in light of the fact that the poet's earliest efforts to enter the Society were frustrated.

...

The scrupulosity regarding affections that informs Southwell's *Spiritual Exercises and Devotions* needs to be read in light of the dejection expressed in his *Querimonia*. After the Jesuits initially reject him, Southwell compensates upon his admission by setting the highest standards for himself and keeping strict account of his failures, among which are frequent temptations to inordinate attractions. The *Querimonia*, written after the Jesuits deferred his application, contains the reasons why Jesuit superiors were reluctant to admit him to the noviceship. It is an exceedingly immature response to rejection, and the qualities which Southwell exhibits therein would account for the postponement of his entrance. Robert was seventeen years old when he applied to the order, which was not unusual at the time. The Jesuit *Constitutions* set the minimum age for entering at fourteen (Loyola *Constitutions*, 160), and during Loyola's generalship 37 percent of men accepted to the Society were between the ages of sixteen and twenty, and 10 percent were younger still (*Constitutions* ed. Ganss, 130–31). Southwell's age does not explain his rejection. But elsewhere the *Constitutions* catalogue other requirements for entrance, some of which Southwell lacks if he is judged on the basis of the *Querimonia*.

According to O'Malley, "the Jesuits were especially concerned with the character and emotional maturity of those who wanted to join them" (56). A related quality, good judgment, was also "recognized as especially necessary in the Jesuit, who almost by definition would often find himself on his own, far removed from his brethren and superiors, in new, strange and difficult situations" (81). The *Constitutions* bear this out. After urging those charged with accepting members to the Society to be "very moderate in [their] desire to admit," Ignatius lists reasons for rejecting candidates. He repeatedly notes the lack of qualities such as "discretion" (*Constitutions*, 154]. Superiors should also turn away men who exhibit "passions that seem uncontrollable" (179), as well as those who "practice indiscreet devotions" (182) or "lack judgment" (184). Finally, he proposes postponing admission in cases where applicants lack constancy (156; 193).

Southwell's inability to choose between the Jesuits and the Carthusians provided evidence that he lacked constancy in his vocation, as his spiritual director pointed out. The *Querimonia* reveals that he was also deficient in other qualities. In the interest of hagiography, however, earlier readers downplayed this document's disclosures. Foley, for example, states that Robert's acceptance was postponed "on account of his extreme youth," and he describes the *Querimonia* as a "pious lamentation" (*Jesuits in Conflict*, 304). He also quotes Henry More who claims that the text "afford[s] the pious reader some idea of the ardent flames of heavenly love which burned in that youthful breast, and the effusions which so tender a pen was enabled, by the grace of the Holy Spirit to pour forth" (305). Christobel Hood describes it as "a lengthy and finely written lament," and Janelle calls it a "beautiful" text in which Southwell expressed his "deep sorrow" (24). According to Devlin, "the lyric ardor" of the piece is "obvious," but he minimalizes its importance, claiming that "it throws only a little light on the conflict that was taking place" (28). In actuality, as Brownlow notes, "the Jesuits thought the teenaged Southwell immature and excitable," and the *Querimonia* confirms their judgment.

As in later works, Robert uses biblical typology to situate himself in relation to God and, in this case, to the Society of Jesus. He casts himself as Agar, the Egyptian maid of Sarah, wife of the patriarch Abraham. In Genesis 6, Agar, or Hagar, becomes Abraham's second wife and pregnant with his child. Southwell manipulates the facts in the story. For him the point is that Sarah, unable to bear children and envious of her maid, deals so harshly with Agar that she flees into the wilderness. The poet finds himself in a similar place emotionally. In Genesis an angel visits Agar, announcing that she will bear a son to be named Ishmael. In Southwell's version, she already has the child before going into exile, and he is "dying of thirst" because his mother is "devoid of all means of succoring him." Southwell heightens the pathos in order to compare his sorrow at being rejected by the Jesuits to that of a mother watching her infant die: "Agar had not so much cause for weeping over her misery as I have at my calamity." The maid has merely been exiled from the tents of Abraham, while he, Robert, is "an exile from a place as far surpassing the house of Abraham in dignity as a body does a shadow, or truth a fiction." In this set of hyperbolic comparisons, himself to Agar and the Society of Jesus to the place where God revealed himself to the father of faith, Southwell establishes the *Querimonia*'s arguments and tone. Throughout the text he uses spousal images to explain his own case, and he describes the Jesuits in preposterously exalted terms.

To his credit, he admits that he bears the blame for his suffering, confessing, "I have erred from the mark at which I aimed." His error, he thinks, amounts to ingratitude and tardiness, and there is some irony involved. He describes how Jesus labored to conquer him in "a two-fold combat." First, when the Son "assaulted" him by "holy inspirations," Southwell resisted. Christ won by "assail[ing] the bulwarks of [Southwell's] heart" with "fresh batteries." But after this initial victory, and just as the poet resigns to enter the Jesuits, Christ plays something of a cruel trick on him. Through Jesuit superiors, the Saviour prevents Southwell from joining the order. "Now," Robert complains, "do I pay the due penalty of my past ingratitude; and rejected from the dignity of thy espousals and fallen to the condition of a miserable captive, too late I weep my past folly and fruitlessly mourn the tardiness of my assent." Southwell's interpretation of events strikes a discordant theological note. Jesus, in his mind, is vindictive. He exiles the young Englishman "to a winter world," where he is "daily tossed about amid the waves of carnal desires, and dashed against the rocks of occasions of sin." If, in the interviews prescribed for those applying to the Society, Southwell articulated such an image of God, superiors justifiably postponed his entrance and encouraged him to more prayer and further religious studies.

Similarly immature is Southwell's unrealistic understanding of Jesuit life. While superiors would want to admit novices who are enthusiastic about the order's works, the poet seeks in the Jesuits mainly a refuge from the world. Upon rejection from the Society, he bids farewell to the "heavenly delights" supposedly enjoyed by Jesuits, "wherewith [Christ's] lambs are fed in the pastures of [His] Society":

> Farewell sweetest savor of devotion which Thou dost pour out into their breasts, and sprinkling their hearts with the choicest dew of heavenly consolation, dost excite delightful tears, the tokens of supernatural consolations. These favors are not communicated to aliens, they are the privileges of souls admitted to the inner chamber of the King: now feeding on the spiritual delights of Paradise, then resting upon the couch of love they take a repose that transcendeth all delights. What budding germs of perfection, what flowers of grace, what abundance of happiness is found in these pastures! Happy souls that are both loved, and love! ... Even as innocent babes in their cradles do you securely rest.

Again, if those charged with admitting Southwell detected that he was looking for love and security, they wisely made him wait before joining their ranks. The poet, away from home and family for several years, might understandably want the asylum and ready companionship which Jesuit life appeared to supply; but from the Jesuits' perspective this desire was not a compelling reason to accept him. Jesuits wanted to recruit *"quamplurimi et quam aptissimi"*—as many as possible of the very best—for the sake of the Society's burgeoning apostolates which were increasingly located in distant and often dangerous places (O'Malley 55). The first generations of Jesuits understood that the Society of Jesus did not exist to meet the affective needs of its members; members existed to meet the apostolic needs of the Society. According to the *Constitutions*:

> The Charity and zeal for souls in which this Society exerts itself according to the purpose of its Institute embrace all kinds of persons, to serve and help them in the Lord of all men to attain beatitude. Nevertheless, when there is a question of incorporating persons into the same Society, that charity and zeal should embrace only those who are judged useful for the end it seeks. (Loyola *Constitutions*, 163)

Southwell does not express in the *Querimonia* a desire to be useful. Instead, he wants to be provided for. He imagines a Society which "presents the full breasts of celestial nourishment to its babes" and "feeds those who are in progress with more solid food," until it ultimately "fortifies the perfect with invincible constancy." Deprived of such sustenance, "doubts of salvation agitate his soul," and such agitation, a classic symptom of desolation, would have been reason enough for the Jesuits to defer him.

The *Querimonia*, filled with exaggerated notions about the Society, likewise serves as an occasion for Southwell to inflate his identity or theatrically bemoan his lack thereof. He represents himself alternately as Christ's intended spouse, his "widow," "his divorced wife," and an "abortion," casting himself in several of these roles in a single sentence. "Remember, O Lord, that already the appointed day of my espousals has passed," he writes, "and I, as yet a widower, am looked down upon by all, and abandoned by Thyself am despised as an abortion." This last and most disturbing image expresses the poet's death wish, which works as a kind of ultimatum. He wants Christ to bring about his acceptance into the Jesuits or let him die:

> Who could wonder if my very soul, oppressed by grief, should attempt to migrate from so dire a tomb, that it may be dissolved and be with Christ? ... I will patiently bear to be rejected by man; but I count not that the

greatest evil. I fear lest these kalends denote a heavier punishment in store, and since I languish with perpetual expectation—an expectation more bitter than death that lessens not, but aggravates my languishing, and while the body, through the grief of the afflicted soul, must succumb, what remains for me to desire, but that my Christ would deliver me from this miserable prison?

There is no evidence that Southwell ever showed this text to anyone. Had he done so, it is unlikely that he would have ever been admitted to the noviceship. And it is telling that he needed to move to Rome before superiors there, who did not know him as well as his teachers at Douai, accepted him into the Society. But if he revealed his immaturity and "uncontrollable passions" in the *Querimonia*, he also soon exhibited tenacity in traveling far to pursue the vocation he was now so certain of. Despite opposition, he walked across Europe to make application in person at the Jesuit headquarters in Rome.

...

Reliable information about Southwell's move to Rome is hard to uncover. Foley thinks he set out for Rome with Deckers, but evidence proves that the latter entered the novitiate at Naples. Moreover, in a letter of 27 September 1580 to Southwell, Deckers remembers his friend's impatience to make the trip compared to his own caution at the time. Deckers had already entered the novitiate once, at Tournai on 25 May 1578, but in three weeks' time anti-Catholic violence struck the city, and on 3 June the novices were sent away for their own safety. After that, the Belgian's desire to re-enter the Jesuits waned for a time. Southwell, notwithstanding the despair expressed in the *Querimonia*, became more determined to press his case at Rome. Two years later Deckers writes to Robert, still curious about his friend's resolve:

> I beseech you, how came it about that we so like in age were so unlike in generosity ... I cannot conceal my insane error. Truly, I wonder at it. Why were you so impatient of delay, why did you trample underfoot all those values which cause worldly men to hesitate, oblivious of your homeland, your parents, your colleagues, not to mention your costly property? You answered: I am hastening without delay whither my vocation urges me. (Devlin 34)

Whether Deckers overestimates his friend's zeal and indifference is difficult to determine. As Janelle suggests, Southwell may not have had much choice in the matter. While the trip to Rome was "a thrilling journey indeed," "perhaps it was not such a self-willed affair as some biographers would suggest." "It was probably decided," Janelle reports, "that some of the most brilliant pupils at Paris or Douai would be sent to the Roman College for the completion of their studies or for their novitiate, and that they should travel in a batch" (21). According to Devlin, this "batch" included four other Englishmen: Matthew Marshall, a relation of Southwell's; two brothers, Harwood and Nicholas Smith; and Edmund Holt, already a priest and a distinguished scholar. Given Holt's status, his acceptance to the Jesuits was assured. Robert, however, took a substantial risk, and one that did not prove immediately fruitful.

Southwell moved into the English College, as opposed to the Jesuit novitiate, upon his arrival in Rome. This College, to which he will return as a Jesuit tutor and Prefect of Studies, was a residence for men from England and Wales, many of whom were preparing for priesthood. It was also a hotbed of nationalist tensions into which the poet will eventually get swept up. As he arrived, a fight between the English and Welsh residents was already underway, involving one of Southwell's relatives. Devlin reports that his grand-uncle, Sir Richard Shelley, "*doyen* of the English colony," was quarreling with a Welshman, Archdeacon Owen Lewis, over the exploits of the Marquis Thomas Stucley. Stucley, who began his career as a Protestant pirate but later converted to Catholicism, was planning an invasion of Ireland. Shelley questioned the wisdom of the plan and was about to be imprisoned by the Inquisition on account of his objections until Robert Persons intervened on his behalf.[29] The tension between Shelley and Lewis spread among the two national groups at the College and was a harbinger of differences to come, differences which Southwell will try to reconcile.

How long Robert remained at the English College and what he did there is not clear. According to Janelle, "the young man thought that upon reaching Rome, he would immediately be allowed to join the Society, but he was again disappointed." Janelle quotes earlier biographies to prove that "at Rome, so that his youth might be tried, and his constancy somewhat proved, hopes were held out to him of obtaining that admission into the Society which he was seeking; but the fulfillment was somewhat put off, and a further period of study prescribed" (23). A letter from Persons to Campion, then stationed in Prague, notes that by the time he entered the Jesuits, Southwell had finished a significant portion of his studies:

> We are here at Rome now twenty-four Englishmen of the Society, whereof five have entered within this month: one named Mr. Holt which was once of Oriel College master of arts; and the other four came hither

from Paris, all excellent towardly youths, and all have ended the courses
of philosophia. (Persons *Letters and Memorials*, 2)

Perhaps Southwell completed this work while living at the College.
However, once he entered the novitiate at San Andrea al Quirinale, his
activities and attitudes are readily known on account of Jesuit documents
and his own *Spiritual Exercises and Devotions.*

The novitiate was already hallowed for having housed one saint,
Stanislas Kostka, a young Polish nobleman, who, like Southwell, walked to
Rome to join the Jesuits in the face of opposition.[30] He suffered greatly
from his travels and died in 1568 after spending only ten months in the
novitiate. During that time, though, his pious reputation spread throughout
Rome. Eyewitness accounts at his beatification in 1605 tell how "he
devoted himself so completely to spiritual things that he frequently became
unconscious." Francis Borgia, then Superior General, reports that at his
death "the entire city proclaimed him a saint" (Farrel *AHSJ* 6, 637).

The piety modeled by Kostka, and to which Southwell ambitions,
also fills a contemporaneous biography of a young Englishman, Edward
Throgmorton, which may have been written by Robert. Throgmorton also
died shortly after professing vows as a Jesuit, and his life was compiled for
the edification of other novices and to recruit young men to the order. As
Foley notes, "the point of its authorship lies between Father Robert
Southwell and Father Alphonsus Agazari, the rector of the English College,
Rome" (*Records* VI, 288).[31] In either case, the short work reveals the kind
of rectitude to which Southwell aspired and, if in fact he is the author, it
exposes more about his anxieties. As Foley explains, Throgmorton was
"distinguished for his high birth and for perfection in every kind of virtue
requisite for constituting a saintly youth, one who left behind him a model
for all future comers from England to that College" (288). The work opens
by emphasizing the "ancient" rank of Throgmorton's family from which he
inherited his virtue (290). As observed elsewhere, this class-consciousness
was a regular feature in works by Southwell and other Catholic apologists.
Throgmorton's pedigree contradicts claims by the English government that
the Jesuits were attracting society's dregs.

Throgmorton's parents sound much like Southwell's. His father
was made the President or Chief Justice of Wales by Queen Mary, during
whose reign he "was a most vigorous champion of the Catholics." Once
Elizabeth gained the throne, however, "following the evil example of
nobles and persons of rank ... he yielded to the time, and lived for a long
period in schism, cut off from the perfect unity of the Church." The author
is quick to note, though, that "still in heart and will he retained an
inclination to the piety and devotion in which he had been educated, and

was so far from becoming a persecutor, that on the contrary, he permitted priests and missionaries to frequent his house, nay, they thought themselves nowhere safer than under the shadow of his roof and the protection of his patronage and authority" (291). Edward's mother, like Southwell's, showed "invincible constancy in the Catholic faith." Throgmorton's parents are typical of many Englishmen who entered the Jesuits, and Southwell could certainly identify with him.

From his parents, Edward acquired great affection for Catholic clergymen. In a chapter entitled "His Faith and Zeal for Souls Even in Boyhood," readers learn that, like Southwell who was called "Fr. Robert" as a boy, Edward early on imagined himself as a priest. "In short," according to the biography, "so devoted was he to priests and sacred things, that while others were whiling away their time with play or gossip, his delight, if he had the chance, was to sit in a room with a priest talking of pious things, and particularly of Holy Orders, to which he had already in his heart dedicated himself" (298).

The romantic aura that appealed to Southwell when he read the Jesuit *Relations* also colors Throgmorton's youth. For example, the boy's departure from England is described in histrionic terms:

> As soon as the report got abroad that Edward had been summoned by his parents with a view to his being sent over shortly to France, it was wonderful how many of his old schoolfellows, and of the common people and gentry, assembled, both to bid farewell to the object of their singular esteem, and congratulate him on his departure to a Catholic country. What tears started to the eyes of relations; what lamentations there were of servants, male and female; what weeping and grief of all! Each one bewailed the great loss which he foresaw he would suffer by the departure of Edward; and, as though about to be deprived forever of one whom they held so dear, they accompanied him on his way as if in a funeral procession, with many sad tokens of their deep affection.

This funereal reference is the first of several in the biography, and they culminate in Edward's own prediction of his early death. The author regards his ability to make this forecast as yet another sign of special virtue, and whenever death crosses Edward's mind, the author notes how he is well prepared. For example, the captain of the ship taking Edward to France worries about his passenger when they encounter rough weather. Instead of the captain consoling the boy, however, Edward comforts him: "there is, therefore, no reason why my danger should give you so much unquietness, for, come what may, thanks to God I feel my mind quite ready for it" (300).

A more remarkable aspect of Edward's death, though, is that he asks permission before dying. In the chapter, "His Singular Virtues, and Especially Obedience," the author emphasizes how "he strove so hard to break his will that as often as he had an opportunity he would ask leave even about the least things, and though the superior's permission was not required for them, he still did not let slip the occasion of conquering himself, and of ascertaining with more certainty the good pleasure of the divine will, which he always recognized in the voice of the superior" (309). "In fine," he continues, "Edward was advanced to such a high degree of virtue, that he was unwilling to depart even to the glory of heavenly bliss without first obtaining his superior's consent" (311). This episode exemplifies what early Jesuits hoped would be a hallmark of their order: perfect or "blind" obedience (Loyola *Constitutions*, 547). Edward and his biographer were well aware of the emphasis Ignatius places on obedience in the *Constitutions*. "All should keep their resolution firm to observe obedience," Loyola writes, "and to distinguish themselves in it, not only in matters of obligation but also in the others, even though nothing else is perceived except the inclination of the superior's will without an expressed command" (547). Southwell's *Spiritual Exercises and Devotions* manifest his own desire to attain such an attitude, and if he authored Throgmorton's biography, then he projects on to his subject an attribute that eluded him.

Edward seemed perfect in the practice of other virtues as well. For example, the author underscores his humility, especially regarding his family's preeminence. "He measured no man by the obscurity of his condition or family," according to the biographer, "and notwithstanding his own high birth he never claimed any more consideration for himself in the college on that account" (Foley *Records* VI, 311). Southwell, who admits in his diary entries that he struggled against the temptation of "singularity," would envy Throgmorton's self-abnegation.

The work does record, though, that some of Throgmorton's peers found so much perfection irritating, and one wonders if Southwell did not share their perceptions on account of the glimpses he allows into the underside of college life. The author notes that some students "accused [Throgmorton] of vainglory in seeking after the applause or goodwill of Superiors under a false pretense of piety" (311). Of course, he adds that when such accusations were made, Edward "betrayed no signs of anger, but maintained his usual serenity of countenance and speech, rather accusing himself by his silence than entering into any explanation of his real motives." Other students also referred to Edward as "the Innocent" on account of the "purity of his mind" and the fact that "the integrity of his body was such that ... he had kept it unsullied and had vowed that he would keep it so for the future." There might be room to read into Throgmorton's nickname some youthful teasing, and the same might be true of an anecdote regarding Edward's behavior on holiday. "On vacation days," the author recounts, "[wh]en the students went out to the country, and were engaged in general conversation, according to the bent of their minds, he, that he might combine relaxation and devotion, used to sing pious hymns with an expression of devotion that sometimes drew tears from his companions" (314).

Perhaps Southwell could not resist the ambiguity here, allowing readers to imagine the incredulous reaction of Edward's peers. If this is the case, then he regrets it later. He devotes an entry in the *Spiritual Exercises and Devotions* to "The Desire of Being Thought Amusing," urging himself to "take care not to be carried away by the desire of popularity with the rest of the brethren and ... not wish to be considered an agreeable companion or to have the talent of keeping others amused or of acting cleverly or speaking wittily." Such a tendency so worries Southwell that he continues to chastise himself about it: "All this comes from pride and is most displeasing to superiors, for it opens the way to violation of the rules and to dissipation of all kinds, as experience has shown in those who indulge in this kind of thing and as each one can easily prove for himself" (*Devotions*, 98). Here, Robert is battling his natural inclinations and talents, which he does throughout his noviceship, and Throgmorton represents the standard against which he measures himself.

Southwell's failure to imitate Throgmorton's virtue is clearest in regard to distractions, including friendship. For example, Edward relentlessly practices "modesty of the eyes," which his biographer documents on practically every page, and especially when quoting from a list of "daily Exercises" which "after his death was found in [Throgmorton's] desk, written in English with his own hand." This list "embraces a distribution of almost the whole day, [and] it proves how carefully he kept to the path of virtue in the most exact regulation of all his actions" (Foley *Records* VI, 303). Conspicuous among these regulations are those policing sight. "As soon as I enter the church," Throgmorton writes, "I will take holy water and be careful not to look about me, but fixing my eyes on the High Altar or on the ground I will go to my usual place, and there kneeling down spend the time of Mass in pious meditations, firmly resolving with myself not to turn my eyes unless I am called." Later, he continues, "on the way between the College and the schools, I will not look about me." "Nothing that may happen," he claims, "shall make me look back or to one side." The same rules apply during class: "If there are disputations or repetitions in class, I will converse with no one at that time, but will listen quietly to the arguments, and will try, if I can, to draw some profit from them, having special care of my eyes not to look about" (307). His resolve seems to have been effective. In the author's summary description of Throgmorton at the end of the biography, we read that "when walking in the streets, he kept his eyes cast down and his gestures humbly composed ... Lastly, he was careful in keeping an exact guard over his senses, and his every movement was so well regulated, that he would neither look at any object without a reason, nor listen to idle tales, nor speak without weighing his words" (321).

Throgmorton was not satisfied with following the rules himself. According to the author, he reminded others of their obligations. He regularly scolded students at the English College, and the author tactfully describes one such occasion:

> As he was most zealous in freeing others from care and trouble, he displayed equal solicitude in bringing back from error any one whom he detected swerving the least from the path of rectitude. Not that he ever used severe words, except in a very grave case, for he was utterly removed from all harshness; but by a gentle and benign rebuke he would modestly remind his companions of their duty. If he saw one looking at any object in the streets with unnecessary intentness, he would address him with a smile: "Now you have seen enough, conquer yourself a little and be satisfied. Do you not know that the eye is the outer gate by which death enters?" This he always said with such gentleness and kindness of expression, that his words seemed to breathe love rather than censure. (317)

If scolding cost him friends, Throgmorton had no regrets because he was careful not "to form a special intimacy with any one, and he did so only when there was a prospect of great profit and advancement in virtue for himself and others." He models indifference and emotional control. When a boyhood friend reminded him of the "ancient ... alliance which they had formed together," and complained that Throgmorton had grown distant, he responded, "Pardon me, I am bound to obey my superiors and the statutes of the College, by which I am forbidden to do anything which appears singular; and it would be altogether against charity, were I to have such an attachment to you as to prefer you to the rest" (319). This attitude sets him far apart from Southwell. If Robert wrote Edward's life, he is implicitly scolding himself, and the chastisement is even harsher because, until the last days of his life, Throgmorton was a lay boarder at the College. He professed vows as a Jesuit on his deathbed. As a boarder he had to keep "the common ordinances and statutes of the College," yet, "Edward, not content with his own duties, prescribed to himself the rules of the ordinary alumni, and resolved to learn how to practice the perfection which he saw was expected of them" (302). If Southwell authored this text, he was a Jesuit at the time; and he was certainly a member of the order when he even more explicitly faults himself for falling short of Throgmorton's example in *Spiritual Exercises and Devotions*.

...

Spiritual Exercises and Devotions is a collection of fragments which Southwell wrote during his early years in Rome. Some portions date from his noviceship, reflecting his experiences while making the month-long retreat based on Loyola's *Spiritual Exercises*. This retreat ranks first among the practices assigned to Jesuit novices, and, as scholars starting with Louis Martz reveal, its influence on Southwell's future works is profound.[32] In some cases, especially the earliest entries, Robert imitates the founder's text word for word. In other instances, he paraphrases the suggestions or "points" for prayer provided by his retreat director. This standard material reveals little about the poet's state of mind. Elsewhere, however, he includes information "arising from the changing and sometimes even capricious inspiration of the moment" (Southwell *Devotions* ed. Buck, 27). In these passages, Southwell wrestles with conflicting desires, thoughts and emotions. Such bouts show him maturing, especially in comparison to the *Querimonia*. The longer Robert stays in religious life, the better he is able to reconcile tensions, though these cause dissonance even to the end of this quasi-diary.

The earliest fragments concern his "entry into religion," and correspond to "The First and General Examen which should be proposed to all who request admission into the Society of Jesus." This document, contained in the Jesuit *Constitutions*, was presented to Southwell during his first weeks, or "period of first probation," at San Andrea.[33] In response to it, the poet commits himself to the two-fold goal shared by all Jesuits:

> As my aim in entering religion was that, by constant mortification of self and by submitting myself to all men for Christ's sake, I might become as like to my crucified Savior as I could, and use my every endeavor to sustain his love; and as my aim in choosing the Society in preference to other religious orders or congregations was that I might not only have the opportunity of carrying out these objects, but in addition labor with all my strength for the salvation of my fellow-men; I am absolutely certain and convinced that my vocation to the religious life in general and to the Society in particular is verily from Almighty God, I must cling to it with all care and gratitude to the very last moment of my life. (*Devotions*, 33–34)

Southwell wants to save his own soul and those of as many others as possible. How and where he will do so remain questions, as they should. Novices must be indifferent about the work they will pursue, and this instruction begins in one of the first passages in Loyola's *Spiritual Exercises*, the previously cited "Principle and Foundation." Here Ignatius instructs novices and others making the *Exercises* to "make ourselves indifferent to all created things in all that is allowed to the choice of our free will and is not prohibited to it; so that on our part, we want not health rather than sickness, riches rather than poverty, honor rather than dishonor, long rather than short life, and so in all the rest" (Loyola *Spiritual Exercises*, 23). Later in his journal, writing about returning to England, Southwell admits to scruples on account of a perceived want of indifference. But early in his formation, entries describe his commitment to the Ignatian ideal. The first several pages of *Spiritual Exercises and Devotions* consist of five "foundations," which are essentially elaborations on Loyola's own.

He strikes one anomalous note, however, when describing himself as "singled out from all my family and kindred and called to enter the Society of Jesus" (*Devotions*, 33). Southwell simultaneously celebrates God's attention to him and worries about making too much of it. The temptation to "singularity" arises regularly in following entries, revealing that the poet struggled with this issue. He is at once gratefully aware of and anxious about his talents, which potentially set him apart from the community, so he resolves to avoid singularity, "for nothing is more harmful to community life" (42).[34] A related issue is Southwell's tendency to dramatize himself, also observable in the *Querimonia*. For example, he wants to experience "the suffering of continuous tribulation so that during the whole course of my life I may not enjoy so much as one hour of repose." "Indeed," he embellishes, "I am to think it an especial mark of God's favor to me if I am burdened with perpetual afflictions and wearied with constant difficulties, especially in this manner alone may I become like unto Christ who passed no single moment of His whole life without some sorrow, and thus attain more completely the end for which I entered religious life" (35–36). Again, there is a tension between wanting to be special and knowing that his manner should be ordinary. His immoderate desire for suffering, as well, constitutes a problem that will irk him for years. He ultimately reconciles it with a gentler outlook on religious life, but that awaits more formation.

Southwell pays scant attention to ordinary novitiate activities in *Spiritual Exercises and Devotions*, and this is possibly explained by Devlin's suggestion that he spent most of his noviceship completing courses at the Roman College, which was "about to assume its new title of the Pontifical Gregorian University" (46). Such a practice was not unusual (Loyola *Constitutions* ed. Ganss, 76, n. 9). Early Jesuit superiors "allowed that three or four months was long enough for the training of a novice in the novitiate, after which he could be sent to a college to teach or study" (O'Malley 362). Robert waited the traditional two years before professing vows, but he never mentions working in hospitals or any of the "experiments" or "trials" which the *Constitutions* prescribe for novices.[35] Also shedding light on Southwell's early assignment to studies was the Jesuits' growing commitment to staffing the national Colleges, or residence halls, which housed students enrolled at the Roman College. For example, immediately after professing vows, Robert became a tutor at the English College, a position for which he was being prepared from his first months as a Jesuit.[36]

There is one passage, however, in which Southwell humorously describes kitchen work. This assignment numbers among the "testing experiences" for novices listed in the *Constitutions*, and, in fact, Loyola treats it at length. "When anyone begins to perform the services of the kitchen or to aid the cook," he writes, "with great humility he must obey him in all things pertaining to his office, by showing him always complete obedience" (*Constitutions*, 84). The cook, according to Loyola, should give orders such as "Do this" or "Do that," rather than request help. In doing so "he will show more clearly that he is speaking as Christ to a man, since he is commanding in His place" (85).

Southwell found this experience difficult, but through it he learned to take himself less seriously. In an entry entitled "Important Considerations Upon Self-Resignation," he considers "how God knows thee better than thou knowest thyself, and He sees not only the present, as thou dost, but also the future" (*Devotions*, 92). As a result, "God knows thy capabilities and He shields thee from dangers to thy soul of which thou art ignorant." In addition, "He knows the talents that seem to fit thee for great things, He knows thy gifts of nature and of grace, [and] He has examined and pondered upon these things and many other considerations with absolute thoroughness." "And," Southwell teases himself, God "has come to the conclusion that no other duty suits thee so admirably as, e.g., the kitchen." "Therefore," he reminds himself, "unless thou dost regard thyself as superior to God in wisdom and prudence, thou must think this duty to be for thee the most excellent and profitable" (92). In this respect, at least, the author of the *Querimonia* has matured. Southwell mocks his own pretensions.

On other counts, however, his concerns remain the same as those in his letter to Deckers. *Spiritual Exercises and Devotions* returns to issues of intimacy and records sins against modesty and chastity. Only toward the end of the work does Southwell seem slightly more comfortable in his attractions, affections and desires. He frequently exaggerates his sinfulness, believing himself to be the worst sinner in the entire Society of Jesus. "Again after a careful examination of thy sins," he writes, "it must surely be clear to thee, that in literal truth and not simply out of humility thou must say that no one, in whatever college or house of the Society thou mayest be, has ever in his former life offended God so grievously as conscience and truth require thee to say that thou hast done, especially after thy vocation to religious life" (48). Part of this claim concerns influencing others. "Consider again," he suggests to himself, "how thou, like a cruel and wicked robber, hast stolen away from Christ some of those whom he had brought under his power and protection by his precious blood, His bitter pains and death."

Another typically dramatic passage occurs in the note "Often Read and Consider with Sorrow of Heart":

> Consider attentively and grieve to think how many, perhaps with thy consent or help, have become servants of the devil, enemies to God and deserving of eternal damnation. Some of them perhaps have died unrepentant and been condemned to suffer for all eternity with the devil the dreadful pains of hell. Now in misery they pay the penalty of thy sin, cursing the day they first saw thee and calling down upon thee the vengeance of God ... What wilt thou do, most miserable wretch? Wilt thou not weep unceasingly and refuse to be comforted? What wilt thou answer to God for those souls deprived through thee of the benefit of his passion and death? Weep therefore, miserable sinner, and do penance, that as at thine instigation they have offended Him so at thy penance they may obtain his forgiveness ... As thou hast yielded thy members to serve uncleanness, so now yield thy members to serve justice unto sanctification. (81–82)

Loyola's *Exercises*, especially the First Week's meditations on sinfulness, inform this passage. As a novice, Robert would have been instructed, for example, to pray for certain "graces": "first, that I may feel an interior knowledge of my sins, and hatred of them; second, that I may feel the disorder of my actions, so that, hating them, I may correct myself and put myself in order; third, to ask knowledge of the world, in order that, hating it, I may put away from me worldly and vain things" (Loyola *Spiritual Exercises*, 63). But Southwell's emphasis on the evil he has done seems inordinate even by Ignatian standards. In another entry, he repeats the phrase about "yield[ing] his members to serve uncleanness and iniquity unto iniquity" and remembers that he had "before been a servant of the devil" who gave "labor and time … to carnal pleasure" (*Devotions*, 80). As he reflects on his past, he prays that God will give him "the water of life to extinguish the fire of [his] passions and cleanse [him]." In a related passage entitled "Rules for Intercourse with Others," he notes how "an undue familiarity has been harmful to thee and that thou shouldst avoid it even with members of the Society and still more those who live in the world" (84). And on the last page of the book he iterates a familiar "foundation": "To allow no creature to take possession of your heart" (118). Reflections on sinfulness in connection with personal relationships dominate Southwell's thinking in this period.

At the heart of *Spiritual Exercises and Devotions* he describes an intense struggle over whether or not he should ask to be sent to England. The struggle comes to a head in two entries called "Important Considerations Upon Self-Resignation" and "Is It Better to Offer Myself or Remain Silent," in which Southwell first asks, "didst thou enter the Society in order to do this or that special work or fill some special office?" (91). He wants to give the correct answer: "Of course not, but simply to ensure the salvation of thy soul, and to live in this Society to which God called thee, in that position, abode, company, under those exercises, rules and superiors which God saw fitting for thy spiritual welfare." However, he admits that he increasingly understands his vocation in relation to "[his] country, relatives and friends" who "need his help" (93). This dilemma stimulates one of the most revelatory entries in the collection, and its candor is suggested by a shift from the second to the first-person pronoun. Instead of addressing an instruction or admonition to himself, he writes "I have been much wondering what would be better." Because he worries that his desire to return to England is tarnished by inappropriate affections, he hesitates to volunteer for the mission. Perhaps it would be better, he thinks, to "leave the whole matter absolutely to the disposition of God." He admits that there might be a good reason for speaking his mind to superiors, since "a good desire, which has lasted for a long time and when dwelt upon in prayer seems to grow stronger, can come, as it would seem, only from God." "On the other side," he agonizes, "it seems still safer to leave the whole matter to God, to say nothing and be ready for either alternative." "There is a danger," according to Robert, "and indeed a grave one," that when we make a request "something of our own judgment will enter in when we state our case." While he never discloses which course he takes in this matter, *Spiritual Exercises and Devotions* reveals his concerns about following personal inclinations and yielding to natural attractions. Starting with his affection for Deckers, such feelings cause Southwell anxiety because they might lead him to transgress the kind of rules which a character such as Throgmorton embodies. For the most part these rules hamper the poet from acting on his deepest desires, and *Spiritual Exercises and Devotions* records frustration caused by an inability to trust that God can work in, and through, earthly vehicles such as passions, patriotism and poetry. Southwell will only alter his perspective on the apostolic potential of such phenomena as he immerses himself further in the incarnational Ignatian world view and the study of theology. *Spiritual Exercises and Devotions* occasionally presents evidence that such an evolution in Southwell's thinking has begun, if only in a nascent way.

Notes

[1] Foley notes that Deckers' letter, dated 29 September 1580, is preserved in a Stonyhurst ms. The section he cites describes its author's happiness in religious life: "Blessed be the God and Father of Our Lord Jesus Christ, Who calleth me to the Society of His Son. Blessed, and forever blessed be Our Lord Jesus Christ, Who has deigned to enroll me, so unmindful of His benefits, in the number of those walking the straight path. Would that I could lay open to you, my brother, my joy, and with how great pleasure and desire I bind myself to spend my life in the service of God. Good God! Thou hast already fulfilled Thy promise. I receive the hundredfold in this life; but rather a thousand than a hundredfold." Foley provides information on Deckers, charting his career as professor of theology and philosophy at various Jesuit colleges including Douai, Louvain, Gratz and Olmutz, where he served as rector (*Records* I, 307–308).

[2] Southwell's hope echoes instructions of Loyola: "I exhort and beg you by [God's] love and reverence to improve your writing and to conceive some esteem for it and a desire to edify your brethren and your neighbor by your letters … So I beg of you, by your love and reverence for the Divine Majesty, put your heart in this matter and work with all diligence; it will contribute so much for the spiritual progress and consolation of souls." See Simon Decloux's *Commentaries on the Letters and Spiritual Diary of St. Ignatius Loyola* (Rome: C.I.S., 1980), 14.

[3] For a description of Carthusian life, see chapter 3 of Laurence Hendriks' *The London Charterhouse: Its Monks and its Martyrs* (London: Kegan Paul, 1889).

[4] For biographies of these men see L.E. Whatmore's *The Carthusians Under King Henry VIII* (Salzburg, Austria: Institüt für Anglistik und Amerikanistik, 1983).

[5] The London Charterhouse became property of the Crown until it was given to the Howards, and it is in this former monastery that Southwell visited and perhaps lived for a time with the Countess of Arundel.

[6] Elsewhere in *Spiritual Exercises and Devotions*, he compares Jesuit duties to the rules of other orders, reminding himself that he "belong[s] to the lowly Society of Jesus which finds perfection in performing even the smallest acts out of love and obedience towards Our Lord." "For the ordinary duties of members of the Society are not difficult in themselves," he continues, "if we compare them with the ordinary duties of other religious, e.g., Carthusians, Capuchins, etc. For if these have nothing else, at least they

have their austerity of life and of dress, their fasting, their chanting of the divine Office, which they offer to God, and which earn for them the title of religious" (100–101).

[7] See *Constitutions* nos. 115, 349, 648.

[8] Lessius entered the Jesuits in 1572, after completing a doctorate in philosophy at age seventeen. He went on to teach at Louvain, Douai and Rome. Southwell was his pupil and friend at the latter two schools. Lessius' theological works are ranked with those of Bellarmine, Suarez, Vasquez and Molina; and he wrote on asceticism as well.

[9] Scholars point out the cultural and personal aspects of the Latin education that Southwell and Deckers experienced. According to Walter Ong, "by the Renaissance ... learned Latin was eminently qualified as an instrument for a puberty rite of [a certain] sort": "Puberty rites are *rites de passage*, transition rites. They are didactic, for in them the initiates are given understanding of more or less secret tribal lore." Moreover, and particularly apt in regard to a college for exiles, Ong observes, such rites "involve calculated hardship: often the boys are snatched with violence or mock violence from the arms of their mothers and established in an all-male extrafamilial environment where they undergo various trials and often physical torture. They emerge with an *esprit de corps*, a feeling that they have gone through rough times together, which helps to establish the typical male 'bonding pattern'" (*Fighting for Life: Contest, Sexuality and Consciousness* [Ithaca: Cornell UP, 1981], 130). Bruce Smith, building on Ong's work, argues that "as a male code, Latin in the Renaissance was the language of law, diplomacy and international trade." It was also, according to Smith, "the language of sexual knowledge": "For Renaissance schoolboys like Marlowe and Shakespeare, Latin was the public language of male power and the private language of male sexual desire—of homosexual desire in particular" (83–84).

[10] Ignatius' attitude toward penances was a reaction against his own rigorous practice early on in his conversion. Through trial and error, he learned that extreme self-inflicted suffering leads to desolation. See *The Autobiography of Ignatius Loyola*.

[11] An argument between Loyola and Simaõ Rodrigues precipitated this letter. Rodrigues, the superior of the Jesuits in Portugal, promoted "penitential practices among Jesuits that caused wonderment among friends and enemies." According to O'Malley, "The practices included severe fasting and self-flagellation in the streets, not a common practice in Portugal at the time" (330). Ignatius also received reports of Portuguese Jesuits "taking a corpse into one's room to meditate on death." Ultimately, Loyola replaced Rodrigues as superior, and his successor dismissed "nearly 20 to 25 percent of the province or more" (331–32). In a letter to Gaspar Berze, a missionary to India, Ignatius expresses similar concerns: "There are two drawbacks in dealing with yourself so severely. The first is that without a miracle your reverence will not last long in the ministries you undertake; rather death will tie your hands. Or you will become so ill that you will no longer be able to continue them, which would be to put quite an obstacle in the way of God's service and the help of souls, in which works you could, with better health, employ yourself for many years to come. The second is that, being so harsh with yourself, you could easily come to be excessively so with those under your charge. And even though you give them no more than your example, it must result in making some of them run too fast, and especially so among the better of your subjects" (Loyola *Counsels for Jesuits*, 92).

[12] Cano, professor of theology at Salamanca, expressed "rabid opposition to the Society" on other counts as well, such as the Jesuits' refusal to chant the Office in choir and disregard for the tradition of cloister. According to O'Malley, Cano loved "the clarity and objectivity" of scholastic theology, "just as he feared the subjectivity of those who placed confidence in internal inspiration" (292).

[13]   See Alan Bray, *Homosexuality in Renaissance England* (London: Gay Men's Press, 1982); Bruce Smith, *Homosexual Desire in Shakespeare's England* (Chicago: U of Chicago P, 1991); Gregory Bredbeck, *Sodomy and Interpretation: Marlowe to Milton* (Ithaca, NY: Cornell UP, 1991); Jonathan Goldberg, *Sodometries: Renaissance Texts, Modern Sexualities* (Stanford, CA: Stanford UP, 1992); and Alan Stewart, *Close Readers: Humanism and Sodomy in Early Modern England* (Princeton, NJ: Princeton UP, 1997).

[14]   O'Malley notes that "of the three vows, the early Jesuits had the least to say about chastity." "The vow formally precludes marriage," he continues, "and to that extent it was clear-cut and needed no explanation." But "besides the obligation of celibacy, ... the vow implied a life that was chaste in every way." Those such as Southwell who were sent on missions were to be especially vigilant. For example, "Provincials from both India and Brazil warned that the special circumstances in those places meant that anybody known to have a weakness in this regard should not be sent from Europe" (348).

[15]   Southwell discusses reasons for dismissal in *Spiritual Exercises and Devotions*, recording an anecdote in which the Queen of Portugal asked a local superior how the Jesuits maintained their spiritual fervor. He answered, "because it opens its veins and lets out the corrupted blood" (195).

[16]   See John Cassian, *Institutes* (The Nicene and Post-Nicene Fathers), bk. II, ch. 15. For Cassian's thought on friendship see *Conferences*, Conference XVI, pp. 450–60. A. Fiske comments on these texts in "Cassian and Monastic Friendship," *American Benedictine Review*, 12 (1961), 190–205.

[17]   See Aelred of Rievaulx, *Of Spiritual Friendship* (Paterson, NJ: St Anthony's Guild Press, 1948). For more on his theology of friendship see A. Fiske, "Aelred of Rievaulx's Idea of Friendship and Love," *Citeaux*, 13 (1962), and Amedee Hallier, *The Monastic Theology of Aelred of Rievaulx* (Spencer, MA: Cistercian Publications, 1969).

[18]   These phrases appear in Lithgow's *Rare Adventures*, 12 and 229.

[19]   This is the title of an anonymous play published in 1658.

[20]   This phrase appears in *The Monarche* in *The Works of Sir David Lindsay* (ed. D. Hammer, vol. 1, The Scottish Text Society, 1931, 197–386).

[21]   Lithgow claimed to have traveled thirty-six thousand miles, and he recorded his adventures in *The Total Discourse of the Rare Adventures and Painful Peregrinations of Long Nineteen Years Travels from Scotland to the Most Famous Kingdoms in Europe, Africa and Asia*. Upon his return to England, he frequently entertained James I with his exotic and anti-Catholic tales.

[22]   Stewart traces these lines to John Marston's *The Scourge of Vilanie*, sig. C6v.

[23]   Smith warns that "change in forms of desire across historical time present a much more difficult challenge to the imagination than do changes in laws, in marriage customs, or in literary conventions." As a result, "concerning sex," more than any other aspect of our humanity, "we use indirections to find directions out" (4–5). Stewart similarly argues that "we are operating here not within empirical history ... but in the realm of powerful cultural fantasies and anxieties, which, nonetheless, ... can come to affect what we accept as empirical history" (xvi).

[24]   Smith sheds light on Sedgwick's observation, asserting that "if fifth and fourth-century Athens exemplifies 'ideological homosexuality,' and if our own society exemplifies 'ideological heterosexuality,' [then] the society of Shakespeare's England clearly exemplifies conflict" (58).

[25]   According to Stewart, "the humanists portrayed their own social relations as drawing on classical notions of friendship and pedagogy, lacking a profit motive and existing directly between men." "These 'humanist relations,'" Stewart thinks, "were vulnerable to accusations of another relationship between men—sodomy" (xxiii).

26   Stewart also identifies *De Amicitia* as "the single most influential text on friendship and one of the few classical texts to be printed in translation by William Caxton," and he notes that "there were to be two further printed translations before the end of the sixteenth century" (126).

27   One translator of *De Amicitia*, Andrew P. Peabody, observes that "the special duties of friendship constituted an essential department of ethics in the ancient world, and that the relation of friend to friend was regarded as on the same plane with that of brother to brother." "No treatise on morals would have been thought complete," according to Peabody, "had this subject been omitted" (vii).

28   See *De Amicitia* in Andrew P. Peabody's *Cicero's Masterpieces* (New York: Thomas Nelson, n.d.).

29   Stucley's exploits are described in stridently anti-Catholic style by John Izon in *Sir Thomas Stucley: Traitor Extraordinary* (London: Andrew Melrose, 1956). His reputation made him notorious in his own age. He is featured in a 1605 play, *The Famous Historye of the life and death of Captaine Thomas Stukeley*, 1605, the authorship of which is ascribed to Peele, Dekker or Thomas Heywood. See the edition published for the Malone Society by Judith C. Levinson in 1974. Anthony Kenny also writes on Stucley's adventures in "From Hospice to College," *The Venerabile* 20 (1960–1962), 3–11, 89–103, 171.

30   This novitiate also housed Rudolph Acquaviva, Henry Garnet, Thomas Cottam, Henry Walpole and Aloysius Gonzaga. Southwell's teacher Robert Bellarmine died there in 1621.

31   Devlin attributes the work to Southwell (18), though neither Janelle nor Brownlow make any mention of it.

32   Among the "six different testing experiences" required by the *Constitutions*, the *Spiritual Exercises* comes first (Loyola *Constitutions*, 65). As Ignatius describes it, "that is to say, in the candidate's examining his conscience, thinking over his whole past life and making a general confession, meditating upon his sins, contemplating the events and mysteries of the life, death, resurrection and ascension of Christ our Lord, exercising himself in praying vocally and mentally according to the capacity of the persons, according to what will be taught to him in our Lord, and so forth."

33   The *Constitutions* describe how "when two or three days have passed after he entered the probation, he will begin to be examined more in detail according to the method explained in the Office of the Examiner. The text of the Examen should be left with him that he may carefully consider it more slowly in private. Subsequently he will carefully read the bulls, Constitutions and rules which must be observed in the Society and the house he enters" (198).

34   In the *Constitutions* Ignatius writes "as far as possible, we should all think alike and speak alike." Moreover, "even in regard to things which are to be done, diversity, which is generally the mother of discord and the enemy of the union of wills, should be avoided as far as possible" (273).

35   This practice of involving the non-ordained in the ordinary works of the order was unique to Jesuits. As O'Malley notes, "although most Jesuits would eventually be ordained, all of them were deeply involved in the ministries of the Society almost from the moment they entered it" (80). The *Constitutions* lists six "principal testing experiences for novices, all of which aim at ministerial preparation: making the month-long retreat based on the *Spiritual Exercises*; serving in hospitals; making a pilgrimage "without money and even in begging from door to door … in order to grow accustomed to discomfort in food and lodging"; employment "in various low and humble offices" in the house; explaining Christian doctrine "to boys and other simple persons"; and

preaching or hearing confessions "in accordance with the times, places and capacity of all" (*Constitutions*, 64–70).

36   Novices are considered members of the Society from the day they enter. According to the *Constitutions*, "the Society, when we speak in the most comprehensive sense of the term, includes all those who live under obedience to its superior general. Thus it comprises even the novices and the persons who, desiring to live and die in the Society, are in probation to be admitted into it" (511).

Chapter 5
Reconciling Spirituality: Intellectual Formation and Divine Artistry

During his Roman years Robert Southwell acquired a major change in perspective on the role of affect in religious life. The magnitude of this transformation can be gauged in a single sentence from the dedicatory epistle accompanying *Mary Magdalene's Funeral Tears*, a prose work that he likely began in Rome and completed in England. Writing to Dorothy Arundell, the daughter of John Arundell of Lanherne, Cornwall, whose "virtuous requests" for spiritual reading "won [Southwell] to satisfy [her] devotion in penning some little Discourse of the blessed Mary Magdalene," he states,

> Passions I allow, and loves I approve; only I would wish that men would alter their object, and better their intent; for Passions being sequels of our nature, and allotted unto us as handmaids of Reason, there can be no doubt but as their Author is good, and their end godly, so their use, tempered in the mean, implieth no offense. (iv)[1]

His new understanding of the nature and function of passions and loves resulted from his immersion in the incarnational spirituality of the Society of Jesus and the study of philosophy and theology at the Jesuit-run Roman College. By the time he leaves Rome for England, Southwell confidently embraces a full range of emotions and perceives in them the potential for encountering God. "Love," he writes, "is but the infancy of true Charity, yet sucking Nature's breast, and swathed in her bands; which then groweth to perfection, when Faith, beside natural motives, proposeth higher and nobler grounds of amity" (iv). Passions and loves, rightly ordered and under the influence of grace, can promote holiness; and the tears Mary Magdalene shed after the crucifixion, "in which she most uttered the great vehemency of her fervent love to Christ," provide an apt example of such a possibility. Her tears are surprisingly not penitential; they are evidence of a great and holy passion for the person of Christ, who rewards Mary for the depth of her feeling by appearing first to her after the resurrection.

The same possibility of finding God in and through emotions also guides Southwell's emerging literary theory. In the epistle prefacing the *Funeral Tears*, "To the Worshipful and Virtuous Gentlewoman, Mistress D.A.," he comments on current poetic practice and offers his prescription for redirecting and redeeming the genre: "For as passion, and especially love, is in these days the chief commander of most men's actions, and the idol to which both tongues and pens do sacrifice their ill-bestowed labors; so there is nothing now more needful to be treated, than how to direct these humors into their due courses, and to draw this flood of affections into the right channel" (iv). As was the case in his appropriation of Dyer's love lyrics for the sake of offering consolation and catechesis to the recusant community, Robert intends to set a precedent which he hopes other poets will follow. Poetry, like passions and loves, when rightly ordered and under the influence of grace, can reconcile writers and readers to God. Southwell's confidence in the ability of grace to perfect nature, a conviction which he gained through eight years of study and prayer, largely determines the contours of his priestly and literary ministries in England, a nation which he loved well enough to court death for the sake of reconciling it to Rome. Though clearly bearing the imprints of Gregory XIII's Rome and the Society of Jesus headquartered in its physical and psychological center, Southwell never lost his natural affection for his native country. That affinity, refined by nearly a decade of spiritual and intellectual formation, leads him to volunteer for the English mission. During his Roman years Southwell gained a motivation much like that of the Jesuits' founder whose "goal was to find God in all things, in the created world as well as the supernatural, and then to communicate that divine presence in the concrete situations of daily life, using every means of communication available, 'like the spoils of Egypt'" (Lucas *Saint, Site and Sacred Strategy*, 18).

...

Most of the years Southwell spent studying and teaching in Rome occurred during the pontificate of Gregory XIII, which seemed, to many observers, a "dawning golden age, a 'tempus Gregorianum'" (Lucas *Landmarking*, 162). Southwell caught the contagious enthusiasm and sense of purpose emanating from the Pope throughout the city and especially among Jesuit ranks, upon whom Gregory relied for the implementation of many of his plans and projects. Gregory, originally known as Ugo Buoncompagni, was elected pope in May 1572 at the age of seventy. His many years of service to the church in a variety of curial and diplomatic offices had not diminished his strength and energy, however. Pledging himself to implement the decrees of the Council of Trent, he launched a variety of reform efforts and was particularly committed to stemming the tide of Protestantism through the rigorous preparation of men for the priesthood. He established twenty-three seminaries, starting with the German College in 1573, which he placed under the jurisdiction of the Jesuits. His other schools in Rome included a Greek College, a college for recently converted Jews and Muslims, a Maronite College and the English College. Students from all these national residential colleges heard lectures at the international Jesuit school, the Collegio Romano, established by Ignatius Loyola in 1551, for which Gregory built a new and much larger home dedicated in 1584.[2]

The elaborate ceremony marking the dedication of the new Collegio Romano, which Southwell likely attended, revealed important and interrelated features of Gregory's reign: his international outlook and his close relationship with the Society of Jesus. For example, speeches were delivered in twenty-five languages at the dedication, including one by a Sicilian Jesuit, Stefano Tuccio. Tuccio's address is described in an *Avisi*, a kind of hand-written newsletter, circulated shortly after the dedication. His speech was, according to the account, "a very worthy display of his training and imagination":

> The abstract points illustrated with various oratorical ornaments were principally these: the very great indebtedness which the [Jesuits] have to his Holiness for his visit, their gratitude for the other and divine blessings they have received, but in particular this memorable visit, because in this case the condescension of the Pontifical Dignity has greatly added to the honor of this Society, which, because of him is now diffused throughout all parts of the world; their true way of winning mastery over nations, and extending over all peoples which in appearance seems a combat with a leaden sword but is in fact waged with the arms of Divine Providence and Pontifical authority, the particular grace granted by the Pope of entrusting to the Society the ministry of teaching the children of so many nations; their gratitude which cannot match their obligation, but which will endure as long as this edifice, as well in their studies and teaching of the arts in every city and place; their obligation to celebrate the name of his Holiness, for whom they would not hesitate to give their very lives. (Lucas *Saint, Site and Sacred Strategy*, 170)

Tuccio's observations on the close collaboration between the Pope and the Jesuits around the world is also borne out by the fact that Gregory underwrote the expenses for two seminaries and a Jesuit College in Japan all founded by Giuseppe Valignano, S.J. In gratitude, Valignano sent an embassy of Japanese Catholics to meet the Pope shortly before his death in 1585, another occasion celebrated with pomp and pageantry in Rome during Southwell's stay there.

Southwell's formative years were spent in a city dominated by Jesuit presence, and he understood himself to be at the hub of the Society's rapidly expanding range of activities to which he contributed prodigiously as a teacher, spiritual director and publicist.[3] He enjoyed and drew energy from his proximity to Jesuit authorities, such as the Superior General, and he regularly interacted with them in person and through correspondence. That the Jesuit central offices and so many Jesuit schools and churches were located in Rome was no accident. According to Thomas Lucas, "Ignatius was the first founder of a major religious order in the history of the church to locate his headquarters in Rome and the first to opt deliberately for the complete insertion of a religious order's works and residences in the center of the urban fabric" (*Landmarking*, 23).[4] Rome had been the most important place in the Jesuit imagination almost from the inception of the order. In a 1547 circular letter from his secretary, Juan Polanco, to Jesuit houses in Portugal, for example, Loyola develops "a somewhat overwrought yet ultimately telling metaphor for the centrality of Rome to the Jesuit vision" (Lucas *Landmarking*, 130):

> I know that everyone there wants to know what our Lord is doing for those who are in Rome, the city that is in one respect the head, and in another the stomach of all Christendom. For this Society it seems to be both the one and the other: and, if one could add a third element, it is the heart of the Society. It is like the head in that it is from here that the Society is directed and moved, and like the stomach in that from here are dispensed and distributed to all its members that which maintains their well-being and fruitful progress. So too one can call it the heart, in as much as it is the [vital] principle of the other members, and also because it seems to be the seat of life of the entire body of the Society. Without the connection to Rome, no matter how much the Society were to increase in numbers, things would surely go badly for its preservation. For this reason, those who know the importance of this house in Rome most reasonably want to know what is going on here in it. (*Letters and Instructions*, MHSJ, I, 208, 609)

Loyola arrived in Rome with two of his original ten companions in 1537, three years before the formal incorporation of the Society. Their first apostolic effort was feeding the sick and hungry during the disastrous winter of 1538. Soon after, "the companions ... embarked on a concentrated blitz of urban preaching that focused on the churches in the medieval core of the city" (Lucas *Landmarking*, 87). In subsequent years, Jesuits acquired Roman churches, apostolic centers and houses of their own to such an extent that an engraving known as "Roma Ignaziana" was published in 1609, the year of Ignatius' beatification. The map, according to Lucas, is "a much reworked version of an earlier rendering of the Renaissance city," showing "an immense Chiesa del Gesu [the order's mother church] dominating the center of the city, surrounded by a corona of out-of-scale buildings housing Jesuit social, pastoral and educational works." It is, Lucas admits, "a celebration of triumphalistic hagiography and Jesuit chauvinism," but, he argues, "there is more": "an articulated relationship of parts to a center and a harmonic relationship of that center to the city center" (*Landmarking*, 171).

Southwell studied and taught as a member of a religious order that imagined itself at the center of things, so much so that two Italian urban historians describe the creation of a "Jesuit Pole" in Rome:

> In 1568 the Church of the Gesu was begun; in 1583 the Collegio Romano. Giving a new thrust to the entire central area of Rome ... these two edifices conditioned and transformed the relationships between the city's buildings, creating in modern terms, a "third pole," that, levering against the renovated fulcrum of the capitol, tended to relegate towards the periphery the traditional religious points of reference, the Vatican and the Lateran. Every other initiative of the new orders—from S. Andrea della Valle, to the Oratorians, to S. Carlo—would in fact be subordinated to the central Jesuit presence, notably reinforced with the construction of the church of S. Ignazio. In the last decades of the Cinquecento and the first decades of the Seicento, first in Rome then in all the other Catholic capitals, we see the Jesuit college and church constituting centers of attraction, and centers of growth within the urban organism. These are quickly surrounded by a series of churches or secondary institutions, always bound to the Society, which form a corona around the principal edifices, invariably located, wheresoever it is possible, in the city center. (Guidoni and Marino 614–15)

Two of these Jesuit-run institutions shaped Southwell's Roman experience, the Collegio Romano, where he studied, and the English College, where he lived and served in a variety of capacities, first as tutor, then as Prefect of Studies and Prefect of the Sodality of the Blessed Virgin. In both places his commitment to the ministry of reconciliation deepened, and he acquired learning, skills and attitudes that would facilitate his future work in England.

. . .

When Ignatius Loyola established the Collegio Romano in 1551 in a rented house provided by a donation from Francis Borgia, former Duke of Gandia and now a Jesuit, he envisioned students engaging in a four-year course in humanities followed by seven years dedicated to philosophy and theology. While this plan was not uncommon at the time, "Ignatius grafted onto it an innovation that was to make it a unique establishment in Europe." "From the beginning," according to Philip Caraman, "he saw it as a unique university at the service of the Holy See in the center of the Catholic world with a staff of professors drawn from whatever country the most proficient in their subjects could be found" (*University of the Nations*, 6). As with most Ignatian paradigms, however, he made room for adapting the curriculum to the needs of individual students. Southwell, for example, followed a considerably abbreviated course of study. He was ordained to the priesthood in 1584 owing to the urgency of the situation at the English College and in England itself. This short course likely pleased him, as he later advocated it for other English seminarians. His views on education were, as Devlin puts it, "ruthlessly pragmatic." For Southwell "Catholic England was the end," according to Devlin, "and studies, higher or lower, means to the end": "With a notion of study as a career he had no sympathy" (64). A letter written to the rector of the College, Alphonso Agazzari, after Robert's arrival in England bears Devlin out. After surveying the needs of English Catholics, the poet writes, "it is true that all priests are useful here, but especially those who are skilled in moral and controversial questions." "As for other branches of sacred learning," he concludes, "they may gratify fastidious ears, but they are rarely of any use to us here" (Southwell *Unpublished Documents*, 315)

Southwell's attitude reflects that of Loyola, who, according to Philip Caraman, "set about organizing the [Collegio's] syllabus with a sense of immediate urgency" (*University*, 11). Even in advance of the Council of Trent, which prescribed a new and far more demanding spiritual and intellectual formation for future priests, Ignatius intuited that rigorous seminary training in controversial theology would best foster the Catholic cause. Ignatius made two choices regarding his syllabus that definitively shaped the Catholic intellectual tradition for centuries to come. He decided that Aristotle ranked first among philosophers and, more importantly, that Thomas Aquinas, rather than Augustine, Peter Lombard or Duns Scotus, would form the basis for theological studies. In the *Constitutions* he specifies that "in theology there should be lectures on the Old and New Testaments and on the scholastic doctrine of St Thomas" (464). Later he adds, "in logic, natural and moral philosophy, and metaphysics, the doctrine of Aristotle should be followed, as also in other liberal arts" (470).[5] While these decisions may seem inevitable in hindsight, they were, according to Caraman, "by no means obvious ... and [were] considered a surprising innovation at the time" (*University*, 11). Ignatius admired the clear style of the *Summa*, considering it to be the best extant compendium of Catholic teaching. He also wanted to make it more widely obtainable, especially for poor students, and to this end he purchased a printing press for the Collegio. Moreover, he commissioned a Jesuit theologian, James Ledesma, to produce a summary edition of Aquinas' enormous work. Ledesma wrote *Christian Doctrine*, which was eventually translated into ten languages, including English.[6]

Ledesma numbers among early faculty members who won acclaim for the fledgling Collegio. Loyola's successor as Superior General, Diego Laynez, determined to make available to a growing number of students from all over Europe a first-rate faculty. He assigned a Spaniard, Juan Mariana, to teach theology and a Portugese, Manoel da Sao, to a chair in philosophy. The Society's third General, Francis Borgia, continued this policy, appointing to the faculty Francesco de Toledo, whose accomplishments included four volumes of commentary on Aquinas, reconciling Henry IV of France to the church, and becoming the first Jesuit Cardinal. Borgia also brought Gian Battista Eliona to Rome, a converted Jew who had entered the Society at Venice. Eliano produced numerous publications including an Arabic edition of the decrees of the Council of Trent as well as an Arabic New Testament. In 1565 Christopher Clavius returned to his alma mater as professor of mathematics, a position he held for forty-seven years during which he revolutionized the discipline and insisted on its place in the curriculum of the Collegio. Clavius also supervised Gregory XIII's reform of the Julian calendar. His colleagues included other luminaries such as Francisco Suarez, who taught philosophy during the years when Southwell was a student. In his lectures Suarez was developing what he later published as *Disputationes Metaphysicae*, a work of over one thousand folio pages, which served as the textbook for modern philosophers such as Descartes, Leibnitz and Schopenhauer (Caraman 25). Towering over all these academic giants, however, was Robert Bellarmine, who came to Rome from Louvain in 1576 at the request of Gregory XIII. The Pope wanted Bellarmine to fill the chair in controversial theology, which he occupied during Southwell's own tenure at the Collegio.

This faculty made the Collegio famous throughout Catholic Europe and infamous in Protestant nations, including England. For example, after visiting Rome, Montaigne wrote, "it is marvelous what a place this College

P. Robertus de Nobilibus Romanus Soc. Iesu,
apud Madureenses 45 annos ob Euangelij predica-
tionem commoratus, sancte obijt Meliapore 16 Ian:
anno Sal: 1656. ætat: 80

5.1 Engraving of Roberto de Nobili, Missionary to India (by courtesy of the Woodstock Theological Center Library, Georgetown University, Washington, D.C.)

holds in Christendom. I think there is no such other ... It is a breeding ground of great men in all sorts of grandeur" (Caraman 23). Among the great men who studied at the Collegio, several of Southwell's contemporaries stand out as indicators of the vibrancy and influence of the school in those years. A native of Bruges, Gregory de St. Vincent, who later became a professor of philosophy at the Jesuit College at Antwerp, did work on conical sections under the tutelage of Clavius. His discoveries caused Leibnitz to count him in the same category as Descartes. Other students, such as Matteo Ricci and Roberto de Nobili, extended the reach of the Collegio to China and India. Ricci, another of Clavius' students, made his way into the court of the Ming emperor by impressing officials with horological instruments, compasses and prisms. Along with translating Euclid into Chinese, Ricci also published Chinese editions of three works by his former teacher, Clavius' *Gnomoica*, *Astrolabe*, and *Practical Arithmetic*. Historians also credit Ricci with first informing the Chinese of the American continents, about which he had learned from reading the *Relations* written by Jesuit missionaries. De Nobili was simultaneously following a similar missionary strategy in India. He revolutionized Christian practice on the subcontinent where earlier, non-Jesuit missionaries required converts to adopt Western names and customs along with the faith. De Nobili followed a more inculturated approach, dressing in the robes of Indian holy men and forming friendships with Brahmin scholars. He is thought to be the first Westerner to study Sanskrit, the Vedas and Vedanta.

Ricci and de Nobili's embrace of other cultures and their confidence in using scientific and linguistic tools for apostolic purposes mirrors Southwell's integration of literature into his own ministry. These alumni of the Collegio Romano came by this approach to natural and created things as a result of the curriculum that molded their thinking as well as their praying. Building on Aristotle and Aquinas, professors such as Bellarmine convinced their students that good could be accomplished and God could be found in the natural world as it was brought to perfection by grace. To appreciate the understanding of the relationship between nature and grace that Aquinas developed and Bellarmine refined, it is helpful to contrast it with that of Augustine, which had been dominant since the latter saint's time.[7] In the final analysis, Aquinas does not differ in essentials from Augustine, whom Thomas considered his master. His systematic analysis of the relationship between nature and grace, however, represents a significant shift that yields quite a different mentality. The key, interrelated factors are Aquinas' starting point and method. Augustine starts from the perspective of the Fall and the subsequent pervasiveness of sin in the world. Sin fractures the relationship between human beings and God; and human nature, the reality of a human being conceived concretely, is profoundly wounded and suffers a loss of integrity. As a result, Augustine construes God's grace as primarily medicinal: because human beings are sinful, they

5.2 Engraving of Matteo Ricci, Missionary to China (by courtesy of the Woodstock Theological Center Library, Georgetown University, Washington, D.C.)

need grace to heal and empower them. Augustine's method, consequently, is phenomenological. He reflects on the relationship between nature and grace in terms of human nature considered as the concrete, existential condition of human beings and their psychological development.

Aquinas' method draws on the philosophy of Aristotle, who saw the world as an ordered cosmos with each nature in the hierarchy of beings having its own proper structure, finality and principles of operation. This perspective yields a far more positive outlook on human potential. In his analysis of the relationship between nature and grace Thomas uses the abstract Aristotelian category of nature. Human nature is a clearly defined substance with its own end or finality and the built-in powers by which it achieves its end. For Aquinas, the human spirit is openness to all being, including the transcendent being of God. However, the end or finality of human nature, a personal union with an utterly transcendent God to whom Christians understand themselves called, transcends the power of human nature, and would even if Adam had not sinned (*Summa Theologica* I–II, 110, 3).[8] God's grace, therefore, is *super*natural, something that transcends human nature in itself, and is consequently gratuitous (*Summa Theologica* I–II, 112, 1). Grace perfects human nature by elevating it to a new level of existence, personal union with God (*Summa Theologica* I–II, 109, 2). To be sure, grace is also medicinal, as Augustine insists, because it heals a human nature that is *de facto* sinful (*Summa Theologica* I–II, 109, 9). But the key factor is human nature considered abstractly, in relation to its end, union with God. In relation to the substance of humanity, grace is a gratuitous accident that informs, elevates and perfects human nature (*Summa Theologica* I–II, 110, 2 and 3). Aquinas' analysis, which Southwell studied at Rome, provides an obvious benefit: a reverence for a fundamentally ordered world and for human nature and its potential to be perfected by grace. Grace can ultimately have the same effect on human artifacts, including poetry. As Southwell puts it at the conclusion of the poem standing first among his works, "[i]t is the sweetest note that man can sing/ When grace in virtues key tunes natures string" ("To the Reader," ll. 17–18).

According to Philip Caraman, Bellarmine, who based his own thinking on that of Aquinas, more than anyone else on the Collegio's faculty at the time, impressed his personality on his students and had the most enduring influence on their spiritual as well as intellectual formation (*University of the Nations*, 38). Through his publications, sermons and "domestic exhortations" he articulated "a vision of life and religion that sees all reality as friendly and working unto good" (Bellarmine *Spiritual Writings* ed. Donnelly and Teske, 9). He based much of his teaching on the works of Aquinas, but gave theology a more historical and less abstract or philosophical orientation. In addition, Bellarmine was innovative in a way that influences Southwell's conciliatory approach to controversies. As John

Patrick Donnelly writes, "his defense of Catholic teaching was remarkably free of the mud-slinging that characterized most of the polemics of the period" (14).

Southwell's relationship with Bellarmine can be established upon evidence that the latter was particularly attentive to his English students. Looking back on his years of teaching in Rome he writes:

> When Pope Gregory XIII, of blessed memory, in his zeal to assist Germany and England, established two great colleges for the young men of those countries, I was appointed to teach them controversial theology in our schools, and thus, as it were, arm these new soldiers of the Church for the war with the powers of darkness which they would have to wage when they returned home. (Brodrick 124)

His biographer, James Brodrick, also notes that Bellarmine was so concerned with the plight of England's Catholics that he volunteered for the mission, offering to "lecture openly against the heretics" (124). Given the needs of the Collegio, the Pope denied his request. Nevertheless, Bellarmine's works and reputation were well known in England. According to Brodrick, "some Englishmen knew their Bellarmine as well as their Bible" (149), and, at least according to legend, Elizabeth herself established academic chairs "for the expressed purpose of refuting [Bellarmine's] *Controversies*," his major work, which was published in three volumes in English starting in 1588. In response to this publication, William Whitaker, Master of St. John's College and Regius Professor of Divinity at Cambridge, one of England's most prominent Protestant theologians, wrote to William Cecil that "the pit of Rome, from the time it was first opened, hath not ceased to exhale perpetual smoke to blind the eyes of men, and hath sent forth innumerable locusts upon earth." "Among these locusts," Whitaker continues, "none ... have ever appeared more keen or better prepared and equipped for doing mischief than are the Jesuits at this present day." Moreover, "amongst these Jesuits, Robert Bellarmine, a native of Italy, hath now for several years obtained a great and celebrated name." "His lectures," according to Whitaker, "were eagerly listened to by his auditors, transcribed, transmitted into every quarter and treasured up as jewels and amulets" (Brodrick 139). Now that Bellarmine's major work is Englished, Whitaker, "in the discharge of the duties of [his] office," plans to "discuss the new sophisms of the Jesuit and vindicate our unadulterated truth from the captious cavils with which the popish professor hath entangled it" (139).

Whitaker, along with numerous other Protestant apologists, began publishing volumes bearing the title "*imprimis Robertum Bellarminum,*

Jesuiticam" [*sic*], a "little codicil ... very popular in the anti-Catholic literature of those specious times, for nearly every Protestant doctor of any consequence, who wrote against the Church, flourished it on his front page" (Brodrick 140). Other examples of anti-Bellarmine works in English include titles such as "On the Pope and his iniquitous Domination, against Robert Bellarmine and the whole tribe of Jebusites"; "On Monks and their Mode of Life and Manners, against Robert Bellarmine and the whole Kennel of Monks and Mendicants"; and "On the Popish Mass, against Robert Bellarmine and the universal Cohort of Jebusites and Canaanites" (Brodrick 149). One such work describes Bellarmine as a "petulant railer," and likens his *Controversies* to "new stables of Augaeus containing an infinite heap of dung" written by "a braggart dunghill of a soldier, a furious and devilish Jebusite, the Hannibal of all the Jebusites" (Brodrick 149). Even ordinary Englishmen were part of this anti-Bellarmine enterprise. For example, Brodrick marks the existence of bottles or jugs with big bellies called "Bellarmines," explaining how "the tipsters of heretical Europe were to be found ... pouring their ale or wine from the top of the tilted Cardinal's head." "It is perfectly plain," he argues, "that they were originally meant in mockery, as a kind of coarse retort to the *Controversies*" (142).[9]

In Rome, Bellarmine pursued a very different tactic, and one that Southwell adopts in his dealings with English Protestants. Bellarmine, like Southwell after him, assumes a conciliatory tone even while insisting on the rightness of his arguments. The theologian, according to Brodrick, responded to his adversaries "leaving out the abuse," because, as Bellarmine writes, "it is not our business to return evil for evil" (178). "At times," Brodrick attests, "we find him assuming the defense of some heretical doctor who had been misrepresented in Catholic books," even to the point of putting "a favorable construction" on Calvin's works.

This tendency to read his opponents in the best possible light is symptomatic of what John Donnelly calls his "optimistic piety," an approach best observed in Bellarmine's *The Mind's Ascent to God by the Ladder of Created Things*. This work, written near the end of his career, serves as a culmination and summary of Bellarmine's thought, and, according to its most recent editor, is based on exhortations that he gave over the course of many years to young Jesuits such as Southwell (Bellarmine *Spiritual Writings* ed. Donnelly and Teske, 20). About the tone of the work, A.O. Lovejoy writes in *The Great Chain of Being* that the *Ascent* is "the most celebrated modern elaboration of the mind's upward movement along the chain of being to the One," and he commends the Cardinal for "avoiding the harshness of St. Bernard and the extreme contempt for creation encouraged by St. John of the Cross," two other spiritual writers who contributed to the same genre (91–92).

Bellarmine's *Ascent*, like Southwell's *Short Rule of Good Life*, is written for busy people engaged in public affairs. "There is nothing," Donnelly observes, "that is not suitable for any educated, serious Christian man or woman" (Bellarmine 25), and "there are few passages in Bellarmine's book that have a mystical tone and none that pretend to give guidance in mystical prayer" (26). Like Loyola before him, Bellarmine takes a conventional notion in the Christian spiritual tradition, that of climbing upward toward God according to a program imagined as a ladder, and he infuses it with his own insights, many gleaned from the Ignatian *Exercises*. For example, he takes St. Bernard's ladder as his model, but informs it with "the spiritual atmosphere of the [Ignatian] Principle and Foundation," found at the start of the *Spiritual Exercises*, as well as "The Contemplation for Attaining Love" in which "Loyola has retreatants reflect on how God dwells in creatures, how he works and labors on our behalf in created things" (Bellarmine ed. Donnelly, 25). As a result, "by showing how creation reflects the Creator, he has not devalued nature but rather transvalued it." According to the philosopher Paul Kuntz, "Bellarmine starts from delight in the beauty of the earth. He shows no contempt for matter when he talks of earth, water, air and fire." For Bellarmine, "the world has a rich variety of forms and a plentitudinous creation is appropriate to a plentitudinous creator" (Kuntz 963).

In dedicating the *Ascent* to Cardinal Pietro Aldobrandini, Bellarmine invites his busy readers to take time for contemplation. He hopes his book will "serve as a sort of counselor." "Should your crowd of business commitments overwhelm you," he writes, "may this book gently advise you to block out that crowd for a short time and recall to your mind your accustomed interior joy" (Bellarmine 49). Later he recommends that readers "recollect ... daily at a set time and enjoy some holy leisure and heavenly repast ... For without sustenance the soul cannot in any way do its duty amid its mass of critical business" (52). The style and content of these passages are reminiscent of Southwell's introduction to his poems. Southwell, writing for a "cousin," as well as a wider recusant readership thoroughly acquainted with stress, encourages his audience to enjoy the same kind of "holy leisure." In a poem entitled "To the Reader," he urges the "[d]earest eye that doest peruse my muses style" to "[g]ive sobrest countenance leave sometime to smyle,/ And gravest wits to take a breathing flight" (ll. 1–2). "Of mirth to make a trade may be a crime," he admits, "[b]ut tyred spirites for mirth must have a time" (ll. 5–6). He then introduces an avian conceit to elucidate his point:

The lofty Eagle soares not still above,
High flightes will force her from the wing to stoupe,
And studious thoughtes at times men must remove,
Least by excesse before their time they droupe.
In coarser studies tis a sweete repose,
With Poets pleasing vaine to temper prose. (ll. 7–12)

He asserts that poetry, like prayer, relaxes and refreshes the anxious spirit. The former can be as helpful, according to Southwell, as the latter is necessary according to his teacher, Robert Bellarmine.

The "soul's duty," as assigned by Bellarmine, is to make its way back to God, and about the best route he is quite certain: "no ladder of ascent to God can lie open except through the works of God" (Bellarmine 53). He comes by this conviction through personal experience, describing how "I tried to build a ladder from the consideration of creatures by which one can somehow ascend to God" (54). In retrospect, he organizes his considerations into fifteen "steps," taking for his inspiration "the fifteen steps by which people ascended to Solomon's temple and the fifteen Psalms which are called the Gradual Psalms" (54). The first step is consideration of the self, since "each of us is a creature and an image of God and nothing is closer to us than ourselves" (55). The self contains more than enough material from which one can build the indispensable ladder: "He who examines his whole self and considers what lies hidden within will find the whole world in shortened form, from which he will ascend without difficulty to the Maker of all things" (55). The intricacies of anatomy, for example, "how many muscles there are in the human body, how many veins and sinews, how many bones large and small, how many fluids and innards and many similar things," disclose that God is "the architect of the whole man," "a craftsman of infinite power" (56–57). In conversation with his soul, Bellarmine learns that God shares his artful powers with humans. "How can man do good things?," he asks himself. The honest answer, he claims, is that "the power by which he acts is given him by God and is not something he produced" (59). By grace "God guides and helps what man does, and without his guidance and help man would accomplish nothing good" (59). With divine help, however, "the form which man is given appears precious and excellent": "The substantial form of man ... is his immortal soul endowed with reason and free choice; it is the image of God modeled on the pattern of the Supreme Godhead" (60).

Contemplation of the self as the image of God gives Bellarmine confidence in humankind's ability to enhance creation. "How great is human genius," he writes, "which has invented skills such that we wonder whether nature surpasses art or art surpasses nature" (73). In the same vein, "the human possesses ... the gift of inventing things [because] the human soul is endowed with reason and judgment and invents countless skills" (135). "If you admire human genius," he continues, "you should admire God more" (136). Then Bellarmine refers specifically to making and admiring art:

> Finally, if you stand in awe at the art of painting pictures and bringing almost living faces out of marble, why should you not be awestruck at the art of your Creator, who formed a true and living man out of mud and built up a true and living woman from his rib (Gn 2:21–22), especially if you also consider that what men make would not happen without God's cooperation, but what God makes is done by him alone without anybody else's cooperation? (136)

Several corollaries from Bellarmine's considerations here find echoes in Southwell's work. The latter considers making art analogous to prayer. Artists imitate the ways of God and participate in the ongoing work of creation. Moreover, sacred scripture sanctions the making of art. According to Southwell, "God, who delivering many parts of scripture in verse, and by his Apostle willing us to exercise our devotion in Himnes and Spiritual Sonnets, warranteth the Arte to be good, and the use allowable." Jesus himself composed and sang hymns after the Last Supper, as the poet observes in "The Author to his loving Cosen":

> And therefore not onely among the Heathens, whose Gods were chiefly canonized by their Poets, and their Painim Divinitie Oracled in verse: But even in the Old and New Testament it hath bene used by men of greatest Pietie, in matters of most devotion, Christ himselfe by making a Himne, the conclusion of his last Supper, and the Prologue to the first Pageant of his Passion, gave his Spouse a method to imitate, as in the office of the Church it appeareth, and all men a paterne to know the true use of this measured and footed stile.

Finally he cites the biblical verses attributed to King David in the poem "To the Reader." In distancing himself from the lot of contemporary love poets he writes, "[p]rophane conceits and fayning fits I flie,/ Such lawlesse stuff doth lawlesse speeches fit:/ With *David* verse to vertue I apply,/ Whose measure best with measured wordes doth sit" (ll. 13–15).

Admiring art can also serve religious purposes. It can raise the mind to reflection on divine artistry, which at once inspires and enables human art while infinitely surpassing it. This is because, as Southwell learned from Bellarmine, "God is in absolutely everything, not only in bodily things, but also in spiritual beings; nothing can come into existence

5.3 Engraving of Cardinal Robert Bellarmine (by courtesy of the Woodstock Theological Center Library, Georgetown University, Washington, D.C.)

without God being in it" (Bellarmine 139). As a result, admiring beauty, whether artistic, physical or spiritual, should not provoke anxiety but rather cause consolation, since such admiration can be considered a religious act:

"God wanted man to know Him somehow through his creatures, and since no creature could fittingly reflect the infinite perfection of the Creator, He multiplied his creatures and gave a certain goodness and perfection to each of them" (69). On this account Bellarmine instructs himself, "My soul, when anything that seems wonderful strikes your eye or your thought, make it a ladder to recognize the Creator's perfection which is incomparably greater and more wonderful" (69).

Such a perspective on mortal beauty would clearly console Southwell. It answers some of the questions raised by his attraction to Deckers and resolves tensions caused by other objects of his affection such as his family, his nation and the kind of work to which he aspires as a Jesuit. Bellarmine helps him understand that Ignatian indifference does not require that he be dispassionate or unappreciative of beauty. "If," as Bellarmine suggests, "we reflect carefully under God's enlightenment, these creatures will have no little power to raise up our heart so that it will be overcome in admiration" (67).

···

Mary Magdalene's Funeral Tears can be read as an example of such careful reflection, under God's enlightenment, on a very human theme: grief resulting from the loss of one loved passionately. Southwell, prompted by Bellarmine's thinking, "examines" Mary Magdalene "and what lies hidden within her," "from which he can ascend without difficulty to the Maker of all things." Southwell's choice of topic is significant, especially in light of his earlier anxieties about the appropriateness of passion in religious life. Unlike most contemporary works inspired by the saint, his lengthy consideration of Mary Magdalene has almost nothing to do with her conversion.[10] Rather it examines and celebrates her attraction and attachment to Jesus. As Devlin observes, "the note that Southwell strikes all through is the divine acceptance of genuine human love however misguided" (79). Even the poet's most recent and severest critic, Brownlow, admits that the *Funeral Tears* "is a clever, charming work, despite the initial discouraging fact that Southwell has expanded a gospel narrative of eighteen verses into a 25,000-word book" (39). The charm of the *Funeral Tears* results from its genre. It is essentially a love story, and "Southwell's method of telling the story is to visualize the scene and the actors clearly, and to track its development through every detail of his heroine's feelings" (Brownlow 40). In conclusion, Brownlow goes so far as to claim, "the revelation of Jesus and the reversal of Mary's grief probably has no equal for sustained emotional and intellectual power in Elizabethan prose" (41).

The power of the *Funeral Tears* has much to do with Southwell's hard-won knowledge of love, which Brownlow describes as "surprising ... both in his treatment of Mary, and in the many apt aphorisms about love and the behavior of lovers that he sprinkles throughout the book" (43). Personal experience grounds this knowledge, as the poet acknowledges in the dedication to the *Funeral Tears*: "I know that no man can express a passion that he feeleth not, nor doth the pen deliver but what it copieth out of the mind." As his letters and *Spiritual Exercises and Devotions* show, Southwell learned about love, even if the process of learning initially caused dissonance and confusion. In the *Funeral Tears* he reveals that his outlook has changed. He comes to regard Mary's very human love, and sustained literary reflection upon it, as a step on the ladder leading to God. Robert wants to show how such love, influenced by grace and considered carefully under God's enlightenment, can bring Mary, along with the poet and his readers, closer to God.

Historically, however, critics have been confused about the nature and purpose of the work. Herbert Thurston, usually an admirer of Southwell's, wrote in *The Month* that the *Funeral Tears* was an example of John Lily's euphuism, "very popular in England at the time and known at the English College through a steady stream of visitors." He describes it as "a curiously affected style ... in favor in Italy, Spain and France and in keeping with the somewhat perverted literary taste of the period" (*The Month* LXXXIII [1895], 233–34). Thurston explains this stylistic move on Southwell's part as a play for acceptance. Adopting euphuism was merely "a passport to the good graces of casual fellow-travelers." Janelle, on the other hand, blames the "curiosity" of the work on its author's classical and theological education. He is primarily concerned with the sources Southwell used, believing that the poet had access to a text on a similar theme attributed to St. Bonaventure. "Thus," he concludes, "what is generally considered as the framework of Lily's preciosity is already present in the meditation ascribed to St. Bonaventura" (192). "As for the fanciful and grotesque similes which diversify every page of *Euphues*, nothing of the kind is to be met with here," according to Janelle, who, typically, reads each of Southwell's prose works as stages in the development of an ultimately rugged, masculine and definitively English style.[11]

Devlin, too, reads the work in light of a developmental scheme, but its creator's progress, as he understands it, is in terms of "judgment." The *Funeral Tears* "shows that while Southwell's judgment had matured [during his years in Rome], his poetic 'sensibility' had not been blunted"

(79). Brownlow concurs on this issue, describing how Robert's Jesuit formation accounts for important features of the *Funeral Tears*. "The book's two most striking literary qualities, its emotional power and its vividly realized scenes," according to Brownlow, "reflect Southwell's professional training as a Jesuit in the arts of meditation and self-examination, often in quite tiny details" (38–39). He concludes that "Southwell's presentation of sacred persons and events as real people of flesh and blood and of concrete realities with all their physical detail is a feature of the art and literature of the baroque age often attributed to the influence of Ignatius and his Exercises" (39).

The influence of the Ignatian *Exercises* on the *Funeral Tears* is undeniable. As Brownlow notes, a few lines from scripture become, in Southwell's version, an elaborate and lengthy love story constructed with an eye for detail. As in the *Exercises*, the purpose of such vividly drawn scenes is to engage the audience and enable them to enter as fully as possible into the incident being described. Most importantly, the poet catalogues and examines Mary's feelings, inviting the reader to experience similar emotions. The point, as in the Ignatian *Exercises*, is that God's work and will can be discerned in and through such feelings, if they receive the kind of serious and sustained attention they deserve. When he introduces Mary, she has returned with Peter and John to Christ's tomb and found it empty. After Peter and John leave to tell the other disciples, she remains to mourn "a second loss." Already devastated by the death of Christ, she wanted to "preserve the relics of his body as the only remnant of all her bliss" (Southwell *Marie Magdalene Funerall Teares*, 13). When she discovers his body gone, "the fire of her true affection inflamed her heart, and her inflamed heart resolved into incessant tears; so that burning and bathing between her love and grief, she led a life ever dying" (11). The paradoxical image of "burning and bathing," as well as her life spent "ever dying," recur in Southwell's "Burning Babe," where they elucidate the mystery of the Incarnation. Here they help underscore Mary's suffering for having twice lost the man whom she loved most in the world. There is a Petrarchan echo here as well, a characteristic emphasis on the double nature of love and the emotional extremes it generates; but while the lovers in Petrarchan poems often feign affection or hold it out for some unattainable object, Mary's love is genuine and intended for a person whom she knew very well. Throughout the work Southwell underscores how her love for Christ far surpassed that of any of the other disciples. Peter and John, for example, left Mary alone at the empty tomb because they were "fearful of further seeking." "Their love was soon conquered with such fear," he writes, "that it suffered them not to stay" (15). Since Mary has lost all she ever loved, she has no reason to fear anything else. Her fearlessness also validates the claims of scripture in the Song of Songs, according to Southwell: "it is proved true in her that love is stronger than death" (16).

In the opening scene the poet also offers one of many aphorisms concerning the effects of love. Mary remains at the tomb, "a haunt for hope," because "when things dearly affected are lost, love's nature is never to be weary of searching even the oftenest-searched corners." This aphorism has the added feature of a scriptural allusion. Southwell has in mind the parable of the lost coin (Luke 15:8–10). He later presents another aphorism on lovers' tenacity in searching for their beloved. "In true lovers," he contends, "every part is an eye, and every thought a look, and therefor so sweet an object among so many eyes, and in so great a light, could never lie so hidden but love would espy it" (23–24). The narrator, who regularly converses with Mary and other characters based on the colloquies prescribed in the Ignatian *Exercises*, tries to reason with Mary, asserting that her search is hopeless. He catches himself, however, and remembers love's impact on reason: "But alas! Why do I urge her with reason, whose reason is altered into love." "Her thoughts," he claims, "were arrested by every thread of Christ's sindon," or winding sheet, and she "had forgotten all things, and herself among all things, only mindful of him she loved above all things" (18). Unable to think clearly or to heed the narrator's instructions, Mary can only weep.

As she begins to cry, the narrator introduces other characters whose presence is caused by Mary's grief. "Thy weeping was for a man," he tells her, "and thy tears have obtained angels" (19). Without his help, Mary cannot see the angels through her tears. Once she does notice them, she refuses to engage them, much to the frustration of the narrator. It seems obvious to him that she should ask them about Christ's whereabouts. "I came not to see angels," she replies, and then she employs the first of several comparisons between the presence of Christ and nourishing food. "Alas," says Mary, "small is the light that a star can yield when the sun is down, and a sorry exchange to go gather crumbs, after the loss of heavenly repast." She implies that the angels can offer little help in the absence of Christ, and the series of food images introduced here reflects Southwell's typical interest in the real presence of Jesus in the Eucharist. One of the poet's most important ministries in England was to provide the sacrament to recusants and to remind them, through poetry and prose, of its significance. In this instance, Mary Magdalene represents most Englishmen who, as members of the established church, no longer have access to the real presence of Christ. As the angels only offer a poor and ineffective substitute for the Saviour, nothing can replace his real presence in the sacrament. Even the beauty of the angels only serves to remind Mary of the greater beauty of Christ, a sentiment recalling Bellarmine's theory articulated in the *Ascent*. The narrator confirms her reaction, admitting, "thy eyes were too well acquainted with the truth to accept a supply of shadows." Then he adds another food reference, observing how Mary "in all other delights … seest no more than some scattered crumbs and hungry morsels of [her] late banquets" (42). The narrator iterates this same notion several pages later when he finally begins to understand Mary's feelings: "That others see the sun does not lighten thy darkness; neither can others eating satisfy thy hunger" (47).

Mary's description of her love for Christ facilitates the narrator's newfound understanding. Prior to her explanation, he asked, "Oh Mary, why dost thou thus torment thyself with these tragical surmises?" Thus cued, she tells him how closely she identified with Jesus, even wishing to die in the same manner, "seeing a part of myself partner in my master's misery" (53):

> If I might be chooser of my own death, O how quickly should the choice
> be made, and how willingly I would run to that execution! I would be
> nailed to the same cross with the same nails, and in the same place; my
> heart should be wounded with the same spear, my head with his thorns,
> my body with his whips!

Elsewhere she likens her love to ownership as well as identification. "He was mine," she claims, "because his love was mine; and when he gave me his love, he gave me himself, since love is no gift unless the giver be given with it" (45). After explaining that her love for Christ was reciprocal, she further asserts, "then dare I boldly to say, that Jesus is mine; for on his body I feed; by his love I live; and for my good, without any need of his own, hath he labored and died … I never mean to resign my interest in him" (47). This eucharistic allusion is followed by yet another reference to food. The narrator, now apprised of the depth of Mary's love, admits, "to ask thee why [it doth so deeply grieve thee that thou knowest not where he is] is in manner, to ask one half-starved why he is hungry: —for as thy Lord is the food of thy thoughts, the relief of thy wishes, the only repast of all thy desires, so is thy love a continual hunger, and his absence an extreme famine" (49).

Once he understands Mary's profound love for the Saviour, the narrator turns his attention to her beloved. He cannot understand why Christ waits so long before appearing to Mary. Jesus' sense of timing perplexes the narrator, who has the advantage over Mary of knowing how the story ends. In a passage where he conflates several scriptural characters into the woman standing at the tomb, he considers earlier effects of Mary's tears on Jesus:

> But, alas! what meaneth this change? And how happeneth this strange alteration? The time hath been, that fewer tears would have wrought greater effect, shorter seeking having sooner found, and less pain having procured more pity: — the time hath been, that thy anointing his feet was accepted and praised, thy washing them with tears highly commended, and thy wiping them with thy hair most courteuosly construed . . . Is it not he that reclaimed thee from thy wandering courses, that dispossessed thee from the damned inhabitants, and from the wilds of sin recovered thee into the fold and family of his flock? Was not thy house his home, his love thy life, thyself his disciple? Did not he defend thee against the Pharisee, plead for thee against Judas, and excuse thee to thy sister? In fine was he not thy patron and protector in all thy necessities? (20–21)

"O good Jesu," he inquires, "what hath thus estranged thee from her?," and "why art thou so hard a judge on so soft a creature?" (21). The implied answer is that Jesus delays in order for the narrator and his readers to learn even more about the nature of love as epitomized in Mary. Observing her grief-inspired efforts to seek out clues regarding the Saviour's disappearance, he offers further observations on the transforming power of love:

> And as men in extremity of thirst are still dreaming of fountains, brooks and streams, being never able to have other thought, but of drink and moisture; so lovers, in the vehemence of their passion, can neither think nor speak but of what they love; and if they be once missing, every part is both an eye to watch, and an ear to listen, for what hope or news soever may be had. (48)

This image recalls the line in the poet's letter to Deckers describing their desire to find time alone. In the letter, Robert looked back uneasily on such an intense desire. In the *Funeral Tears*, Mary's longing is exemplary. Here, Southwell does more than merely "allow passions;" he celebrates them when they are rightly ordered. No object of Mary's affection, or that of Robert and his readers, could be more appropriate than Christ. "Once again," as Brownlow observes, "Southwell is writing about a theme of his own formation as a Jesuit, in this case the redirection of the passions, and especially love, from an earthly to a heavenly object." "In fact," he points out, "the *Funeral Tears* is really a story, cast in the form of a homiletic meditation, about a woman's overwhelming love for an infinite object" (37).

Southwell's description of the power of love rises to a crescendo after Jesus finally appears to Mary, only to go unrecognized and taken for a gardener. According to the narrator, she cannot identify the Saviour because she did not believe his prophecies about the resurrection. "If thou hadst remembered God's promise," he informs her, "that his holy one should not see corruption—if thou hadst believed ... thy faith had been more worthy of praise, but thy love less worthy of admiration" (*Funerall Teares*, 67). Nevertheless, her admirable love will make up for her lack of belief. "Why, then, canst thou not as well see what in truth he is, as what in shew he seemeth?" he asks Mary. Answering his own question, he suggests, "it is because thou trusted more to thy senses than to thy belief, and sufferest thy fancy to find more than faith will avouch: it is for this cause that thy love was thought worthy to see him, yet thy faith unworthy to know him." "I cannot say that thou art faultless," he concludes, "because thou art so unwilling in thy belief; but thy fault deserveth favor, because thy charity is so great; and therefore, O merciful Jesu, let an excuse be pleaded for her whom thou art minded to forgive." Then, the narrator, in one of the most poignant and powerful passages in all of Southwell's works, convinces Jesus that the merits of love make up for unbelief:

> Love is not controlled by reason. It neither regardeth what can be, nor what shall be done, but only what itself desireth to do. No difficulty can daunt, no impossibility appall it. Love is title just enough, and armor strong enough, for all assaults, and is itself a sufficient reward for all labors. It asketh no recompense, it expecteth no advantage. Love's fruits are love's effects, and its pains prove its gains: it considers behoof more than benefit, and what of its duty it should, not what of its power it can. (66)

Such can be love's effect even on women, according to the narrator, who asks Mary, "is thy courage so high above thy nature, thy strength so far beyond thy sex, and thy love so far above measure, that thou neither does remember that all women are weak, nor that thyself art but a woman?" (65). In recognizing her weakness, he can then chide her for failing to recognize her Lord: "Hath thy Lord lived so long, laboured so much, died with such pain and shed such showers of blood, and hast thou bestowed such cost, so much sorrow and so many tears, for no better man than a gardener?" But then he realizes abruptly, and for the sake of introducing an ornate literary turn, that her "mistaking hath in it a further mystery." Her error allows him to enter into an elaborate exercise in typology, listing various scriptural gardens in which revelations have occurred. "Thou thinkest not amiss," he assures Mary, "for as our first Father, in the state of grace and innocence, was placed in a garden of pleasure, and as the first office allotted him was to be a gardener, so the first man that ever was in glory, and presenteth himself in a gardener's likeness, that the beginnings of glory might resemble the entrance of innocence and grace." There is nothing especially original in this juxtaposition of Adam and Christ. St. Paul makes the same point in Romans, but Southwell further develops it by adding some allusions of his own:

> And as a gardener caused the fall of mankind, and was the parent of sin, and the author of death; so is this gardener the raiser of our ruins, the ransom of our offenses, and the restorer of life. In a garden, Adam was deceived, and taken captive by the devil: —in a garden, Christ was betrayed and taken prisoner by the Jews: —in a garden Adam was condemned to earn his bread by the sweat of his brow; and after a free gift of the bread of angels, in the last supper, in a garden Christ did earn it us by a bloody sweat of his whole body. By disobediently eating the fruit of a tree, our right to that garden was by Adam forfeited; and by the obedient death by Christ upon a tree, a far better right is now recovered. (60)

Southwell also makes Jesus' agony in the garden the subject of one of his most intricately witty poems, "Christs bloody sweat." Here, too, the reference allows an exercise of wit, providing a clever way to underscore the eucharistic motif running through the *Funeral Tears*. In the end, Mary's mistaking Christ for a gardener also proves an innovative variation on the *felix culpa* theme. "For this also was Mary permitted to mistake," the poet concludes, "that we might be informed of the mystery, and see how aptly the course of our redemption did answer the process of our condemnation" (60).

After concluding this ornate typological digression, and enabling his readers to learn from Mary's mistake, Southwell returns to the issue of Mary's powerful love and Christ's response to it. He exhorts Jesus to reveal himself and "minister unto her the true bread, and provide her with the food that hath in it the taste of all sweetness" (68). Then he tells Mary "to fear not" because "thy tears will prevail: they are too mighty orators to let any suit fail." Offering an aphorism about tears he remarks how, "when they seem most pitiful, they possess the greatest power." Making a rare reference to Mary's past life, he notes how, "penitent tears are sweetened by grace, and rendered more purely beautiful by returning innocence." "It is the dew of devotion," he explains, "which the sun of justice draweth up; and upon what face soever it falleth, it maketh it amiable in the eye of God" (69). Once Jesus reveals himself to Mary by speaking her name, she is "ravished ... with his voice," and except for uttering one word, "*Rabboni*," she remains speechless. Her silence permits the narrator to offer a final observation on the nature of her love, which "coveteth not only to be united, but, if it were possible, to be wholly transformed out of itself into the thing it loveth" (74). This desire causes Mary to fall down at Christ's feet in order to once again kiss them and wash them with her tears, for "to see him did not suffice her; to hear him did not quiet her; to speak with him, was not enough for her; and except she might touch him, nothing could please her" (74). Jesus, however, eschews her advance for reasons that initially confuse the narrator. He first takes it as another form of punishment for a woman who has already suffered enough on account of love. Ultimately, though, after sustained reflection, this new mystery yields up its two-fold meaning. The narrator explains that Christ "didst only defer her consolation in order to increase it," and the Saviour teaches her a lesson that she needs to learn in light of his anticipated Ascension. Jesus tells her,

> Embrace me first in a firm faith, and then thou shalt touch me with more worthy hands. It is now necessary to wean thee from the comfort of my external presence, that thou mayest learn to lodge in me the secrets of my heart, and teach thy thoughts to supply the offices of outward sense: for in this visible shape I am not long to be seen here, being shortly to ascend unto my Father. But what thine eye then seeth not, thy heart shall feel, and my silent parley will find audience in thine ear. (76)

The narrator appreciates the lesson, but his sense of justice is nevertheless still offended on account of Mary's "wounded love" (80). He takes up her cause, urging Christ to "therefore ... admit[test] her to kiss thy feet ... renewing her a charter of thy unchanged love and accepting from her the sacrifice of her sanctified soul" (81). He seems to succeed in his plea as he ends by describing "a gracious Lord" who, once Mary's belief grows strong enough, has finally "quieted her fears, assured her hopes, fulfilled her desires, satisfied her love, dried up her tears, perfected her joy, and made the period of her expiring griefs the preamble to her never-ending pleasures" (81).

The familiarity that such an argument implies, as well as his narrator's certainty about the persuasive power of love, reveals that Southwell's development during his Roman years made him more confident in his relationship with Christ and more willing to understand the religious significance of emotions. The kind of wariness on both counts observable in early letters and the *Spiritual Exercises and Devotions* is gone. Anxieties are replaced by affective assurance, enabling him to be more apostolically focused. In the end of the *Funeral Tears* he underscores the apostolic nature of this literary work. For example, his readers learn what "the continued tears of constant love are able to attain." "O Christian Soul!" he writes, "take Mary for thy mirror. Follow her affection, that like effects may follow thine own" (81). He urges his readers to imitate Mary Magdalene by "roll[ing] away the stone of [their] former hardness" and searching for Christ in their hearts: "seek him truly, and no other for him; seek him purely, and no other with him; seek him only, and nothing beside him" (83). Jesus will "answer thy tears with his presence, and assure thee of his presence with his own words; that having seen him thyself, thou mayest make him known to others—saying with Mary, *I have seen our Lord, and these things he said unto me*" (84). Consolation in Mary's case, as well as that of Southwell and his readers, spurs apostolic efforts. Certainly, that was true at least in the case of Dorothy Arundell, for whom he initially composed the *Funeral Tears*, who died a Benedictine nun in Brussels.

. . .

Readers who criticize Southwell for expanding the relatively brief gospel narrative regarding Mary Magdalene at the empty tomb into such a lengthy meditation can find consolation in a much-abbreviated version found in a 42-line poem entitled "Marie Magdalenes complaint at Christs death." The poem functions as a precis of the *Funeral Tears*, managing to cover most of the work's major points. Even the syntactic similarity is obvious. Mary is the speaker in the poem, and at the start she expresses her desire to die, since "my life from life is parted" (l. 1). "Who survives, when life is murdred," she complains, "live by mere extortion" (3–4). Mary speaks aphoristically here as well. For example, the first stanza ends with a plainly didactic couplet: "All that live, and not in God:/ Couch their life in deaths abod" (5–6). The second stanza turns toward figurative language, offering two conceits that Southwell also employed in the *Funeral Tears*. Here Mary's loss is likened to "[s]eely stars" who "must needes leave shining,/ When the sunne is shadowed," and "borrowed streames" that must "refraine their running,/ When head springs are hindered" (7–10). Another aphorism on lost love completes the stanza: "One that lives by others breath,/ Dieth also by his death" (11–12). Once Mary has established her emotional state, she addresses an absent Christ, "O true life, sith thou hast left me,/ Mortal life is tedious" (13–14). Then she raises an intriguing possibility which introduces the poem's subtle eucharistic undertones. Mary asks Christ to let her die or, somehow, "live thou in me" (18). The third stanza hints at how this might be possible, and the allusions to England under the established church are not difficult to discern. "Where truth once was, and is not," according to Mary, "shaddowes are but vanitie:/ Shewing want, that helpe they cannot:/ Signes, not salves of miserie" (19–22). At the close of this stanza Southwell employs the same references to food that punctuate the *Funeral Tears*. Here "[p]aynted meate no hunger feeds" (23). Mary desires not empty signs but the real presence of Christ. Lacking it, "[d]ying life each death exceedes" (24).

In the poem, as well as in the *Funeral Tears*, Southwell permits Mary a nostalgic moment for the sake of heightening the pathos of the scene. She remembers how "[w]ith my love, my life was nestled/ In the sonne of happiness" (25–26). Now, however, "From my love, my life is wrested/ To a world of heaviness" from which she begs to be removed (27– 29). The similarities between the poem and the *Funeral Tears* break down toward the poem's end, however, and Mary is left between confusion and consolation. She has questions that seem to go unanswered, though she holds out hope for resolution. She cannot understand what did "unloose" her "soule," or Christ, from the "sweete captivity" of the grave. She realizes that Jesus belonged to God more than to her, and she describes the Son as God's "happy thrall" who would sacrifice his "libertie" to his Father's will. The empty tomb, she anticipates, might be part of God's plan, though she does not fully grasp it. Christ never appears to her in the poem. In the last stanza she is still mourning the "double treason" of his death and disappearance. In the final couplet, though, she continues to hope in the power of love. She wonders if perhaps her love for Christ might cause him to be present to her in some new way: "Though my life thou drav'st away,/ Maugre thee my love shall stay" (41–42). The poem, though less satisfactory on account of Jesus' absence, still reveals Southwell's newfound reverence for emotions as well as his appreciation for the power of love, rightly ordered and under the influence of grace. Mary's hope at the poem's end, that somehow love will precipitate an encounter with Christ really present, was Southwell's own as he leaves Rome for England.

Notes

[1]   According to Janelle, Southwell knew Dorothy through her father, who sponsored Robert's colleague, John Cornelius, at the English College. Returning to Rome as a Jesuit, Cornelius contacted John Arundell and introduced him to Southwell, who wanted to establish ties "with the powerful feudal aristocracy of the Western Counties." "Neither Dorothy Arundell ... nor her father," writes Janelle, "seem to have much to do with literary life; but their social position was the highest, John Arundell being called on account of his wealth and domestic splendor, 'the great Arundell'" (59).
The Collegio Romano opened in rented rooms in 1551 as "a free school of grammar, humanities and Christian doctrine." In 1556 Paul IV authorized the conferral degrees in philosophy and theology. Owing to the growth of the student body, it relocated several times before occupying the space provided by Gregory XIII.

3   The growth of the Society during Southwell's lifetime was remarkable. In 1579 there were 5,165 Jesuits living in 200 houses on four continents. By 1600 the order numbered 8,500, dispersed among 350 houses.

4   According to Lucas, "[The Jesuits'] willingness to enter into conversations with the urban environments they inhabited gave them an intimate knowledge of the social scene and a liberating ability to move back and forth across lines otherwise closed by prejudice, class distinctions and fear." "For them," Lucas argues, "the city was a vast proscenium on which they could improvise their *Opera Pietatis* with delight and virtuosity" (104).

5   As Ganss notes in his edition of the *Constitutions*, "until well into the 1500's, Peter Lombard's *Sentences* was the most widely used textbook on theology. But in the first half of the sixteenth century, the use of St. Thomas' *Summa Theologica* was much furthered by the Dominican Cajetan in Italy, Vitoria and others in Spain, and Crockaert, Vitoria and Peter of Nijmegen at Paris from about 1504 to 1526." "Ignatius," he points out, "was within this influence during his study of theology under Dominicans in Paris in 1534" and "ever afterwards he and the early Jesuits, especially Nadal, had the esteem of St. Thomas manifested in ... legislation" (Loyola *Constitutions*, 219).

6   Ledesma's *The Christian Doctrine* was published in English in 1597 (See *English Recusant Literature* vol. 2). Another edition, in French, was translated by St. Jean de Brebeuf, one of the North American Jesuit martyrs. As a result of so many translations, Ledesma's name became "famous from Lithuania to the savage tribes of Canada" (Caraman *University of Nations*, 12).

7   For a full exposition of this contrast see Henri Rondet, S.J., *The Grace of Christ*, tr. and ed. Thad W. Guzie, S.J. (Westminster, MD: Newman Press, 1967), 209 [ff].

8   For these citations from the *Summa Theologica* see *Nature and Grace: Selections from the Summa Theologica of Thomas Aquinas*, vol. XI, The Library of Christian Classics, tr. and ed. A.M. Fairweather (Philadelphia, PA: The Westminster Press, 1944).

9   Brodrick's biography contains information on Bellarmine jugs: "As a household vessel the bellarmine is now obsolete, but that it once enjoyed much popularity in the taverns and stately homes of England is evident from the many specimens which are to be found in museums and private collections up and down the country. The London Museum alone possesses more than a hundred, nearly all dug up in the city and its suburbs ... The first and best specimens were good attempts at caricature, and the Cardinal is easily recognized in them." He observes that "there are some references to the jug in the by-ways of English literature," including Ben Jonson's *Bartholomew Fair* and Cartwright's "forgotten comedy" (*The Ordinary* 142–44).

10   Janelle lists various texts on Mary Magdalene, all underscoring her conversion. He speculates that "there was especial reason why the Counter-reformation, with its mood of self-reproachfulness, should grant paramount honor to her, who was dwelling in perpetual sorrow for the sins of her past life." The reason, he believes, is "the remorse felt for the moral perversion of the Renaissance period," which accounts for "the tearfulness in fashion after the Council of Trent" (189). Among Italian works on Mary Magdalene published in the sixteenth century are: Erasmo Valvasone's *Le lagrime della Maddalena*, Giuseppe Policreti's *La conversione di Maddalena*, Giovanni Ralli's *Le lagrime de Santa Maddelena*, and Torquato Tasso's *Stanze ... per le lagrime di Maria Vergine santissima, di Chiesu Christo Nostro Signore*. There is also an anonymous French work, *La Magdelene repentie*, published in Paris in 1597, and a Spanish poem, *Breve Suma de la admirable conversion y vida de le gloriosa Magdalena* (Janelle 189–90).

11   Janelle maps Southwell's stylistic "progress." His earliest works, including the *Funeral Tears* and the *Epistle of Comfort*, are "strongly Euphuistic," filled with "parallel and

contrasted prose [and] conceits." His middle period includes his letter to his father and *Triumphs Over Death*, which Janelle describes as "detached paragraphs of parallel cast." Finally, in the *Short Rule of Good Life* and the *Humble Supplication* he achieves "clear, direct and forcible controversial prose" (155).

Chapter 6
Reconciling Mortality:
Triumphs over Death

Study and prayer in Rome enabled Southwell to reconcile, through redirection, personal and artistic passions to religious life in the Society of Jesus. During the same years, while residing at the English College, he also started down the road to England and toward reconciliation with a martyr's fate. There is no exaggerating the degree to which students and faculty at the English College contemplated dying for their faith. Anticipation of martyrdom and news of martyrs determined the atmosphere, especially during Southwell's first years there. Edmund Campion was executed on 1 December 1581, shortly after Robert moved from the novitiate to the College.[1] This event changed utterly both Southwell and the institution that was his home for the next five years. After the martyrdom of Edmund Campion and his companions, "the life of the College was geared to an heroic pitch" (51). Responding to Campion's death, and those of other priests, occupied a significant amount of the poet's time and energy. It also prepared him psychologically and spiritually to face his own likely death under the same circumstances.

Campion's execution after only a year in England surprised many in Rome, and might have precipitated a public relations disaster for the Jesuits and a calamity for their English mission. As Michael E. Williams observes:

> One should not underestimate the shock that Campion's trial and subsequent execution created. The mission had raised great expectations. On leaving Rome the company had been accompanied by a procession of dignitaries to the Milvian Bridge, they had been received with great joy at Rheims and news of success in England was eagerly awaited. The martyrdom of Campion, Sherwin and Briant was seen as a serious check to the idea of winning back the English people to Catholicism by a campaign of preaching the Gospel and ministering the sacraments to the Catholic community. ("Campion and the English Continental Seminaries," 290)[2]

Jesuits, including Southwell, averted this potential disaster through artistic and public relations efforts, thereby turning a defeat at Tyburn to their advantage. In doing so, they articulated an aesthetics of martyrdom grounded in the Jesuits' "way of proceeding." At once emotionally charged and eminently practical, the artifacts produced after Campion's death respond in characteristically Jesuit ways to the risks inherent in the English mission and the reality of dying for one's faith.

Some of Campion's contemporaries recognized the Jesuit's return to England as risky for him, for his order and for recusants. For example, Edmund's death would have confirmed the fears of Everard Mercurian, the recently deceased Jesuit General, who allowed Campion to return home at the urging of Allen and Persons. After years of hesitation, Mercurian acquiesced to the requests of Englishmen in the Society to work among their own people who faced increased pressures to abandon their faith.[3] William Allen ultimately persuaded Mercurian that his subjects were especially suited for this work. Responding to claims that the Society already had too many apostolic commitments, Allen writes:

> But most approachable Father, Allen ... asks, or rather the nation and our native land asks, and suppliantly requests some part of the charity and concern which you bestow on all nations, Christian and barbarous. Father do not repel us as we ask for justice. And you who go about collecting sheep for the flock of Christ in far-off Indies, do not be disdainful of seeking with us the lost British lamb. (Knox *Letters and Memorials of William Cardinal Allen*, 68–69)

It was not disdain, however, that made Mercurian reluctant; he anticipated the death that Campion would meet and its possible implications for the Society. As Thomas McCoog observes, "[t]he dangers of the English mission were too great to be overlooked ... Even if many, perhaps attracted by the dangers and the possibility of martyrdom, would volunteer for the mission, would the good gained by their labors outweigh the loss of these men?" (*The Society of Jesus in England, Ireland and Scotland*, 132). Another objection concerned the difficulty of sustaining the integrity of Jesuit life. Mercurian and others feared that Jesuits in England would be out of regular touch with their superiors and with one another. Moreover, Mercurian perceived that the Society's image was at stake:

> [He] ... feared that the English government would depict the missionary expedition as a political enterprise, a fear very understandable because of Papal Spanish machinations still under consideration. If the government did interpret the Jesuit mission as political, it would make the English Jesuits odious to their countrymen and their actions suspect—perhaps not to the wiser but certainly to the greater part of the people. (McCoog 132)

Mercurian might have proved prescient had not Southwell and others launched a public relations campaign after Campion's death. The crisis of losing a prominent member of the order to an early and ignominious end spurred prodigious creativity. Jesuits promoted through literary, pictorial and dramatic representations the cult of England's newest martyr and those who suffered and died after him. These usually fervent depictions served four pragmatic purposes: they shored up the reputations of martyrs such as Campion, already known as "one of the diamonds of England" and "the chief pearl of Christendom"; they promoted vocations; they prepared English Jesuits to meet similar fates; and they encouraged benefactions to Jesuit enterprises.⁴ Moreover, they achieved this in a manner consistent with methods of Ignatian prayer and related forms of Jesuit practice. The artifacts produced by Campion's confreres, including Southwell, constitute a characteristically Jesuit response to the death of one of their own.

Protestants who attacked Campion's credibility as a martyr and questioned the integrity of his order shaped the context for the Jesuits' response. Three attempts to undermine Campion and the Society were written by men who spent, or who claimed to have spent, time in Rome. The first attack, *John Nichols Pilgrimage, wherein is displaied the lives of Proude Popes, ambitious cardinals, lecherous bishops, fat bellied Monkes, and hypocritical Jesuits*, was written in the year of Campion's death. Nichols, a Welshman, aspired to the priesthood but was found wanting by the English College faculty. Upon his return to England he was arrested and became the government's spokesman in debates between Catholics and Anglican officials.⁵ Before impugning Campion, Nichols levels charges against Roman Jesuits, accusing them, for example, of having sex with their students. "These Jesuits are full of scoffs and mocks," he writes, "they have vowed chastity, but I do not like the things that were practiced in the dark between some of the Jesuits and the English Seminarie, and some of the fairest complexion of the English students, whose names I remember, but for modesty's sake I conceal them." He did not hesitate, however, to name imprisoned Jesuits. He refers to Campion as "Ignatius di Loyolas priest," who is "highly promoted in England, for he is archbishop of the Tower of London, and retaineth in his service many a stout prelate." Nichols facetiously invites more Jesuits to join Campion: "Let us bid them make haste to return home, they shall want no preferment: the bishopric of Newgate is void, the Archdeaconship of the King's Bench is vacant, and many rich benefices in the Tower to wait and tarry their coming home."

The following year Anthony Munday, who testified in the proceedings against Campion, published *The English Roman Life*, an account similar to Nichols' of time spent in Rome.⁶ At Campion's trial

Munday gave testimony about a meeting between Campion and Allen during which they conspired against the Queen.[7] Edmund never denied the fact of the meeting, but argued that Munday's claims about its agenda were false (Simpson *Edmund Campion*, 421). After the death of Campion and his companions, Munday reports their allegedly unedifying behavior on the scaffold:

> You may note a special example in these our countrymen lately executed, that neither their cause was esteemed of God, nor perfectly persuaded in themselves; yet they would die in a bravery, to be accounted martyrs at Rome, and in the midst of their bravery all the world might know their false and feint hearts ... Campion, their glorious captain, he looked death in the face so soon as he saw the pace of execution, and remained quaking and trembling unto the death ... These are the martyrs of Rome, not one of them patient, penitent, nor endued with courage to the extremity of death, but dismaying, trembling and fearful as the eyewitnesses can bear me record. (Howell *State of Trials* vol. 11, 1860–85 [see note 7])[8]

Charles Sledd, who spent eight months in Rome in 1579–1580, made a third effort to disassociate the Jesuits' cause from God's. In his diary, Sledd traffics in rumors about Jesuit support for Fitzmaurice's invasion of Ireland and other real or imagined plots against Elizabeth (South 19–20). He claims to have been privy to conversations with Allen, which he weaves into elaborate fantasies of Jesuit intrigue. Altogether, Nichols, Munday and Sledd contributed to disproportionate panic among Englishmen about the aims of the Jesuit mission as well as to the government's tarring of Campion's reputation.

Southwell and others quickly offered their own version of these people and events, and typically letters first conveyed news to houses of the Society and supporters of the order throughout the world. As noted in material on the Jesuit *Relations*, such correspondence is mandated in the Jesuit *Constitutions*, which describes epistolary exchanges as "a very special help" in promoting the union of members. Loyola orders local superiors to supervise this, "providing an arrangement through which each region can learn from the others whatever promotes mutual consolation and edification in our Lord" (*Constitutions*, 673). Letters written in proximity to Campion's arrest already show Jesuits turning a coming tragedy into a cause for consolation and edification. Claudio Aquaviva, Mercurian's successor as General, writes:

> [Campion's] exertions ... gave us great consolation and we were daily looking for great results; yet since it seemed good to the Lord, to whose honor those achievements were devoted, we have more hope that, in as

much as there is more merit in enduring torture rather than toil, so for the conversion of that people Fr. Campion will have greater influence in prison or being racked than on the platform or by preaching, or any of his former occupations.[9]

Edward's influence in death is subsequently taken up by Southwell. In a letter to Persons probably written in early 1582 and mostly concerning worries about his family, he begins by noting "how well Ours [i.e., members of the Society] have comported themselves, especially he with whom you started [i.e., Campion], your trusty and inseparable companion in labor." Writing in code, Southwell underscores that the latter's death has inspired conversions and vocations. "He has had the start of you," the poet tells Persons, "in loading his vessel with English wares, and has successfully returned to the desired port" (Southwell *Unpublished Documents*, 302). The "vessel" to which he refers is the church or, perhaps more specifically, the Society of Jesus. The "English wares" are recruits to the order. In the months after Campion's death twenty-two Englishmen came to Rome, inspired by the martyr's example. Edmund's "desired port" is heaven.

Robert Persons also contributes to this epistolary campaign. He reports to Aquaviva how "a good many [witnesses] related to me with how fearless and glad a countenance Fr. Edmund and the others endured that ignominy." Persons takes the measure of Campion's influence on recusants, especially candidates for the priesthood. He describes how the martyr "melted the hearts of a number of Catholics, mainly young men of the upper class, to such an extent, that, being unable to keep back their tears there at the spot, they returned hurriedly to their homes, and then for a long time afterwards continued to weep."[10] Weeping, according to the Ignatian tradition, signifies consolation, and it becomes something of a trope in accounts of Campion's martyrdom which, according to Persons, are numerous. He notes that:

> ... countless is the number of books, dialogues, treatises, poems and satires which have been composed and published, some in print, some in manuscript, in praise of these martyrs and in blame of their adversaries ... The enemy rages, but to know purpose, for even boys stand up to their faces and reproach them with their cruelties. They cannot or dare not with Campion dispute. (*Letters and Memorials*, 133)[11]

One such boy was Henry Walpole, who resolved to enter the Jesuits after being splattered with Campion's blood when the martyr's severed quarters were thrown into a boiling cauldron.[12]

Edmund Campian, Jesuit.

Ob. 1581. Ætatis Suæ 41.

Published 1st Dec.r 1819. by T.RODD Jun.r & H.RODD. 17. Little Newport St. Leicester Sq.r

6.1 Engraving of Edmund Campion, Martyr, 1 December 1581 (by courtesy of the Woodstock Theological Center Library, Georgetown University, Washington, D.C.)

This inspired Walpole to write a poem of thirty stanzas, many of which are typically tear-soaked.[13] As Walpole's biographer, Augustus Jessop, puts it, the poem "was calculated to produce profound sensation."[14] Walpole describes Campion in martial terms typical of early Jesuit discourse: "The cawse to conquyre synne,/ his armor praier, the word his terdge & shield/ ... / his capteine Christe, which ever durying is" (ll. 13–18). He then connects Campion with the planting of the faith in England. Along with tears and other vehicles for producing "profound sensation," iterations of this argument occur in many other Jesuit works, including Southwell's *Epistle of Comfort* and the *Humble Supplication*. Walpole identifies Edmund as "our new apostle cumying to restore the feith wich Austen planted here before" (23–24). Referring to Augustine of Canterbury here and elsewhere in literary and pictorial representations contradicts critics of the Jesuits who identified the order as a Tridentine innovation incongruent with traditional Christianity.[15] In fact, Campion made this argument from antiquity at his trial. In his concluding statement, he accused those who convicted him of analogously censuring "all the ancient priests, bishops and kings—all that was once the glory of England, the island of saints, the most devoted child of the See of Peter" (South 114). Southwell employs this same thesis in his *Humble Supplication*, when he reminds Elizabeth that he stands in an ancient line of pastors and prelates:

> Yea, if to be a Priest made by th'authority of the See of Rome, and present within your Highnes dominions, be a just title of treason, ... then all the glorious Saints of this land were no better than Traytors, and their Abettors felons ... then St. Augustine and his Company, that converted our Realme in St. Gregories time were all within the Compass of Treason, sith their Functions and ours were all one, equally derived from the See of Rome, from whence they were directly from the Popes, Eleutherius and Gregory sent into this Kingdome, being Priests and Religious Men, as all antiquity doth witness. (*Supplication*, 29)

Southwell's strategy, like that of Campion and Walpole, involves witty playfulness with historical parallels. The Company of Jesus, led by Campion, replaces the company of monks led by Augustine; and, serendipitously, both missions to England occurred under popes named Gregory.

After arguing from antiquity, Walpole turns his attentions to the advantages of martyrdom over other forms of ministry, a tactic observed earlier in letters written by Southwell, Persons and Aquaviva. Campion's "pacience in death," Walpole claims, "dyd worke so much nor more,/ as his heavenlie speaches done before" (ll. 35–36). The priest's death also confounds his enemies, including Sledd and Munday:

The wittnes false, Sledd, Munday and the rest
Which had your slanders noted in your bokes,
Confesse your fault beforehand, it were best,
Lest God do fynde it written, when he lookes,
In dreadful doome upon the sowles of men,
It will be late, alas, to mend it then. (85–90)

Walpole acquits Elizabeth alone of those involved in the execution because she has been "mysinfoorme[d]" by enemies: "My sovereigne Liege, behold your subjects end./ Your secret foees do mysinfoorme your grace" (67–68). This sensitivity to Elizabeth, whether feigned or genuine, also occurs in other Jesuit works, including Southwell's *Humble Supplication*. Southwell describes for Elizabeth the treatment of Catholics as though she were unaware of it. "We presume," he writes, "that your Maiestie seldome or never heareth the truth of our persecutions, your lenity and tendernes, being knowne to be soe professed an enemy to these Cruelties, that you would never permit their Continuance, if they were expressed to your Highnes as they are practiced upon us" (*Supplication*, 44). The strategy here involves professions of loyalty by Elizabeth's Catholic subjects. They hope, perhaps naively, to promote the martyrs' cult and the Catholic cause without antagonizing the Queen.

Having made a diplomatic appeal to the Queen, Walpole widens his scope. He addresses England, encouraging it to "look up" and recognize that "thy soil is stained with bloode/ thou hast made martyrs manie of thine owne,/ if thou hadst grace, thire deathes wuld do thee good" (ll. 73–75). Next he reports how all Europe "wonders at a man so rare" (121). The effect is two-fold. Walpole acknowledges how his poem disseminates news of the martyrs to the Society's members and friends in other countries. At the same time, he implies that England should be embarrassed. Other nations know of her policy of cruel religious intolerance. In fact, as in Luke's Gospel where Jesus tells the Pharisees that if the people were silent "the very stones would cry out" (19:40), Walpole predicts that "the streets, the stones, the steps" of London (l. 125), along with the Tower (127), and Tyburn itself (129), will "proclaim the caws, for which these martyrs dye" (126). Then Walpole follows an agenda that is characteristic of other Jesuit writers and artists. He vividly describes the martyr's execution while showing how so much suffering is paradoxically all to the good: "His prison now, the citie of the Kynge,/ his racke and torture joies and hevenlie blysse,/ for me[n]s reproche wyth angells he doth synge/ a sacred songe, wich everlasting ys" (139–42). Walpole observes Campion's "quartered lymmes" and "every droppe of blood," and concludes that with these "he purchast hath an ever durynge crowne" (144–45).

By inverting the outcomes of Campion's death, Walpole applies a line of thinking frequently found in Southwell's works on martyrdom, the best example of which is his poem "Decease, release," in which the speaker, usually thought to be Mary Queen of Scots, meditates on the details of her own execution and finds in them consolation. The first stanza contains four conceits, all figures for the mystery of death and resurrection. Mary compares herself to "pounded spice" which "both taste and sent doth please." Secondly, she is like "fading smoke" which "the force doth incense show." Then she alludes to an image used by Jesus in the gospel of John 12:24, noting how "[t]he perished kernell springeth with encrease." Finally, and most bluntly, she is like "[t]he lopped tree" which "doth best and soonest grow." In the second stanza she unravels these figurative enigmas, identifying herself, for example, as "Gods spice":

> Gods spice I was and pounding was my due,
> In fading breath my incense savored best,
> Death was the meane my kyrnell to renew,
> By lopping shot I up to heavenly rest. (5–8)

The third stanza opens by aphoristically stating the poem's thesis: "[s]ome things more perfect are in their decaye" (9), and then offers a simile that illuminates Mary's present state: "Like sparke that going out gives clerest light,/ Such was my happ whose doleful dying daye/ Beganne my joy and termed fortune's spite" (10–12). Beyond fortune's reach, Mary is lifted up by God, raised to her rightful preeminence of which she had been denied during her earthly life. "Alive a Queene, now dead I am a Sainte," she claims, "from earthly raigne debarred by restaint,/ In liew wherof I raigne in heavenly blisse" (13–16). From her new perspective, she understands the paradox underlying the mystery of her death and that of every martyr. As though to underscore the complexities of comprehending the paradox, however, Southwell makes the first two lines of the fifth stanza syntactically obscure: "My life my griefe, my death hath wrought my joy,/ My frendes my foyle, my foes my weale procur'd" (17–18). But the stanza's final couplet resolves any lingering confusion. "My speedy death," Mary informs her audience, "hath shortned longe annoye,/ And losse of life an endless life assur'd" (19–20).

In the sixth stanza Southwell, like Walpole and other Jesuit writers and artists, concentrates on the details of execution, focusing on the instruments of Mary's death. Even the executioner and his tools reveal the paradoxical truth about martyrdom. Mary looks back on her beheading and sees that "[m]y scaffold was the bedd where ease I found,/ the blocke a pillowe of Etrernall [*sic*] reste" (21–22). Most startlingly, at least to twenty-first-century readers, are the claims she makes about the man immediately responsible for her "loppinge": "My hedman cast me in a blisfull swounde,/ His axe cutt off my cares from combred breste" (23–24). Southwell's poem, like Walpole's, ends on a didactic note. Mary directly addresses the readers, instructing them, "[r]ue not my death, rejoyce at my repose" (25). Given the difficulty of the lessons, she resorts again to explanation. "It was no death to me," she reminds her audience, "but to my woe," and she offers another image to illustrate her point: "The bud was opened to lett out the Rose" (27). Before ending, she underscores how poorly she had fared during life, describing the downward trajectory of her political career. "A prince by birth, a prisoner by mishap," she begins, "from Crown to crosse, from throne to thrall I fell." Her "rights," "titles," and "weale" ultimately caused her nothing but "woe." Like Campion in Walpole's poem, she is to be envied in death:

> By death from prisoner to a prince enhaunc'd,
> From Crosse to Crowne, from thrall to throne againe,
> My ruth my right, my trapp my stile advaunc'd,
> From wor to weale, from trapp to heaveny raigne. (33–36)

In making Mary Stuart the speaker of the poem, as opposed to simply describing her in the third person, Southwell achieves immediacy and a degree of intimacy with readers, encouraging them to enter into Mary's situation and emulate her feelings as well as her heroic behavior. Walpole ends his poem in a similar and a characteristically Ignatian fashion. Walpole, like Southwell and other Jesuit artists, attempts to draw readers into a scene through an exercise of imagination designed to elicit emotions. His poem's conclusion emphasizes how this kind of Ignatian contemplation affects readers' hearts. Walpole wants readers to witness Campion's death and then imitate him:

> We ca[n] not feare a mortal torment, we.
> Theise martyrs bloods hath moistened all our harts,
> Whose parted quarters when we chawnce to see,
> We learn to plaie the constant Christian parts.
> His head doth speake, and heavenlie precepts gyve,
> How we it looke, shuld frame our selfs to lyve. (157–62)

Walpole hopes Campion's hurdle "drawes us wyth him to the crosse./ his speaches there provoke us for to die./ his death doth saie, this life is but a loss./ his martyred blood from heaven to us doth cry" (169–72).

This technique of incorporating the audience into the scene is also characteristic of another medium used by Jesuits to promote their martyrs. In 1583 the chapel walls of the English College, Rome, named in honor of England's most famous martyr, were covered with thirty-five frescoes depicting ancient and contemporary English martyrs.[16] The series starts with St. Peter ordaining Joseph of Arimathea before the latter sets out for Britain. It includes images of the deaths of Saints Alban, Winifred, Thomas Becket, and Hugh of Lincoln. The penultimate frescoes feature Thomas More, John Fisher, and three bays depicting stages in the execution of Campion, Sherwin and Briant. Finally, the painter, Nicolo Circignani, shows Gregory XIII surrounded by the students and faculty who prayed in the chapel as the artist completed his work. Southwell, of course, served there as a tutor at the time. These images presented him and his compatriots with opportunities to enter imaginatively into experiences that likely awaited them. Meditations sparked by the paintings were propaedeutic to martyrdom, and the method of prayer is typically Ignatian. The frescoes are conducive to what Loyola calls "a composition of place" in which a retreatant asks for what he desires while imagining the behaviors of exemplary people so as to "draw profit" from what can be seen in the mind's eye and felt in the heart. This exercise does not approach the truth through theological understanding; it leads through imagination and affect, and Southwell provides a classic sample of just such a "composition" in his *Spiritual Exercises and Devotions*:

> Consider thy companions at present in the service of the Lord and see how fervent they are, how regular in their observance, how eager for perfection. Think of the virtues of those members of the Society who … in England … devote themselves to the salvation of souls with the greatest zeal and amidst extraordinary difficulties. Some lie in their dungeons in chains, amidst squalor and filth indescribable, but bear all with astonishing cheerfulness and a desire to suffer still more … Notice how what they have done is higher even than the reach of thy desires, so now thou shouldst not only desire, but actually do, more for him. (88)

Jesuits also used the art produced in response to martyrdom to elicit generosity and support among benefactors. Circignani's frescoes, for example, circulated among a wider audience when copies were made by G.B. Cavalieri in a book of engravings entitled *Ecclesiae Anglicanea Trophaea*. The book cultivated interest among Continental Catholics in the plight of England's recusants. This publication and others like it aimed at gathering assistance for the Jesuit mission. For example, six engravings were published from copper plates in the first Italian translation of Allen's

Briefe Historie of the Glorious Martyrdom of Twelve Reverend Priests, Father Edmund Campion and His Companions (1583). J.H. Pollen, who edited the unique copy of Allen's book in the British Museum, speculates that the plates were originally engraved for Persons' *De Persecutione Anglicana*, which, he claims, "made a great impression abroad." According to Pollen, "these pictures give the earliest representations of the sufferings of the English martyrs, and so Allen's book was "the seed ... of subsequent martyrologies." "These pictures," Pollen contends, "afforded ideas to various subsequent artists," including Circignani (121). The plates that accompanied Allen's *Briefe Historie* are remarkable for providing a record of the costumes and practices of the day. Circignani, and Cavalieri after him, represent all characters, except the martyrs, in classical attire. The classicism underscored the parallels between the church's earliest martyrs and those of sixteenth-century England. Regarding the scope of the publication's circulation, an Annual Letter published by the English College reports that:

> ... a book on the persecution has been published at the expense of the College, to which have been added plates descriptive of the tortures which the enemies of the faith inflict upon our brethren. We have spread copies of this work far and wide, even to the Indies, that the infamy of this disastrous persecution, the phrenzied rage of the heretics, may be made known everywhere. (Foley *Records* VI, 83)

The subject of martyrdom thus absorbed the energies of Jesuits throughout Europe and especially at Rome, through which all information flowed. Some Jesuits, Southwell prominent among them, devoted most of their time to publicizing the matter. The poet, in fact, was reprimanded for neglecting academic responsibilities while generating promotional materials. Persons urges Southwell's superior to "tell Robert not to spend so much time in writing news letters, but to get on with his studies" (Persons *Letters and Memorials*, 226). The newsletters to which Persons refers are the Annual Letters published for the English College, and Southwell collaborated on these throughout his years in Rome. The Letters provide a month-by-month account of important events in the life of the College and celebrate the accomplishment of its faculty, students and alumni. For example, an entry dated 18 April 1580 is typical:

> On April 18 we sent forth to the English mission the following students of this College: the Rev. Edward Rishton, Ralph Sherwin, Luke Kirby, John Pascal and Thomas Bruce. Having received from his Holiness his blessing and funds for their journey, they were most graciously allowed to depart

in the company of the Rev. Fathers Roberts Parsons [*sic*] and Edmund
Campion, the first of the Society of Jesus whom, at the permission of
Most Rv. W. Allen, His Holiness sent to England for the conversion of
heretics and the assistance of Catholics. (Foley *Records* VI, 69)

Elsewhere the Letters serve as the equivalent of a modern university's
mission statement and admissions brochure. The 1580 Letter ends with a
lengthy description of the purpose of the College and the quality of its
faculty, students and course offerings. "The College was lately opened," it
reads, "for the spiritual benefit of the English nation," and it thanks the
Pope for his generosity: "Over and above the immunities and privileges His
Holiness had bestowed on this new institution, he has given numerous other
tokens of his concern for unhappy England, now so long shrouded in the
mists of error, in order to return from darkness to light, from death to life"
(*Records*, 70). Intended in part for future benefactors, the Annual Letter
wants them to know that they will join good company in donating to the
College. Moreover, the seventy-some students who will benefit from their
support are mostly "of noble or gentle parentage." This quality, mentioned
first in 1580, is repeatedly touted. These high-born young men are also
worthy of assistance because of their zeal. Many of them suffered for the
faith even before enrolling in the College. "It is indeed amazing to behold
such fervor in these young men," the Letter observes, "of whom not a few
have, in the cause of religion, tasted of threatenings, outrage, and crosses,
thus experiencing the sweetness of suffering for the name of Christ" (71).
In an exemplary case, "[o]ne of them was cruelly flogged, his ears ... bored
through with a red-hot iron, and he himself thrust into a foul dungeon,
when, in consideration of his youth, he was released after a confinement of
some months." "Others," the Letter continues, "who have been kept three
days hanging by their feet, or subjected to no less cruel torments, give proof
of the same fortitude":

> Despite these experiences, the students want to return to England as
> quickly as possible, cognizant that martyrdom awaits them: But, omitting
> for the present further mention of their piety and virtue, their detachment
> from earthly desires, and the goods and conveniences of this life, the
> loftiness of their purpose to aim at nothing merely transitory or mortal,
> and many similar virtues, it were hardly possible to express their great
> zeal for martyrdom. So eager are they to shed their life-blood for Christ,
> that this forms the constant topic of their conversation, and of the trial-
> sermons delivered in the refectory at meals ... The louder the boastings of
> the heretics, and the more terrible the reports of the cruelties committed in
> England, the more ardent are their desires. So much so that, brooking no
> delay, many would shorten the time of their studies to be the sooner free

to rush into the fray, reckoning little of the fame and honor to be acquired by a full course of the more arduous branches of learning. (70–71)

The Letter for 1585 makes similar claims:

> Such is the zeal of all for the souls led astray by heresy in England, that the details which reach us about the hardships of imprisonment, the tortures, and the atrocious butchering of their fellows, only increases their yearnings to return to that most arduous mission. Hence it comes that several of them, finding the four years of the scholastic course too long, have petitioned to be allowed to make the shorter course of two years. (113)

Given Southwell's experience and his utilitarian attitude toward studies, he may have authored these entries. If so, he gives credit for his inspiration to the faculty, noting how the Fathers of the Society cannot "in their domestic exhortations awaken a livelier interest than by urging [the students] to shed their blood and to lay down their lives for the faith."

The entry immediately following upon the report of the deaths of Campion, Briant and Sherwin notes that Gregory XIII has paid for additional rooms built to accommodate the influx of students inspired by the martyrs' example. All of these students are said to be conspicuous for "obedience, prayer, modesty, self-restraint ... and other extraordinary virtues" and "intent only on procuring the salvation of souls, and eager to shed blood for their religion" (75). "To do this," the Letters add, "they encourage each other, and when news is brought from England of some fresh outburst of heretical rage and cruelty, it enkindles their desires to undergo in their turn the like inflictions and tortures." For example, when Campion's benefactor and protector, George Gilbert, arrived some months later, he came as the bearer of such news.[17] The Annual Letter records his arrival and its effects. He is described as "a young man ... who has proved of immense use to the Catholic cause, and is no less illustrious for his services to religion than for his rank" (76–77). The Letter provides Gilbert's resume, noting how "from the first entrance of the Fathers of the Society upon the English mission he became their constant guide and companion, he maintained them at his own cost, set up a printing press, and hired workmen to print such works as they wished to publish, defraying all expenses" (77). It also explains his reason for coming to Rome. "Having been despoiled of all his estates and property, and sought out for death as the chief abettor of Jesuits and other priests," he heeds "the advice of the fathers to keep himself in reserve till better times." Gilbert is lauded as a generous benefactor. Before leaving England he "left to Father Parsons a large sum of money and seven horses for the use of priests on their excursions." He also gave an alms of two-hundred and fifty gold pieces to nuns while passing through Rouen as well as eighty gold pieces to the College there. Upon his arrival at Rome, he paid for Circignani's decorations in the College chapel.

Gilbert embodies the attitudes common among men at the English College during Southwell's tenure. Though not a seminarian himself, he ardently desired martyrdom. According to his biography:

> He often discoursed with the English students in the College upon the joys and glories of martyrdom, and these discourses were beneficial alike to both parties; to himself as an opportunity of giving vent to the flames of divine love that consumed him, whilst they tended to enkindle similar flames in theirs; although, on his part, he never conversed with them upon this subject without many sighs, accusing himself as unworthy of the honor of martyrdom, since he had lived in the immediate presence of it for so long and yet, through his own faults and demerits, he had never attained to its glorious palm. (Foley *Records* III, 682)

The Annual Letter of 1583 reports Gilbert's untimely death from illness and recalls his many acts of piety, most of them honoring martyrs. He had "a singular affection for all who died for the Catholic religion." As a result, "[h]e frequently made ... visits to basilicas of martyrs, and venerated the places where traces of their precious blood were still to be found; for the same reason, he at his own expense beautifully decorated the College chapel with the pictures of those who, from the very first conversion of England to this present day, had given their lives for the faith" (Foley *Records* VI, 109). Finally the Letter describes his death, immediately before which he was given permission to profess vows as a Jesuit. On a mission for Gregory XIII, Gilbert contracted "an acute fever ... which soon brought his life to a close." "The day previous to his death," according to the Letter, "as he beheld some of the bystanders weeping round his bed: 'Cease to mourn,' said he, 'you who have the hope of martyrdom.'" "Leave tears and sobs to me," he continued, "who, having all but attained the chance thereof, and had resolved to yield my soul to God amid tortures, am now hurried away by death on this soft bed" (110). His eulogy summarizes the piety that the young Englishman epitomized:

> [Gilbert] showed a very great veneration for the martyrs on account of the ardent desire which he entertained to become their companion in torments and death. Hence the holy youth took great pains to learn the names of all the English martyrs of former and modern times, and caused their acts of martyrdom to be represented in paintings, with which he adorned the whole Church of this College in the way that your paternity has seen,

placing also the holy confessors alternately with the martyrs over the capitals of the columns. (Lucas *Saint, Site and Sacred Strategy*, 186)

This desire for martyrdom, which, according to the Annual Letters, was typical among many at the College, depended upon a certain logic already found in the poems of Walpole and Southwell. The Letters argue, as well, that martyrdom is the most effective ministry available to English priests and ought to be preferred to long life. The 1581 Letter makes this point in relation to Campion, Briant and Sherwin. After describing the efforts of priests who arrived to replace the martyrs, the Letter records "the reconciliation of no less than ten thousand who have been received into the church, though," it adds, "as we are aware, a great, not to say the greater part of this abundant harvest is, under God, to be ascribed to the blessed martyrs, Campion, Briant and Sherwin":

> Their precious deaths, the iniquity of which is confessed by many even of the heretics, have born so much fruit, that both Catholics and their adversaries confirm that, had they lived a hundred years, their lives could never have availed so much as their brief but glorious death, for of the heretics nearly four thousand have been reconciled to the Church, and many Catholics who heretofore were timid and disposed to yield now stand forth boldly and undauntedly. (Foley *Records* VI, 78)

The Letters also note the range of activities which the College sponsored for the people of the city and their reactions to the presence of future martyrs among them. These reactions would have confirmed in the Englishmen the rightness of the cause for which they were willing to die. St. Philip Neri, founder of the Oratorians and a neighbor of the College, greeted the students by calling out, "Salvate Flores Martyrum."[18] Often a student was invited to preach to the Papal court, usually as he was leaving for England. For example, in March 1581, William Hart "made a short address to His Holiness, which both moved and consoled the Pontiff and all who were present" (72). Hart made a point of thanking the Pope for having "opened up and cleared of its obstacles the way of return to the faith and practice of our ancestral religion ... by opposing to the barbarous rage of the heretics those schools of virtue and learning, the Seminaries of Rome and of Rheims" (73). Students also preached to large crowds on the feasts of martyrs and in the course of Forty Hours Eucharistic devotions. The Pope, for example, ordered an annual sermon on 26 December, the feast of the first Christian martyr, Stephen: "[t]he pope commanded that some one of our students should be appointed every year to preach on the subject, deeming it admirably suited to those whose main end is to win the martyr's crown" (98). The feast of St. Thomas of Canterbury was another occasion for such a sermon, and the Letter for 1586 contains news of a dinner during which "a panegyric of St. Thomas was given" as well as "a description of the deplorable state of England" which "moved the Cardinals and the rest of the audience to deepest compassion" (116). The Letter for 1582 likewise reports that "the Forty Hours Exposition has been held twice in the College church, for relief of the spiritual needs of England, His Holiness having granted a Plenary Indulgence for all who were present." The account continues:

> Besides an immense concourse of people, the Cardinals, many members of the prelacy, confraternities, the Roman, German and Greek colleges, together with that of the newly baptized, assembled in due order and spent a whole hour in prayer. At fixed intervals the students discoursed in Latin, and the Fathers of the Society in Italian, on the troubles of that ill-fated island. The impression made not only on the vulgar and humbler sort, but on the prelates and dignitaries present, manifested itself in the length and fervour of their visit, and their abundant tears. (82)

A 1583 Forty Hours celebration is similarly described in the Letter for that year. "The chapel was splendidly decorated," according to the author, "and strains of devout music, composed for the occasion, added not a little to the impressiveness of the function, which drew an immense concourse" (110). Among those in attendance were students from the German College, also preparing to return to a Protestant country. The Letter thanks them for their "general edification" and their "brotherly love of which they have given proof in sympathizing with the calamities of England, as if they were their own." In fact, "they joined with the English in this function with such devout earnestness that it had been difficult to tell whether the cause of Germany or England was the object of their prayers."

The public also visited the College to venerate its growing collection of relics. Along with the forearm of Thomas Becket, a gift of Gregory XIII, the College possessed relics of recent martyrs. The Letter for 1582 records how, after the execution of Luke Kirby and John Shert, Englishmen preserved their bones and sent some of them to Rome:

> Their quarters, which were parboiled, would have been placed over the city gates, were it not that the people, moved by the fate of others who had been lately executed for the same cause, and with the like barbarity, began to murmur. Hence after burning their entrails, they buried the mutilated remains of the martyrs under the gibbet. Certain Catholic noblemen, having marked the spot, took counsel to have these precious relics removed, which was successfully accomplished under favor of the night.

> Not only have several parts of England been enriched by this priceless treasure, but portions of it have been brought even to this College. The Divine Goodness has had regard to the ardent devotion wherewith the Catholics venerate these hallowed remains. (86)

The same William Hart who addressed the Pope was executed in 1583. The crowd in attendance mobbed the gibbet before he was disemboweled. According to the Letter for that year, "some took his shirt, others his shoes, while portions of his flesh were cut off by some to be kept as relics." Some of these were sent to the College. In 1584 Campion's printer, Stephen Brinkley, brought the College "a great treasure, viz. the ropes wherewith this blessed martyr [Campion] had been racked and the crucifix which the glorious martyr Briant held in his hands when receiving the sentence of death" (111). These objects attracted the keen attention of the Roman faithful, who made the College chapel a place of pilgrimage and held the seminarians in great esteem. According to the Letter for 1582, "so high is the account in which [our students] are held by the Roman public, that they make many large presents and are eager to be recommended in [their] prayers" (98).

While theatricality underlies most of the Jesuits' efforts to celebrate the martyrs, perhaps the most effective medium of all was the stage. Records at the English College show that during the last decades of the sixteenth century, plays featuring martyrs were staged annually. The phenomenon also occurred at other Jesuit schools throughout Europe, the number of which exceeded 500 by the middle of the next century. The productions were lavish, and local audiences flocked to them. Special "ladies performances" were added at some schools because women were so overwhelmed by what they witnessed that their highly emotional reactions disturbed male viewers. As with Jesuit correspondence, the poems of Walpole and Southwell, and Circignani's paintings, the plays' methods for moving the audience are consistent with formulae prescribed in Loyola's *Spiritual Exercises*.[19] The emphasis is on imagination and affect, while the aims are to defend the reputation of the Society, inspire vocations, prepare future martyrs, and encourage benefactions.

Theatrical representations of Campion are apt because he was a dramatist. While in Prague from 1574 to 1580, he wrote three Latin plays which were performed by students at the Jesuit college.[20] The plays, staged on great feast days or school events, educated the boys on stage and edified audiences. Fittingly enough, Campion's extant play features Ambrose of Milan, who negotiated with an heretical female ruler. He wrote the play two years before Mercurian sent Jesuits to England, but, as Alison Shell speculates, "*Ambrosia* is not merely historical drama, but a compellingly imaginative and profoundly practical preparation for a possible future." The play, she contends, is "an arena for anticipatory role play," a phrase that aptly describes life at the English College, as well. According to Shell, "the play explores the various ways in which Church and state can collude and collide: in particular, the means by which a priest can assert ecclesiastical power and retain spiritual integrity when the state is against him" ("Campion's Dramas," 110–11). Whether or not this play is, in fact, autodidactic in the sense that the author employed it as preparation for his own martyrdom, scripts written by Jesuits after his death certainly educated audiences about Edmund's heroic qualities. For example, his praises are sung along with those of Southwell and other missionaries in Act 4, Scene 2 of *S. Thomas Cantuar* (1613). An angel visits Thomas Becket before his death to reveal the future of the English church:

> Great danger crowns the pious with eternal leafy garlands. Do you see how great a band, defended on all side by the flower of virtues, rises up against the enemy? Robert Persons leads with the banner; spreading the name JESUS, he shields the cares of the standard-bearer with a sacred cover. See the labors of the uphill struggle. Edmund Campion will accord you a great and famous triumph, and Robert Southwell in equal measure, Henry Walpole on a false charge and Henry Garnet, hurt very little: happily and innocently he approaches the stars, and the miracles of his countenance remain on the earth ... Given these preludes, you, Thomas, seize the fragrant crowns that holy liberty weaves and displays. (Shell 117)

This speech does what it describes: it turns the martyrs' deaths into "triumphs" and makes them "famous" in the process. Students enacting the play, as well as those in the audience, are encouraged to aspire to the same renown, or, at least, to support by their prayers and benefactions those who do.

The outcomes of these efforts are, in some respects, difficult to determine, though anecdotes provide evidence that Southwell and other Jesuits succeeded. Within a decade after Campion's death, Jesuits established seminaries for Englishmen at Valladolid and Seville. Vocations to the Society among English Catholics were robust, and numerous novices adopted Campion's name as part of their own (Simpson *Edmund Campion*, 467). As a result of so many joining the mission, the demand for places in the Spanish colleges was great. These schools benefited from the generosity of local donors, one of whom, Louisa de Carvajal, had a particular devotion to Campion and the recently martyred Henry Walpole. She knew Walpole while the future martyr was on the faculty at Valladolid. After his death, she moved to London and established a religious community. De Carvajal died in London before being deported by the government of James I (Williams "Campion and the English Continental Seminaries," 296). Meanwhile in Portugal, a military officer, Pedro Coutinho, was so moved by a book of engravings on the English martyrs that he endowed a seminary in Lisbon (Williams "The Origins of the English College, Lisbon," 478–92). From as far away as Prague, pilgrims visited Campion's Roman rooms where an altar was erected in his honor.

Even in England, despite the efforts of Elizabeth's government to suppress all memory of the martyrs, their influence endured. In a letter to the Earl of Leicester, the Oxford Regius Professor of Divinity writes:

> I can say with truth, that the ghost of the dead Campion has given me more trouble than the *Rationes* of the living—not only because he has left his poison behind him, like the fabled Bonasus, which in its flight burns up its pursuers with its droppings, but much more because his friends dig him up from his grave, defend his cause, and write his epitaph in English, French and Latin. It used to be said, "Dead men bite not," and yet Campion dead bites with his friends' teeth, and to the old proverb; for as fresh heads grow on the hydra when the old are cut off, as wave succeeds wave, as a harvest of new men rose from the seeds of the dragon's teeth, so one labor of ours only begets another, and in the place of a single Campion, champions upon champions have swarmed to keep us engaged. (Simpson *Edmund Campion*, 462)

The professor exaggerates in estimating the "swarms" of men influenced by the martyrs, but he is correct about their intensity, especially in Southwell's case, whose desire to return to England grew steadily during his years in Rome. His *Spiritual Exercises and Devotions*, written early on in his stay, showed him wavering about asking permission to return to England. After spending five years in an atmosphere charged with energies generated by men dying for their faith, he confidently writes to the Superior General about his convictions:

> About myself I will add only one thing: nothing is more in my prayers, nothing more welcome could ever happen to me, than this. It is your Paternity's decision that I devote myself to the English here in Rome. May it also be your decision, by God's inspiration, that I do the same for England herself, with the supreme goal of martyrdom in view. I will not cease to strive with God in prayer that he may grant me this in his mercy, and that he may keep your Paternity long years to rule over us (X Cal. Feb. 1585).

...

Southwell's *The Triumphs Over Death*, a work he completed after five years in England, best reflects his reconciliation to his own death. *Triumphs*, along with *A Short Rule of Good Life* and the *Humble Supplication*, was written during the "hectic and harried months" of late 1591 (Devlin 231). The ostensible reason for the poet's attention to the subject of death was the passing of Lady Margaret Sackville, half-sister to Philip Arundel, at the age of twenty-nine. Margaret, whom Southwell never met, was the devoutly Catholic wife of Robert Sackville, second Earl of Dorset. Along with their ties to the Arundels, the Sackvilles also provided Southwell with "another link with the world of fortune and literary fashion" (Janelle 58). Margaret's father-in-law, Thomas, wrote the Introduction and "The Complaint of Buckingham" for *A Mirror for Magistrates* and collaborated with Thomas Norton on the blank verse tragedy *Gorboduc*.[21] The Sackvilles, like the Southwells, represented the variety of religious allegiances available at the time. Thomas Sackville was related to Anne Boleyn and, as a staunchly Protestant member of Parliament, participated in the trials of Thomas Howard in 1572 and Philip Arundel in 1589. A year later, his youngest son, also Thomas, became a Catholic, perhaps through Southwell's intervention. According to Devlin, "it is a reasonable conjecture that he was one of the 'many principal persons' whom Southwell is said by his earliest biographer to have converted" (231). Given the family's complicated religious history, Southwell, in *Triumphs*, emphasizes that Margaret "made a good death, that she died a Catholic, and that there were Catholics in attendance at her death" (Brownlow 59).

The central portion of *Triumphs* celebrates the virtues of the woman it memorializes. Southwell intended the work for Philip Arundel's consolation, but he also ambitions that it will reach and edify a wider readership. He worries that the imprisoned Arundel will never see the text, "that it shall be last in execution that was first designed, and he last enjoy the effect that was the first mover of the cause." This being the case, the poet continues, "[t]his let chance overrule sith choice may not, and into whatsoever of their hands it shall fortune, much honor and happiness may it carry with it, and leave in their hearts as much joy as it found sorrow" (Southwell *Triumphs Over Death*, xv).

In many ways Margaret embodies all the practices and virtues prescribed in Southwell's *Short Rule of Good Life*, which he was composing at the same time as *Triumphs*. He praises her for her noble birth as well as her piety, humility and modesty. "Even those that least liked her religion," according to the poet, "were in love with her demeanor" (*Triumphs*, 6). "Of feeding she was reasonable," he tells readers, and "regular in prayers." "In sum," he concludes, "she was an honor to her predecessors, a light to her age, and a pattern to her posterity" (8). His primary interest, however, is Margaret's acceptance of death. "Neither was her conclusion different from her premises or her death from her life," he observes. Most importantly, "[s]he showed no dismay being warned of her danger ... but with a mild countenance and a most calm mind, in more hope than fear, she expected her own passage" (8). Southwell's thesis is that he and his readers should live with the same expectation. As Brownlow notes, Robert's audience can read the piece from more than one perspective: it is addressed to Philip Arundel about his sister's death; it is addressed to a wider readership urging them to consider their own eventual ends; and, finally, it is "Southwell's premonitory statement about his own death as well as on all those other deaths" (56).

In making a statement about his own death, most likely as a martyr, Southwell grounds *Triumphs* on his own experience, both his years at the English College, suffused with literary and visual exhortations to dying for one's faith, and his time in England facing "death's real presence" (Brownlow 58). These experiences made him realize the need for rigorous discipline as a means of preparing for a good death; and, according to Brownlow, the prose style of *Triumphs* "is as disciplined as the frame of mind it recommends" (58). Devlin concurs, commenting on the work's "fine, clipped, and philosophical" expression. Janelle, too, notes its careful design. Likening *Triumphs* to the *Epistle to His Father*, he describes how both contain "a succession of detached paragraphs, each enclosing one definite thought and complete in itself" (150).[22] Detachment not only marks the division of paragraphs in the treatise, it also constitutes a major theme. Detachment, or "indifference" in Ignatian terms, is a corollary to the discipline Southwell mandates. It even applies to family relationships. Once again, the poet "allows" passions, including grief over the death of loved ones, but passions must be checked and kept in proper proportion by reason. It is "natural," he believes, to mourn, "but as not to feel sorrow in sorrowful chances is to want sense, so not to bear it with moderation is to want understanding" (*Triumphs*, 2). Too much sorrow for the dead, he posits, is "either the child of self-love or of rash judgment" (4). This is especially true when virtuous people die. As he states aphoristically, "a good departure craveth small condoling, being but a harbour for storms and an entrance into felicity" (4). "[Margaret] being in a place where no grief can annoy her," Southwell argues, "hath little need—and less—of your sorrow." "Why then," he asks rhetorically, "should her lot be lamented whom high favor hath raised from the dust to sit with the Princes of God's people?" (11).

The argument here, as in so much of the Jesuit discourse of martyrdom, is that we are better off dead, or, as Southwell puts it, "[h]er death to time was her birth to eternity; the loss of this world an exchange for a better" (24). He claims that Margaret Sackville, like Campion and Mary Queen of Scots, understood this. As a result of "how mildly she accepted the check of fortune—fallen upon her without desert," she exemplifies the kind of wise discipline Southwell urges upon his readers. She is, he thinks, "a miracle in her sex" (6). Moreover, "[s]o blessed a death is rather to be wished of us than pitied in her, whose soul triumpheth in God, whose virtue still breatheth in the mouths of infinite praises and liveth in the memories of all to whom either experience made her known or fame was not envious in concealing her deserts" (10).

For those such as Margaret who exercise the proper discipline in life, death constitutes a "homecoming," "a return into a most blissful country" (10). Here Southwell alludes again to the Augustinian motifs found in the *Epistle of Comfort*. Discipline requires that we relinquish disordered attachments to earthly things, even to our lives, which we borrow rather than own. "Our life is a lent good," Robert reminds readers, "to make thereof during the loan our best commodity." Moreover, "[i]t is a due debt to a more certain Owner than ourselves [and] when we are deprived of it, we have no wrong." He then ornaments his argument with a metaphor. "This clayey form," the human body, "is an inn, not a home" (12).

Southwell also situates death in the context of the wider category of suffering, which, like death, ought to be always expected. "Nature did promise a weeping life," he argues, "exacting tears for custom at our first entrance—suiting our whole course for this doleful beginning." He understands necessary suffering in aesthetic terms, noting how "[n]o picture can be drawn of the brightest colors nor a harmony consorted only of trebles." "Shadows are needful in expressing proportions," according to the poet, "and the bass is a principal part in perfect music" (25). If suffering is to life what shadows are to painting and the bass clef is to music, then Southwell suggests that suffering purifies and perfects people; and just as all must suffer, all must die, and by dying be improved: "Yet the general tide wafteth all passengers to the same shore, some sooner, some later, but all at the last." In a similar passage he personifies death, describing how it is "too ordinary a thing to seem any novelty, being a familiar guest in every home; and sith his coming is expected and his errand known, neither his presence should be feared nor his effects lamented" (22). Elsewhere, he employs a conceit from "Decease, release" to hone his point. "What wonder is it," he asks, "to see fuel burned, spice pounded, or snow melted?" "And as little sure, it is," he concludes, "to see those dead that were born upon condition once to die" (22). This being the case, "we must settle our minds to take our course as it cometh, never fearing a thing so necessary, yet ever expecting a thing so certain" (13). He advocates fearlessness throughout the text. It becomes something of a refrain, in fact, and he regularly returns to the question of how one can cultivate this quality. Harkening back to the *memento mori* tradition that he employed in the *Epistle to His Father*, he suggests that readers dwell on suffering and death rather than "delights." Schooled in Rome to prepare for suffering and death, he wants to toughen up his readers lest they become "effeminate":

> Soft minds that think only upon delights and admit no other considerations but of soothing things, become so effeminate that they are apt to bleed with every sharp impression; but he that useth his thoughts to expectation of troubles, making them travel through all hazards and opposing his resolution against the sharpest encounters, findeth in the proof facility in patience, and easeth the load of the most heavy combers. (28)

Southwell, after years of using "his thoughts to expectation of troubles," is in a position to articulate hard truths about facing death. First, death is determined by God, and over that determination humans have no control. Moreover, God always acts for the good, even through death, so we should "[l]et Him, with good leave, gather the grapes of his own vine and pluck the fruit of his own planting." He has learned the advantage of thinking "so curious works," such as the death of young people, "ever surest in the Artificer's hand, Who is likeliest to love them and best able to preserve them" (10). Using a slightly less deliberate image, he later compares death to a game of chance: "God casteth the dice and giveth us our chance; the most we can do is take the best point that the cast will afford us" (26). The duty incumbent upon humans is to "die willingly," and he praises Margaret for doing so, hoping he himself acts accordingly when his time comes. And when suffering and death near, we should not try to elude them because "affliction resembleth the crocodile: fly it—it pursueth; follow it—it fleeth and feareth, a slave to the constant, a tyrant over the timorous" (27).

For five years in England Southwell was following a path that almost certainly leads to death. It is important to distinguish, though, that this need not be interpreted as suicidal behavior. While Robert knows how his mission is likely to end, he has gone to great lengths to stay alive while remaining open to the possibility of martyrdom. As Brad Gregory explains, distinguishing between martyrs and "holy suicides," "the phrase 'to martyr oneself' is an oxymoron when applied to the early modern period":

People could, however, enter or remain in situations overshadowed by the threat of death. Frequently this is highly praised, as with missionaries or itinerant preachers, who, if they were killed, were recognized as martyrs. Such missionaries did not value the prolongation of their lives above everything else. Rather they were willing to risk a shorter life that might end in a brutal death to help guide others to external salvation ... The issue was rather whether certain commitments were worth dying for, and if so, which ones. The challenge of comprehending deep religious commitment looms once more. (105)

Southwell's Jesuit formation prepared him very specifically for this willingness. The *Exercises'* "First Principle and Foundation" calls retreatants to make themselves indifferent to all created things in all that is allowed to the free choice of our will ... so that on [their] part they want not health or sickness, riches rather than poverty, honor rather than dishonor, long rather than short life" (Loyola *Spiritual Exercises*, 23). By the time Southwell writes *Triumphs*, he had been praying over this passage for thirteen years, five of which he spent guiding his own people to their salvation. *Triumphs* reveals a readiness on his part, a desire even, to imitate Margaret Sackville's willingness to embrace death in an edifying manner. He emphasizes the pattern of her death as *in imitatio Christi*. She empties herself after the *kenosis* described in Philippians 2:7. She lets go of her life as death approaches, emptying herself of control or any pretensions to it. The poet urges the same upon his readers and, perhaps especially, himself: "Let God strip you to the skin—yea, to the soul—so He stay with you Himself. Let His reproach be your honor; His poverty your riches; and He in lieu of all other friends. Think Him enough in this world that must be all your possessions for a whole eternity" (*Triumphs*, 31). Here Southwell shows himself reconciled to the "profoundly paradoxical" nature of martyrdom:

> The martyr's agency depended upon relinquishing control, their strength upon a naked admission of utter impotence and total dependence on God. The project of perseverance came not from gearing up but from emptying out, being acutely aware that only total reliance on God could sustain the horror of being burned alive or being hanged, drawn and quartered. There is nothing esoteric or mysterious about this. (Gregory 133)

Again, he consoles his readers and himself by rehearsing the benefits of dying sooner rather than later. It is "not the quantity but the quality commendeth our life," he argues, "the ordinary gain of long-livers being only a greater burden of sin" (*Triumphs*, 24). As for those left behind,

Southwell recommends that they consider the death of loved ones as a lure used by God to bring their thoughts to him:

> God thither sendeth your adamants whither he could draw your heart, and casteth your anchors where your thoughts should lie at road; that seeing your loves taken out of this world and your hopes disanchored from this stormy shore, you might settle your desires where God seemeth to require them. (21)

Notes

1. Campion sailed to England in April 1580, along with Robert Persons and Ralph Emerson. Joining these Jesuits were "seminary priests," trained on the Continent. Other secular priests preceded them, arriving in England in 1574. Campion was the first Jesuit executed by Elizabeth's government. Two secular priests, Cuthbert Mayne and John Nelson, were killed in 1577 and 1578 respectively. These executions strengthened William Allen's resolve. As Malcolm H. South contends, "[t]he executions did not change Allen's mind about the importance of the work of the missionary priests. He was convinced that the priests were the main hope of English Catholicism ... He felt that most of the English people were still essentially Catholic in sympathy and outlook and that the country could be won back to Catholicism" (*The Jesuits and the Joint Mission to England*, xv).

2. Ralph Sherwin and Alexander Briant, secular priests, tried along with Campion, also died on 1 December. Sherwin, an Oxford alumnus like Campion, was the first to enroll in the English College, Rome. Briant studied at Rheims. In selecting these men to die together, Elizabeth's government played into the hands of Catholics who considered this fortuitous. Each constituency responsible for the mission had a martyr. As Persons notes in a report to Rome, "[m]any people have taken note that it was a special providence in choosing these three men for martyrdom; as though [God] had wished to pluck three flowers from the Gardens, one [Campion] from the Society [of Jesus], another [Sherwin] from the College in Rome, a third [Briant] from the Seminary at Rheims" (*Letters and Memorials of Fr. Robert Persons*, vol. 1, 135).

3. Parliamentary acts banned priests from England and levied fines against recusants. See John LaRocca, S.J., "Popery and Pounds: The Effects of the Jesuit Mission on Penal Legislation," in McCoog, *The Reckoned Expense*, 249–64).

4. Francis Everyman, imprisoned for distributing Allen's apology for the seminaries, likens Campion to a "pearl" in a letter written to his brother. Everyman understands Campion's death as atonement for the sins of previous generations. "All men," he claims, "are of the opinion that the offences and negligences of our predecessors and forefathers were so great, and our own sins so many, as they must needs be redeemed by the blood of martyrs" (Simpson, *Edmund Campion: A Biography* [London: John Hodges, 1896], 466).

5. Nichols' first salvo in the propaganda war was a sermon in the Tower. He then published *A Declaration of the Recantation of John Nichols*, relating his Roman experiences. Nichols also was a pursuivant, but ultimately returned to the Catholic church (South *The Jesuits*, 71). Nichols' attack was answered when Persons published *A Discovery Of John Nichols* (1581), challenging Nichol's credibility.

6. Munday published anti-Jesuit material until he met with success, including a possible collaboration with Shakespeare on *Sir Thomas More*. In 1582 he published *A Breefe*

Answer made unto two seditious pamphlets, responding to texts celebrating Campion. Munday reprinted four Catholic ballads, refuting the arguments of each in the same meter and style. See Phebe Jensen, "Ballads and Brags: Free Speech and Recusant Culture in Elizabethan England," *Criticism,* 140 (3) (1998), 342.

[7]   On Munday's role see *A Complete Collection of State Trials ... to the Year 1783,* ed. T. B. Howell, 21 volumes (London, 1816), vol. 1, 1049–72; Simpson, *Edmund Campion,* 393–442; and South, *The Jesuits,* 421.

[8]   In the same year, Munday published two attacks on the martyrs. The first is entitled *A breefe and true reporte, of the Execution of certaine Traytors at Tyburn, the xxvii day of May, 1582.* The second is *A Discoverie of Edmund Campion, and his Confederates, their most horrible and traiterous practices, against her Maiesties most royall person, and the Realme.*

[9]   Patrick Ryan (ed.), "Some Correspondence of Cardinal Allen 1579–85," in *Miscellanea,* 7, Catholic Record Society (London, 1911), 81.

[10]   Persons, *Letters and Memorials,* 93. Charges that the Jesuits attracted disreputables with no other livelihood occasioned Persons' class-consciousness. His response is congruent with Southwell's argument in his *Humble Supplication*: "This may we only say in answer to our objected baseness; that of the small number of Catholique priests of our Nations, (which reacheth not to the tenth of the Protestant ministry), there are very neare as many, yea, happily more gentlemen, then in all the other Clergy of the whole Realme" (7).

[11]   Simpson preserves ballads that circulated during Campion's trial. Prior to the trial, the government advertised that Campion cracked under torture and identified those who aided him. As Simpson notes, "these ideas were overthrown root and branch by his public appearances ... and when they were suppressed, the voice of the people was heard in ballads, which were nonetheless effectual for their lack of melody and grammar" (*Edmund Campion,* 378). The most sophisticated ballad follows:

A Jebusite, a Jebusite, Wherefore, I you pray?
Because he doth teach you the only right way?
He professeth the same by learning to prove,
And shall we from learning to rack him remove?

His reasons were ready, his grounds were most sure,
The enemy cannot his force long endure;
Campion, in camping on spiritual field,
In God's cause his life is ready to yield.
Our preachers have preached in pastime and pleasure,
And now they be hated for passing all measure;
Their wives and their wealth have made them so mute.

[12]   Augustus Jessop reports that Walpole's biographies disagree about the anecdote's veracity. Relying on Bartoli's *Dell' Istoria della Compagnia di Gesu,* he imagines how "[when] the executioner had finished his bloody work and flung Campion's quarters into the cauldron was simmering hard by, the blood spurted out upon Henry Walpole, and bespattered his garment." "The beating heart of the young enthusiast throbbed with new emotion," according to Jessop, "every impulse of indignation and horror stirred within him; and it seemed that there had come to him a call from heaven to take up the work which had been so cruelly cut short, and to follow the path which Campion had trodden" (*One Generation of a Norfolk House* [London, 1879], 100). Walpole arrived at Rheims in July 1582. In 1584 he moved to the English College, Rome, where

Southwell was tutor. After some years of study he entered the novitiate at Naples. According to Devlin, Walpole's entrance pleased Southwell, but also exacerbated his difficulties at the College, where factions were causing unrest. When Walpole left the College, Southwell lost proximity to a friend and a fellow Norfolk man. As a newly ordained priest, Walpole was sent to Flanders where he was arrested and imprisoned for a year by Calvinists. Upon his release he worked at the colleges for English exiles in Seville and Valladolid. In December 1593 he finally returned to England, where he was arrested within twenty-four hours of arriving. He spent two years in prison and was tortured fourteen times, often by Southwell's own torturer, Topcliffe. Like Southwell, Walpole was executed in 1595.

[13] Henry Garnet attests that Walpole wrote the poem before leaving England in 1582. In a letter dated the day Walpole died, Garnet writes:

In prison he had nothing but one poor mat three feet long, on which he made his prayer upon his knees for a greater part of the night; and when he slept, it was upon the ground, leaning upon the same mat. And besides this long prayer in the night, he spent not a little time making English verses, in which he had a particular talent and grace; for before he left the Kingdom, he had made a poem on the martyrdom of Father Campion, which was so much taken notice of by the public, that the author not being known, the Gentleman who published it was condemned by the Council to lose his ears and pass the remainder of his days in prison, in which, after some years, he made a pious end.

(Challoner *Memoirs of Missionary Priests*, 221–22).

[14] Walpole's poem appeared immediately after Campion's death, circulating anonymously, first in manuscripts, four of which survive, and then in print (STC 4537). Another copy of the poem is in the hand of Sir John Harrington, Sr., in the Arundel Harington manuscript. See *The Arundel Harington Manuscript of Tudor Poetry*, ed. Ruth Hughey, vol. 1, 106–11.

[15] See John Donne, for example, in *Ignatius His Conclave*. Loyola lists among such innovators as Copernicus, Paracelsus, Machiavelli and Columbus. According to Donne, all are worthy of similar scorn, though he proves Ignatius most despicable.

[16] The wall paintings were razed, along with the chapel itself, in the nineteenth century. The only surviving decoration is the high altar painting by Durante Alberti of *The Trinity with Sts. Thomas of Canterbury and Edward* that can be viewed in the Gothic Revival church built on the site in 1866.

[17] Volume VI of Foley's *Records* contains Gilbert's biography.

[18] Williams explains that Neri lived close to the College at San Girolomo. See no. 43, "Campion and the English Continental Seminaries," 294.

[19] On Jesuit spirituality and drama, see William H. McCabe, *An Introduction to Jesuit Theater* (St. Louis, MO: Institute of Jesuit Sources, 1983).

[20] Two of the plays are known through extra-textual evidence. The first was a reworking of Abraham's sacrificing of Isaac. According to Alison Shell, this episode was popular with Jesuit dramatists because "of the opportunity it gave for a boy's part, and also because its message of youthful sacrifice was appropriate to an order which gave high priority to both teaching and missionary work." "Jesuits who faced spectacular dangers abroad, in the Far East and in America as well as in England, were," Shell notes, "constantly commended to the pupils' admiration and possible emulation" ("'We are Made a Spectacle': Campion's Drama," 105). The second script recounts the life of St. Paul as a missionary and martyr.

21   Most scholars agree that Sackville wrote only the last two acts of the play, which was performed in 1561. Sidney praised the play, based on a Senecan tragedy and the legendary history of Britain, in his *Defense of Poesy*.

22   Janelle's verdict on *Triumphs* is unfavorable. He decries the allegedly overwhelming stoicism of the work. "Even what is Christian," he writes, "is prompted more by prudence than by enthusiasm" (233). Moreover, he argues that *Triumphs* reveals an "almost Pagan fatalism," and, "despite occasional flashes of lyrical beauty, the chief merit to which the work can lay claim is its concinnity" (238).

Chapter 7
Reconciling Religious
Opponents

Sharp divisions among students and faculty at the English College during Southwell's tenure there made him appreciate even more the importance of reconciliation, and he later brought this appreciation to bear when composing his remaining and most conciliatory prose work, *An Humble Supplication to her Majesty the Queen.* His first two years at the College, in the immediate wake of the martyrdom of Campion, Sherwin and Briant, were peaceful and productive. Dedication to promoting the martyrs' cause "swept all discord out of the College" (Devlin 50). In previous years, however, tensions between English and Welsh factions had deeply scarred the institution, and though the martyrs' fresh wounds had a paradoxical healing effect, at least temporarily, former tensions resurfaced during Southwell's career as tutor, Prefect of Studies and Prefect of the Sodality of the Blessed Virgin. These teaching and administrative responsibilities alone would have kept the poet busy, but he also actively sought to mediate a variety of disputes, and his superiors relied on him to do so. As Henry More reports:

> [t]he English College at that time was crowded with young men [who] ... could not be easily led except by one who gained from all the ornaments of learning. Now this Southwell lacked neither sharpness in the quick conception of things, nor soundness in judging them, nor ease of expression in explaining them clearly; and besides there was in him an innate suavity and modesty joined with gravity, and a ceaseless striving after virtue amidst the heat of studies, and thus both in the ruling of students with authority, and in inciting souls to virtue, he bound himself to the will of everyone. (13)

More's hagiographic hyperbole aside, he nevertheless explains why Robert's superiors expected him to reconcile opponents.

Negotiating among antagonistic factions, especially after his priestly ordination in 1584, preoccupied Southwell such that it adversely affected his health, but despite over-extension he continued to generate and execute strategies for reconciliation. These strategies shape his later rhetorical approach to Elizabeth and other officials in the *Humble Supplication*. During this same period, he also became averse to politics, both civil and ecclesiastical, which marked him for life. In the sole letter that survives from these years, he writes to Persons endorsing the conciliatory position regarding the Queen's supremacy in temporal matters articulated by Campion at his trial:

> One thing occurs to me, though I am aware you know it already, seems good to mention, in order to confirm you in that course. It is greatly desired that there should be great conformity among Ours [the Jesuits] in their method of doing business, and that all who are of this firm, should, when the occasion presents itself, copy as far as possible the conduct in all business matters that was noticeable in the relations (both in word and in deed) between your first companion [i.e., Campion] and those who prepared him for the banquet. (Southwell *Unpublished Documents*, 303)

Deciphering Southwell's code reveals his hope that all missionaries, when similarly interrogated, will repeat Campion's politically neutral answers. Robert grounds his hope in the previously discussed instructions given by the Jesuit General at the inception of the English mission. He remains mindful, and implies that Persons should as well, that Jesuits "are not to mix themselves in the affairs of States, nor should they recount news about political matters in their letters to this place [Rome], or to that [England]; and there also they are to refrain from all talk against the Queen and not allow it in others" (*Documents*, 303). He obeys this command throughout his career, and this compliance, along with his sensitivity to the plight of those to whom he ministered, determined the substance and style of his *Supplication*.

. . .

The fractious history of the College warrants attention because of its effect on Southwell's character. The poet's life in Rome was "closely bound up with events in the College, and, therefore, those events will have to be treated at a length that would otherwise be disproportionate" (Devlin 47). Years later Robert vividly remembered College infighting and still regretted it. From England in 1586 he sends his sympathies to Alfonso Agazzari, the College's rector, recalling "the troubles [Agazzari has] had." "I marvel," he writes, "that the devil should be able to stir up dissension among those, who here live in perfect harmony with us and among themselves." Commenting upon the situation in England he adds, "[h]ere, forsooth we have so many enemies in common, that there is no time for internal factions." Finally, he apologizes for the behavior of his countrymen and their Welsh co-religionists in Rome: "Be patient, dear Father, with our shortcomings, if occasionally the breath of storms ruffle your sea" (*Documents*, 317–18). Unfortunately for Agazzari and other administrators, these "storms" were more than occasional. They were regular features of English College life almost from its foundation. Its first historian, Cardinal Gasquet, understatedly notes that "the beginnings of the College were not tranquil" (69). Its early history is marked by revolts, reassignments and resignations, starting with a movement led by Ralph Sherwin in 1579, demanding that the school be placed under Jesuit jurisdiction.[1] Governance of the College was debated from the time when the former English Hospice in Rome was transformed into a residence for seminarians. Older occupants, mostly retired priests, resisted this change and undermined the efforts of early superiors.[2]

Two Welshmen, the previously mentioned Owen Lewis and Morys Clynnog, eventually established a modicum of control over the new College, until the larger English population began to complain "that the Welsh were a quarrelsome and uncooth set, with whom it was impossible to live in peace" (Gasquet 70).[3] An even more serious difference of opinion concerned the work for which students were being prepared. Lewis and Clynnog belonged to a generation that remained reticent about missionary activity in England. Rather than sending men during Elizabeth's reign, they preferred to wait until she was deposed or dead. Younger men, such as Sherwin, hoped to return home soon after ordination regardless of the Queen and her government. Hostilities reached the point "that there was even danger of bloodshed in the College walls" (Gasquet 71). Most of the English students saw a solution in handing over the reins of the College to the Jesuits, with whom they were familiar from spiritual direction, classes and lectures.[4] The Jesuits, they believed, would best prepare them for their eventual return to a hostile England, since members of the Society were already supervising the formation of missionaries for Germany. When their request came to Mercurian, he rejected it on account of the order's overwhelming number of commitments and his wariness of things English. Allen, however, was urging the Pope to overrule the General. Allen opposed Clynnog's appointment as rector, and his resistance was more than nationalistic. He hoped that if Jesuits ran the College they would eventually want to accompany their former students on missions to England. Under Allen's influence, the English students, who outnumbered the Welsh thirty-three to seven, sent disputations to, and ultimately appeared before, the Pope, and their moving appeals swayed his opinion. Gregory XIII ordered the Jesuits to take charge of the College in March 1579. Mercurian reluctantly appointed Agazzari as the first rector, and he began a long and frustrating campaign to raise external funds to support the growing enterprise.

Internally, except for the tranquil interlude inspired by the martyrs, tensions simmered for reasons including nationalism, rivalries between Jesuits and secular priests, and the presence of spies such as Munday, Sledd, Solomon Aldred, Thomas Morgan, Edward Grately, and Gilbert and William Gifford (Devlin 50).[5] Many of these men worked for Walsingham, and Owen Lewis, deposed but still agitating from a distance, allowed himself to become their rallying point (Devlin 49). Fomenting divisions at the College served Walsingham's aims, as did the spies' ability to inform about priests' names, appearances, whereabouts and plans.[6] This was especially valuable information now that students took an oath on admittance to the College to return to England.[7] The College's Annual Letters, some written by Southwell, cite the spies' efforts, claiming "[t]his College can count as a high honour the cunning arts by which the English government tries to overthrow it, as well as the failure of these wicked plans" (i).

Once "the presence of hostile agents" became known, Jesuit administrators imposed strict rules on College students, which some came to resent.[8] Southwell acknowledges this strictness in *Humble Supplication*, comparing life at the English College to Oxford and Cambridge:

> We must limit our minds to the restrained and severe course of the Society of Jesus or the Seminaries, where the place is in exile, the rules strict, the government austere, our wills broken, the least fault chastised, and most absolute virtue exacted ... [W]e are there tied to so precise terms in diet, apparel, exercise and all other things, that we are much more shortened of our scope than in any College of our English Universities. (*Supplication*, 7–8)

Opposition to this "shortness of scope" was especially common among older students training for the secular priesthood who resented what they perceived as efforts to "Jesuitize" them. Moreover, they complained that they were being infantilized, a situation exacerbated because oftentimes the prefects who had charge over them, including Southwell, were younger than they. A complaint lodged by disgruntled residents alleges that "[a]t times a priest has to make way for a beardless youth appointed prefect of a room over his head" (Foley *Records* VI, 24). Prefects were largely responsible for implementing the *camerata* system imposed on the College by Jesuit superiors. The system stipulated an internal organizing principle whereby students were divided into groups and placed under the supervision of a prefect who had charge over their studies and discipline. For example, a prefect would review with students in his *camerata* the materials presented in lectures at the Collegio Romano. In terms of discipline, when students were able to leave the College and venture out, it was always with their *camerata*. The purpose of the system can be debated. On the one hand, seminarians in smaller groups could receive more individual attention and care from prefects, an advantage consistent with the Jesuit notion of *cura personalis*. Conversely, "it was sometimes a convenient means of detecting religious and political dissenters" (Williams *Venerable English College*, 23, no. 55). Students, while admitting the utility of such a system in forming members of a religious order, grumbled that it was not suited for secular priests (Gasquet 89).

In addition to resentment over rules, there were disputes regarding curriculum. One student argued that the Jesuits' "trade of syllogizing there is not fit use for our people" (Gasquet 81). The length of studies was also debated. At approximately the same time that Southwell became Prefect of Studies in 1584, the College saw an influx of arrivals with university backgrounds, some of whom were likely government agents such as Christopher Bagshaw, John Cecil and Stephen Gosson.[9] These older academicians took exception to the pragmatic policy of a shorter course of study urged by Southwell and other Jesuits, and they were aided in their opposition by a returning Owen Lewis. Jesuits on the faculty resisted lengthy studies owing to their sense of urgency about the situation in England. Since so few of their own were sent on the mission, however, Lewis and his faction complained that secular priests were being turned out of the College quickly so that they could provide "gallows-fodder to the missionfield" (Devlin 66). There was truth to this charge: during the years 1584–1585, William Weston was the only Jesuit in England, while hundreds of secular priests had been sent. Making matters worse were charges that the Jesuits were "putting their sickles into other men's harvests, and making use of their position in the College to entice their pupils into their own Order" (Gasquet 81). One complaint notes that "our pious founder [i.e., Gregory XIII] never meant the College to be a Jesuit novitiate" (Foley *Records* VI, 25). This concern caused a rare rift between Southwell and Agazzari. The latter, more sensitive to complaints about Jesuit recruitment efforts, cautioned the poet to be less aggressive in recommending the Society to those under his charge. Southwell complained to the General that these men were being "injuriously prevented" from their authentic vocations. He also enlisted Allen in his argument, and the Cardinal, a consistent admirer of the Society, wrote to Agazzari to support Southwell (Devlin 66).

For this and other reasons, Robert was the object of grievances. As a relatively young man of twenty-three, his position of authority irked the more seasoned Bagshaw and his cohorts. His influence was also advanced by Agazzari's forced attention to finances. While the latter was cultivating curial officials who might provide scholarships for students, Southwell was left to administrate the College. In addition, he was influential among younger men and instrumental in recruiting them to the Society. As a result, when Persons requested that Robert be sent to England in 1584, Aquaviva refused: "The morale of the college was being so thoroughly threatened that if [Southwell] were withdrawn it might collapse" (Devlin 69).

Southwell's own morale suffered as a result. He wrote to Persons for advice in dealing with Bagshaw, to which Persons responded to Agazzari, "All the things which my dear brother Robert has written to me about the College and about Father Bagshaw are not strange to me or unexpected; because God our Lord has given me some experience of what the devil can do to strew thorns and obstacles in the way of good" (Persons *Letters and Memorials*, 200). Ultimately, Southwell and Agazzari managed to have Bagshaw expelled by the College's Cardinal Protector for causing "such tumults there as had never been known before" (Persons *Letters and Memorials*, 119). This caused Persons to write to the rector, "God bless the zeal of your Reverence and of Father Southwell ... I am very glad that you have scotched Father Bagshaw and his companions, but I am inclined to think that more drastic measures may be necessary" (*Letters and Memorials*, 200).

Applying "drastic" disciplinary measures was not easy for Southwell, as he admits in *Spiritual Exercises and Devotions*. It made him revert to the exacting self-scrutiny which his years of formation had mostly helped him overcome. Administrative responsibility sometimes ran contrary to his preference for reconciliation over conflict, and this dissonance disturbed him enough to write to himself about it at length:

> By the heart of Jesus Christ and by the Most Precious Blood which flowed from His wounds, I beg thee to take thyself in hand, observe the greatest modesty in thy exterior conduct and the most exact diligence in self-examination, and show thyself truly to be the light of the world and the salt of the earth. Thou knowest how highly important is an innocent and blameless life in those whose duty it is to point out and upbraid the defects and sins of others, and to correct them by word and example ... Consider what a scandal it would be to others if thou shouldst upbraid them for their defects without amending thine own ... There are some, however, who in addition to their private pursuit of virtue and perfection, have the office of guiding others to the heights of perfection, of noting

their faults and giving due remedies for their correction, or carrying them to others who will correct them. In these persons, a thing which in others would be without blame, wouldst be not only a defect, but something more; whilst a want of custody of the eyes, loud laughter, some immoderate gesture or external act, would seem to be almost a mortal sin. Their behavior and actions are scrutinized and examined more than those of any others, as we can see in the case of superiors, all of whose actions are clearly subjected to all the closer scrutiny, just because they are superiors and bound to set the standard and give an example to their subjects. (*Devotions*, 108–109)

Southwell was not alone in scrutinizing College disciplinary policies. Student grievances occasioned an investigation and report by Cardinal Sega, and though the Jesuits were exonerated, Robert was named in students' complaints.[10] The visitation was ordered by the new Pope, Sixtus V, a Franciscan, who was, at least initially, less favorably inclined toward the Jesuits than his predecessor.[11] Though the report concludes that Sega and his Commissioners "bore witness to the satisfactory state of the College, to the general contentment and progress of all the students, with but few exceptions" (Foley *Records* VI, 112), "the Acts of the Visit disclose that there was serious discontent" (Gasquet 89).[12] One result of the students' accusations was the removal, at Allen's suggestion, of Agazzari as rector. He was replaced by an English Jesuit, William Holt, satisfying the students' request that they be governed by a compatriot rather than an Italian.[13] In addition, the College received a new and more detailed constitution, *Omnis Republicae Status*, confirming most of the Jesuit structures already in place, including the influential and controversial presence of the Sodality of the Blessed Virgin Mary, supervised by Southwell.

The Sodality was a feature at all Jesuit schools, and was established at the English College in 1581. Such organizations predate the official founding of the Jesuits, with Peter Faber composing rules for a Sodality at Parma early in 1540. These rules, which were confirmed in various later documents, stipulated daily meditation, examination of conscience, spiritual confession, frequent reception of communion, and charitable works. From the first, Sodalities recruited from among elites, based on Loyola's conviction that it was important to attend in a special manner to those "who by their authority, their learning, and their example are in a better position to spread the good" (*Constitutions*, 622). While Loyola and his first companions established proto-Sodalities, especially at churches in major cities, the form of the organization familiar to Southwell was established by the peripatetic Jesuit, John Leunis, who, as a Prefect at the

Roman College in 1560, organized his students into small groups which fostered their sanctification. Leunis spent the rest of his career traveling to Jesuit schools throughout Europe and establishing similar groups characterized by "a strong and tender devotion to Mary, the interior source of an intensely Christian life, [and] an unwearied activity in the exercise of charity and zeal" (Villaret 26). Leunis' work was promoted by Aquaviva, under whose leadership Sodalities spread to Africa, Brazil and Japan. Gregory XIII also endorsed the movement, confirming it in the 1584 Bull, *Omnipotentis Dei*, which made normative the practices of the Sodality at the Collegio Romano. His successor, Sixtus V, also attested to their usefulness, and instructed Aquaviva to draw up universal rules. Aquaviva's legislation and the history of the Sodality stress the movement's integral "Marianity" (Villaret 34). All Sodalists made an obligatory act of consecration to Mary, and, after a series of probations based on experiments prescribed for Jesuit novices, professed a formula very similar to the first vows of Jesuits. The diction of the formula reveals the strong Marian element in the spirituality of Sodalists:

> Most Holy Mary, Virgin Mother of God, I, *N.*, most unworthy though I am to be thy servant, yet touched by thy motherly care for me, and longing to serve thee, do, in the presence of my Guardian angel and all the court of heaven, choose thee this day to be my Queen, my Advocate, and my Mother, and I firmly purpose to serve thee evermore myself and to do what I can that all may render faithful service to thee. Therefore, most devoted Mother, through the Precious Blood thy Son poured out for me, I beg thee and beseech thee, deign to take me among thy clients and receive me as thy servant forever. Aid me in my every action, and beg for me the grace never by word or deed or thought to be displeasing in thy sight, and that of thy most holy Son. Think of me, my dearest Mother, and desert me not at the hour of death. Amen. (Villaret 37)

The obvious stress on fidelity to Mary and her centrality in the scheme of salvation soon resulted in a willingness of some Sodalists to pledge to defend Marian doctrines, such as the Immaculate Conception, even to the point of death.[14] When the young Jesuit and future saint, John Berchmans, did so, he was praised by Southwell's teacher, Robert Bellarmine. Upon hearing of Berchmans' vow, Bellarmine reportedly exclaimed, "Oh, the wonderful idea of thus signing with his blood a statement which, as the young man himself says, is as certain as can be. For my part, I believe that this is the Blessed Virgin herself who has inspired this act of devotion" (Villaret 40). Early Sodalists also acquired apologetical skills, though these skills were not always welcome. Some Protestants found the young men to be "worse than Jesuits": "These at least leave us in peace by our firesides, but these brats are always and everywhere dinning their Mary into our ears, their confession and their Mass" (Villaret 52). Sodalities at the English College, Rome and other schools for English exiles were especially famous for emphasizing apologetics. At St. Omers, for example, Sodalists added to the universal rules an English accent: "The proper end of this Sodality is to train in all the virtues whoever is admitted, and principally in those virtues which will make of him a suitable instrument to cooperate with almighty God for the conversion of our poor country bowed down under the yoke of heresy" (Villaret 55). As a Sodalist, Southwell professed the movement's formulae, taking upon himself the obligation to recite daily the Office of the Blessed Mother or the rosary.[15] As prefect of the Sodality in Rome, he had the obligation of instilling in his charges the same style of devotion.

The Sodality's "Marianity" later colors Southwell's poetry, in which Mary features prominently, especially in "The Sequence on the Virgin Mary and Christ." "The Sequence" consists of fourteen poems, mostly three six-line stanzas, concerning an episode in the life of Mary or her son. Each stanza explores a different aspect of the episode's significance, serving as something akin to "points" for prayer. At first, the episodes Southwell chooses seem odd since he omits the events of Christ's ministry, Passion, death and resurrection. Instead, there are three poems on Mary's life prior to conceiving her son and one each on Mary's death and Assumption. The other nine poems consider only Christ's gestation, infancy and early childhood. Catholics commonly meditated on some of these events by saying the rosary, usually in the manner prescribed by Dominicans. According to this tradition, dating back to the fourteenth century, the lives of Mary and Christ are divided into fifteen episodes, each considered as a topic for one "decade" of the Rosary, or ten "Hail Marys." These events are divided into three groups: the "Joyful" mysteries (recalling Christ's birth and early life), the "Sorrowful" mysteries (recalling his Passion), and the "Glorious" mysteries (commemorating the resurrection and concluding with the coronation of Mary in heaven). Southwell's "Sequence," while related to this Dominican tradition, obviously does not match it. As Martz reports, however, "[t]here was in Southwell's time another kind of rosary, now almost forgotten but then very widely used: it was known as 'the *corona* of our Lady.'" Martz, relying on Thurston, notes that "the *Libellus Precum*, the manual of the Jesuit Sodalities, 'seems to contemplate nothing else but' the use of the corona" (106). The corona consists of sixty-three "Hail Marys," one for each year of Mary's life, as legend has it. These prayers are divided into six groups of ten and a final group of three. Along with the *Libellus Precum*, there are also three books in English, *The Society of the Rosary* (c. 1600), the Jesuit Sabin Chambers' *The Garden of Our B. Lady. Or a devout manual, how to serve her in her Rosary* [St. Omer, 1619], and Thomas Worthington's *The Rosary of Our Lady* [Antwerp, 1600], which explain "how the usual procedure was to divide the material for meditation into seven parts, either distributing the events considered into seven sections, or using the seventh part—the appendage of three Aves and the Pater—for some sort of concluding topic, such as the merits of Mary" (Martz 106). The six "decades" of the corona focus on the Marian feasts then in the liturgical year: her conception, birth, presentation, visitation, Christ's presentation and Mary's Assumption. "Most important" about this version of the rosary in terms of understanding Southwell's "Sequence" is "the fact that the corona was used to throw special emphasis on the life of the Virgin before and after the life of Christ" (Martz 106). Southwell's poems share this emphasis and afford him the opportunity to express thoughts and sentiments he would have acquired as a Sodalist and then passed on to his students at the English College. "The Sequence" supplements the Christologically-focused Ignatian *Exercises* by highlighting Mary's role in salvation history. They also reveal theological sophistication matched by witty ornament.

The first poems show Robert's attraction to the epigrammatic tradition despite its traditional association with "satire and scatological comment" (Scallon 97). As in his renditions of Dyer's Petrarchan love poems, in "The Sequence" Southwell is redeeming a secular and, to his mind, tainted genre, and making it serve religion. He uses three epigrammatic statements, for example, in the fourth poem of "The Sequence," "The Virgins Salutation," to illuminate Marian doctrine and praise the Virgin's virtue:

> SPELL *Eva* backe and *Ave* shall you finde,
> The first began, the last reverst our harmes'
> An angels witching wordes did *Eva* blinde,
> An angels *Ave* disinchants the charmes,
> Death first by womans weakness entered in,
> In womans vertue life doth now begin. (1–6)

The epigrams all depend upon the juxtaposition of two scriptural events. Eve's temptation in the Garden of Eden (Genesis 3) is compared to Mary's Annunciation (Luke 1). The acrostic which introduces the comparison is an ancient one found in Patristic authors whom Southwell frequently cites. There are also liturgical references to the relationship between the name "Eve" and the Latin word "ave" with which the angel Gabriel greeted Mary when appearing to her in Nazareth to announce that she is pregnant with God's son. The hymn *Ave Maris Stella*, for example, which Robert and fellow Sodalists would have sung during Vespers on Saturdays and Marian feasts, contains the stanza "*Sumens illud Ave/ Gabrielis ore/ Funda nos in pace,/ Mutans Hevae nomen.*"[16] The appeal of this word play is that it underscores how the Incarnation reverses humankind's fall which, in typical sixteenth-century fashion, Southwell blames entirely on Eve. The first angel to whom he refers is Lucifer, cast here as a sorcerer. Centuries later, Gabriel, using the same words which Catholics repeat sixty-three times while praying the corona, undoes Lucifer's spell. As the last couplet stresses, Eve's "blindness" resulted in sin and its consequence, death. Mary's generous response to Gabriel's news, "Behold, I am the handmaid of the Lord; let it be to me according to your word" (Luke 1:38), creates the condition of possibility for humankind to regain eternal life.

This stanza epitomizes Southwell's strategy throughout "The Sequence": he relies for form upon a customary prayer prescribed for theologically unsophisticated people. As for matter, he mines his training in classical literature and Patristic theology. The result merges simplicity with sophistication, keeping alive a traditional Catholic devotional practice, while infusing it with the church's new Tridentine and, more specifically Jesuit, intellectual energy. He invites readers to meditate on the mystery of the Incarnation, which he explicates through an exercise of wit. This would likely have well suited an audience of Sodalists drawn from the English College's intellectual elite, as well as English aristocrats to whom Southwell later ministered.

The first poem in "The Sequence" also reveals its author's approach throughout by deliberately, and in the very first line, inviting others into the poem's considerations. These are apostolic poems, as opposed to personal reflections. Southwell indicates his desire to include others, for example, by using first person plural pronouns. In "The Virgine Maries Conception" Mary belongs to all of us. She is "[o]ur second Eve" (1). Nowhere in the poems does the speaker reveal anything of himself or his own spiritual state. "The Sequence" is without idiosyncracy. The lack of personal detail, meant to open space for readers to enter into Southwell's poems, is consistent with advice given at the start of the Ignatian *Exercises*. A spiritual director should never let himself get between God and the person making the *Exercises*. The director can help by explaining forms of prayer and suggesting matter for prayer, as Southwell does throughout "the Sequence," but should not hinder God's movements in the retreatant by revealing much about himself.[17] This also reflects the poet's Jesuit approach to the priesthood and sacramental ministry. Robert writes as though he were presiding at a sacrament, pointing away from himself and toward some other, more significant presence. After his conversion, John Henry Newman appreciated this distinction, describing how "[t]he preacher is different from the minister of sacrament": "The latter is, as it were, impersonal. The former is personal or definite. In particular the ... preacher comes to his audience with a name and history" (*The Idea of a University*, 412). Southwell's poems rarely even hint at the author's "name and history." To the contrary, he cultivates a kind of sacramental or ritual anonymity. The first person singular pronoun occurs only once in all 234 lines of "The Sequence," and then it reminds the otherwise unidentified speaker that he should make himself a gift to God: "God is my gift, himselfe he freely gave me:/ Gods gift am I, and none but God shall have me" ("The Nativitie of Christ," 17–18). In "The Sequence" the poet sacrifices self-concern for the sake of helping readers enter more fully through imagination, intellect and emotion into Marian mysteries.[18]

"The Sequence" also opens with typical Southwellian stress on the effect of grace on nature. Mary epitomizes this reconciliation. In "The Virgine Maries Conception," he notes how "[b]oth Grace and Nature did their force unite,/ To make this babe the summe of all their best" (7–8). Her greatness at birth is attributed to the ontological company she keeps. She is one of only four "wights bred without fault ... / And all the rest conceived were in sinnne" (13–14). Southwell, after introducing the riddle, uses the last four lines of the stanza to solve it. Adam "[w]ithout both man and wife was ... framde" (15). Eve "[o]f man, but not of wife did ... beginne" (16). Christ was born of woman but "without touch of man" (17), and "[o]f man and wife this babe [i.e., Mary] was bred in grace" (18). By implication, Mary's Immaculate Conception is the most remarkable of all these events. God created Adam out of nothing, so, therefore, in a state of grace. Eve, though shaped by Adam's flesh, was created before sin entered the world. Christ's sinlessness is explained by the Virgin Birth, since, according to Catholic thinking after Augustine, original sin was passed on through the concupiscence associated with sexual intercourse. Because Mary was the product of two humans, and therefore sinful parents, that she was conceived without sin is most mysterious. At her conception, nature's post-lapsarian inherent defects are perfected by grace. As a result, "[e]arth breeds a heaven, for God's new dwelling place," i.e., Mary's womb (2). Later, in a poem on her marriage to Joseph, Southwell speculates that because of grace's effect on Mary's nature, she fulfills all the roles available to women. Because "[n]o carnall love this sacred league [Mary and Joseph] procured,/ ... Though both in wedlocke bandes themselves assurde," "[t]hus had she Virgins, wives and widowes crown,/ And by chast child-birth dubled her renowne" (13–18).

Finally, "The Sequence" shows its author incorporating yet another contemporary literary motif into his work. Most stanzas contain images from the emblematic tradition popular among poets of the period, especially among Jesuits, who used the genre for religious instruction. Emblematic poets employed traditional symbols to illustrate mysterious phenomena, spiritual or otherwise. Many of these symbols had acquired a variety of intellectual and emotional associations, and the associations could be playfully arranged to instruct and inspire. Southwell, for example, likens Mary to both "the Orient starre" and a "loade-Starre." The first reference underscores how Mary's birth marks a new start in salvation history, just as the morning star rising in the east signals a new day. It also allows the poet to introduce the kind of sportive paradox he enjoyed. He finds "[j]oy in the rising of our Orient starre,/ That shall bring forth the Sunne that lent her light" ("Her Nativitie," 1–2). Later, in "The Nativitie of Christ," he works this same theme of the nature of Christ's relationship with his mother, summoning readers to "[b]eholde the father is his daughters sonne:/ The bird that built the nest, is hatched therein" (1–2). In this initial iteration, however, he revels in the fact that Mary can be two stars simultaneously, anticipating the dual nature of her son. At once she inaugurates a new era and provides a model for Christians to follow. Mindful of his English audience, he underscores how Mary is especially exemplary for those "all engolfd in worldy waves" (5). She is "the card and compasse that from ship-wracke saves" (6). An imperilled ship numbers among Southwell's favorite images for describing English Catholics, and he places it here to recall England's ancient devotion to the Mother of God. These poems praising Mary might also have "struck a chord in the hearts of the great majority of Englishmen who, with characteristic conservatism, deplored the disappearance of the cult of the Virgin in the newly established religion and the destruction of her shrines in the isle which in earlier centuries was proud to style itself 'the dowry of Mary'" (Scallon 105). If so, then Southwell is typically trying to reach out to the lapsed, attempting to reconcile them to the church.

The poet is most effusively emblematic in the last stanza of "Her Nativitie," in which he employs a different image in every line, thereby invoking a wide range of associations and attendant emotions:

> For God on earth she is the royall throne,
> The chosen cloth to make his mortall weede,
> The quarry to cut out our cornerstone,
> Soile ful of fruit, yet free from mortal seede,

For heavenly flowre shee is the *Jesse* rod,
The child of man, the parent of a God. (13–18)

The notion of Mary as a "throne" recalls one of the many titles awarded to
the Virgin by believers in the course of church history: *sedes sapientia.*
This and other titles were familiar to Southwell because they appear in the
Litany of Loreto, a prayer that gained popularity in the sixteenth century.
While the origins of this Litany are unknown, it was definitively approved
in 1587, though in the years leading up to this it had been the subject of
panegyrics and ascetical writings. Its first use was associated with the Holy
House of Loreto, which was believed to have been Mary's house in
Nazareth transported to Italy by angels in 1294. *Sedes Sapientia,* or "Seat
of Wisdom," is one of dozens of figurative Marian titles that devotees
would exclaim in honor of their patroness. Imagining Mary as the source of
wisdom is likely related to the opening of John's Gospel, where Jesus is
word of God made flesh (1:14). The second image of Mary as "chosen
cloth" is harder to account for, since it has no scriptural or liturgical
analogue. It might be a product of Southwell's own wit inspired by the
image that follows. In Matthew's Gospel (21:42), the evangelist invokes
Psalm 117:22, which describes Christ as "the stone which the builders
rejected." If Christ is stone, then Mary is "the quarry to cut out our
cornerstone" (15). The next image alludes again to the corona's sixty-three
"Hail Marys," each one of which contains a reference to Christ, the
"blessed fruit" of Mary's womb. If Jesus is fruit, then Mary is the soil in
which he was planted. She is not like other soil, however, since she is "free
from mortal seede," or original sin (16). Here Southwell is adding layer
upon layer of allusive reference. The connection between fruit and sin
refers back to Genesis 3, reminding readers that Mary reverses Eve's
punishment for eating the only thing forbidden her in Eden. Given
Southwell's abiding attention to the eucharist, it is also likely that he has in
mind the salvific effect of consuming consecrated bread and wine, both
made from fruits of the earth. If Eve and Adam were damned for eating
Eden's fruit, then Southwell's readers can be saved by receiving Mary's
fruit via the sacrament. Finally, the poet invokes a Marian image grounded
in Isaiah 11:1, referring to Christ's Davidic ancestry: "For heavenly flowre
shee is the *Jesse* rod" (17). Jesse was the father of King David, and, as
recorded in Luke 1:32, the Lord God will give Jesus "the throne of his
father David." The author of Luke also notes Jesus' lineage in the Canticle
of Zechariah (1:69) and in narrating the journey of Mary and Joseph to
Bethlehem (2:4). Southwell may also be playing with a legend associated
with Mary's betrothal to Joseph, since this line appears immediately before
the poem "Her Spousals." According to apocryphal literature, Joseph was

chosen among potential suitors for Mary when a branch that he was holding burst miraculously into bloom. Upon this flowering, "God lent his Paradise [i.e., Mary] to *Joseph's* care/ Wherein he was to plant the tree of life" ("Her Spousals," 7–8). Mary is no longer simply "[o]ur second *Eve*," she has become Paradise regained in which God will "plant" the "tree of life," Jesus, on the cross, who will cancel the tree in the middle of Eden that was not to be touched.

Southwell's "Marianity" reaches its peak in the last two poems in "The Sequence." In "The death of our Ladie" he apostrophizes nature, instructing all "living things" to weep for "[t]he world doth loose the summ of all her blisse" (1–2). Because we have lost "[t]he Queen of Earth, the Empresse of the skyes,/ ... mankind an orphan is." Typically, however, the poet turns our loss into Mary's gain. As in "Decease, release" and *Triumphs Over Death*, from the Virgin's perspective "[i]t was no death to her but to her woe/ By which her joyes beganne, her grieves did end" (7–8). Because humankind so depended on Mary, her "[death] was ... to us a foe." After having suffered so much in life, she found in death "a frende" (9). According to Southwell, she shares this perspective with all who lead good lives, and especially those who suffer for their faith, such as his recusant readers. Again, Mary models for them how they should face adversities, confident in ultimate vindication. Her faith is so strong that she can transform death from frightful to fortuitous: "Not pray of death but praise to death she was,/ Whose ugly shape seemd glorious in her face" (12–13). That face receives Petrarchan praise in the poem's last stanza. Finally, Southwell has found an object worthy of the lavish adulation that secular poets waste, from his perspective, on the women they love. Mary's face is "a heaven." In typical Petrarchan fashion, the poet focuses on her eyes which, to him, are "two planettes ... [w]hose gracious light did make our clearest day" (14–15). As death "eclipses" that light, Southwell instructs the sun to hide its light: "thy beames untimely shine,/ Trew light sith we have lost we crave not thine" (17–18). This is reminiscent of passages in *Mary Magdalene's Funeral Tears* where Mary finds wanting any possible substitutes for Christ's real presence. This sense of irreplaceable people or presences runs throughout much of Southwell's work and seems related to his mournful observations on life in England. England, from his vantage point, sadly lacks that which he is trying to provide through reconciliation, namely full communion with the Catholic church.

The ultimate poem in "The Sequence" celebrates Mary's Assumption, a dogma for which he argues through epigrams and illuminates through an emblem.[19] Since there is no mention of Mary's Assumption in scripture, this ancient teaching would have been scrutinized by reformers. Southwell responds by restating in verse traditional arguments for the belief. In the poem's opening lines, he not only defends the Assumption, but also renders an opinion on the still open question of whether or not Mary died.[20] Robert's syllogistic opening implies that the Virgin did not die: "If sinne be captive grace must finde release,/ From curse of synne the innocente is free" (1–2). The "curse of synne," according to Genesis 3:19, is death. Since Mary was free from original sin, Southwell argues, she does not deserve to die. This opinion is at odds with most Catholic thinkers, including the Fathers of the Church upon whom the poet normally relies, and evinces the ardor with which he and his fellow Sodalists promoted Mary's cult. Instead of burial in a tomb, therefore, the Virgin is enthroned. Southwell also defends the Assumption on the basis of a distinction between Mary and the rest of humankind. The rest of us are "[f]aynte winged soule[s]" who "by grounde doth fayntly flye" (11), while Mary is "[o]ur Princely Eagle" who "mountes unto the skye" (13). As an eagle, she can look directly into the light of God's presence, which would be so great as to blind all others. All save Mary need time in the grave, or, perhaps Purgatory: "The daseled eye doth dymmed light require/ And dying sightes repose in shrowdinge shades" (7–8). Mary's eyes, like those of an eagle, "to brightest light aspire/ And living lookes delight in loftye glades" (9–10).[21] This set of images also recalls *Mary Magdalene's Funeral Tears* where Southwell accounts for Mary's inability to recognize the risen Christ: "He is nowe to bright a sunne for so weake a sight: your looks are limited to meaner light, you [have] the eies of a bat, and not of an Eagle." Mary, the Mother of God, however, looks into the pure light of heaven and sees her son, becoming "Queene to her heavenly kinge,/ Whose court with solemne pompe on her attends,/ And Quires of Saintes with greeting notes do singe" (14–16).

. . .

The only other woman whom Southwell praises so effusively in any of his works is Elizabeth I, and he does so in his *Humble Supplication*, a plea for tolerance written in response to the royal proclamation, *A declaration of great troubles pretended against the realme by a number of Seminarie Priests and Jesuits, sent, and very secretly dispersed in the same, to worke great Treasons under a false pretense of Religion, with a provision very necessary for remedy thereof.*[22] Southwell had been in England for five years when Elizabeth issued this latest in a series of decrees that made more difficult the lives of English Catholics.[23] Elizabeth in Council was responding to the threat posed by the presence in Normandy of Spanish troops trying to expel Henri IV.[24] These Spaniards were poised to seize ports from which they could launch another Armada. Elizabeth dispatched armies to the aid of Protestant allies and then set her sights on Catholics at home. Southwell, staying in London when the proclamation was issued, responded immediately.[25]

Two features of the proclamation account for his urgency: regulations on the movement of and communication among Catholics and, more importantly, scurrilous charges leveled against priests. Commissions were appointed throughout England to examine anyone who might have had dealings with Catholics on the Continent. Property owners were to provide lists "of all manner of persons that have been admitted, or suffered to have usual resort, diet, lodging, residence in their houses, or in any place by their appointment within the space of one whole year now passed" (64). This was to expose families who provided refuge for Southwell and other priests. Any failing to cooperate would be "punished as abettors and maintainers of traitors" (65). More pressing, however, from Southwell's perspective were attacks on priests, starting with the Pope. Gregory XIII is figured as a "Milanois vassal" who has been "seduced" by Philip II "to exhaust the treasures of the Church, and therewith levy forces in Italy ... and in many other places" (60). The proclamation pictures the Pope "hanging at the girdle" of the Spanish King and insinuates that the two of them are practicing "with certain principal seditious heads," namely Persons and Allen, "to gather together with great labors ... a multitude of dissolute young men, who have partly for lack of living, partly for crimes committed, become Fugitives, Rebels, and traitors" (60). The seminaries where these "seedmen of treason" prepare "to be secretly and by stealth conveyed into [Elizabeth's] Dominions" constitute "receptacles made to live in and there be instructed in School points of sedition" (60). Elizabeth and her Councilors want to "discover these venomous vipers, or to chase them away as soon as they come ... by secret creeks or landing places, disguised both as in their names and persons" (63–64). Should they fail, these "Seminaries, Jesuits and Traitors ... by falsehood, by hypocrisy, and by underminings of [the Queen's] good subjects under a false color and face of holiness" will spread "secret infection of treasons in the bowels of our Realm" (63).

As noted earlier, attacks on the seminaries and their graduates have plenty of precedent among English polemicists such as Nichols, Sledd and Munday. The 1591 proclamation feeds upon and nourishes the anxieties they generated, and receiving royal endorsement accords them special status, establishing their place in the dominant discourse of the day. While much in the text is familiar, the proclamation underscores the "unnaturalness" of those loyal to Rome and pays special attention to social class. Catholic priests, it declares, are "of very base birth," so greed is their motive for conspiring against the Queen. They renounce their "natural allegiance ... upon hope by a Spanish invasion to be enriched and endowed with the possessions and dignities of our other good subjects" (60). These emphases cause Southwell to write immediately.[26] His *Supplication* answers all charges and, more significantly, it attempts to alter the cultural ethos by employing a novel rhetorical strategy for the sake of reconciliation.

. . .

Southwell's novelty can be appreciated when his *Supplication* is compared to responses offered by other Catholics, especially those in exile. Typically, Persons is the most vitriolic and obviously at cross purposes with Southwell. From Spain he writes to incite fury and rage among Catholics, "far outdoing the proclamation in its scurrility" (Southwell *Supplication* ed. Bald, x). Persons' context and constituencies were much different from Southwell's, and these disparities determine his response, entitled *Elizabethae Angliae Reginae ... saevissimum in Catholicos sui regni edictum ... cum responsione ad singula capita.*[27] Persons learned of the proclamation while recuperating at Valladolid after two taxing years of diplomatic and fundraising missions. Against this background he responds to what he terms "the most vicious edict of the Queen of England" (*Elizabethae*, 1). Her motive, he asserts, is to "defend the Calvinist heresy" by hurling "most undignified insults against all the Catholics of her kingdom." Taking the pseudonym Andrea Philopatrus, "Presbyter and Roman theologian, long ago rising from the English," he offers a "response to each point of the edict, in which not only is there viciousness and impiety ... but also lying." He seeks to expose the "iniquitous and barbaric" proclamation's "deceptions and stage playing." His opening paragraph establishes enmity toward Elizabeth, and the same hostility is everywhere in the document. She is "a wicked tyrant," and her treatment of Catholics puts her in the company of Julian the Apostate, "who, since lacking in his faith, attempted to dismantle the Christian perseverence with occult plans and plots rather than fight it openly" (5).

As for the lies against the colleges and seminaries, Persons counters that they are "houses of virtue and Catholic letters." News of such holy establishments "inflamed [Elizabeth] more against Catholics," so she "immediately planned the atrocious document, harsh and insulting ... with not the least bit of contradiction allowed by her group of advisors" (2).

Contrary to Southwell, who will exonerate the Queen, Persons holds her personally responsible for the edict's contents and for the cruel treatment of Catholics. Moreover, she acts as Persons would expect a female ruler to: her motive is "a woman's anger," compounded by the insecurity which, he alleges, is characteristic of her sex. She is a woman "scared to death" (3). At the same time, she, and not her Catholic subjects, is greedy: "[e]asily she judged that she was about to kindle so great a hatred against Catholics that she could steal their goods under the pretense of suspension of business" (3). These, he contends, "are the most true reasons of that edict." Therefore, "a thing of such great wickedness and of such ignorance" must be "silenced openly and publicly." To this end he published his response in Italy, Germany, the Netherlands and France (Meyer 251–52).[28] He wants all of Europe informed of his exasperation with Elizabeth: "Enough time has been given, enough hope has been spent, hope which has been given by others about that woman's coming to her senses." "Why don't we speak out at last," he asks his Continental readers, "why do we not stand in the way of so wicked a tyrant?" (*Elizabethae*, 4). In every case, Persons' response to charges reveals his anger. On the issue of the class origins of clergymen, for example, he cannot rest after praising the quality of Catholic priests. After asserting that "in the three English seminaries of Rome, Rheims and Valladolid there are more flowers of nobility than among all your clergy" (Meyer 353), he points out how "[t]hey are not descended from the dregs of mankind like your ministers of the word." The only way to restore the missionaries' honor, for Persons, is to impugn that of all others. Finally, he rails again about Elizabeth: "You are fighting against God. You, savage, are fighting against the Church. You are chasing after holy men. You are hating the spokesmen of Christ" (7).

Other Catholic responses, such as John Creswell's *Exemplar Literarum e Germania ad Guilielmum Cecilum*, Thomas Stapleton's *Apologia pro Rege Catholico Philippo II ... contra varias & falsas Accusationes Elisabethae Angliae Reginae per edictum suum 18 Octobris datum*, and Richard Verstegan's *A Declaration of the true Causes of the great Troubles*, share the tenor of Persons' work, and "the violence of these replies did more harm than good, and their only result was to provoke still more severe legislation against Catholics at the next meeting of Parliament" (*Supplication* ed. Bald, x–xi).

. . .

Southwell took another approach entirely. On the ground in England, he knew from experience that vitriolic rhetoric would only exacerbate the plight of the people to whom he ministered. Having been scarred by deep divisions at the English College, and sensitized to the precarious predicament of English Catholics, he was committed to the course of reconciliation; and that commitment is nowhere more obvious than in his *Humble Supplication*. Most critics are in agreement on the conciliatory style and content which the Jesuit achieved in his last prose work. R.C. Bald, for example, in the introduction to his edition of *Humble Supplication*, states that "Southwell's own feelings, no less than his experience in the mission, had taught him the vital necessity, if English Catholicism was to survive, of reconciling loyalty to Church and State" (xxii). Bald judges the work to be "deeply moving" on account of its straightforward style and possession of "continuity and unity in an unusual degree":

> It is animated by an orator's passion. Southwell wrote of thoughts ever present to his mind and of things that were part of his daily experience. His sense of mission, with its almost inevitable martyrdom, and his feeling for the sufferings of his fellow Catholics, were the impulses that prompted the work. (xvii)

Janelle concurs, describing the work as "aflame with the most ardent sincerity" (238). It is, he thinks, "the ablest, fullest and most powerful plea ever put forward in defense of the English Catholics in the time of Queen Elizabeth." "Its chief beauty lies in the author's feelings, and in the naked, moving simplicity with which they are voiced" (238). The authenticity of the work makes "the Jesuit's straightforward defense of his Catholic countrymen ... more than a document on Elizabethan England." "It is," he argues, "a document by which to judge him," because "[i]t reveals his single minded love of souls, his moral greatness; it is a fitting preface to the ordeal—which he no doubt foresaw—of his trial and execution" (248). Devlin, typically more interested in the events surrounding the production of the text, writes that "[t]his is Southwell in his happiest vein" (245). In the *Supplication*, he writes "with the ease of a true-born gentleman" (246). Even Brownlow admits that writing the *Supplication* is "a courageous and momentous step" (66). Moreover, in its statement of rights of conscience, what Southwell calls 'soul rights,' (28) against the power of the crown, the *Supplication* can claim a distinguished place in the history of English civil liberties as well as in the history of English prose" (72).

Before arguing for "soul" rights, Southwell happily recognizes the prerogatives that belong to his Queen. At the start of the *Supplication*, the poet flatters her while acknowledging her legitimate authority in civil matters. As "a prince supplying the place, and resembling the person of

Almighty God," she has an undisputed claim on the loyalty of her Catholic subjects (*Supplication*, 1). This validation of the authority of an excommunicated monarch by a Catholic priest, referencing her relationship to God, marks the first of several attempts to assure Elizabeth that she enjoys the support of Catholics, in particular, among all her subjects. She is their "most beloved Princesse," "perfect in all Princely virtues," and "the shoot-anchor of her [Catholic subjects'] last hopes" (1). Unfortunately, he submits, these loyal subjects have been misrepresented by her advisors who, on account of "unjust and lawless motives," have created "Counterfeit illusions" (2). These advisors are avaricious, according to Southwell. "They water their fortunes with the showers of our tenderest veines," he complains in a characteristic conceit, "and [they] build their howses with the ruynes of ours, tempering the morter of their foundations with our Innocent bloud" (43).

Positioning himself as spokesperson for a persecuted and powerless community, Robert feels compelled to respond on behalf of Catholics by "lay[ing] open [their] manifold extremities" of which the Queen must, he wants to believe, be uninformed. "We presume that your Maiestie seldome or never heareth the truth of our persecutions," he avers, "your lenity and tendernes being knowne to soe professed an enemy of these Cruelties, that you would never permitt their continuance, if they were expressed to your Highness as they are practiced upon us" (44). He repeatedly states his preference for avoiding a public appeal, but the Queen's interests, as much as those of recusants, demand that he make one. "Both your Majesty's sex, inclined to pity, and the mildness of your own disposition," he claims, render it impossible that Elizabeth is cognizant of her Catholic subjects' condition. Adding to this impossibility is Southwell's accustomed nationalism. His patriotic streak, noted earlier, seems to have grown during his years in England, despite the atrocities he witnessed and the hardships he endured. After the Armada of 1588, he wrote to Aquaviva about the intensified persecution of Catholics, but before providing details he admits his hesitation to do so. He worries that his account will "bring more hatred on the English name than the constancy of our martyrs would win praise for it." To avoid embarrassing the country he loves, he offers Aquaviva an interpretation of the recent behavior of his compatriots:

> Your Paternity should regard the situation in this light. The constancy of the Catholics is such as is always admired in a people naturally inclined to piety, but the fury and cruelty of the enemy is not to be regarded as a disgrace on the nation, but as the outcome of the pestilent heresy, which does violence not only to religion, but to the laws and restraints of nature. (Southwell *Unpublished Documents*, 328)

The majority of English people, inherently good, according to Southwell, are behaving cruelly on account of harmful foreign and domestic influences.

Southwell's patriotic streak also colors his lengthy account in the *Supplication* of the Babington Plot, a bungled attempt to liberate Mary Queen of Scots and spark a general rebellion among England's Catholics, leading to Elizabeth's demise. In the end, the plot caused Mary's death along with the executions of several of Robert's friends and relatives. Despite these ties, the poet's immediate reaction to the plot was anger, which he expressed in a letter of 21 December 1586 to Aquaviva. After describing the severe suffering recently endured by Catholics in the wake of "this new storm," i.e., the conspiracy, he accounts for the government's harsh treatment:

> The occasion for this outburst was given by the men who set on foot that wicked and ill-fated conspiracy, which did to the Catholic cause so great mischief, that even our enemies, had they the choice, could never have chosen aught more mischievous to us or more to their mind. (*CRS* 1, 314)

In the *Supplication*, defending the innocence of Catholics in general, he claims that those arrested in the intrigue against the Queen, though guilty, were manipulated by Walsingham and his agents. The "plot" amounts to a government operation "to draw into the nett such greene witts as (partly fearing the general oppression, partly angled with golden hookes) might easily be overwrought by Master Secretaries subtill and shifting witt" (*Supplication*, 18). While he condemns those Catholics immediately involved, he tempers his denunciation by placing most of the responsibility on government agents who, he believes, committed treason by leading others into treason. Walsingham and those in his employ, while working for the government, undermined its legitimacy. Elizabeth should not trust them, he implies, because they serve their own interests rather than hers. He points this out in order to show that he, and not those closest to the Queen, deals honestly in the present situation. For the time being, he argues, England is not herself, and not even the Queen can see this as she has been misled by her Councilors. Southwell, as a patriot, feels bound to tell her the truth. He writes to his monarch, whom he styles as kindly and maternal, so that he might recruit her in his campaign of reconciliation.

Facilitating reconciliation, the poet gently refutes all charges in the proclamation. For example, he explains the purpose of the colleges, claiming that "nothing in those Seminaries is either intended or practiced, but the relief and good education of such forsaken men, as from the storms of our English shore flee thither for a calmer Road, till perfected in the Course of learning and virtue, they may return to offer their blood for the recovery of souls" (5). Like Elizabeth, Southwell also references social-class consciousness. "As for [Catholic] priests," he boasts, "how many of them are Knights' and Esquires' sons, and otherwise allied both to worshipful and noble houses, and heirs to fair Revenues, let their own Friends and Parents dispersed through the whole realm bear witness" (7). Invoking his own family's prominence, he asserts, "this only may we say in answer of our objected baseness; that in the small number of the Catholic priests in our Nation ... there are very nearly as many, yea happily more gentlemen, than in all the other Clergy of the whole Realm" (7).

These specific rebuttals contribute to a strategic whole. Southwell pursues a two-pronged approach throughout his *Supplication*, insisting on the loyalty of misrepresented Catholics to a misinformed Elizabeth, and pleading the case of a persecuted population that has been denied its voice. His tone remains respectful and mollifying. He never qualifies his commitment to Catholicism's claims on truths necessary for salvation, but he affirms Elizabeth's authority in temporal matters. His hopes for reconciliation rest on his Queen, whom he wishes he could address in person. That course of action being unavailable, he apologizes that he, speaking for the English Catholic community, is "forced" to "divulge our petitions." He publishes "to the multitude" only because he has no recourse to "so easy and gracious a judge as [Elizabeth's] sacred self" (45).

Because Elizabeth is both wise judge and God's agent, Southwell describes as "strange" the proclamation's style and content. Its "apparent and uncolorable untruth" makes even the Queen's most devoted subjects doubtful of its authorship. "The due respect everyone carrieth to your gracious person," he insists, "acquitteth you in their knowledge from any meaning to have falsehood masked under the veil of your Majesty" (1–2). Likewise he absolves members of Council from involvement. Southwell presumes that, on account of their familiarity with Elizabeth's "style," none of them would deliver in "[her] name a discourse so full farced with contumelious terms, as better suited a Clamorous tongue, than your Highness' pen" (2). This is a far gentler tone than that of Persons, who describes Walsingham as "well nigh crazy" (Meyer 353). Southwell attributes the proclamation to an anonymous "Inditor, ever forgetting truth when he remembereth us" (*Supplication*, 8). Even regarding this mendacious writer, however, the poet offers amity. After citing a passage that maligns the colleges of the Society, Robert calls the author "our friend" (13). For reconciliation's sake he befriends a severe critic.

If Southwell can include the "Inditor" among his friends, then he hopes Elizabeth will count Catholics as her most trustworthy constituency. "Disloyalty," he assures her, "shall never be found the Sequel of any article of our religion; which more than any other tieth us to almost exact submission to your temporal authority" (16). He disabuses her of the notion that Catholics are "Unnatural Subjects" by inviting her to picture the details of their difficult situation: "If we live at home as Catholics, ... we are imprisoned for Recusancy, impoverished, troubled and defamed. And yet if we leave all, and seek free use of our Conscience, and depart the Realm, taking such helps as the Charity of other Countries affordeth us, we are straight reckoned for *unnatural subjects*" (3). Later he elaborates on their condition to make Elizabeth marvel all the more at their obedience, and he does so by specifically answering the "Bloody Question," which was the ultimate test of Catholic loyalty: "If the Pope do by his Bull or sentence pronounce her majesty to be deprived, and no lawful Queen, and her subjects to be discharged of their allegiance and obedience unto her; and after, the pope or any other by his appointment of authority, do invade this realm; which part would you take, or which part ought a good subject of England to take?" (Hughes and Larkin III, 357–62). Responding to charges that Catholics under torture had confessed how they would "take part with any army of the Pope against our Realm," Southwell claims that divulging such information "must be urged upon torture with other odious Interrogatories, far from our knowledge, [and] much farther from our action" (*Supplication*, 33). Death is more preferable than the sufferings that imprisoned Catholics endure, which Robert lists for the perusal of Elizabeth and his wider audience:

> Some are hanged by the hands, eight or nyne or twelve howers together, till not only their witts, but even their sences faile them; ... Some are whipped naked ... Some, besides their tortures, have bene forced to lie continually booted and Cloathed many weekes together, pined in their diett, Consumed with vermyne, and almost stifeled with stench ... Some have bene tortured in such parts, as it is almost a torture to Christian eares to heare it ... Divers have bene throwne into unsavory and darke dungeons, and brought soe neere starvinge, that some for famine have licked the very moisture of the walls ... Some with instruments have been rolled up together like a ball, and so Crushed, that blood sprouted out at diverse parts of their bodies. (34)

For all this, Southwell argues, Catholics will never take up arms with any who would usurp their Queen's temporal power. Instead, they will "defend [her] Realme, as the Catholique subjects of your Maiestiess Auncestors, or any other Prince were, are, or ever shall be ... we doe assure your Maistie, that what Army soever should come against you, we will rather yield our brests to be broached by our Countrie swords, then use our swords to th'effusion of our Cuntries bloud" (35). His statement is ambiguous in the sense that it is not clear whether Catholics will die at the hands of invaders or their fellow Englishmen. What stands clear, however, is that Catholics will never fight against their Queen, despite her status outside their church. At the same time, they cling to their religion because "we are upon soe mighty and warrantable proofs assured by all Antiquity, that our Catholic faith is the only true faith (to which all that have been or shall be saved must owe their fidelity)." It would, in fact, be "an unnatural thing to disobey the Author of nature for any Creature, in forsaking that Faith by which only we hope to be saved" (3). Nevertheless, Southwell insists, "in all other Civil and temporal respects, we are submitted and pliable as any of your Maiesties best beloved subject" (16).

Southwell, in his *Supplication*, claims to speak for all Catholics, and since the proclamation attacks his mentor, Persons, the poet defends him, unaware that Persons is pursuing a strategy quite contrary to his own. "And what cause [has he] given," Southwell asks, "to this slander, unless it be accounted Sedition to gather the ruins of God's afflicted Church, and to have provided sanctuaries for persecuted and succourless souls" (4). Moreover, he argues, Persons serves England's interests abroad, especially in Spain, where "he has used such mean for the mitigation of their enmity towards us" (38). Finally, Southwell makes Persons a partner in his project of reconciliation, claiming that the latter has been laboring on the Continent to "incline fury to Clemency, and rage to Compassion" (38). How much Robert knew of Persons' plots and schemes is difficult to determine, but seemingly he was unaware of his confrere's machinations as he wrote his *Supplication*. Perhaps he presumed that all Jesuits were as obedient to the instructions of superiors as he was.

. . .

Whether Elizabeth ever saw the *Supplication* is difficult to determine. In the Roman proceedings surrounding the Archpriest controversy in the 1590s, there is some mention of the text being presented to the Queen: "ad reginam Angliae praeteritiis annis ... a religioso quodam viro ... exhibitus" and "libellis iste supplex scriptus ac reginae oblatus est" (*Supplication* ed. Bald, xii). But Southwell himself was not hopeful of a royal reading. This lack of hope accounts, he claims, for his plan to publish the *Supplication* on a secret press:

> We are forced to divulge our Petitions, and by many mouthes to open unto your Highnes our humble suites. For neither daring ourselves to present them in person ... nor having the favour of any such Patron, as would be willing to make himself Mediator to your Maiestie, we are forced to commit it to the multitude, hoping that among soe many as shall peruse this short and true Relation of our troubles, god will touch some merciful heart to let your Highnes understand th'extremity of them. (45)

The work in manuscript did reach a wide audience, including Topcliffe and Francis Bacon, and, at one point in its circulation history, Jesuit superiors tried to limit access to it. As noted, Southwell's acquiescent approach to Elizabeth and, more significantly, his recognition of her secular authority for the sake of reconciliation, stood at odds with the arguments of Persons and other Continental English Catholic writers. In the years after Southwell's death, Persons and those of his opinion became even more entrenched in their position. They insisted on papal supremacy in England without exception. During arguments between secular priests and Jesuits in England, this intransigence became a sticking point, since the secular priests urged a position similar to Southwell's. They found his *Supplication* so congenial that they printed it in 1600 to embarrass his increasingly stringent religious order.[29] The secular priests were appealing the appointment of the archpriest, George Blackwell, who seemed to favor the Jesuits. The government, of course, was happy to encourage them because of benefits gained by dividing Catholics into factions. As a result, the *Supplication* was printed on a press in London with the support of the Bishop of London.

The government's strategy in reprinting the text proved a disaster on two counts. Rather than embarrassing the Jesuits who disagreed with Southwell's mediating position, the publication exposed the horrific treatment of Catholics as recorded by the poet, as well as his treatment of the Babington Plot, which, if true, impugned the loyalty of Elizabeth's closest Councilors. Government agents seized and destroyed as many copies as they could find and executed two men responsible for distributing the text, Peter Bullock and James Duckett. In Rome, the battle between secular priests and Jesuits was waged before the Pope, who ultimately ruled that the publication of rival pamphlets by both parties, including Southwell's *Supplication*, must cease. As a result, the text was rarely cited in following centuries and unavailable to Grossart in 1872 because it was catalogued as an anonymous work in the British Museum (*Supplication* ed. Bald, xvii).

Jesuits first embraced and subsequently suppressed Southwell's *Supplication*. The government initially suppressed it, then encouraged its publication, and then, in the end, suppressed it again. All of this highlights the nuance and power of the text. There was room in the treatise for all parties to find a rhetorical, religious and political home, at least temporarily. Since it never entirely endorsed the position of either party, however, it made them uncomfortable enough to abandon it. Southwell's *Supplication*, at its conciliatory best, required readers to stretch beyond their increasingly inflexible categories of thought. The concept of Catholic "soul rights" sharing textual space with a recognition of the legitimate authority of an excommunicated Queen created tensions that seemingly few sixteenth-century imaginations could fathom. After an apostolic lifetime of negotiating or living creatively with tensions and competing allegiances, Southwell's imagination could stretch far enough to generate and embrace so radical an instance of reconciliation.

Notes

[1] While Gasquet's history is valuable, Devlin and others dispute his reporting on "the stirs" of the 1580s and other criticisms of Jesuit administration as "untenable" (327). Gasquet, according to Devlin, makes two centuries of Jesuit rule sound like "an unfortunate incident" (327).

[2] See McCoog, *The Society of Jesus* (104). He describes how the "lives of the clerics at the English Hospice retained the characteristics of a collegiate senior common room": "Many residents devoted too much time to drinking, gambling, quarreling and associating with rather dubious female companions."

[3] Clynnog was appointed warden in 1565 after a distinguished career as a canon lawyer and *confidante* of Cardinal Pole. In 1578 he was named rector despite the objections of the resident clergy who had elected an Englishman, Henry Henshaw. Clynnog and Lewis also conspired with Thomas Stuckely in his crusade against Elizabeth (McCoog 104–105).

[4] Two Jesuits were "lent" for two months to the College by Mercurian prior to this episode. According to McCoog, "Mercurian's decision was more significant than anyone involved would have known: it was the first commitment that the Society had to England" (*The Society of Jesus*, 106).

[5] Haynes explains the willingness of so many young men to spy for Walsingham on economic as well as religious grounds (52). College admission policies changed as a result, and it "had to learn from experience how much care was needed in admitting guests and scholars and from time to time there were warnings about who should be accepted and refused admission" (Williams *Venerable English College*, 13).

[6] Haynes reports that "Walsingham's rise to power coincided with the founding of Douai and surveillance began as early as 1571 ... Walsingham's intention was to recruit men who could be infiltrated into the colleges to wreck them" (40–41).

[7] Persons suggested that the oath be imposed on students who were supported by papal funds, as opposed to those who were paid for by their families. Ralph Sherwin was the first to be asked to swear it, and his response, "potius hodie quam cras" (today rather than tomorrow), "not only stands for his personal zeal, fitting for the canonized

protomartyr of the Venerabile, but also for the new spirit that marked the regime established in 1579" (Williams *Venerable English College*, 7).

[8] The strict rules also responded to dangers posed by Roman living, explaining why the Roman regime was much harsher than that of Douai (Williams *Venerable English College*, 15).

[9] Cecil and Bagshaw feature in Southwell's demise and demonization. Cecil implicated Southwell in plans to recruit Lord Strange, the son of Henry VII's great-granddaughter, and therefore a somewhat legitimate claimant to the throne, in a plot to overthrow Elizabeth. After Southwell's death, Bagshaw continued to attack him endorsing equivocation.

[10] See A.O. Meyer (436) for Sega's report.

[11] See Williams' *Venerable English College* (16) on the confusion surrounding the reason for this visitation. It may have been occasioned by "special trouble" or "it was only a part of a much bigger inquiry of Sixtus V." The new Pope also had a dispute with the Society over "the nature of their vows," which resulted in an inquiry into all four Jesuit seminaries in Rome (McCoog *The Society of Jesus*, 224–25).

[12] See Meyer (492–519) for Sega's report.

[13] Holt was in turn succeeded by Persons, but Agazzari was later returned as rector for a second term, precipitating another visitation and report (Williams *Venerable English College*, 15).

[14] The dogma of the Immaculate Conception was not formally promulgated until the nineteenth century. Prior to that, Catholic scholars could disagree about it. In the late sixteenth and early seventeenth centuries, requests for clarification were denied by various Popes. According to Gregory XV, for example, "The Holy Spirit, although besought by the most constant prayers, has not yet opened to His Church the secrets of this mystery."

[15] See Janelle (19) who claims that "it cannot be reasonably doubted that Southwell" was a member of this "spiritual elite" at Douai and at Paris.

[16] See *The Hymns of the Breviary and Missal*, ed. Matthew Britt, O.S.B. (New York, 1924), 317.

[17] See David Fleming's "contemporary reading" of the *Exercises* (Loyola *Spiritual Exercises*, 11).

[18] Southwell's selflessness in "The Sequence" stands out, for example, in comparison to John Donne's "La Corona." Donne considers similar events, but his poem is self-absorbed. "La Corona" opens with as many references to Donne as it does to God: "my hands" (1); "my low devout melancholie" (2); "my muses white sincerity" (6); "give me/ A crown of glory" (7–8). And it ends on a similarly self-referential note: "Bright torch, which shin'st, that I the way may see,/ Oh, with thy own blood quench thy owne just wrath,/ And if thy Holy Spirit, my muse did raise,/ *Deigne at my hands the crown of prayer and praise*" ("Ascension," 11–14). For Donne, sacred poetry is a means for self-exploration and expression; for Southwell, it is an exercise of ministry, of priestly service.

[19] Describing the Assumption as "dogma" is an anachronism in the sixteenth century, since it did not officially have this status until 1950. However, Christians believed for centuries that Mary, having completed the course of her earthly life, was assumed body and soul into heavenly glory.

[20] Even in 1950 this issue was left open. The wording of the apostolic constitution defining the teaching avoids settling the argument between "mortalists" and "immortalists."

[21] "Galdes" are the clear light of heaven (Southwell *The Poems of Robert Southwell, S.J.*, 123).

[22] See Bald (Southwell *Supplication*, 59).

23   As Bald notes, "Elizabethan enactments against Catholics came in waves, and were invariably related to political events, either at home or abroad" (*Supplication*, ix). The first recusancy laws were promulgated in 1571, after the excommunication of Elizabeth. In 1581 the arrival of the first Jesuits and the presence of papal forces in Ireland resulted in more statutes. In 1584 Spanish military victories caused still more, as did the anticipation of the Armada in 1588.

24   The reason that the proclamation was issued in Council was that no Parliament was sitting at the time.

25   See Bald (*Supplication*, x) on Southwell's urgency: "the allusion in *Humble Supplication* to 'the last Arraignment of three priests at Westminster, even since this proclamation,' refers to the trials of Edmund Jennings, Eustachius White and Polydore Plasden on December 4; they were executed on December 10, and the fact that Southwell makes no mention of their executions suggests that they were still alive when this passage was written."

26   Southwell probably composed the *Supplication* in a house just north of London, which Garnet had rented and reserved for times "when there was serious writing to be done of great importance" (Devlin 241 cites Garnet's letter preserved in the English Province Archives).

27   Quotations here are from an unpublished translation by Otto Hentz, S.J., of a 1605 edition in the Joseph Mark Lauinger Library at Georgetown University, Washington, D.C.

28   There was also an abbreviated version in English, *An Advertisement written to a Secretarie of my L. Treasurers in Ingand* (1592).

29   The publication was falsely dated 1595.

Chapter 8
Reconciling Sinners to God and the Church

One-third of the poems Southwell wrote in England aim to reconcile sinners to God. This preponderance reflects the nature of his work among England's Catholics, especially the lapsed and lukewarm, work assigned by his superiors, whose will he followed scrupulously. The instructions given by the Superior General at the inception of the English mission clarify the Jesuits' objectives:

> The object aimed at by this mission is, firstly, to preserve, if God is propitious, and to advance in the faith and in our Catholic religion all who are found to be Catholics in England; and, secondly, to bring back to it whoever may have strayed from it either through ignorance or at the instigation of others. (Persons *Letters and Memorials*, 319)

These instructions, with emphasis on reconciling "whoever may have strayed," also stipulated a methodology. "As regards intercourse with strangers," the General writes, "this should be at first with the upper classes rather than with the common people" (320). This elitism is grounded, as previously mentioned, in Loyola's conviction that powerful people, once converted, most effectively serve faith and promote the common good. Among them "there is greater fruit to be gathered" (320). In England there was a self-interested reason as well: the upper classes "will be able to protect [the Jesuits] against violence of all sorts" (320).

Among their own, especially the lapsed, Jesuits were to help people "put away fury and hatred." For their own behavior, "they should refrain from biting and intemperate words" and "make use of solid arguments in preference to bitter wrangling" (320). If forced into conversation with heretics, according to the General, Jesuits "are to be brief and avoid quarrels and altercations" (320). "Finally," the instructions end, "let them bear themselves in such a way that all can see that their sole purpose is the gain of souls" (321). Underscoring this point, the General specifies that "[t]hey are not to mix themselves in the affairs of State, nor should they recount news about political matters in their letters from this place [Rome], or to that [England]; and there also they are to refrain from talk against the Queen and not allow it in others" (321).[1]

The same attitude colors the mandate issued to Garnet and Southwell on 24 March 1586. After appointing Garnet Southwell's superior until they join William Weston in England, Aquaviva defines the work they can do on their journey, namely preaching and, most importantly, hearing confessions (Persons *Letters and Memorials*, 356). The same labors await them upon reaching their destination, in addition to the ministry of printing. Aquaviva notes that "[l]eave is given for some pamphlets to be printed for the defense of the faith and the edification of Catholics at the discretion of Fr. Weston" (356). Southwell, in penning and publishing poems that promote reconciliation, fulfills two apostolic aims in one effort. He edifies Catholics by urging them to remorse, repentance and confession through the written word.

. . .

A work written by George Gilbert, who had ample opportunity to observe the Jesuits' way of proceeding in England before he was forced to seek refuge in Rome, best elucidates the methodology contained in these mission statements. Gilbert's 1583 account, included among Persons' *Letters and Memorials*, is entitled, *A way to Deal with Persons of All Sorts so as to Convert Them and Bring Them Back to a Better Way of Life—Based on the System and Methods of Fr. Robert Persons and Fr. Edmund Campion* (331–40). Gilbert begins by describing the assistance he provided for Jesuit friends. He encourages every Jesuit missionary to "seek out some gentleman to be his companion" (331). Ideally, this companion "should be a man who has many relations and friends and much local information" (331). Such an association has numerous advantages. With a gentleman's aid, a Jesuit can "mix freely everywhere, both in public and in private, dressed as a gentleman and with various kinds of get-up and disguises." More practically, a gentleman can provide a Jesuit with "a reliable and satisfactory livelihood" (332). With these benefits secured, missionaries can set up quasi-parishes wherein they can console the faithful:

> It will be necessary also for the priests to be stationed in various parts of the country and for each of them to stay at the house of some gentleman or other, as though he were a relation, friend or steward, or in some office of dignity but little work, so as not to interfere with his own calling; and he should also undertake the charge (unless the family with whom he is staying is a very large one) of a certain district in the neighborhood, or of

a number of neighboring families, because it will be very difficult to find
priests enough for every family. (332)

"Besides Catholics," Gilbert continues, "there are three classes of persons
who are to be dealt with: heretics, schismatics and lukewarm Catholics"
(333). A Jesuit's gentleman friend introduces the missionary to people in
every category, all needing reconciliation. Gilbert then describes "how a
Father can deal with each," anticipating the style, emphasis and tone of
Southwell's conciliatory poems. The process of reconciliation, even for
heretics, begins by approaching them on their own terms. Southwell
follows this advice by adopting popular poetic styles for religious purposes.
According to Gilbert, "it is necessary for the Father, as soon as he comes, to
take note of the gentleman's inclinations and what pleases him most, so as
to suit himself to his humors and thus gain his good will":

> If for instance it is study, letters, affairs of state, politics, discussion, or if
> it is active pursuits and praiseworthy bodily exercises, it is necessary for
> him to show that he takes pleasure in them, so far as is seemly: if he takes
> pleasure in regrettable things such as cutting a fine figure, gambling,
> hunting or other vanities, this should not be found fault with at first but he
> should bear with it in word and deed with a compliant countenance and
> yield, so far as he can without sin, to his tastes, until greater confidence
> and friendship is established between them. (333)

Gilbert advises this strategy in dealing with all who need conversion.
Characteristic lines urge Jesuits "to avoid talking about matters of religion
until the time seems opportune, when there has been a greater increase of
familiarity and friendship between them" (334). Heretics should be met
quite literally where they are. "The place is also to be taken into
consideration," Gilbert writes, "for instance, if the man happens to be in the
city one can walk in the park or in a garden; if at his country house one can
saunter through the fields or woods, or preferably in the neighborhood of
some stream" (335). By extension, Southwell meets his readers on familiar
literary grounds and then moves them in new religious directions. There are
as many ways of reconciling sinners as there are sinners to be reconciled,
and Southwell believes that poetry numbers among them.

    "God," Gilbert insists, "will suggest a thousand other means to the
man who is tireless in his efforts to gain souls which cannot be written
down in detail" (335). In general, however, there are rules to follow. The
first recommends a gentle approach with sinners, as opposed to "touch[ing]
too much on the raw, especially in the presence of others." Gilbert suggests
that Jesuits not "be too hasty in showing awareness of … imperfections."

He recommends, instead, "indirect methods" (335). This requires intimacy with those to be reconciled, "a knowledge of all particulars," which can serve to "frame private discourse." "Hearers," he insists, "must feel themselves intimately touched" before conversion can commence. As noted, this approach influenced Southwell's prose, especially the *Epistle of Comfort*, in which he first and then frequently invoked familiar aspects of his readers' lives, rendering them well disposed to the challenges that followed. He will do the same in poetry, employing stylish genres and tropes while urging unfashionable, counter cultural religious commitments.

Gilbert is especially confident in the power of gentle and well-chosen words to move sinners to contrition and reconciliation. "I know of no other ground why God opens the intellect and moves the will more freely," he writes. His highest hopes are on sermons, for "it is found by experience that more are converted by sermons than by the other way [i.e., theological disputes]" (336). Sermons, like spiritual conversations, should be tailored "to suit the humor of the individual" (337). He gives the example of reconciling schismatical priests:

> In the same way he must deal with schismatical priests gently and with sweetness, giving them kind words; he must put them in the first place at table, show reverence for their old age and politeness of that sort so as to bring about familiarity and friendship; and he must bring back to their memories the happy times when they exercised their ministries; he must talk about the number of souls in their parish, the devotion that existed at that time; he must praise the excellence of the priestly state, the benefit that comes through the most holy Sacrifice. (339)

Finally, Gilbert recommends "spiritual books to stir devotion," especially those promoting "frequent confession and communion," as opposed to once a year at Easter (339).[2] Southwell's poems often aim to do the same.

. . .

The centrality of reconciling sinners in the instructions given to English Jesuit missionaries, in Gilbert's recommendations, and in many of Southwell's poems, stems from a similar stress in Jesuit foundational documents and ministerial practice. Amidst their various works, the earliest members of the Society insisted that the sacrament of confession was "the centerpiece of Jesuit ministry." It should not be surprising, then, that it enjoys preeminence among the sacraments in Southwell's verse. The Jesuit approach to confession was typical of their way of proceeding in other matters:

> The way the Jesuits approached the sacrament of penance and their insistence upon its consolatory features were symptomatic of the way they dealt with many traditional institutions. The Jesuits were, on the one hand, quite conventional, and they accepted the institutions and much of the practice surrounding them. On the other hand, they employed and interpreted them within a framework that to some extent refashioned them, even when they were not fully aware that they were doing so. (O'Malley 20)

The importance of confession for Jesuits was grounded in their experience of the Ignatian *Exercises*. The First Week of the retreat, as noted, climaxes with a general confession of all the sins of one's life. Given their own consoling experience of the sacrament, "Jesuits consistently recommended it to others from all walks of life as the keystone and expression of their conversion," and they were quite specific about their priestly role in the consoling "drama" of confession (O'Malley 139). Jesuit confessors were instructed always to "incline in the more humane direction," and to fashion themselves "vicars of the mild Christ" (O'Malley 142). This phrase occurs in Peter Favre's 1544 instruction to Jesuit confessors, and among the first Jesuits, Loyola singled out Favre as best embodying the spirit of the order and as being the most accomplished director of the *Exercises*. The basic theme in Favre's instructions is that Jesuits "should never be harsh but always sweet ... and they must ward off in themselves all pharisaical self-righteousness." One report of Favre hearing a general confession shows him exemplifying these dispositions:

> Showing mercy to another in this sacrament brought tears to his eyes, for it helped him discover anew the mercy God had shown to Favre himself. He concluded by observing that if a just person wanted God to show kindness and not act out of the rigor justice required, that person must be kind to all, "not stringent and overly just" (O'Malley 142).

Confessional practice received considerable attention during Southwell's formative years in Rome. In part, this was owing to the renewed significance that the Council of Trent bestowed on the sacrament in response to Protestant attacks. After condemning "the vain confidence of heretics," Council members unambiguously restated the need for sacramental confession: "[t]hose who fall away by sin from the grace of justification which they had received [at baptism], can again be justified when at God's prompting they have made the effort through the sacrament of penance to recover, by the merit of Christ, the grace which was lost" (Tanner II, 677). This same Decree condemned the doctrine of predestination and insisted on the efficacy of good works "wrought in God," such as "labors, watchings, alms, deeds, prayers and offerings, ... fastings and chastity" (676). Those who perform such works can "expect and hope for an eternal reward from God through his mercy and the merits of Christ, if by acting rightly and keeping the divine commandments they persevere to the end" (680). Underlying these teachings is a reaffirmation of the freedom of the will, the exercise of which, under the influence of grace and through sacramental confession, can lead to justification. In two canons following the Decree on Justification, the teaching is pellucidly clear:

> 4. If anyone says that a person's free will when moved and roused by God, gives no cooperation by responding to God's summons and inspiration to dispose and prepare itself for the grace of justification, and that it cannot, if it so wishes, dissent but, like something inanimate, can do nothing at all but remains merely passive: let him be anathema.

> 5. If anyone says that, after the sin of Adam, human free will was lost or blotted out, or that its existence is purely nominal, a name without a substance, indeed a fiction introduced into the church by Satan: let him be anathema.

A later decree, entirely devoted to the "teaching concerning the most holy sacrament of penance," also begins by referencing reformers. "So great is the accumulation of errors about this sacrament during our time," it states, that "public advantage will come from giving a more detailed and full definition" (Tanner II, 703). In the sacrament, "the benefit of Christ's death is applied to those who have fallen away after baptism." Contradicting Protestants who hold that baptism suffices for justification, the Council teaches that "this sacrament of penance is necessary for salvation for those who have fallen after baptism, just as baptism itself is for those not yet regenerated" (704). The "matter" of the sacrament is "Contrition, confession and satisfaction," and "the meaning and fruit ... is reconciliation with God, which in devout persons who are receiving this sacrament with devotion is often followed by a peace and a serenity of conscience accompanied by an intense spirit of consolation" (704). The Council defines contrition, "which holds the first place among the above-mentioned acts of the penitent," as "a grief and detestation of mind of the sin committed, together with the resolution not to sin in the future" (705).[3] This necessitates a "movement of sorrow," but while the movement is necessary, it is not sufficient: "[t]he Council further teaches that, though it sometimes happens that this contrition is made perfect by love, and a person is reconciled with God before this sacrament is actually received;

nevertheless, the reconciliation is not to be attributed to the contrition without a desire for the sacrament being included within it" (705). Sorrow for sins without desiring the sacrament is "attrition," which cannot of itself lead the sinner to justification, but "disposes him to beg and obtain the grace of God in this sacrament of penance" (705). Many of Southwell's poems, which never specifically refer to sacramental confession, seem dedicated to encouraging this disposition.

Regarding ministers of the sacrament, the Council refutes Protestant claims that the faculty of forgiving sins extends to all believers "indiscriminately, in addition to bishops and priests" (707). It stresses that, "although a priest's absolution is a stewardship of another's gift [i.e., Christ's], nevertheless it is not only a bare service, either of proclaiming the gospel or of declaring that sins have been forgiven; but it is like a judicial act in which a verdict is pronounced by him like a judge" (707). This judicial quality, while never contradicted by Jesuits in writing or in practice, is tempered by them. Another early Jesuit, Jeronimo Nadal, for instance, describes confessors as "sometimes encouraging with kind words like a father, sometimes expostulating and reprehending like a judge, sometimes applying remedies for sickness like a doctor." In general, "[i]nsistence upon the consolatory aspects of the sacrament within the judicial framework ... characterized the Jesuits' approach to confession and marked it with its many ambivalences" (O'Malley 141). Even when hearing general confessions, for example, a Jesuit confessor was encouraged to "disclose 'in general terms' something from his own life" to console and comfort penitents. Moreover, Jesuit leaders such as Francis Xavier "typically insisted that the confessor try not to incite fear in the penitents but move them by consideration of 'the abundant mercy of God'" (O'Malley 139). Confidence in this mercy led Jesuits to steer penitents away from scrupulosity and toward thinking about "the therapeutic aspects of confession." Rather than an occasion for receiving judgment, penitents should look forward to hearing "guidance, counsel and encouragement as the means for accomplishing the healing" (O'Malley 139).[4]

Southwell learned to hear confessions at the Collegio Romano, and, typical of most aspects of Jesuit education, this training was practical, driven, in part, by special confessional privileges granted to Jesuits by the Pope. For example, Jesuits could absolve heretics without consulting the Inquisition or local bishops. As a result, they paid careful attention to how they leveraged their special faculties, and developed, in response, the study of "cases of conscience," or casuistry, through which they facilitated "the application of general norms like the Decalogue to different sets of circumstances according to consistent principles" (O'Malley 144). To a large extent, casuistry responded to "the scope of the dilemmas facing the sixteenth century," such as "the explosion of new data from an expanded vision of the world; a turn to the subject as singularly responsible to account for one's actions both religiously and ethically; the failure of existing principles to resolve satisfactorily urgent issues; and the inability to achieve consensus among moral thinkers, church and political leaders, and the general population" (Keenan and Shannon xvi). Because of these new realities, "scholars turned to the immediate and practical, nearly abandoning the methodological, speculative and metaphysical" (xvii). The philosophical underpinning of the system was nominalism, and the focus was on choices made through which a person moved closer to or away from God. While casuistry was practiced by some, especially the Franciscans, in the middle ages, the sixteenth century was "casuistry's century of maturity" (Jonsen and Toulmin 142). It was the Society of Jesus, in particular, "whose name almost came to be equated with 'casuistry,'" that was responsible for this development. Because of Jesuit involvement in the world, as a result of their freedom from monastic restrictions, the order's members "were forced to acknowledge the genuine problems of practical decisions faced by agents in complex circumstances involving conflicts of principle" (Jonsen and Toulmin 148). They faced this task head on in their course of studies:

> All students ... as well as most of the members of the community, were required to attend a weekly case conference, at which the Professor of Cases presented and resolved several difficult cases of conscience; participants were admonished to come prepared "to ask and be asked questions." On occasion the students themselves, described in the text of the document as *casistae*, were given the task of resolving the case in the presence of their critical brethren. (Jonsen and Toulmin 149)

As a result, every Jesuit knew well casuistical methodology and was likely to make use of it in his ministry. It was an especially valuable tool for men such as Southwell who were hearing confessions in new and extraordinary circumstances. "As confessors ... in a time of rapid social, economic and religious change," he and other missionaries to England "encountered many perplexing moral cases," and "[i]n all this a knowledge of principles needed to be supplemented by a sharp perception of the novel and unprecedented nature of these problems, and by a refined capacity to discern the morally relevant similarities and differences between cases" (Jonsen and Toulmin 151). Southwell often provided models of this kind of discernment and other aspects of exemplary confessional practice in his poems.

. . .

In many of Southwell's poems he urges readers to reconcile themselves to God and the church, and, at the same time, he models the mildness that was to characterize Jesuit confessors. One such poem is the shorter and earlier of his two efforts entitled "Saint Peter's Complaynte," in which he urges propositions on readers "through a series of tightly worked conceits and paradoxes" (Woolf 371). Southwell starts the poem with word play to score intellectual points among readers who admired exercises of wit:

> How can I live, that have my life deny'de?
> What can I hope, that lost my hope in feare?
> What trust to one that trewth it self defyde?
> What good in him that did his God forswere? (1–4)

These rhetorical questions expose Peter's miserable situation. In language reminiscent of Southwell thinking himself in his *Spiritual Exercises and Devotions* the most egregious sinner in the Society of Jesus, Peter admits to committing the "synne of synnes, of eveells the very worste" (6). As a result his is a "synfull wretch, of synners most accurste" (6). He, like many former Catholics in England, has abandoned Christ and the church out of fear, and what makes this fear so despicable is that it was occasioned by a woman: "But o infamous foyle: a maydens breathe/ Did blowe me down, and blast my soule to death" (17–18). Southwell is alluding to Matthew 26:69–75, wherein Peter, when asked by a maid whether he was in the company of Jesus, three times denies knowing him, fulfilling Jesus' prediction earlier in the same chapter (26:34).

Several scholars have investigated whether this woman represents Elizabeth I. Given that elsewhere in his works, and most notably in *Humble Supplication*, Southwell treats the Queen with deference, an attack is unlikely here. The *Supplication* was written as a response to anti-Catholic propaganda, but unlike other Catholic authors who replied "in language that yielded little in scurrility" to Protestant polemicists, "Southwell ... wrote in dignified phrases direct to the Queen, whom in total sincerity he addressed as 'Most Mighty and merciful, most feared and best beloved Princess'" (Caraman, 63). The reference to the "mayden," then, sharpens the focus on Peter's transgressions, which are compounded by his over-weaning pride. Peter ruefully remembers how he "vaunted erst though all his frendes had fayld',/ Alone with Christe all fortunes to have try'de" (7–8). When threatened with exposure, however, Peter "craven first of all was quaild" (9). Southwell, recalling Loyola's assertion that "love ought to be put more in deeds than in words" (*Spiritual Exercises*, 231), has Peter reflect on how "[s]uch distance is betwene highe wordes and deedes:/ In proof the greatest vaunter seldome speedes" (11–12).

The church's "Chosen rocke," on account of being overthrown by "so soft a gale," has become "a rocke of ruyne, not a rest to staye:/ a pastor, not to feede but to betray" (19–24). He failed to heed the advice Southwell urged in *Triumphs Over Death*, letting fear of death, "rendring natures dewe,/ Whiche grouth in yeres was shortly like to clayme," eclipse his faith and fortitude (25–26). Disappointment with himself brings him to the point of despair, and he wants to "dye: dye: disloyall wretch, thy life detest" (29).

Employing such strong language, Southwell reminds readers that Peter is no ordinary penitent. He has Peter accuse himself of "spitting [his] poison in [his] makers face" (52): "O impious tongue, no torture but vipers stinge,/ [t]hat could with cursing othes forsweare thy kinge" (59–60). He also recounts the apostle's deeds and the privileges granted him by Christ, including the power to forgive sins: "I once designed Judge to loose and bynde/ Now pleade at mercyes barr as guilty thrall" (43–44). The preeminent disciple must now become the model penitent. Moreover, Southwell references Tridentine emphasis on the confessor as judge, but tempers it by noting how the sometime judge is himself a sinner. This recalls the Jesuit practice of confessors mentioning to penitents, in some general way, their own sinfulness. Peter, who once had faith enough to confess earlier than any other apostle that Jesus was Lord (Matthew 16:16), must now find courage enough to confess his sins:

> O tongue, the first that did his godhedd sounde,
> How couldst thow utter such detesting wordes,
> That every word was to his hart a wounde,
> And lawnc'd him deeper than a thowsand swords? (61–64)

Peter, in examining his own conscience, a process which Jesuits recommended to penitents, expresses Southwellian confidence in the power of words, but in this case to do harm. Much of the poet's work focuses on the horrendous suffering experienced by Christ. Here he argues that Peter's words of denial were more painful. But his words in the poem have a power of their own to work toward good. In speaking his tortured mind, Peter is moved to "deep remorse" signaled by "tears." In hope of consolation, the apostle asks Jesus to follow the advice of Nadal and Favre to Jesuit confessors. He begs him to "lett myldness temper ... deserved hate" (70):

> With mercye, Jesu, measure my offence:
> Lett deepe remorse thy due revenge abate:
> Lett teares appeace when trespas doth incense:

> Lett myldness temper thy deserved hate.
> Lett grace forgive, lett love forgett my fall:
> With feare I crave, with hope I humbly call. (67–72)

In a companion piece, "S. Peter's remorse," the roles prescribed for penitent and priest are reenforced. Again, the examination of a "self blaming conscience" results in "streames of weeping eies" (2–4). Peter understands and admits that fear has led him to "highest treasons," but he trusts that "mercy may relent and temper justice rod" (24–25). The sinner again sounds Nadal's and Favre's note in reminding himself and readers that God, whom the confessor represents, is a "milde Lorde" who wants to provide "comfort":

> O milde and mighty Lorde,
>   Amend what is amisse:
> My sinne my soare, thy love my salve,
>   Thy cure my comfort is. (53–56)

Similar modeling is found in other poems featuring repentant sinners from the Old and New Testaments. In "David's Peccavi," the King of Israel laments his behavior after his marriage to Bathsheba. David acknowledges a former "blisful time" when virtue was "[a]yme to my thoughtes, guide to my word and deede" (5–6). "But feares now are my Pheares," he complains, "[n]urse of unrest the night" (7–9). The inversion he experiences recalls Psalm 102, thought in Southwell's time to have been written by David, in which the God who once lifted the speaker up has cast him down (10). David takes responsibility for his new situation, confessing, "[t]his is the change of my ill changed choyse" (13). Like Peter, he is filled with self-hatred. He listens to the "doleful ecchoe of [his] wayling minde" (16). That same mind, "[w]hich taught to know the worth of vertues joyes,/ Doth hate itself for loving fancies toyes" (17–18). He also admits that he did not act out of ignorance. Instead, "wit and will must now confesse with shame,/ [b]oth deede and doome, to have deserved blame" (23–24). The power to think and choose was employed in the pursuit of an unworthy object. Echoing his poetic theory articulated in "The Author to his loving Cosen" and in his reworkings of Dyer's verse, Southwell underscores temptations presented by "Fancie":

> I Fancie deem'd for guide to leade my way,
>   And as I deem'd, I did pursue her track;
> Wit lost his ayme, and will was Fancies pray,
>   The Rebell wan, the Ruler went to wrack: (25–28)

Readers observe in David an exemplarily honest and remorseful soul suffering appropriate torment while always hoping that he can "mend" his ways with the aid of God's help (30).

The mild nature of Southwell's forgiving God is best outlined in the poet's most frequently anthologized work, "The Burning Babe." The speaker employs an Ignatian composition of place, summoning up images of a "newly borne" Christ Child. This "pretty Babe" is in tears because "none approach to warme their harts" (15). Were they to do so, their "shame and scorne" would be reduced to ashes by the "fire" of his love. "Defiled souls" are invited to approach Jesus who wants only "to work them to their good" (26). The Christ Child models Jesuit penitential practice. The speaker learns that his initial anxieties, which caused him to lift "a fearful eye" toward this vision, prove groundless. There is nothing threatening about this scene, just as there ought to be nothing threatening about sacramental reconciliation gently administered. Even the purifying fire toward which the penitent is drawn seems more comforting than dangerous. Rather than raging out of control, "mercie blows on the coales," keeping the fire alive. Only in the last lines of the theophanic poem, which invokes a typological allusion to Moses' encounter with the burning bush in Exodus 3, is it clear that the occasion for the contemplation is Christmas:

> With this he vanisht out of sight,
> And swiftly shrunk away,
> And straight I called unto minde,
> That it was Christmas day. (29–32)

Writing a penitential poem on a festive day may seem odd, but it fits Southwell's scheme of connecting confession and consolation. Christmas, as opposed to Lent, is not a penitential season, but Robert suggests that it is appropriate for confessors and penitents alike to consider qualities evinced by Christ as early as his birth.

In another poem also grounded in an Ignatian composition of place, "Sinnes heavie load," the speaker watches Jesus on the way of the cross, and the familiar point here is to foreground Christ's kindness to repentant sinners. The poem's central images all concern falling: the sinful speaker has obviously fallen as has Christ under the weight of the cross. The fall of the former is metaphorical, whereas that of the latter is literal. According to a traditional form of Catholic devotion, the Stations of the Cross, Jesus stumbled three times while being led from Pilate's court to Calvary.[5] Loyola incorporates and adapts the Stations in his *Exercises*, and Southwell takes the further step of relating the scenes to sacramental confession. Again, Christ is modeling for confessors. They should follow him in avoiding severity, even when there is just cause for it. If Jesus, in excruciating pain, could be kind to sinners, all the more must confessors avoid rigor in the sacramental context. The poem opens with a prayer in which the speaker admits that his own sins have contributed to Christ's fall:

> O Lord my sinne doth over-charge thy brest,
> The poyse thereof doth force thy knees to bow;
> Yea flat thou fallest with my faults opprest,
> And bloody sweat runs trickling from the brow. (1–4)

The image of Christ's bloody sweat, a favorite of Southwell's, has a spiritually salubrious effect on the speaker. He is glad of it. Had his sins not caused Christ "to earth thus prest," "[m]uch more they would in hell have pestered mee" (5–6). This represents a new slant on the *felix culpa* tradition, and in a flash of wit the poet shows how the sinner's transgressions must be heavier than the earth itself. Christ, figured as a new Atlas, could easily prop "the Globe of earth" on "one finger" without so much as breaking a "sweat," but sin has caused Christ to "fall flat to the ground" (7–12).

     The following stanza is an apostrophe to sin, acknowledging its "huge and heavie" weight and asking the rhetorical question "[a]las if God himselfe sinke under sinne,/ What will become of man that dies therein?" (17–18). All of Christ's "falls" are understood as acts of love which increase the sinner's consolation and serve as a source of hope. The speaker celebrates the Messiah's gentle treatment of those who are "the cause of [his] unrest," a quality epitomized in an imagined kiss. As Jesus falls to the ground, he "seal'st a peace with bleeding kisse" (28). Even though the earth "shortly was to drink [Christ's] dearest blood," Jesus shows his love for it and, by extension, all who will ultimately lie under the earth in death. The poem ends in a colloquy with Christ, following closely the Ignatian paradigm. The poem is an exercise which begins by summoning up sensual apprehension of an event for the sake of provoking a strong emotional reaction. It then invites rational consideration of the event's meaning. Such consideration leads to spoken prayer and, ultimately, action, namely reconciliation. The sinner asks a "prostrate Christ" to "erect [his] crooked minde" so that he might share in the resurrection.

. . .

Southwell's poems on reconciliation culminate in his 792-line work, *Saint Peter's Complaint.* This poem, certainly his longest and perhaps his best, incorporates materials from earlier poems on St. Peter, and indicates the process by which Southwell produced his *magnum opus*. Full accounts of the poem's history are attempted by several scholars, all of whom agree that, to some extent, Robert is indebted to Luigi Tansillo's *Le lagrime di San Pietro*, a popular Italian poem based on Peter's denial of Christ in Pilate's court (Matthew 26:69–75 and Luke 22:54–62). Tansillo's poem, in anticipation of Southwell's own, was revised over the course of several years, and was known in various forms by different publics. It is difficult to determine with certainty which version Robert knew. In any case, he seems at first to have attempted a translation of the Italian poem while still in Rome. In England, in response to the needs of those whom he served, Southwell greatly altered his intention and the poem's aim. According to Devlin, "[h]e had begun work on the Italian original as early as 1584, and he kept on refurbishing it at intervals" (258). Brownlow adds how "the poem and its theme must have been a continual preoccupation for him," which makes sense in light of the work of reconciliation he vigorously pursued.

Critical response to this poem has varied widely over centuries. The prefatory poem that accompanies it, "The Author to the Reader," indicates that Southwell was preparing it for publication and that manuscript versions were already in circulation. His imagined audience consisted of Catholics needing courage, those who had abandoned Catholicism out of fear or to obtain worldly security, other writers who were abusing poetry by focusing on unworthy subjects, and, perhaps in this work more clearly than elsewhere, himself. Given this range of readers, it is not surprising that critics have faulted the work. Robert is trying to sum up his priestly and poetic insights and package them for very diverse publics. He was bound to disappoint some.

His contemporaries, especially other writers, seem to have appreciated the work. Devlin, for instance, argues for the *Complaint*'s effect on Shakespeare's *Rape of Lucrece*, in particular, as well as a more general reform of Shakespeare's literary interests (269–73). Devlin lines up parallel passages to prove that "the real debt of Shakespeare ... would seem to be an inspiration rather than a set of conceits" (272). Shakespeare, he believes, found inspiration in Southwell's exploration of the effect of sin on the soul of the sinner. "The general impression one gets," according to Devlin, "is that Shakespeare, pricked by Southwell's example, had tried his hand at tapping a loftier and more metaphysical vein" (273). "Thus it may be claimed with some probability," he concludes, "that Robert Southwell's last service to English letters, ... was to rouse up Shakespeare to a loftier conception of the divine spark within him" (273). Brownlow, reconsidering Devlin's argument, judges it "impressive, although it was weakened for some original readers because he combined with it an argument for a personal acquaintance between Southwell and Shakespeare that the evidence, interesting though it is, will not support" (94). He does allow, though, "that Shakespeare took a strong writerly and literary interest in Southwell's work," based on "the rather unusual use of 'spotted' in a moral and religious sense" (95):

> It occurs twice in the *Complaint*: "spotted soul" (l.18) and "spotted frame" (l.493). Shakespeare's uses of the word are concentrated in a trio of early works. He first used it twice in *Lucrece*, "spotted princess" (l.172) and "her [Lucrece's soul's] sacred temple spotted," both times in relation to the soul. The words appear in *Richard II* (3.2. 134), "their spotted souls," an exact repetition of Southwell's usage, and in *A Midsummer Night's Dream* (1.1.110), "This spotted and inconstant man." It seems very likely that Shakespeare picked up the word from Southwell and that he was struck by the idiosyncratic force of its moral and religious meaning. (95–96)

Other readers, such as Janelle, have been unfavorably struck by some of the work's stylistic idiosyncrasies. Janelle, always straining to fit particular works of Southwell's into his scheme of stylistic development, admits how, for the majority of readers, himself included, the *Complaint*, "on a first reading," is "disappointing" (205). The reason is two-fold. Janelle blames the poet's "juvenile partiality for literary 'elegance,'" and lingering Italian influence. But while the work's style irks him, Janelle admits that "Southwell excelled his contemporaries in that very exactness and subtlety of psychological and intellectual analysis on which they most prided themselves" (223). The most sophisticated appreciation of Robert's exactness and subtlety is offered by Scallon. Relying on Nancy Pollard Brown's "The Structure of Southwell's 'Saint Peter's Complaint,'" which highlights the poem's relationship to Tridentine confessional theory and practice, Scallon deems the *Complaint* "a remarkable poem for several reasons" (181). First, he acknowledges the increasingly dangerous circumstances in which Southwell found himself while finishing the work. Secondly, he notes how the poet, after starting on a translation, "succeeded in achieving a remarkably original work" (181). Scallon also uncovers how the poem concerns more than internal movements in its central character. He reads it as referring to English apostates in need of reconciliation and to Southwell's own "failures and faults and longing to give consolation and absolution" (181–82). Scallon also best understands the influences working in the poem and its author's intuitive appropriation of them:

> The meditative framework of Peter's effusions, the shadowy outlines of preludes, points and colloquies, which can be discerned in the poem,

confirm, I believe, the impression that the teachings of Trent, like the ascetical doctrines of Ignatius of Loyola, had become so much a part of Southwell's intellectual equipment that he could call upon them in his poetry without having to use proper names. (186)

Southwell introduces his poem with four stanzas addressed to the reader which, in themselves, reveal some of the poet's most frequently used intellectual equipment. His affection for his audience is palpable, as is his admiration for Peter in all his humanity. He warns readers that the poem will document "sad memories" of Peter's sins, but these should console rather than scandalize: "They once were brittle mould, that now are Saintes./ Their weaknesse is no warrant to offend:/ Learne by their faultes, what in thine owne to mend" (4–6). This interjection is reminiscent of Jesuit stress on confessors admitting their own sinfulness to penitents, and it also makes clear from the first of Southwell's 136 six-line stanzas that the poem is as much about his readers as it is about Peter. One of its primary aims, as Devlin grasps, is an "apostolic" one: "to attract imaginative souls to repentance and the life of the spirit" (259). There is also a note of sadness at the start, perhaps revealing difficulties Robert encountered on the mission. "The world doth waxe in evill," he laments, "but waine in good" (12). Nonetheless, he does not abandon hope, especially not in the power of literary persuasion. He resolves again, as in "The Author to his loving Cosen," to reform contemporary poetry. The state of his world "makes [his] mourning muse resolve in teares" (13). His sorrow is compounded because "[s]till finest wits are [di]stilling *Venus* Rose," and "[t]o Christian workes, few have their tallents lent" (16–18). In reaction, he asks for inspiration from "heavenly sparkes of wit" to "shew native light" through his "single penne." With their aid, through *Saint Peter's Complaint*, he can "learne [poetry] once to levell right" (22), and, simultaneously, win sinners back to God and encourage Catholics, including himself, to fortitude and fidelity.

At the start of the poem proper, readers overhear Peter addressing his soul, which he wants to "launche foorth ... into a main of tears" (1). The first several stanzas of the poem contain nautical language and imagery appropriate to the fisherman who speaks them. This authenticity, however, does not last. In time, Southwell's Peter accesses a range of knowledge beyond the scope of the biblical character upon whom he is based. At first, though, "remorse" is his "pilot" and he studies "the Carde," or map, of his misdeeds. He has been deservedly shipwrecked for his sins. Peter is encouraging himself to "vent ... the vapours of [his] brest" and be rebaptized by his weeping: "Where life was lost, recover life with cries./ Thy trespasse foule: let not thy teares be few:/ Baptize thy spotted soule in weeping dewe"

(16–8). Understanding sacramental confession in relationship to baptism echoes Tridentine teaching. Peter underscores how grace is restored to baptized sinners through proper penitential practice, though, in fact, the sacrament, per se, was not available at the time of his betrayal.

Peter, from the start, recognizes an audience of sinners. One reason for "sobbing out [his] sorrowes, fruites of [his] untruth," is to "[t]ell hartes that languish in the soriest plight,/ There is on earth a farre more sorry wight" (20–24). The apostle, throughout the poem, repeats that he is the worst of sinners, a "matchless wretch, O catife most accurst" (50). Southwell did the same in his *Spiritual Exercises and Devotions*. Implicitly, Peter and Southwell argue, if they can be forgiven, all others can. He also fashions himself "[t]he morrour of mishap" in which others can see the pattern of sin (27). Helping readers understand that pattern, Robert shows Peter struggling to name the nature of his transgression. First, he accuses himself of being "to God ungratefull" (30). Three stanzas later, however, his sin was fear in the face of death: "I fear'd with life to die; by death, to live" (49). Looking back he sees the error of his ways. Instead of remaining loyal to a "heavenly raigne," he lost courage when confronted with "an earthly rod" (52). Southwell, making this distinction between sacred and secular power, has English readers in mind. They can learn about disordered fears from Peter's example. The saint regrets being beguiled by the "fancies" and "follies" of earthly life. They cheated him of the promise of heaven. Underscoring how this can easily happen in the contemporary English context, Peter adds three stanzas criticizing life at court. While the court in question is Pilate's, the behaviors described point to that of Elizabeth I. Peter betrayed Christ "in so ill a court,/ Where rayling mouthes with blasphemies did swell,/ With taynted breath infecting all resort" (230–32). The atmosphere of court, whether in the ancient near east or sixteenth-century England, breeds corruption:

> It seems no fault to doe that all have done:
> The nomber of offenders hides the sinne:
> Coatch drawne with many horse doth easily runne.
> Soone followeth one where multitudes begin.
> O, had I in that court much stronger bene:
> Or not so strong as first to enter in.

Peter's epigrammatic admission allows the poet to address another audience, namely other writers. They, like Peter, are deceived by objects unworthy of their attention. Southwell describes them as "ambitious heades" who "dreame ... of fortunes pride" (31). They "[f]ill volumes with ... forged Goddesse praise," and "[d]evote [their] fabling wits to lovers layes" (32–

34). As Peter was too much in love with life, most poets are too much in love with love. After betraying Christ, Peter's new "theame" is grief:

> Sad subject of my sinne hath stoard my mind
> With everlasting matter of complaint:
> My threnes an endlesse Alphabet do find,
> Beyond the panges which *Jeremy* doth paint. (40)

The allusion to Jeremiah is the first reference to Old Testament figures to whom Peter compares himself. In this case, he claims that his "complaint," because of his sin's gravity, is more sorrowful than the prophet's lamentations. Most comparisons illustrate the magnitude of Peter's duplicity in the face of fear. His betrayal was occasioned by a "womans wordes," so he associates himself with Samson who lost his strength on account of Delilah's beauty (Judges 16). Later, he compares his weakness to Goliath's. As the Philistine giant was undone by a mere boy, so the first among the apostles abandoned Christ when questioned by a serving woman. Likewise, as "[s]mall gnats enforst th'Egyptian king to stoupe," so Peter "quayld at wordes that neither bit nor stonge,/ And those delivered from a womans tounge" (289–94).

To emphasize fully the senselessness of Peter's fear, Southwell exploits the misogyny characteristic of contemporary poets. One stanza, in particular, shows him indulging in anti-feminist invective to explain Peter's reason for remorse:

> O women, woe to men: traps for their falls,
> Still actors in all tragicall mischaunces:
> Earthes necesssarie evils, captivating thralles,
> Now murdring with your tongs, now with your glances,
> Parents of life and love: spoylers of both,
> The theefes of Harts: false do you love or loth. (319–24)

These charges are cultural commonplaces, and typically Southwell adapts them for his own purposes. Most poets employ these notions to explain their lack of luck in love, blaming fickle women for terminating relationships. Southwell uses them to explore a sinner's guilt. While other biblical characters, such as Adam, David, Solomon and Samson, succumbed to temptations presented by or in women, Peter considers himself worse than all of these. They, at least, were tempted by beauty:

> The blaze of beauties beames allured their lookes,
> Their lookes, by seeing oft, conceived love:
> Love, by affecting, swallowed pleasures hookes:

> Thus beauty, love and pleasure them did moove.
> These Syrens sugred tunes rockt them asleepe:
> Enough, to damme, yet not to damme so deepe. (307–12)

Peter is damned deeper than his biblical prototypes. He was a coward who, for fear of losing his life, lied about knowing Christ. Moreover, Southwell imagines that the woman who provoked the lies was unattractive:

> But gratious features dasled not mine eies,
> Two homely droyles were authors of my death:
> Not love, but feare my sences did suprize:
> Nor feare of force, but feare of womans breath.
> And those unarm'd, ill grac'd, despisde, unknowne:
> So base a blast my truthe hath overthrowne. (319–24)

Peter's "truthe," loyalty to Christ, was based on graces and privileges Jesus bestowed on him. In betraying Christ, Peter considers himself guilty of ingratitude, which he deems unnatural. Explaining his sin, the apostle draws a metaphor from nature. "The mother sea," he writes, "from overflowing deepes,/ Sendes foorth her issue by divided vaines:/ Yet back her offspring to their mother creepes,/ To pay their purest streames with added gaines" (103–106). Unlike such streams, Peter, "who dronke the drops of heavenly flood./ Bemyred the giver with returning mud" (107–108). The "drops" likely refer to the wine consumed at the Last Supper, which Southwell understood to be Christ's blood. This greatest gift, which Peter received along with the rest of the apostles, makes him remember privileges that were shared by fewer and some by himself alone. He recalls, for example, being present at Christ's Transfiguration (Matthew 17:1–8): "In Thabord joyes I egre was to dwell,/ An earnest friend while pleasures light did shine" (181–82). James and John were also present at this event when Moses and Elijah appeared with Jesus. It was only Peter who spoke, however, offering to make tents for the prophets, so that they might remain. Peter wanted to prolong this ecstatic experience. After betraying Christ, the memory of such an experience only exacerbates his guilt. "But when eclipsed glory prostrate fell," he confesses, "[t]hese zealous heates to sleepe I did resigne,/ And now my mouth hath thrice his name defil'd,/ That cryed so loud three dwellings there to build" (183–86).

The number three, representing the times Peter denied knowing Christ, features prominently throughout the poem. For example, there are three stanzas on the cock that crowed three times after Peter's third denial (Matthew 26 and Mark 14). The bird is described as "wakefull," "unhappy," "the just rebuker of [Peter's] crime," and the "milde revenger

P.Robertus *Soutbuuellus*, Nobili *fanguine in* Anglia natus, Soc.IESV.
pro Religione Catholica *fufpenfus et fectus* Londini. A.1595.3.Mar.
C.S.d. *M.K.f.*

8.1 Engraving of the martyrdom of Robert Southwell from Tanner's
Martyrology (by courtesy of the Woodstock Theological Center
Library, Georgetown University, Washington, D.C.)

of aspiring pride" (259–76), and like all else in Peter's memory, it moves
him toward despair. There is a fair amount of repetition on episodes in the
last days of Christ's life, such as the cock crowing three times, and this
reveals again the influence of the Ignatian *Exercises*. Ignatius suggests that

one praying the *Exercises*, especially during the Third Week, which considers Christ's Passion and death, return several times to the same passage or points for prayer to spark intense feelings and gain deeper insights (Loyola *Spiritual Exercises*, 204). Repetition serves this purpose in Peter's case. His remorse grows steadily through the first fifty-four stanzas of the poem, leading him to conclude that good cannot possibly come out of the evil he has done. Invoking the Parable of the Sower, he decides that Christ wasted his efforts on him, asking rhetorically, "[i]s this the harvest of his sowing toil?" (109). After an awkward metaphor describing how the Saviour "manured" his heart only "to breed him bryars," he decides that he can accomplish nothing on his own and doubts whether Jesus can accomplish anything in him: "[n]o: no: the Marle that perjuries do yield,/ May spoyle a good, not fat a barraine field" (113–14). Peter's instinct is to retreat into darkness and despair. He wants to "lurke in eternal night" and "[c]rouche in darkest caves from loathed light" (119–20). Finally, he wishes he had perished prior to all this, and especially regrets that he did not drown when he failed to trust Christ enough to walk with him on water (Matthew 14:23–33). He knows now how right Jesus was in calling him a "man of little faith." While that was true even when he enjoyed the Messiah's companionship, it is now even more certain. "Parted from Christ" his "force declin'd" entirely, and "[b]ase feare out of [his] hart his love unshrinde" (194–95). Having surrendered his love for Jesus to save his life, Peter feels at odds with himself. His contrary inclinations, and that he succumbed to the baser of these, result in a disintegration of identity. Peter describes how he chose to live and "lost my selfe" (222).

He is saved, however, exactly half way through the poem when Christ looks at him. This glance enables him to see beyond his own sinfulness and recognize the Son's saving power exercised specifically in the moment of his suffering: "In time, O Lord, thine eyes with mine did meet,/ In them I read the ruines of my fall" (325–26). Because Christ's eyes, described as "chearing raies," "blist where they beheld," Peter can begin to hope that he can rise through Jesus' mercy. The power of this single glance is so effective, that Peter cannot say enough about it. Twenty stanzas rhapsodize Jesus' eyes, far surpassing the ocular fixation found among Petrarchan-inspired poets. Christ's eyes do more than make Peter feel restored to grace. They are "springs of living light" that enable him to see more clearly his "deathful plight" as well as the possibility that he can be saved from it. They are "[s]weet volumes stoarde with learning fit for Saints," and their contents are inexhaustible. When one is lost in them "eternal studie never faints,/ Still finding all, yet seeking all it findes" (339–40). Southwell concludes this stanza, as he does many in the poem, with a witty paradox. Looking at Christ's eyes he asks, "[h]ow endlesse is your labyrinth of blisse,/ Where to be lost the sweetest finding is?" (341–42).

Lost in Christ's eyes Peter can find himself and be restored to integrity through remorse and reconciliation. In a stanza recalling "The Burning Babe," Jesus' eyes become "flames divine" which "warme" Peter's "cold breast" (349–54). Simultaneously, he compares them to "nectared Aumbryes," or cupboards for sacramental vessels found near a "church's altar." These, Peter claims, contain "soule feeding meats" upon which his "famishde breast" feasts. Lastly, they are metaphorically "graceful quivers of loves dearest darts" which wound his "stony" breast. There is an obvious poetic exuberance in this compilation of figures of speech. Southwell stresses that the effects of remorse and reconciliation are manifold. In the following stanzas, Christ's eyes and their effects are likened to a range wide enough to include "blazing comets" (361), "living mirrors" (367), the "pooles of *Hesebon*" (380), "Sunnes" (397), "Little worldes, the summes of all the best" (409), and twin turtle doves "all bath'd in virgins milk" (434). Crying as he speaks these lines, Peter understands that the boundlessly merciful Christ whom he encounters in disgrace loves him still. This is clearest in the stanza comparing Jesus' eyes to spheres:

> O gracious spheres, where love the Center is,
> A native place for our selfe-laden soules:
> The compasse, love, a cope that none can mis:
> The motion, love, that round about us rowles,
> O Spheres of love, whose Center cope and motion,
> Is love of us, love that invites devotion. (403–408)

Feeling loved, Peter is changed, as he explains to Christ:

> I, though too hard, learnd softness in thine eye,
> Which iron knots of stubborne will unbinds,
> Offering them love, that love with love wil buy,
> This did I learne, yet they could not discerne it,
> But wo, that I had now such need to learne it. (392–96)

Peter remains conscious of his sin and its effects. He still calls himself "cheefest Saint in Calender of shame" (497), and he asks for more shame: "Come shame, the lincea of offending mind,/ The ougly shroud, that overshadoweth blame:/ ... Light shame on me, I best deserve thy scourge" (517–22), and he compares himself unfavorably to Cain, whose motive for fratricide was at least under the "pretense of good" (525). Moreover, Southwell has Peter employ the allusion to Hagar that he used for himself in the *Querimonia*. The apostle wants Hagar to "bequeath" her tears for her dying son to him because his soul was even nearer to death. The depth of feelings is compounded when Peter considers how his friends, including Mary, the mother of Jesus, Mary and Martha, Lazarus, John and James, will react to him. His sin had consequences for the community which he was called to lead. The "corde" that bound them together "was broken with [Peter's] worde" (603). He dashed their high expectations of him: "Our rocke (say they) is riven, ... / Our Eagles wings are clipt, that wrought so hie" (613–14). He even worries that he is no longer a priest, describing his desires as "lay unconsecrated" (636). But he can also speak out his new and hard won knowledge about himself and the nature of sin. Sin is "the nothing that doth all things [de]file" (637), "Parent of death" (638), the cause of "selfe ruine" (642), and "a thing most done, yet more than God can doe" (643). Sin works by deceit, "seeming a heaven, yet banishing all from blisse" (646) and "first, seeming light, proving in fine a load" (650). The "load" Peter carries is a hellish circle from which he fears he cannot escape:

> My eye, reades mournefull lessons to my hart,
> My hart, doth to my thought the griefes expound,
> My thought, the same doth to my tounge impart,
> My tounge, the message in the eares doth sound.
> My eares, backe to my hart their sorrowes send:
> Thus circling griefes runne round without an end. (673–79)

But he now also understands that Christ can "revive and save him," and this knowledge is based on experience that becomes a prayer:

> Christ, health of feverd soule, heaven of the minde,
> Force of the feeble, nurse of Infant loves,
> Guide to the wandring foote, light of the blind,
> Whome weeping winnes, repentant sorrow moved,
> Father in care, mother in tender hart:
> Revive and save me slaine with sinfull dart. (751–56)

As a loved sinner, he acknowledges his dependence on grace. As a result of committing and confessing so serious a sin, his "pride is checkt" (764). He places himself in Christ's hands and speaks a two-stanza prayer that can serve as a model for any penitent:

> With mildnesse, *Jesu*, measure my offense:
> Let true remorse thy due revenge abate:
> Let teares appease when trespasse doth incense:

Let pittie temper thy deserved hate.
Let grace forgive, let love forget my fall:
With feare I crave, with hope I humbly call.

Redeeme my lapse with raunsome of thy love,
Traverse th'inditement, rigors dome suspend:
Let frailtie favour, sorrow succour move:
Be thou thy selfe, though chaungling I offend.
Tender my suite, clense this defiled denne,
Cancel my debtes, sweete *Jesu*, say Amen.

This prayer is at once brutally honest and hopeful. Just as Adam and Eve could recognize their nakedness after the Fall, so Peter, in the wake of betraying Christ, can see himself as he truly is. Fortunately, he can see God with a similar degree of clarity. The process of remorse and reconciliation restores him to grace, results in new knowledge and repairs his relationship with his closest friend. Grace, knowledge and love, Southwell wants to argue, are causes for consolation experienced through confession. Other Jesuit missionaries to England articulated this same argument because it was an integral part of their self-understanding and the way of proceeding prescribed for them by their religious superior. Southwell's poetic version of the argument may have proved most compelling. It is unquestionably the most enduring, not only for its sound, structure and sense, but also because it is so revelatory of the author himself. Robert, like Peter, knew well his own weaknesses and feared they would cause him to compromise when confronted by the possibilities of suffering and death. Like Peter, too, he wanted to place all his trust in God. Southwell likely had torture and martyrdom in mind when he put in Peter's mouth lines that admit self-doubt and hope for God's help: "I dare not say, I will; but wish, I may:/ ... / My good, O lord, thy gift; thy strength my stay:/ Give what thou bidst, and then bid what thou wilt./ Worke with me what thou of me doest request:/ then will I dare the most, and vow the best" (763–68).

Notes

1   This same prohibition on politics appears in the instructions for William Holt and Joseph Creswell on their mission to Scotland. In conversation with James VI they are to "behave modestly and on no account obtrude themselves in affairs of state" (Persons *Letters and Memorials*, 362). Instead they must "apply themselves … to spiritual occupations" (363).

2   In 1215 the Fourth Lateran Council made annual confession and the reception of communion during the Easter season a requirement for all Catholics. See Tanner I, 245.

3   Canon 5 following the Decree further defines contrition as "prepared for by means of examination, recapitulation and formal renunciation of sins, in which one reflects over one's years in bitterness of soul, by weighing up the seriousness, great number and foulness of one's sins" (Tanner II, 712). Southwell's poems will explore these issues in detail.

4   Teresa of Avila gives an account of confessing to a Jesuit who "greatly encouraged" her. "He left me consoled and encouraged," she writes, "and the Lord helped me and him to understand my situation and how I should be guided." Looking back on her life she concludes, "[p]raised the Lord who has given me the grace to obey my confessors, even though imperfectly; they have almost always been these blessed men from the Society of Jesus—although, as I say, I have followed them imperfectly" (*Collected Works* I, 158). As Jodi Bilinkoff notes, "[i]n the Fathers of the Society of Jesus, many of whom were twenty years younger than she, Teresa finally found confessors who could understand her experiences, her emotions and her methods of prayer" (119).

5   The antiquity of this devotion is difficult to determine. Some historians trace it back to the fifth century. In the sixteenth century, however, a series of sculptures commemorating events along the "way of the cross" or *Via dolorosa* was frequently reproduced throughout Europe (Walsh 251).

Epilogue

Christian martyrs in early modern Europe will remain opaque to the extent that their religiosity—with all that that entails—remains alien, obscured by modern and/or postmodern assumptions ... If martyrdom seems bizarre or incomprehensible, we should suspect that we have insufficiently grasped the religious convictions at its heart. (Gregory 8)

Southwell's religious convictions can be grasped in an especially trenchant way in the letters he wrote from England to his superiors and fellow Jesuits in Rome. These letters present the struggles he endured and his apostolic motivation for such endurance. More than accounts of his death, which are thoroughly hagiographical, they enable us to understand his willingness to surrender his life for the Catholic cause. They reveal the logic that led him to the inevitable conclusion of martyrdom. They also show how his perspective on martyrdom matured during his years on mission. A 1582 letter to Persons, for example, written from the relative comfort of a Continental Jesuit house of formation, illustrates Southwell's youthful and naive views. Upon hearing news of Campion's death, he refers to the latter as Persons' "trusty and inseparable companion in labour." Robert notes how the protomartyr "has had the start of [Persons] in loading his vessel with English wares, and has successfully returned to the desired port." He then urges Persons to his own death: "Day by day we are looking forward to hear something similar of you" (Southwell *Unpublished Documents*, 302). The poet, with no experience of life as a missionary, sees martyrdom as an end in itself, as opposed to one of several means to advance Catholicism.

During his years in England, this perspective changed. His early and "excessive desire for martyrdom" is moderated (Devlin 180). Southwell never stops thinking about martyrdom, nor does he discount its effectiveness, but he ceases to rush headlong toward it. He remained alive and apostolically engaged longer than most other missionaries, exercising great care to elude pursuivants. This exercise required him to wear disguises and use an alias. In a report to his superiors on his activities, he notes that wearing a disguise enabled him to penetrate even into government circles:

In the arrangement for my tour and the risks involved, there have been two young men, both burning with desire to join our Society, whose good breeding and intelligence and personal appearance have greatly helped me. And indeed there have been very many—the sons and heirs of great personages—who have been continually ready to give me not only their companionship but their personal service. I have sometimes been to call on the Protestant Sheriffs to look after secret Catholics in their households; and they, seeing my fine clothes and my bevy of aristocratic youths, and suspecting nothing so little as the reality, have received me with imposing ceremony and truly sumptuous banquets. (Devlin 182)

Doing so, he exemplifies the assertion that "[d]espite aspirations to imitate Christ in death, the English missionaries and their supporters were not carried away by an unrestrained rush to die for their faith." To the contrary, "evidence suggests that the yearning for martyrdom coexisted with a caution that was instilled during the missionaries' education and that remained part of their mentality" (Gregory 285).

Southwell's letters and those of other Jesuits are filled with evidence of his desire to elude imprisonment and death for as long as possible. These accounts also provide insight into their dramatic and anxious lives. Describing a happy respite with other priests at Baddesley Clinton, the country home of the Vaux family, the poet notes how "sorrow pounced on us at the height of our joy, we scattered in some alarm, but escaped fortunately with more danger than damage. My companion and I, having avoided Scylla, proceeded to steer into Charybdis; but by a special mercy of God we circumvented both, and are now riding safely at anchor" (Devlin 209). This safety was always temporary. An account written by John Gerard documents in detail the common experience of Southwell and his circle. The event recounted here occurred upon the celebration of the feast of St. Luke, the anniversary of Robert's entrance into the Jesuits and the day he pronounced his vows:

> Father Southwell was beginning Mass and the rest were at prayer, when suddenly I heard a great uproar outside the main door. Then I heard a voice shouting and swearing at a servant who was refusing them entrance ... Father Southwell heard the din. He guessed what it was all about, slipped off his vestments and stripped the altar bare. While he was doing this, we laid hold of all our personal belongings; nothing was left to betray the presence of a priest ... Some of us went and turned the beds and put up the cold side to delude anyone who put his hand to feel them. Outside the ruffians were bawling and yelling, but the servants held the door fast. They said the mistress of the house, a widow, was not yet up, but was coming down at once to answer them. This gave us enough time to stow ourselves and all our belongings into a very cleverly built sort of cave ... Then they set about searching the house. Everything was turned upside down; everything was closely examined—storerooms, chests, and even every bed

were carefully ransacked, on the off chance of finding Rosaries or picture books or an *Agnus Dei* hidden in them. I have no idea with what patience Ladies in Italy would put up with this! ... The hiding place was below ground level; the floor was covered with water and I was standing with my feet in it all the time. Father Garnet was there, also Father Southwell and Father Oldcorne, Father Stanney and myself, two secular priests and two or three laymen. So we were all saved that day. The next day Father Southwell rode off, as we had come, in company. (Gerard 41–43)

Southwell was cautious as a result of his desire to live for the sake of ministering to England's Catholics, and this desire grew as the sufferings of his community increased. Even before returning to England, Robert saw himself as a spokesman for a beleaguered minority. Writing in 1584 to the Jesuit provincial superior in Naples, he reports how "everything in England is in great trouble" and "Catholics suffer much" (Southwell *Unpublished Documents*, 305). In order to solicit the sympathy of non-English Jesuits, he informs them that "poor peasants, who will not go to the Protestant churches and are unable to pay the fine or sum of money that the heretics have imposed, are whipped through the streets." Even more appalling to the young man with aristocratic leanings, "marvellous cruelty ... has been shown towards certain gentlemen of noble family who were kept for some years in a stinking place." "Moreover," he reports with outrage, "they were kept tied to a manger like beasts, and not content with this, the heretics had a mill made, such as is usually turned by horses, so that the Catholics and priests may be employed in turning it, and when they have not done the tasks imposed, they are whipped like galley slaves." In time, he was no longer content to spread such news among European Jesuit houses. He wanted to make news.

In his first letter from England to the Superior General, Southwell already shows his awareness that the mission needs more than martyrs though he signals his willingness to accept that fate. "On reaching London," he writes, "I met with Catholics first amid swords and then in prison, portents (if it be lawful to play the augur) of a fate to me not unwelcome" (*Unpublished Documents*, 308). This is the last reference to himself in the letter. The rest concerns the sufferings of his people and fellow priests for whom he feels increasingly responsible. He urges the General to send more men, not to die, but to minister to Catholics who have felt "practically abandoned by the Society" after Campion's death and Persons' return to the Continent. These people "were full of misgivings" prior to the arrival of Southwell and Garnet, "thinking that their pastors, dismayed by difficulties, were abandoning the flock that never stood in greater need of their care." Southwell, on the ground in England, asks the

General to send more men for whose deployment the poet is developing a strategic plan:

> For want of missionaries, however, some who then grew faint-hearted, have not yet been restored to their former spirit. It is certainly a matter for regret that there are many counties, each containing not a few Catholics, in which there is not a single priest, though earnestly begged for by many. Unless new supplies are soon sent the Catholic cause will suffer greatly. The evil is further increased by the fact that the priests actually working in the harvest betake themselves in great numbers to one or two counties, leaving the others devoid of pastors. (309)

Later, Southwell's plans become even more specific, especially in light of his assignment in London. It was his responsibility to meet newly arrived missionaries, escort them to safe houses which he had established, and later dispatch them outside the city to places that required their service. Waiting for the arrival of new missionaries, he writes to Aquaviva:

> This is the plan we have agreed on for the glory of God, when there shall be a greater number of ours here. Two should be stationed at London—or one in London and one in the environment. The others should be assigned to each one a province or county in which each can work for all he is worth to promote religion. There will not be lacking other priests, men of outstanding holiness and learning, who will come to their assistance—and to this we most of all can testify by experience. The field will be theirs to take over from our labors, and the harvest from it will be beyond measure, owing to Him who guides the work of our hands unceasingly. (Devlin 161)

Southwell also informs the General about his own work, which he embraces enthusiastically despite difficulties. "I am devoting myself to sermons, hearing confessions, and other priestly duties," he writes, "hemmed in by daily perils, never safe for even the smallest space of time." "But," he continues, "I derive fresh courage from my very difficulties: and the multitude of terrors, which keep following each other, prevent any from lasting long, and blunts them almost all" (*Documents*, 309).

The most treacherous of Southwell's "difficulties" is the possibility of arrest by pursuivants who "prowl about the city linx-eyed" in search of him. They are aware of his presence because "news of our arrival has already got abroad from the lips of those who are members of the Queen's council" (308). Southwell is also troubled by a canonical concern. Even in the midst of strife and mortal danger, he worries about lacking certain ecclesiastical "faculties," or permissions to perform certain rituals. After reporting on exorcisms, "which have had the effect of converting many to the faith and greatly rallying the wavering," he notes how "there is a keen desire here and great need of the privileges and faculties we asked for in our last [letter]: which, if granted, will greatly advantage the Catholic cause" (309). This issue receives attention in subsequent letters as well, wherein he asks, for example, "to have sent unto us those faculties we sought for, especially to consecrate chalices and superaltars." "Of this there is very great need," he explains, "for that by reason of these long searchings of houses, many such things have fallen into the hands of pursuivants, so we are in great want" (314). Later, in a 1585 letter to Persons, Robert sounds exasperated about this issue:

> I have only to ask of you, and I do so most earnestly, that you would see our faculties being sent at the first opportunity. It would be a great boon and meet a great want, if the Pope would give us faculties, like those granted to the English College, to bless 2,000 rosaries and 6,000 grains, for here all are asking for such objects and we are unable to gratify them. (319)

Southwell's concern for such matters, which he seems to share with other missionaries, reveals the religious sensibilities characteristic of these men. It also provides insight into the world view out of which they operate. Given their circumstances, a less rigorous approach to seemingly minor issues would be understandable. If they observed so seriously rules and regulations about blessing rosaries, however, the larger matter of remaining faithful to the church would have weighed heavily on them, forcing them to concentrate their energies and cultivate their convictions. There was nothing relative about their obligations to the church. This helps postmodern readers grasp how martyrdom needs to be "understood from the inside, rather than explained from the outside." Moreover, "[i]t appears 'crazy' only if one considers Christian conviction and devotion crazy; on the martyrs' own terms, its meaning and logic are crystal clear" (Gregory 137).

. . .

Southwell's apostolic understanding of martyrdom crystalizes in his last extant work, a letter to Robert Cecil dated 6 April 1593. The unique copy of this text is found in a manuscript purchased by the Folger Shakespeare Library in 1964, which has been edited by Nancy Pollard Brown, who notes that "[n]othing is known of the history of the letter" (lxii). For example, she points out that "whether it was ever received by Cecil is a matter of conjecture." She is certain, however, that "the text is largely undisturbed" by its editor, who was clearly "a Catholic scribe, one of those faithful followers who carried on the literary apostolate of the Jesuit priest" (lxiii). At the end of Southwell's own apostolate, the last three years of which he spent in various prisons, he explains the course of his life and spiritual formation and how they led him to endanger himself by returning to England, knowing well that he would likely die a traitor's death. The letter's main purpose, in fact, is to ask for that death sooner rather than later, or release from prison so that he can resume other forms of work:

> But my humble request is that though I am bound so I be also resolved to expose this poor body to all extremities rather than to admit the least blemish unto my soul, yet I may find the favor, if my mishaps may not die till I die with them, to be soon put to the last punishment of the law and not further urged by my former torments. (ll. 195–99)

Typically, Southwell mixes honesty about his own faults and fears with a bold admission of his faith and its consequences. To the end, he never resolved doubts about his own fortitude in the face of suffering. His fears of betraying the church and the Society of Jesus, that so permeate *Saint Peter's Complaint*, linger, even after Southwell silently endured brutal tortures at the hands of Topcliffe. In his letter to Cecil, he precipitates his trial and the death that will follow from it by providing evidence that warrants this punishment: "I give evidence against myself and am become suitor for mine own execution" (l. 82). He confesses "with all humility" that he is "a Catholic priest, a state in God's church ever counted venerable and holy as instituted by Christ, succeeding his apostles, inheriting their grace and exercising their function" (l. 79). He is also "a religious man of the Society of Jesus, an Order that abandoning the world hath sacrificed itself to the service of God, wherein nature is perfected by learning, both accomplished by virtue, all ordered by a singular discretion" (ll. 79–80). He even brags to Cecil about the Jesuits' reputation. The "common consent" is that Jesuits have "hearts of judges for themselves, affections of mothers toward their children, [and] the dutiful minds of children to God and his Church" (l. 80).

Previously, Southwell had remained silent to protect the Bellamy family at whose home he was arrested. He felt a "mother's affection" for them, even though their daughter, Anne, had given him up. As a result, he was "[s]traited then to this unfortunate election, either to conceal what I was or to undo whom I loved" (ll. 65–66). He vowed silence on their behalf —"till I saw them either out of danger or past my remedy" (ll. 72–73). He has recently learned, however, "that besides the deposition of the daughter, which I presumed the state would never use to the condemning of her own parents, there had been more averred by her other friends than avowed by her" (ll. 74–77). As a result of this new evidence, which may have been falsified, Southwell thinks his silence can no longer save the Bellamys. Moreover, his silence is being used against him by Topcliffe, his "heaviest friend,"—who publicly interprets it as a result of the prisoner being "ashamed" of his profession (l. 86). He is "enforced to crave the use of [his] pen, that since I may not be publicly heard, I might at the least to a public personage [i.e., Cecil] and the principal in my causes discover that which before public authority I had as yet covered though never denied" (ll. 90–93). Not being heard from or about, for Southwell, means he has been rendered apostolically useless. Release would enable him to resume his activity even in exile. A martyr's death, he believed, would make him equally, if not more, helpful to the Catholic cause.

As he asks for death or release, he takes pains to convince Cecil that he is not worried about enduring more suffering, and he does not complain about his present circumstances. The letter begins with a resume of his Jesuit training, stating that he was prepared for harsh conditions. He admits that "[t]he usual effect of a languishing and afflicted life is an unwillingness to live," but he asserts that this does not apply in his case. "Since time uncradled my thoughts out of the folly of childhood and ripeness of years enabled reason to look with a Christian eye into the labyrinth of worldly dangers," he argues, "I esteemed it better to spend my days in poverty and penance, providing for such an end as might begin my endless comfort" (ll. 9–12). In making his request, Southwell engages in an exercise of wit in constructing these lines, still convinced of the power of words to persuade. In this case, he wants to persuade Cecil that it is frustration about not being apostolically effective either in work or in death, as opposed to the fear of suffering, that motivates him. Pointing to his preparation for priesthood, he describes how "having heretofore so long weaned my senses from their liking and inured my will to crosses and contempt, abridgement of delight is no new want, nor experience of pains any strange occurrence" (ll. 15–17). Nor is he driven to this request by "the unquiet motions of an impatient mind," "any new inclination to death" or the "tediousness of an irksome life" (ll. 16–19). Rather he writes concerning "that only care which every Christian ought to tender, his credit," or reputation (l. 21). This credit, he explains to Cecil, is "that which the wise man valued above all treasures, the Apostle [Paul] above life itself, whereof the root is virtue, the fruit edification, the possession necessary, the want offensive" (ll. 26–28). Southwell asserts that his own credit depends on fidelity and effectiveness:

> And as my religion and Order are more precious to me than a thousand other lives, so to live by relenting in the one or swerving from the other in the least duty I reckon more odious than as many deaths, judging no death

> as intolerable as his infamies are that surviveth his credit and outliveth the due respect of his faith and calling. (l. 82)

Since he long recognized reconciliation as primary among his duties, he practices it in this last letter. Despite his harsh treatment by Topcliffe and his betrayal by the hands of those who "were the authors of my evils and could be content to cast me into this furnace of afflictions," he forgives them:

> But whether ambition, careless by whose fall it riseth, or a despairing impatience, not caring on whom it throw misery from itself, taught them to choose me as the fittest step for their assent or ransom for their delivery, from my very heart I most entirely forgive them, wishing them no worse corrector than grace, no sharper scourge than conscience, no more sorrow than remorse shall beget of their own shames. (ll. 204–210)

How much Robert knew about Anne Bellamy's reason for betraying him is unclear. In January 1592, she had been placed in Gatehouse prison for recusancy. It was there where she had become pregnant with Topcliffe's child, either through rape or seduction. Topcliffe then promised to arrange for her to marry Nicholas Jones, who was in his employ, if Anne would lure Southwell to her family's home which he was accustomed to visiting. Anne, "in despairing impatience," agreed to do so upon Topcliffe's unkept promise that he would preserve her family and their property as well as Anne's reputation. Topcliffe released her, and she invited Southwell to visit her family on 25 June. After saying Mass and retiring for the night, the poet was arrested by Topcliffe and his men who had surrounded the Bellamy home. Topcliffe's motive in this intrigue was more obvious. He ambitioned after Elizabeth's affections, and a letter written soon after he apprehended Southwell reveals how he thought this arrest, in particular, would secure his rise:

> Most Gracious Sovereign, Having F. Robert Southwell (of my knowledge) the Jesuit in my strong chamber in Westminster ... I have presumed (after my little sleep) to run over this examination enclosed, faithfully taken and of him foully and suspiciously answered, and, somewhat knowing the nature and doings of the man, may it please your Majesty to see my simple opinion. Constrained in duty to utter it. Upon this present taking of him it is good forthwith to enforce him to answer truly and directly, and so to prove his answers true in haste, to the end as such as be deeply concerned in his treacheries have no time to start or make shift. To use any means in common prisons either to stand upon or against the wall (which above all things excels and hurteth not) will give warning. But if your Highness' pleasure be to know anything in his heart,

to stand against the wall, his feet standing upon the ground and his hands struck as high as he can reach against the wall, ... will enforce him to tell all, and the truth proved by the sequel.

    ... So humble submitting myself to your majesty's direction in this, or in any service with any hazard, I cease until I hear your pleasure here at Westminster with my charge and ghostly father this Monday the 26th of June 1592.

This was the first of several torture sessions inflicted upon Southwell by Topcliffe. In writing to Cecil, who witnessed at least one of these sessions, Robert still holds out hope that he and his torturer and his betrayer can be reconciled in the same church, even if the reconciliation needs to be worked by his own death. "And it may be," he writes, "that when they shall see my wounds to weep innocent blood, it will draw into their eyes some drops of repentant tears and then move them to think their ill deed not so well done, especially to a child of their own mother [i.e., the Catholic church], as passion persuaded them while it was hot in the doing" (ll. 210–14).

While Southwell understands martyrdom as apostolically effective, he nevertheless admits his fear. When he first anticipated his "painful agonies," he informs Cecil that "[his] body trembled and [his] tears bewrayed grief" (ll. 189–90). His consolation, though, is two-fold. First, calling to mind the agony in the garden of Gethsemane about which he wrote several poems, he remembers that such fear "is a thing incident unto Christ himself" (l. 191). Second, he "believes that the cause maketh this last duty of nature the worthiest price of eternity" (ll. 227–28). This cause made him come to England in the first place. He explains how his mission was motivated by love for his parents to whom he is "indebted ... for my very being" and his "friends for many benefits" (ll. 48–49). He could not remain in Rome and "neglect their miseries." Comparing himself to Lazarus, the rich man who "even in hell retained a feeling towards his friends," he tells Cecil that he wanted to return and risk death because he feared their damnation should they remain deprived of the sacraments and unreconciled to the church. "How could I fear and not seek to repent," he asks rhetorically, "How could I prevent and not come into the realm?":

> Answer for me nature; defend me grace. I was the child of a Christian woman and not the whelp of a tiger; I could not fear, and foresee, and not forewarn; I had not the crueller heart than a damned caitiff, to despise their bodies and souls by whom I received mine ... And God almighty is my witness, I came with no other intention into the realm; and as for the blindness thereof, I appeal to the eyes of all antiquity and to the most and happily not to the dimmest of all Christendom, who both protest and

prove that they have read and seen in this faith the surest and soundest
grounds of all human and divine belief. (ll. 155–67)

Southwell remains committed to restoring England's sight through works
of reconciliation, either as part of an active apostolic life, or in the kind of
death that he is confident can occasion conversion. Since neither course is
currently available to him, he sends Cecil this letter which he imagines as
"a sharp sword, yet as I suppose, well sheathed" (l. 243). In one last
typological reference, he compares himself to Isaac in Genesis 22. In this
instance, his letter becomes "the fuel wherein [Isaac] was to be the
oblation." This gives Cecil two options. He can play Abraham "resolute to
strike," or "the good angel, addresses to stay the blow" (ll. 253–54).
Southwell claims Ignatian indifference, since either decision will enable
him to advance the mission: "I being here ready bound and prepared either
to receive the stroke with patience or to register the favor of life in a
thankful remembrance" (l. 255). He is hardly rushing toward martyrdom
but he understands it as an apostolic work to which he might be consigned.
The important issue is not the kind of work he can do, whether in an active
apostolate or in acceptance of death, but the ability itself to work for
reconciliation. The only things to which the poet cannot be reconciled are
isolation and inactivity. Apologizing to Cecil for putting him in so difficult
a spot, Southwell writes, "the importance of the matter bear[s] the blame of
my boldness" (ll. 301–303).

. . .

Save this letter to Cecil, it is relatively certain that Southwell wrote nothing
while in prison. As Alagambe reports in his martyrology, "Robert, under
close supervision, … was never permitted to use ink; truly, never during the
entire time of his confinement was he granted the benefit of composition."[1]
After his death, his breviary revealed that he used a pin to make marks on
several pages, spelling out ejaculations such as, "[m]y God and my
everything" and "God gave himself to you; you give yourself to God"
(Alagambe 17). At the end of his three-year solitude, he was determined to
use the occasion of his trial and death to speak one final time on
reconciliation. Just before his trial, the date of which he was kept unaware,
Robert was moved to "a subterranean cave whose baseness and harshness
earned it the name 'Limbo'" (Alagambe 19). The name of this cell
corresponds to the state of suspension the poet experienced during his
imprisonment. Released from "Limbo," Southwell makes the courtroom an
arena for apostolic activity. Typically, he eschews belligerence in favor of

respect for his enemies. According to Alagambe, "[w]hen Robert was then led to the bench, he showed reverence to his Inquisitors with his head hung low" (20). Leake also makes mention of the fact that he "put of his hat and made obesance" (Southwell *Unpublished Documents*, 334). When allowed to address the jury, Southwell first clarified the apolitical aim of his work in England. He admits to being "carried to the sacred order of the Priesthood in the Roman Catholic Church," but, he insists, "I testify by God, the avenger of perjury, that I have hatched neither plans nor conspiracies against the Queen or the Kingdom; I have come only to offer aid to those desiring sacraments in the Catholic rites" (Alagambe 21). Throughout the trial, at every question, he insisted that "he was a stranger to treachery in every charge" (Alagambe 21).

In response, the prosecutors catalogued every plot and conspiracy associated with Jesuits and their sympathizers, such as "the treasons of Ballard and Babington," "printing and sending over seditious books," and erecting seminaries "where youths were trained up to be sent to England to disuade Her Majesties' subjects from their natural obedience" (*Documents*, 334). Most notoriously, "they practiced for invasion and now of late their designments have been to make a Spanish or open rebellion." Then, upon the testimony of Anne Bellamy, they linked Southwell with the practice of equivocation. According to Leake's account of the trial "[h]er deposition was that Father S. told them, that if in case any should inquire for him and propose to them an oath whether they had seen him, that they might deny it by oath; although they had seen him that same day; reserving this intention: —'Not with a purpose to tell you'" (*Documents*, 334).

This was the only specific charge to which Southwell responded. After several interrupted attempts to explain the notion of reserved judgment, he posed a case to the court:

> Put the case that the Queen should be pursued by her enemies (whom God bless), and should come to your house, and the enemies following should urge you upon your oath to declare to them where she was, in refusing to swear were a plain discovery; for so must the case be put … That which I then taught, I will defend by the law of God, by the common law civil and the law of all nations. No civil society can be maintained, if the contrary be admitted. (*Documents*, 335)

Southwell's example caused outrage among court officers, as was the subject of equivocation to do for years to come. Immediately, the poet backed away from this contentious issue, and made a plea for the more humane treatment of future prisoners. Exposing Topcliffe's cruelty, he explains how he had been tortured ten times, and would "have rather endured ten executions." He wants this included in the trial record not for himself, "but for others; that they may not be handled so inhumanely, to drive men to desperation, if it were possible." Topcliffe objects that he never subjected Southwell to the rack, but simply "set him against a wall." This obfuscation resulted in the harshest words Southwell spoke during this entire ordeal: "Thou art a bad man" (*Documents*, 335).

Southwell's execution, like most that occurred in the sixteenth century, was highly ritualized. He, his executioners, and the spectators, hostile or sympathetic, were all aware of the prescribed form and their roles within it. Rules of style and decorum had developed or been imposed. Tropes, typologies and expectations—aesthetic, political, and religious— were well known. Southwell understood all this, just as he grasped the nature and purpose of contemporary poetry and prose. He likewise adapted the ritual of execution for his own apostolic purposes, underscoring as often as he could the importance of reconciliation. Through early accounts of his death scene, Alagambe, Tanner and Leake agree in most respects. All record, for example, the procession on a hurdle to Tyburn and Southwell's composure. In Alagambe's account, "[a]s he arrived closer to Tyburn, ... happy and beaming he greeted the death-dealing pyre" (27). According to Leake, "his countenance appeared very modest, yet cheerful, like the sun when it breaketh out after that it hath dispersed the clouds" (*Documents*, 336). Tanner concurs: "He was calm both in countenance and spirit, as if he were approaching a most peaceful place" (13). They also record many of the same lines delivered by Robert and others in the scene. He is, by all accounts, adamant about his loyalty to the Queen. Leake summarizes how "[h]e prayed for the Queen, that she might enjoy all the gifts of nature and grace, all helps of friends and faithful counselors whereby she might reign to God his glory, and after this life be inheritos of the kingdom of heaven; and wished she would pardon him, for that he had come into her kingdom without license" (*Documents*, 336). Tanner offers a fuller and purportedly *verbatim* account:

> At the same time I bear witness that I have never perpetrated anything against the majesty of the Queen, but that I have been accustomed to daily pour forth prayers on her behalf. And now at this boundary of life and death I pray with all my strength to God that he grant eternal safety to her; and mournfully I pray that God in his beneficence grant the very thing for which all our people aspire, namely that a light preserves this our Fatherland ... If my arrival here offends the Queen, I most humble pray to her that it be blotted out, and I even submit to the very act of supplication, and I bear it with a level mind: a benign God reveals work for me, and the pure Virgin Mary Mother of God with all the Angels and Saints of God assist me.

Southwell pursued a conciliatory course until the last moments of his life, seizing a brutal death scene as an opportunity to underscore the work he had been preparing for since he entered the Jesuits and performing since his arrival in England. His acts before dying may strike us as self-conscious but that is true of most of Southwell's performances—personal and literary. Jesuit spirituality and his academic formation had trained him to be especially aware of himself and his place in the world. His many years of preparation for ministry equipped him with a sensitivity for reading and responding to the signs of the time. He was acutely sensitive to the needs of his family, friends, nation, religious order and church. These needs were born of tensions and anxieties that drove apart people whom, and institutions which, he loved. Over time he understood that his ministry was to move against these divisions and draw people back to the center through reconciliation. This understanding was hard won and, by the standards of the twenty-first century, imperfect.

Robert's remaining work was to die. He did so, in *imitatio Christi*, paraphrasing the words of Jesus recorded in Luke 24:46, "into your hands I commend my spirit." The immediate effect of his death would have gratified him. By all accounts, the crowd seemed reconciled, if only momentarily, and Southwell was spared the most horrific aspects of his death sentence. He was not cut down alive to be disemboweled. When the cart was pulled out from under him, "he remained hanging alive a good space, knocking his breast and making divers times as well as he could, the sign of the Cross, turning his eyes up and down wide open, until the hangman pulled him downwards by the legs, at which time he most happily yielding up his spirit closed his eyes and looked most cheerful":

> One of the officers proffered three times to have cut him down alive, according to the sentence, but the people cried, "Stay, stay!" and the Lord Montrouge forbade him likewise ... The people were so much moved by his charitable ending, that no one of them (contrary to their accustomed wont) did speak any evil words against him ... His head being cut off, and by the hangman lifted up to be shown to the people, no one was heard to cry, "Traitor, traitor!" as before times they were wont to do, but passed the matter over in silence. (Foley *Records* I, 375)

Throughout his life as a Jesuit priest, Robert Southwell shaped the body of his literary work for the sake of his mission. In death, his misshapen physical body effected the same apostolic purpose: reconciliation. While literary history has largely overlooked his artistic achievement in comparison to other writers of the time, Southwell, in making art and giving his life for the sake of reconciliation, stands ahead of his contemporaries and, perhaps, ours as well. Writing reconciliation in an era of religious strife and sectarian violence remains an imperative and compelling mission.

Notes

[1]   When citing Alagambe and Tanner here I am relying on unpublished translations by Carey Smith.

Bibliography

Primary Sources

Aelred of Rievaulx. *Of Spiritual Friendship*. Paterson, NJ: St. Anthony's Guild Press, 1948.

[Alfield, Thomas]. *A true report of the death & martyrdome of M Campion jesuite*. [London, 1582]. ARCR II, no. 4; STC 4537.

Allen, William. *A Briefe Historie of the Glorious Martyrdom of XII Reverend Priests*. Rheims, 1582. ARCR II, no. 7; STC 369.5.

_____. *An Apologie and True Declaration of the Institution and Endeavors of the Two English Colleges*. [Mons, 1581]. ARCR II, no. 6; STC 369.

Augustine of Hippo. *The City of God*. trans. Marcus Dods. NY: Modern Library, 1950.

Bacon, Francis. *The Works of Francis Bacon*. ed. Spedding. Boston: H.O. Houghton, 1878.

Bellarmine, Robert. *Robert Bellarmine: Spiritual Writings*. trans. and eds. John Patrick Donnelly and Roland J. Teske. NY: Paulist Press, 1989.

Bruno, Vincenzo, S.J. *The Third Part of the Meditations* (1599) [trans. from Italian]; and *A Treatise of Schisme* (1578) [by Gregory Martin]. Menston: Scholar Press, 1972.

Campion, Edmund. *Campion's Ten Reasons*. ed. John H. Pollen, S.J. London, 1914.

Cicero, *De Amicitia*. trans. Andrew P. Peabody. NY: Thomas Nelson and Sons, 1978.

Copley, Anthony. *A Fig for Fortune*. London: The Spenser Society, 1883.

Copley, Thomas. *Letters of Sir Thomas Copley*. ed. Richard Copley Christie. NY: Burt Franklin, 1897.

Davies, John. *The Complete Works*. ed. Alexander B. Grosart. Hildesheim: Olms, 1968.

De Sales, Francis. *Introduction to the Devout Life*. NY: Harper, 1952.

Donne, John. *The Complete English Poems*. ed. C.A. Patrides. NY: Alfred A. Knopf, 1991.

_____. *Ignatius His Conclave*. ed. Timothy Healy, S.J. Oxford: Clarendon, 1969.

_____. *Pseudo-Martyr: Wherein out of Certaine Propositions and Gradations, this Conclusion is Evicted that those which are of the Romaine Religion in this Kingdome, may and ought to take the*

Oath of Allegiance. ed. Anthony Raspa. Montreal: McGill-Queens UP, 1993.

_____. *Ecclesiae Anglicanae Trophae.* Rome, 1584. ARCP II, nos. 944–946.

Foxe, John. *The Acts and Monuments of John Foxe: With a Life of the Martyrologist, and Vindication of the Work by George Townsend.* 8 vols. NY: AMS Press, 1965.

Gerard, John. *The Autobiography of an Elizabethan.* ed. Philip Caraman, S.J. London, 1951.

Hall, Joseph. *Poems of Joseph Hall.* ed. A. Davenport. Liverpool, UK: Liverpool UP, 1949.

Hicks, Leo, ed. *Letters and Memorials of Father Robert Persons, S.J.* London, 1942, CRS 39.

Hide, Thomas A. *A Consolatorie Epistle to the Afflicted Catholikes* [1560]. Menston: Scholar Press, 1972 (*English Recusant Literature*, vol. 105).

Howard, Henry. *The Poems of Henry Howard, Earl of Surrey.* NY: Haskell House, 1966.

Hudson, Winthrop S. *John Ponet: Advocate of Limited Monarchy.* Chicago: U of Chicago P, 1942.

Hughes, Paul L. and James F. Larkin, C.V.S., eds. *Tudor Royal Proclamations.* 3 vols. New Haven, CT: Yale UP, 1964–1969.

Hughey, Ruth, ed. *The Arundel Harrington Manuscript of Tudor Poetry.* 2 vols. Columbus, OH: U of Ohio P, 1960.

Jonson, Ben. *Timber, or Discoveries: made upon men and matter.* ed. Felix E. Schelling. Boston, MA: Ginn & Co., 1892.

Kleist, James A., ed. *The Epistles of St. Clement of Rome and St. Ignatius of Antioch.* Westminster, MD, 1949.

Knox, Thomas Francis, ed. *The Letters and Memorials of William Cardinal Allen.* London, 1882.

_____. *The First and Second Diaries of the English College, Douay.* London: Nutt, 1878.

Lodge, Thomas. *The Complete Works of Thomas Lodge.* vol. 3. NY: Russell & Russell, 1963.

Loyola, Ignatius, S.J. *A Pilgrim's Journey: The Autobiography of Ignatius Loyola.* trans. Joseph N. Tylenda, S.J. Wilmington, DE: Michael Glazier, 1985.

_____. *The Constitutions of the Society of Jesus.* ed. George Ganss, S.J. St. Louis: The Institute of Jesuit Sources, 1969.

_____. *Counsels for Jesuits: Selected Letters and Instructions of St. Ignatius Loyola.* ed. Joseph N. Tylenda. Chicago, IL: Loyola Press, 1985.

_____. *The Spiritual Exercises.* ed. David Fleming, S.J. St Louis, MO: The Institute of Jesuit Sources, 1978.

_____. *Rules of the Society of Jesus.* Roehampton, UK: Manresa Press, 1929.

Marston, John. *The Poems of John Marston.* ed. Arnold Davenport. Liverpool, UK: Liverpool UP, 1961.

Munday, Anthony. *The English Roman Life.* ed. Philip J. Ayres. NY: Oxford UP, 1980.

Nashe, Thomas. *The Works of Thomas Nashe.* ed. Ronald B. McKerrow. London: Sidgwick and Jackson, 1910.

Persons, Robert. *A Brief Discors Contayning Certayne Reasons Why Catholiques Refuse to go to Church.* (1580). Menston: Scholar Press, 1972.

_____. *Letters and Memorials of Robert Persons, S.J.* ed. Leo Hicks. vol. 1 (to 1588). London: Catholic Record Society, 1942.

Roper, William. *The Life of Syr Thomas More, 1626.* Menston: Scholar Press, 1970.

Southwell, Robert, S.J. *The Complete Poems of Robert Southwell, S.J., for the First Time Fully Collected and Collated with the Original and Early Editions and MSS. and Enlarged with Hitherto Unprinted and Inedited Poems from MSS. at Stonyhurst College, Lancashire.* ed. Alexander Grossart. 1872.

_____. *An Epistle of Comfort to the Reverend Priests, and to the Honourable, Worshipful, and Other of the Lay Sort, Restrained in Durance for the Catholic Faith.* ed. Margaret Waugh. Chicago, IL, 1966.

_____. *An Humble Supplication to Her Maiestie.* ed. R.C. Bald. Cambridge, UK: Cambridge UP, 1953.

_____. *Letters to Various Persons. Unpublished Documents Relating to the English Martyrs.* vol. I (1584–1603). ed. and trans. John Hungerford Pollen. This work, which also contains other documents of interest to students of Southwell, is vol. 5 (1903) of *Publications of the Catholic Record Society.*

_____. *Marie Magdalene Funerall Teares.* London, 1602. STC 22952.

_____. *The Poems of Robert Southwell, S.J.* eds. James H. McDonald and Nancy Pollard Brown. Oxford, 1967.

_____. *Spiritual Exercises and Devotions.* ed. J.M. Buck. NY: Benzinger Press, 1931.

_____. *The Triumphs Over Death.* ed. John W. Trotman. London: B. Herder, 1914.

_____. *Two Letters and Short Rules of a Good Life.* Ed. Nancy Pollard Brown. Washington, D.C.: Folger Shakespeare Library, 1973.

Stephens, Thomas. *Letters of Thomas Stephens.* Stonyhurst MSS., Collectio Cardiwelli, F.16.

Strype, John, ed. *Ecclesiastical Memoirs.* 3 vols. Oxford, 1721.

_____. *Annals of the Reformation and Establishment of Religion.* 4 vols. Oxford, 1820–1840.

Tanner, Norman P. *Decrees of the Ecumenical Councils.* 2 vols. Washington, DC: Georgetown UP, 1990.

Weston, William. *William Weston, 1550–1615: An Autobiography from the Jesuit Underground.* trans. and ed. Philip Caraman. NY, 1955.

Wood, Anthony Á. *Athenae Oxonienses: An Exact History of all the Writers and Bishops who have had their Education in the University of Oxford: To which are added the Fasti, or Annals of said University.* London: F. C. and J. Ribington, et. al., 1813.

Wright, Thomas, ed. *Letters Relating to the Suppression of the Monasteries.* London: Camden Society, 1843.

Secondary Sources

Allen, Morse A. *The Satire of John Marston.* NY: Haskell House, 1965.

Basset, Bernard. *The English Jesuits.* London, 1967.

Beales, A.C.F. *Education Under Penalty: English Catholic Education from the Reformation to the Fall of James II.* London: The Athlone Press, 1963.

Bettenson, Henry. *The Early Christian Fathers: A Selection from the Writings of the Fathers from St. Clement of Rome to St. Athanasius.* Oxford: Oxford UP, [1959] 1984, 7th ed.

Bouwsma, William J. "Anxiety and the Formation of Early Modern Culture," in *After the Reformation: Essays in Honor of J. H. Hexter.* ed. Barbara C. Malalent. Manchester, UK: Manchester UP, 1980, 215–46.

Bray, Allen. *Homosexuality in Renaissance England.* London: Gay Men's Press, 1982.

Bredbeck, Gregory W. *Sodomy and Interpretation: Marlowe to Milton.* Ithaca, NY: Cornell UP, 1991.

Brodrick, James J. *The Life and Works of Blessed Robert Francis Cardinal Bellarmine.* 2 vols. London: Burns, Oates and Washbourne, 1928.

Brown, Carleton, ed. *Religious Lyrics of the Fifteenth Century.* Oxford, 1939.

Brown, Nancy Pollard. "Paperchase: The Dissemination of Catholic Texts in Elizabethan England," in *English Manuscript Studies 1100–1700 (Volume 1).* eds. Peter Beal and Jeremy Griffith. London: Basil Blackwell, 1989.

—————————. "Robert Southwell: The Mission of the Written Word," in *The Reckoned Expense: Edmund Campion and the Early English Jesuits.* ed. Thomas McCoog, S.J. Woodbridge, UK: Boydell Press, 1996, 285–300.

—————————. "The Structure of Southwell's 'St. Peter's Complaint,'" *MLR*, LXI (1966), 3–11.

Brownlow, F.W. *Robert Southwell.* NY: Twayne, 1996.

Byman, Seymour. "Ritualistic Acts and Compulsive Behaviors: The Pattern of Tudor Martyrdom," *American Historical Review*, 83 (1978).

Caraman, Philip, S.J. *Henry Garnet, 1555–1606, and the Gunpowder Plot.* London, 1964.

—————————. *The Other Face: Catholic Life under Elizabeth I.* London, 1960.

—————————. *University of the Nations: The Story of the Gregorian University of Rome from 1551 to Vatican II.* NY: Paulist Press, 1981.

—————————. *Saint Robert Southwell and Henry Garnet: A Study in Friendship.* St. Louis: The Institute of Jesuit Sources, 1995.

Cavendish, George. *Two Early Tudor Lives.* New Haven, CT: Yale UP, 1962.

Challoner, Richard. *Memoirs of Missionary Priests and Other Catholics of Both Sexes, That Have Suffered Death in England on Religious Accounts From the Year 1577 to 1684.* 2 vols. Derby, UK: Burns, Oates & Washbourne, 1924.

Chambers, E.K. *The Elizabethan Stage.* Oxford: Clarendon Press, 1923.

Clancy, Thomas H., S.J. *Papist Pamphleteers: The Allen–Persons Party and the Political Thought of the Counter-Reformation in England, 1572–1615.* Chicago, IL: Loyola UP, 1964.

—————————. "Spiritual Publications of the English Jesuits, 1615–1640," *Recusant History*, 19 (1989), 426–46.

_____. "The First Generation of English Jesuits," AHSI 57 (1988), 137–62.

Cleveland, Charles D. *A Compendium of English Literature: chronologically arranged from Sir John Mandeville to William Cowper*. NY: American Book Co., 1847.

Codino, Gabriel. "The 'Modus Parisiensis,'" in *The Jesuit Ratio Studiorum: 400th Anniversary Perspectives*. ed. Vincent J. Duminuco. NY: Fordham UP, 2000.

Conner, Paul M. *Celibate Love*. Huntington, IN: Our Sunday Visitor, 1978.

Corthell, Ronald J. "'The Secrecy of Man': Recusant Discourse and the Elizabethan Subject," *Elizabethan Literary Renaissance* 19:3 (1989), 272–90.

Craik, George L. *A Compendious History of English Literature and of the English Language from the Norman Conquest, with Numerous Specimens*. NY: Scribner, 1863.

Cunnar, Eugene and Jeffrey Johnson, eds. *Discovering and (Re)covering the Seventeenth Century Religious Lyric*. Pittsburgh, PA: Duquesne UP, 2001.

Decloux, Simon. *Commentaries on the Letters and Spiritual Diary of St. Ignatius Loyola*. Rome: C.I.S., 1980.

Devlin, Christopher. *The Life of Robert Southwell, Poet and Martyr*. NY, 1956.

Donahue, John, S.J. *Jesuit Education: An Essay on the Foundation of Its Idea*. NY: Fordham UP, 1963.

Donnelly, John Patrick and Michael W. Maher, S.J., eds. *Confraternities and Catholic Reform in Italy, France and Spain*. Kirkville, MO: Thomas Jefferson UP, 1999.

Dorsey, Katherine C. *The Life of Father Thomas Copley, The Founder of Maryland*. Woodstock, MD, 1885.

Duffy, Eamon. *The Stripping of the Altars: Traditional Religion in England, 1400 –1580*. New Haven, CT: Yale UP, 1992.

Duffy, Stephen J. *The Graced Horizon: Nature and Grace in Modern Catholic Thought*. Collegeville, MN: The Liturgical Press, 1992.

Edwards, Francis, S.J. *The Elizabethan Jesuits*. London: Phillimore, 1981.

_____. *Robert Persons: The Biography of an Elizabethan Jesuit*. St. Louis, MO: The Institute of Jesuit Sources, 1999.

Elton, G.R. *Policy and Police: The Enforcement of the Reformation in the Age of Thomas Cromwell*. Cambridge, UK: Cambridge UP, 1972.

Fairweather, A.M., ed. *Nature and Grace: Selections from the Summa Theologica of Thomas Aquinas*. vol XI, *The Library of Christian Classics*. Philadelphia, PA: Westminster Press, 1944.

Fiske, A. "Cassian and Monastic Friendship," *American Benedictine Review*, vol. 12 (1961), 190–205.

Foley, Henry, S.J. *Jesuits in Conflict.* London, 1873.

_____. *Records of the English Province of the Society of Jesus: Historical Facts Illustrative of the Labours and Sufferings of its Members in the Sixteenth and Seventeenth Centuries.* 7 vols. London: Burns and Oates, 1878.

Fuller, Thomas. *The Worthies of England.* London: Allen and Unwin, 1952.

Fultrell, John Carroll. *Making an Apostolic Community of Love: the Role of the Superior According to St. Ignatius of Loyola.* St. Louis, MO: Institute of Jesuit Sources, 1970.

Gasquet, Francis A. *A History of The Venerable English College, Rome.* London: Longman's Greene & Co., 1920.

Goergen, Donald. *The Sexual Celibate.* NY: Seabury, 1974.

Goldberg, Jonathan. *Sodometries: Renaissance Texts, Modern Sexualities.* Stanford, CA: Stanford UP, 1992.

Gregory, Brad S. *Salvation at Stake: Christian Martyrdom in Early Modern Europe.* Cambridge, MA: Harvard UP, 1999.

Gruggen, George and Joseph Keating. *Stonyhurst College: Its Past History and Life in the Present.* London: Kegan Paul, 1901.

Guiney, Imogen. *Recusant Poets.* NY: Sheed & Ward, 1939.

Gunn, S.J. *Charles Brandon, Duke of Suffolk.* Oxford: Basil Blackwell, 1988.

Haigh, Christopher. *English Reformations: Religion, Politics and Society under the Tudors.* Oxford: Clarendon Press, 1993.

Hales, John W. *Longer English Poems, With Notes, Philological and Explanitory, and an Introduction on the Teaching of English.* London: Macmillan, 1880.

Hallam, Henry. *Introduction to the Literature of Europe in the Fifteenth, Sixteenth and Seventeenth Centuries.* London: J. Murray, 1854.

Hallier, Amedee. *The Monastic Theology of Aelred of Rievaulx.* Spencer, MA: Cistercian Publications, 1969.

Harley, John. *William Byrd: Gentleman of the Chapel Royal.* Aldershot, UK: Ashgate, 1999.

Haynes, Alan. *The Elizabethan Secret Services.* London: Sutton, 2000.

Head, David M. *The Ebbs and Flows of Fortune: The Life of Thomas Howard, Third Duke of Norfolk.* Athens, GA: U of Georgia P, 1995.

Hendriks, Lawrence. *The London Charterhouse: Its Monks and Its Martyrs.* London: Kegan Paul, 1889.

Hicks, Leo. "Father Parsons and the Book of Succession," *Recusant History*, vol. 4 (1975), 104–37.

Hill, Geoffrey. *The Lords of Limit: Essays on Literature and Ideas.* NY: Oxford UP, 1984.

Hodgetts, Michael. *Secret Hiding Places.* Dublin: Veritas, 1989.

Holmer, Joan Ozark. *The Merchant of Venice: Choice, Hazard and Consequence.* London: Macmillan, 1995.

Hood, Christobel M. *The Book of Robert Southwell: Priest, Poet, Prisoner.* Oxford: Basil Blackwell, 1926.

Houliston, Victor. "Why Robert Persons would not be Pacified: Edmund Bunny's Theft of *The Book of Resolution,*" in *The Reckoned Expense: Edmund Campion and the Early English Jesuits.* ed. Thomas McCoog, S.J. Woodbridge, UK: Boydell Press, 1996, 159–78.

Ives, E.W. *Anne Boleyn.* Oxford: Basil Blackwell, 1986.

Izon, John. *Sir Thomas Stucley, Traitor Extraordinary.* London: Melrose, 1956.

Janelle, Pierre. *Robert Southwell, the Writer: A Study in Religious Inspiration.* NY, 1935.

Jenson, Phebe. "Ballads and Brags: Free Speech and Recusant Culture in Elizabethan England," *Criticism*, vol. 140.3 (1998).

Jessop, Augustus. *One Generation of a Norfolk Family: A Contribution to Elizabethan History.* NY, 1914.

Jordan, W.K. *Edward VI, The Threshold of Power; The Dominance of the Duke of Northumberland.* London: Allen & Unwin, 1970.

Jusserand, J.J. *A Literary History of the English People from the Origins to the Civil War.* London: Unwin, 1925.

Kenny, Anthony. "From Hospice to College," *The Venerabile*, vol. 20 (1960).

_____, ed. *The Responsa Scholarum of the English College, Rome, Part One: 1598–1621.* Newport, Monmouthshire, 1962.

King, John N. "Recent Studies in Southwell," *English Literary Renaissance*, vol. 13.2 (Spring, 1983), 221–27.

Knowles, Leo. *The Prey of the Priest Catchers: The Lives of the Forty Martyrs.* St Paul, MN: Carillion, 1980.

Knox, Thomas F. *The First and Second Diaries of the English College, Douay.* London: Nutt, 1878.

Kuntz, Paul Grimley. *The Concept of Order.* ed. Paul Grimley Kuntz. Seattle, WA: pub. for Grinnell College by the U of Washington P, 1968.

Lake, Peter with Michael Questier. *The Antichrist's Lewd Hat: Protestants, Papists and Players in Post-Reformation England.* New Haven, CT: Yale UP, 2002.

Lewalski, Barbara Kiefer. *Protestant Poetics and the Seventeenth-Century Religious Lyric*. Princeton, NJ: Princeton UP, 1979.

Lewis, C.S. *English Literature in the Sixteenth Century Excluding Drama*. Oxford, 1954.

Loach, Jennifer. *Edward VI*. New Haven, CT: Yale UP, 1999.

Lovejoy, Arthur Oncken. *The Great Chain of Being: A Study of the History of an Idea*. NY: Harper & Row, 1960, c1936, Notes: pp. [335]–371.

Lowell, James Russell. *The Works of James Russell Lowell*. vol. 1. Boston, MA: Houghton, Mifflin, 1864.

Lucas, Thomas M., S.J. *Landmarking: City, Church & Jesuit Urban Strategy*. Chicago, IL: Loyola Press, 1997.

_____, ed. *Saint, Site and Sacred Strategy: Ignatius, Rome and Jesuit Urbanism, Catalogue of the Exhibition Biblioteca Apostolica Vaticana*. Rome, 1990.

Marius, Richard. *Thomas More: A Biography*. NY: Alfred A. Knopf, 1984.

Markham, Clements R. *King Edward VI*. London: Smith, Elder, 1907.

Martz, Louis. *The Poetry of Meditation: A Study in English Religious Literature of the Seventeenth Century*. New Haven, CT: Yale UP, 1954.

McCabe, Richard A. *Joseph Hall: A Study in Satire and Meditation*. Oxford: Clarendon, 1982.

McCabe, William. *An Introduction to Jesuit Theater*. ed. Louis J. Oldani. St. Louis, MO: Institute of Jesuit Sources, 1983.

McCoog, Thomas M., S.J., ed. *The Reckoned Expense: Edmund Campion and the Early English Jesuits*. Woodbridge, UK: Boydell Press, 1996.

_____. *The Society of Jesus in Ireland, Scotland and England 1541–1588: "Our Way of Proceeding."* NY: E.J. Brill, 1996.

McDannell, Colleen and Bernhard Lang. *Heaven: A History*. New Haven, CT: Yale UP, 1988.

McGlinchee, Claire. *James Russell Lowell*. NY: Twayne, 1967.

Meyer, Arnold Oskar. *England and the Catholic Church under Queen Elizabeth*. London, 1916.

Morey, Adrian. *The Catholic Subjects of Elizabeth I*. London: George Allen & Unwin, 1978.

Morris, John. *Jesuits in Conflict: or Historic Facts*. London: Burns and Oates, 1873.

_____, ed. *The Letter-Books of Sir Amias Poulet, Keeper of Mary Queen of Scots*. London: Pickering and Co., 1874.

_____. *The Troubles of Our Catholic Forefathers Related by Themselves*. 3 vols. London: Burns and Oates, 1872.

Moseley, D.H. *Blessed Robert Southwell*. NY: Sheed and Ward, 1957.

Mullan, Elder. *The Sodality of Our Lady: Studied in the Documents*. NY: P.J. Kennedy & Sons, 1912.

Newdigate, C.A. "A New Chapter in the Life of Blessed Robert Southwell, S.J.," *The Month*, CLVII (1931), 246–54.

Norman, E.R. *Anti-Catholicism in Victorian England*. NY: Barnes & Noble, 1968.

O'Malley, John W. *The First Jesuits*. Cambridge MA: Harvard UP, 1993.

Ong, Walter, S.J. *Fighting for Life: Contest, Sexuality and Consciousness*. Ithaca, NY: Cornell UP, 1981.

Parmiter, Geoffrey de C. *Elizabethan Popish Recusancy in the Inns of Court*. London: U of London P, 1976.

Partridge, A.C. *The Tribe of Ben: Pre-Augustan Verse in English*. Columbia, SC: U of South Carolina P, 1966.

Pilarz, Scott, S.J. "'To Help Souls': Recovering the Purpose of Southwell's Poetry and Prose," in *Discovering and (Re)Covering the Seventeenth Century Religious Lyric*. eds. Eugene Cunnar and Jeffrey Johnson. Pittsburg, PA: Duquesne UP, 2001.

Pollard, A.F. *England under Protector Somerset; An Essay*. NY: Russell & Russell, 1966.

_____. *The History of England from the Accession of Edward VI to the Death of Elizabeth (1547–1603)*. London, NY: Longmans, Green, 1910.

Prescott, H.F.M. *Mary Tudor*. NY: Macmillan, 1953.

Pritchard, Arnold. *Catholic Loyalism in Elizabethan England*. Chapel Hill, NC: U of North Carolina P, 1979.

Roberts, John R. "The Rosary in Elizabethan England," *The Month*, XXXII (1964), 192–97.

Robertson, D.W. *A Preface to Chaucer: Studies in Medieval Perspectives*. Princeton, NJ: Princeton UP, 1962.

Rondet, Henri, S.J. *The Grace of Christ*. ed. Thad W. Guzie, S.J. Westminster, MD: Newman Press, 1967.

Ross, Malcolm MacKenzie. *Poetry and Dogma: The Transfiguration of Eucharistic Symbols in Seventeenth-Century English Poetry*. New York, 1954.

Russell, Jeffrey B. *A History of Heaven: The Singing Silence*. Princeton, NJ: Princeton UP, 1997.

Sargent, Ralph M. *The Life and Lyrics of Sir Edward Dyer*. Oxford: Clarendon Press, 1935.

Scallon, Joseph D. *The Poetry of Robert Southwell, S.J.*. Salzburg, Austria: Intitüt für Englische Sprache und Literatür, 1975.

Sedgwick, Eve Kosovsky. *Between Men: English Literature and Male Homosocial Desire*. NY: Columbia UP, 1985.

Sessions, William A. *Henry Howard, Earl of Surrey*. Boston, MA: Twayne, 1986.

Shell, Alison. *Catholicism, Controversy and the English Literary Imagination, 1558–1660*. Cambridge, UK: Cambridge UP, 1999.

_____. "'We are made a spectacle': Campion's Dramas," in *The Reckoned Expense: Edmund Campion and the Early English Jesuits*. ed. Thomas McCoog, S.J.Woodbridge, UK: Boydell Press, 1996, 103–18.

Simmons, Joseph. *Jesuit Theater Englished: Five Tragedies of Joseph Simmons*. eds. Louis J. Oldani and Philip C. Fischer. St. Louis, MO: Institute of Jesuit Sources, 1989.

Simpson, Edmund. "Biographical Sketch of Thomas Pounde," *The Rambler*, vol. 2, 1857.

Simpson, Richard. *Edmund Campion: A Biography*. London: John Hodges, 1896.

Smith, Bruce R. *Homosexual Desire in Shakespeare's England: A Cultural Poetics*. Chicago: U of Chicago P, 1991.

South, Malcolm H. *The Jesuits and the Joint Mission to England 1580–81*. Lewiston, NY: The Edward Mellon Press, 1999.

Southern, A.C. "'The Best Wits out of England': University Men in Exile under Elizabeth I," *The Month*, CXCIII (1952), 12–21.

Spingarn, Joel E. *Critical Essays of the Seventeenth Century*. Oxford: Clarendon, 1908.

Stewart, Alan. *Close Readers: Humanism and Sodomy in Early Modern England*. Princeton, NJ: Princeton UP, 1997.

Strier, Richard. "Sanctifying the Aristocracy: 'Devout Humanism' in Francois de Sales, John Donne and George Herbert," *Journal of Religion* (1989), 36–58.

Strong, Roy C. *The Cult of Elizabeth: Elizabethan Portraiture and Pageantry*. Berkeley, CA: U of California P, 1986 c1977.

Taunton, Ethelred. *The History of the Jesuits in England*. London: Methuen & Co., 1901.

Tierney, M.A., ed. *Dodd's Church History of England*. 5 vols. London, 1839.

Thurston, Herbert, S.J. "An Autograph Manuscript of the Venerable Robert Southwell, S.J.," *The Month*, CXLIII (1924), 353–55.

_____. "Catholic Writers and Elizabethan Readers, I: Father Parsons' *Christian Directory*," *The Month*, LXXXII (1894), 457–76.

_____. "Catholic Writers and Elizabethan Readers, II: Father Southwell, the Euphuist," *The Month*, LXXXIII (1895), 231–45.

_____. "Catholic Writers and Elizabethan Readers, III: Father Southwell, the Popular Poet," *The Month*, LXXX (1895), 383–99.

_____. "A Memorial for Two Lady Margarets," *The Month*, CXV (1900), 596–607.

_____. "An Unknown Poem of Father Southwell the Martyr," *The Month*, LXXII (1894), 230–44.

Tourney, Leonard D. *Joseph Hall*. Boston: Twayne Publishers, 1979.

Unset, Sigrid. *Stages in the Road*. trans. Arthur G. Chater. NY: Knopf, 1934.

Villaret, Emil. *An Abridged History of the Sodality of Our Lady*. St. Louis, MO: The Queens Work, 1957.

Walsh, Michael. *Dictionary of Catholic Devotions*. San Francisco, CA: Harper, 1993.

Walsham, Alexandra. *Church Papists: Catholicism, Conformity, and Confessional Polemic in Early Modern England*. Woodbridge, UK: Boydell Press, 1993.

Welsh, Alfred. *The Development of English Language and Literature*. Chicago, IL: S.C. Griggs, 1882.

Whatmore, L.E. *The Carthusians Under King Henry VIII*. Salzburg: Institüt für Anglistik und Amerikanistik, 1983.

White, Helen C. *English Devotional Literature (Prose) 1600–1640*. Madison, WI: U of Wisconsin P, 1931.

_____. *Tudor Books of Saints and Martyrs*. Madison, WI: U of Wisconsin P, 1963.

Williams, Michael E. "Campion and the English Continental Seminaries," in *The Reckoned Expense: Edmund Campion and the Early English Jesuits*. ed. Thomas McCoog, S.J. Woodbridge, UK: Boydell Press, 1996, 285–300.

_____. "The Origins of the English College, Lisbon," *Recusant History*, vol. 20 (1991), 478–92.

_____. *The Venerable English College Rome: A History, 1579–1979*. London, UK: Associated Catholic Publications Ltd., 1979.

Wolffe, John. *The Protestant Crusade in Great Britain 1829–1860*. Oxford: Clarendon Press, 1991.

Index

(Robert Southwell is abbreviated to RS throughout, except under his own main entry)